Pro Windows Small Business Server 2003

■ ■ ■

Tony Campbell

Apress®

Pro Windows Small Business Server 2003

Copyright © 2006 by Tony Campbell

ISBN-13 (pbk): 978-1-59059-703-3

ISBN-10 (pbk): 1-59059-703-6

Lead Editor: Jonathan Hassell
Editorial Board: Steve Anglin, Ewan Buckingham, Gary Cornell, Jason Gilmore, Jonathan Gennick, Jonathan Hassell, James Huddleston, Chris Mills, Matthew Moodie, Dominic Shakeshaft, Jim Sumser, Keir Thomas, Matt Wade
Project Manager: Beth Christmas
Copy Edit Manager: Nicole LeClerc
Copy Editor: Sharon Wilkey
Assistant Production Director: Kari Brooks-Copony
Production Editor: Katie Stence
Compositor and Artist: Van Winkle Design Group
Proofreader: Lori Bring
Indexer: Toma Mulligan
Cover Designer: Kurt Krames
Manufacturing Director: Tom Debolski

Distributed to the book trade worldwide by Springer-Verlag New York, Inc., 233 Spring Street, 6th Floor, New York, NY 10013. Phone 1-800-SPRINGER, fax 201-348-4505, e-mail orders-ny@springer-sbm.com, or visit http://www.springeronline.com.

For information on translations, please contact Apress directly at 2560 Ninth Street, Suite 219, Berkeley, CA 94710. Phone 510-549-5930, fax 510-549-5939, e-mail info@apress.com, or visit http://www.apress.com.

This book is dedicated to my wife, Sharon.
Without her support, guidance, and encouragement,
I would never have put pen to paper and started to write.

Contents at a Glance

Contents

Foreword

By virtue of having this book in your hands, you are part of the engine that is turning the world's economy.

Small businesses are the epicenter of worldwide commerce. Sure, global corporations throw their billions of dollars of weight around, but small businesses—those with somewhere between 1 and 75 employees—contribute the majority of the capital, the majority of the transactions, the majority of the jobs that make up the global market. You would think that with all of this aggregate clout, small businesses would be on the cutting edge of technology, able to move more nimbly and ride new waves in computing to make their lives more efficient and their bank accounts fatter.

Sadly, this very typically isn't the case. You need more than 40 hours a week to run the world's economy. (Who knew?) So technology often gets relegated to the back burner, an unfortunate outcome of an overloaded schedule. It's unfortunate because technology can help small businesses stay in touch with existing customers, reach new ones, figure out what's profitable and what isn't, and make sure their finances stay strong and long-lasting.

Microsoft saw this problem of "tech as a last priority" a while ago and has attempted to address it at least since the mid-1990s by offering special versions of their back-office server software systems and applications, packaged in one box with easy-to-follow wizards for configuration, allowing small businesses to have the same hard-hitting tech as larger corporations with significant IT budgets. It's a great idea, and this product—Windows Small Business Server—gets better and better with each passing year.

I've always been fascinated with SBS and its implications to the success of small business—so fascinated, in fact, that I wrote a book on it. As the author of *Using Microsoft Windows Small Business Server 2003*, I gave readers enough information to get started integrating and managing the SBS product into their daily lives. Sometimes, that's enough. But the story of SBS and what it has to offer goes far deeper than what I included in my book, and Tony Campbell has taken the torch and run with it in writing the tome you hold in your hands now. In this book, Tony turns over every rock, shines a flashlight in every cave, and fully explores every nook and cranny that SBS has to offer. He then puts it in context for you, so you can easily imagine how such a feature or process can contribute to your business success. It's the most useful book I've read on the subject.

Tony Campbell has a fine book on Small Business Server here. I've bought a copy already. The bottom line is that you should too.

I wish you much success in your future.

Jonathan Hassell
Author, consultant, editor, speaker, trainer
www.jonathanhassell.com

About the Author

TONY CAMPBELL is a veteran Microsoft consultant specializing in the architecture and design of secure Microsoft-centric business solutions. He also has vast experience in many other industry niches such as networking, collaboration, security, business logic, and disaster recovery and resilience. Tony has been involved with all sizes of business, from the very small to the very large, and has successfully delivered secure, reliable, robust solutions to over 150,000 clients in his 18 years in the business. Tony started his career back in the '80s as a "green screen" mainframe programmer for the British Meteorological Office, finally arriving after a long journey in his current role as a self-employed IT consultant with more than a dozen full-time customers.

Tony is a regular contributor to various IT journals distributed across the globe and has been involved in the production of software manuals, user guides, white papers, hardware manuals, and training courses for many of his clients in the past decade. His love of writing has led to the publication of his fiction in a variety of small presses and magazines.

Acknowledgments

This book was most definitely a labor of love. A bystander might throw a cursory glance at my life over the last six months to see a man who just knocked out one of those big IT manuals in his "spare time," but the word *spare*, in this case, should be used with extreme caution. Picture this: a 35-year-old IT guy, sleep deprived, sitting at his dimly lit desk in the wee hours of the night, knocking back cup after cup of max-strength Java like it was going out of fashion, all in order to get the next five pages of his manuscript completed and keep the deadline stress monster off his back for another few hours. Imagine if you will, an exhausted, hungry, unshaven grouch, huddled over his laptop in the back seat of his car during his lunch breaks, bashing out page after page to keep on top of things. Well, finally the ordeal is over, and here I am, emerging from the other side, a happier, wiser, and more carefree individual.

To anyone I have forgotten to mention explicitly, I apologize now; but to everyone who has helped me at any time throughout this book's production, I applaud you. Thank you all!

For putting up with me, my moods, and the lack of intelligible conversation during initial drafting, I want to first and foremost thank my beautiful, patient, caring wife, Sharon, for bringing me coffee when I needed it, doing research when I asked her (nicely), and primarily for keeping out of my hair and letting me get on with my work when I needed the time. Thanks also have to go to Lara, the three-year-old prima ballerina who lives under our roof, for her regular visitations to my office, bringing me cuddly toys, serving me virtual drinks and meals, and for playacting Spiderman and Batman while I stared at the screen mentally screaming out for silence and solitude. Of course, I smiled, nodding as any good parent should, saying, "Thank you, Lara. . .are you sure Mummy doesn't need you for anything? I think I can hear her calling you. . ."

David Pyke, a good friend and colleague, is one of my long-term cohorts in the industry, since the early days of us rolling out countless SBS 2000 systems to unsuspecting clients. David runs a successful IT security consultancy (Intanetworking) and has been certified as an ITSec consultant under various UK government initiatives. He manages Small Business Server clients alongside his day job, keeping them as happy as possible (and as remote as possible) from his, and in his spare time enjoys a good bottle of Rioja.

Andrew Edney is a good friend and colleague and has helped me tremendously with all the research I undertook during the writing of this book. I've never before worked with someone so dedicated to the online world of the Internet and I know for a fact that when Andrew's time comes, he'll spring up somewhere as a web service, more significant even than that of Google. On top of all of this, Andrew runs his own IT consulting company—Firebird Consulting—and is a highly qualified Microsoft professional and information security consultant.

Michael Jenkin, MCP, MVP, IT manager, and senior engineer for the Australian national solutions company, Copyworld, has been nothing less than a godsend for me. His careful and diligent criticism of every word on every page of my manuscript has helped tighten up the facts, correct some glaring errors (instigated in the darkest hours of the night when I was too wired on caffeine to think straight), and added countless helpful hints and tips from his vast experience with many, many SBS 2003 users across Australia. Michael can be contacted through his website: http://www.mickyj.com.

Thanks also goes out to the rest of the review team who did an excellent job of reviewing what I'd written, who without a doubt have made the final product as good as it could possibly be. Thanks go to David Shackelford for his direct no-nonsense approach to my work and to Susan Bradley for her diligence, honesty, and courtesy.

Preface

Toward the end of 2003, Microsoft announced the release of their latest small business server solution. This product launch turned out to be the turning point in Microsoft's penetration of the small business marketplace as finally they delivered a fully integrated set of applications that worked seamlessly and securely together. The product I'm referring to, of course, is Microsoft Windows Small Business Server 2003.

With the subsequent introduction of Small Business Server 2003 Service Pack 1 for both the Standard and Premium editions of the product, Microsoft has dramatically improved the reliability of the underlying product set, raising each of the components to the latest patch/service pack level and replacing Internet Security and Acceleration Server 2000 (Microsoft ISA Server 2000) with the latest version of the product: Microsoft ISA Server 2004 with its own associated Service Pack 1.

Introduction

It's true to say that the previous versions of Small Business Server were buggy, with applications appearing more cobbled together than "tightly integrated," as they were purported to be. But all that's in the past. No more sales spin blowing the product's capabilities out of proportion, and with much tighter integration of the component products, Microsoft Windows Small Business Server 2003 (from now on it will be referred to mainly as SBS 2003) works in harmony rather than resounding discord.

SBS 2003 is easily the best "total solution" that a small business could invest in, delivering a plethora of scalable capabilities, all on a shoestring budget. The main strength comes from being built upon Microsoft's well-matured server technology, Microsoft Windows Server 2003, meaning you get all the reliability, availability, scalability, and security features bestowed upon even the largest of Microsoft's enterprise customers—something that's been sorely missed from the lower budgets of the small business guys until now. However, the value SBS 2003 delivers on top of Windows Server 2003 comes from being enhanced with plenty of easy-to-use wizards allowing you to perform all manner of administrative tasks by using straightforward, plain-English interfaces.

The commitment Microsoft is now showing to the small business marketplace (exemplified with offerings such as the free upgrade of Microsoft ISA Server 2000 to Microsoft ISA Server 2004 with Service Pack 1) shows they are dedicated to making the power of a total Microsoft Windows Server infrastructure as accessible to small business customers as it is to their larger enterprise clients. From Microsoft's strategic perspective, this makes perfect business sense (it's a big, big market to take a slice of). From your own perspective in the small business world, it's certainly the right time to buy into this product because it's now mature enough and developed to underpin your own business needs, all coming with the support and dedication of the biggest software manufacturer on the planet.

The following list offers a brief overview of the components included with SBS 2003 (SP1). At the end of this preface, I've included a brief explanation of what SP1 delivers.

SBS 2003 Standard Edition includes the following components:

- *Microsoft Exchange Server 2003*: This messaging core of SBS 2003 offers enterprise email, ISP integration, shared calendar services, meeting arrangement, and free/busy information services.

- *Microsoft Office Outlook 2003*: This is the client-side messaging product connecting to Microsoft Exchange Server 2003. This product is the primary user interface to all of the information services listed for Microsoft Exchange Server 2003 in the preceding paragraph.

- *Windows SharePoint Services*: This web-based collaboration tool allows you to easily create your own business intranet containing message boards, announcements, document stores, and connections to other information sources, such as Microsoft Exchange Server 2003.

- *Windows Shared Fax Services*: With a single fax modem, you can send faxes from any Windows desktop, as well as routing incoming faxes to either your intranet site, an email address, or directly to a printer.

- *Health Monitor*: The Health Monitor is a useful add-in for displaying server performance details and helping with fault finding.

If you opt for the enhanced capabilities of SBS 2003 Premium Edition, you'll also get the following additional components:

- *Microsoft SQL Server 2000*: This is Microsoft's enterprise database solution, providing a scalable relational database engine that you can build the most complex data structure and indexes upon.

- *Microsoft ISA Server 2004*: This is an industrial-strength firewall, web cache, and web publishing service that offers the same levels of confidentiality and integrity required by even the most secure of government establishments.

- *Microsoft Office FrontPage 2003*: With Microsoft Office FrontPage 2003, you can easily develop and publish your own websites to the Internet or manipulate your Windows SharePoint Services intranet site.

As long as you take care to plan your infrastructure before rushing in, SBS 2003 can be used in practically any business environment to yield great results. By following the simple guidelines in this book, it shouldn't be long before you're ready to grow your business into the 21st century.

Who Should Read This Book?

This book is aimed at anyone who might wish to exploit the services offered by SBS 2003. Over the course of the book, you'll learn how to set up remote-access solutions for home workers, create collaboration systems for enhanced teamwork, enhance your system security policies to keep out intruders, and leverage the power of electronic communication to boost sales.

Business executives will quickly learn how to exploit the features of SBS 2003 to their best advantage, while IT consultants will gain an understanding of how to advise their customers of the best way to approach the small business community.

By leveraging Internet technologies, electronic messaging, collaboration facilities, web publishing, and centralized systems-management solutions, small businesses can now easily grow into modern, competitive players, capable of delivering exceptional customer service at the same time as maintaining healthy profit margins.

The following people will benefit from reading this book:

- Business owners

- IT consultants

- Business managers

- Sales and marketing executives

- Key decision makers

- Technical support specialists

Every type of business—from well-established service companies wanting to take advantage of newly presented Internet opportunities, to newly conceived commodity start-ups depending solely on their ability to exploit electronic trading—will benefit from the services offered by SBS 2003.

The key to understanding how best to leverage SBS 2003 in the targeted environment is to gain an unbiased understanding of the business's shortfalls. In other words, to gain this insight into how to improve a business, it's vital that you first identify its weaknesses. This might sound like Sun Tzu's *Art of War* guide to SBS 2003, but it's the fundamental methodology used by business consultants when they try to figure out how to fix something that, at first glance, might not appear to be broken.

So where can cost savings be made? You might have too many staff members performing inefficient routine jobs. Procurement processes might be so complicated that they are producing nothing but mountains of paperwork with no real benefit. You'll need to look at each process and procedure that defines your business and match these against the services SBS 2003 has to offer. Only then can you begin to determine how you might improve your business. That's exactly what this book is about: helping transform your business from a 10-year-old Ford Escort to a brand new Porsche 911 in a few short weeks.

I always intended this book to be much more than just a straightforward point-and-click manual. It should not be thought of as an administrator's guide, although it does cover setting up and configuring the products (as any good book should). It's more of a consultant/manager's guide to SBS 2003, meaning you can get up and running, and manage and configure each of the applications, without getting so low-level that you get lost in technobabble.

So don't expect a long explanation of every Registry key in Windows Server 2003—you'll be disappointed—or a detailed explanation of every check box, radio button, and configuration file inside Microsoft Exchange Server 2003. There are plenty of other books that do just that; the important thing you'll gain from this book is how SBS 2003 can be employed to help run a business more smoothly and efficiently, freeing up the business owner's time to concentrate on the real task at hand: running a small business and making money.

This book provides the following:

- An insight into modern technology in business

- An explanation of the SBS 2003 components in context

- Guidance on the best way to install and configure SBS 2003

- Guidelines on maintenance, administration, and troubleshooting tasks

- Practical examples of how common tasks are tackled with SBS 2003

Because I want this book to be useful rather than simply a door prop, I've concentrated on three angles, each of which you could use to approach the book: first, it can be read cover to cover (the way I'd recommend at least the first reading) to gain a good understanding of how the technology, at each stage, is used in context; second, it can be used as a straightforward subject matter guide, detailing the technology, installation options, settings, and systems configuration; and last, it can be read as a guide to IT in business, concentrating on the case studies to see how real-world problems are tackled.

So, if you own or manage a small business of between 5 and 75 employees and intend to explore the benefits of SBS 2003, this book is for you. If you are an IT consultant, looking after some small business ventures, this book is certainly for you. And finally, if you already have SBS 2003 and are looking to further leverage its vast range of services, this book is undoubtedly the one to go for.

Note IT consultants in the small business sector will benefit from this book's insight into the many diverse problems faced by their customers. It will help consultants deliver a comprehensive plan to customers, with an IT integration initiative that will allow the business to grow beyond the constraints imposed by the current environment.

Organization and Structure

This book is split into four sections, each concentrating on specific aspects of using, installing, and managing SBS 2003.

SBS Standard Edition

Chapters 1 though 7 offer an in-depth introduction to small business computing, looking primarily at the challenges facing small businesses that are trying to compete in today's global, web-enabled marketplace. Throughout each chapter, you'll be exposed to the IT components that can be used to help your business grow; you'll see how to draw out business requirements, match them to IT capabilities, and create a comprehensive plan of what you need to install, configure, and develop.

You will be taken through exactly what constitutes a successful IT system, looking at the fundamentals of services, maintenance, and security, all in the context of what a small business requires. You will be shown the best way to capture your business requirements and to map these requirements to the capabilities offered in SBS 2003.

This section also goes into the details of modern networking components, covering aspects of wired and wireless networking before proceeding to cover the installation and configuration of all the major features of SBS 2003 Standard Edition. Each component of SBS 2003 is covered in its own dedicated chapter.

SBS Premium Components

Chapters 8 through 10 concentrate on the components supplied in SBS 2003 Premium Edition. These chapters cover the following topics:

- Microsoft ISA Server 2004

- Microsoft SQL Server 2000

- Microsoft Office FrontPage 2003

The section details the installation and administration of each additional component and shows how each can be exploited by your business.

Information Security

Chapter 11 provides a comprehensive guide for the layman on all aspects of information security. The intention of this section is to highlight the importance of information security in your business, taking a long look at security risks and domain modeling and then offering cost-effective solutions to the problems posed by hackers, viruses, and data corruption.

You'll obtain good insight into each topic, looking in detail at domain-based security modeling (a methodology exploited by IT security professionals) in order to design your system securely from the beginning, as well as looking at specific threat countermeasures for eradicating problems such as mail-bomb attacks. You'll learn about spyware and how to get rid of it, as well as about hacking and what to do about protecting yourself against Internet criminals.

Finally, you'll take a look at the aspects of information security that fall outside the bounds of what's enforceable electronically, such as password phishing and social engineering.

Help and Troubleshooting

Finally, Chapter 12 is a guide to troubleshooting your SBS 2003 infrastructure. Here you'll learn about the tools of the trade used by IT troubleshooters when diagnosing problems on your system. You'll also take a look inside the facilities available on the server, on workstations, and on the Internet so you can see where you should go for help.

Case Studies

Throughout this book, each topic is addressed from the perspective of real and fictitious businesses.

Thanks must go out to Michael Jenkin, IT manager from Copyworld, Australia, who has contributed many of the real-world case studies scattered throughout this book and given his permission for publication.

Each fictitious business exists within the bounds of its own ethics and business goals and in no way relates to any real company that might have the same name or goals. Although these three companies are fictitious, the concepts and initiatives detailed for each are drawn from my own personal experiences with my customers over the last few years.

Copyworld

Copyworld is a leading national Australian IT solution provider for small and medium-sized businesses. It has three main state offices, with mobile technicians, a phone department, photocopier department, Microsoft Office products, and IT departments. The site is a heavy user of email, the Internet, and application software.

Until February 2005, Copyworld had three offices, each on a different SBS platform (SBS 4.5 to SBS 2000) with little to no connectivity or centralized administration. The servers were not handling the load—SBS 4.5 was unsupported and failing badly—and did not meet the company's expanding needs. Remote access was nonexistent, therefore limiting the mobile workforce strategy they were adopting.

Reporting on system performance was a tedious manual task, and user management was a nightmare. The Internet connectivity was unreliable, and Microsoft Exchange Server mailboxes were filling up regularly. To top it all, the backup software was unable to cope with the load.

In February 2005, Copyworld adopted SBS 2003 internally as well as using it to manage their growing client portfolio. Clients range from 5 users to an average of 30 users.

The Copyworld implementation team has found the core components of SBS 2003 work just as well in small companies as in their own larger network.

Copyworld currently runs 74 computer systems with 100 staff members across Australia.

Fictitious Businesses

A brief outline of the fictitious case study companies follows, listing the key aspirations of each with regard to the services of SBS 2003.

Planthire

Planthire leases large site machinery to the building trade. The company employs ten permanent employees who maintain and service their stock of machinery, two desk clerks who talk to customers and take orders over the phone, the business owner himself, and his personal assistant. Their current IT infrastructure consists of three PCs running Windows 98 and two directly connected printers. There is no network. The company has no web presence, but the manager is aware of what benefit a website might bring to the company. The PCs are located in the manager's office area, which doubles as the sales point for the desk clerks and the secretary's office. Most company data is held in paper files, with only the sales ledgers and some aspects of finances held on the computers. The manager of this company sees the business lagging behind other businesses in this market sector. To address this problem, he took the time to speak to Microsoft and learned the benefits of the Microsoft Windows Small Business Server 2003 solution.

Goals for deploying SBS 2003 in Planthire:

- Analysis of business processes

- Analysis of IT-unfriendly environment

- Connecting systems for better corporate communication

- Better usage of employee time

- Automation

- Resilience

- Marketing through web presence

- Online ordering

- Spares management

- Remote access

- Corporate email connectivity to suppliers

- Reduced costs, increased customer base, higher profit

Servideal

Servideal is a brand new start-up company, not yet off the ground. Because they have never before traded, this husband and wife team are open to suggestions of how they might best accomplish their goals. They intend to carry out all sales and marketing on the Internet and are content that they have a unique set of products and services to sustain a business. Their intention is to set up a fully automated e-commerce solution to facilitate their plans. After much research into possible technology platforms that might support such a venture, Microsoft Windows Small Business Server 2003 was selected to help deliver their dream.

Goals for deploying SBS 2003 in Servideal:

- Analysis of business processes

- Analysis of IT server placement

- Customer security

- Full automation of e-commerce system

- Resilience and comprehensive database/server backup solution

- Electronic marketing through web presence

- Web hosting

- Inventory management

- Remote access–secure VPN

- Supplier management

Country Estates

Country Estates is a well-established local estate agency in the United Kingdom, spanning three locations and employing 60 staff members with 40 workstations. They currently use a Windows NT 4.0 workstation peer-to-peer solution Although it's capable of offering a reasonably good solution for what they wanted up to now, they are having problems with occasional data loss, the distribution of important company information, and the lack of individual control on workstations (leading to a much higher overhead for total cost of ownership for each user access device). The managing director is constantly worried about corporate security because this is one of the most worrisome concerns for any uncontrolled network. As a result of a recent audit, the managing director employed a business consultant for five days to help him identify where the business could be improved. As a result, he has a fully defined business process analysis that needs updating with technology. He was advised to purchase Microsoft Windows Small Business Server 2003 as the best fit for his company's needs.

Goals for deploying SBS 2003 in Country Estates:

- Automation of previously cumbersome business processes

- Centralization of control of IT policy

- Modernization of web capability

- Remote access for staff via secure VPN solution

- Upgrade of workstations and migration of old data to new system

- Comprehensive resilience and backup solution

- Firewall security and user workstation clampdown using server-driven policy

- Customer contacts database and complaint logging system

What's New in Service Pack 1

In the summer of 2005, Microsoft released SP1 for SBS 2003, sending a ripple of excitement through the product's user community. As usual, Microsoft included the typical set of component-level fixes for the underlying products, such as Windows Server 2003 hotfixes and improvements, Exchange Server 2003 Service Pack 1, an uplifted MSDE to Service Pack 4, and a plethora of patches and fixes wrapped up as Windows SharePoint Services Service Pack 1. However, the inclusion of ISA Server 2004 as a free upgrade was the most indicative gesture of Microsoft's commitment to growing their small business customer base. Under normal licensing circumstances, ISA 2004 would incur a fee to upgrade. By giving this vastly improved product away for free to their small business customers, Microsoft has exposed ISA 2004 to a much wider audience than just the small business community. Table 1 outlines the changes you can expect in a system running SBS 2003 with Service Pack 1.

Table 1. *Components Upgraded in SBS 2003 Service Pack 1*

Component	Description
Windows Server 2003	Service Pack 1
Exchange Server 2003	Service Pack 1
Windows SharePoint Services 2.0	Service Pack 1
MSDE	Service Pack 4
SQL 2000 (Premium customers)	Service Pack 4
ISA 2000 (Premium customers)	Upgrade to ISA 2004 Service Pack 1
Windows XP	Service Pack 2
ActiveSync	ActiveSync 3.8
Microsoft Office Outlook 2003	Service Pack 1

Many of these service packs and fixes have already been rolled out across the enterprise versions of the underlying products, so in a way you are getting a consolidated version of the individual service packs already available. However, there are additional fixes that are specific to SBS 2003 that you should also understand. Most notably, these are outlined in Table 2.

Table 2. *Specific SBS 2003 Fixes in SP1*

SBS Component	Fix
Email and POP3	A fix for the POP3 scheduler has been introduced to ensure that your scheduled downloads from your ISP always work (at least from the SBS 2003 point of view, as it can't govern what goes on the ISP's server).
	A separate fix preventing unsolicited email from appearing in the Microsoft Exchange Server's SMTP outbox is included, stopping your outbox from getting clogged with unwanted, undeliverable messages.
	A feature known as *tar pitting* has also been enabled to slow down the proliferation of spam by creating a delay in the enumeration of commonly associated spam email addresses on your system. The spam effectively sticks in the tar pit.
Microsoft Exchange Server	Exchange SP1 changes the message store limit from a meager 16 GB to 75 GB. This change has been a long time in the coming and will alleviate the problems being experienced by many small businesses that have run out of space on their current message store. The Exchange message store is where all company email is located on the SBS 2003 server.
	Outlook Web Access has been updated to accept forms-based authentication, stopping an annoying alert message when you try to connect.
Backup and Restore	An update to the backup and restore system fixed a problem of certain media not mounting on the backup device.
SBS 2003 Firewall	A fix to allow Windows Firewall on your SBS 2003 server to be configured from a Windows XP (SP2) computer was included.
SharePoint Services	A fix has been introduced to rectify a problem with Windows SharePoint Services that prevented users from connecting to the intranet site by using the normal intranet address of http://companyweb.
Client Installation	An updated version of the client deployment tool vastly improves the SBS 2003 server's ability to easily deploy Windows XP Service Pack 2 to clients on your network.

SBS 2003 Release 2 (R2)

In conjunction with the release of Microsoft Windows Server 2003 R2, a purchasable upgrade to the Microsoft Windows Server 2003 system, Microsoft also announced an SBS 2003 version of Release 2. This upgrade requires a new server license to operate it (although the cost is not as high as that of the counterpart enterprise license for Microsoft Windows Server 2003 R2) and delivers a plethora of updated or new technology that may or may not be of interest to you as a business owner or consultant.

R2 is not mandatory and is not to be confused with a service pack. It does not provide security hotfixes, and any system not running R2 will receive the same level of support and maintenance from Microsoft as those customers who do upgrade.

What's Included in R2?

There are many new features in R2, some more applicable to the large enterprise customers while others service both small and large businesses alike. The version of R2 being shipped for SBS 2003 Premium customers has one additional feature available for the small business above and beyond those available for Microsoft Windows Server 2003 R2 customers, namely the inclusion of an update license for Microsoft SQL Server 2005. A short description of what's new in Microsoft SQL Server 2005 is included in Chapter 9 of this book and should allow SBS 2003 Premium customers to decide whether the R2 upgrade is right for them.

■**Note** If you have purchased Microsoft Software Assurance (and many small businesses have not), the R2 update for SBS 2003 will be shipped as part of this contract. Otherwise, you will have to pay for it.

Aside from the obvious inclusion of the Microsoft SQL Server 2005 package, further facilities and modifications to functionality have also been included. Active Directory Federation Services (ADFS) is a new way of providing extensible security collaboration across disparate organizations using a model of trust and delegation that is not possible without ADFS. There are further improvements in replication services, saving on precious bandwidth and removing the need for backup at remote branch offices. This is beneficial to small businesses that are distributed over many sites so long as additional domain controllers have been provisioned for localized authentication and directory services.

A prerequisite for upgrading to R2 is that you have already applied Service Pack 1.

Should You Upgrade?

There is no requirement to upgrade to SBS 2003 R2. It is not a prerequisite for future upgrades (to Longhorn, for example) and will not in any way negate your support and maintenance contract with Microsoft or third-party service providers. All future service packs for SBS 2003 will install on both the standard version and the R2 version, so there are no future foreseen compatibility issues with the upgrade that Microsoft is aware of.

Another point to mention is that some of your servers can run the R2 version of the operating system while others that don't need the extended functionality don't have to. In this way, you can, for example, upgrade your SBS 2003 Premium Edition server to R2 to acquire the Microsoft SQL Server 2005 upgrade license while still keeping your Microsoft Server 2003 application servers as standard.

More Information on R2

For more information on Microsoft Windows Server 2003 R2 and SBS 2003 R2, see the following links:

- http://www.microsoft.com/windowsserver2003/R2/R2FAQ.mspx

- http://www.microsoft.com/windowsserver2003/R2/overview/default.mspx

- http://www.microsoft.com/windowsserver2003/sbs/techinfo/overview/generalfaq.mspx

CHAPTER 1

∎∎∎

Small Business Computing

According to recent statistics published by IDC (an independent market research company specializing in industry information from the IT sector), there are more than 40 million enterprises throughout the world that could be classified as small businesses. In the United States alone there are around 7.5 million such businesses, every one of them having the same underlying requirement—you've guessed it: *to make money*. Without the drive to make money that fuels every entrepreneurial business manager, a small business would not survive when faced with the challenges of competing with corporations.

Needless to say, at the helm of every successful small business is a visionary: the entrepreneurial manager who makes sure his brainchild survives in the face of all adversity. An entrepreneur is a person who is happy to take the risk in setting up a business where the sole aim is to become as profitable as possible. An entrepreneur will make sure that whatever needs to be done to make a business survive gets done. If a business needs a change of focus or direction, the entrepreneur will spot this and make it happen.

With careful planning and a determined mind, the entrepreneur can take an idea, a dream, to the next stage of reality: a profitable, streamlined small business venture capable of organic growth to its full potential.

∎**Note** *Organic growth* refers to the way a business might grow naturally as opposed to depending on large amounts of investment capital to facilitate expansion.

What Makes a Small Business Small?

So, what classifies a business as small? It's all a matter of opinion. The definition of *small* varies from organization to organization, and country to country, with the answer often being attributed to local government legislation determining exactly where the line is drawn.

∎**Note** Most often the division between what constitutes a micro-sized business, a small-to-medium business, or a large business is related to the government's view of taxes and benefits. Service providers and private business communities have also been known to set their own arbitrary thresholds for specific purposes. Many organizations use volumetric measurements such as annual turnover or numbers of employees to create a banded system for determining the benefits or rights a company might be entitled to receive.

To understand the context of *this* book, it's vital you understand Microsoft's view of what makes a small business small.

Small Business Server in a Nutshell

Microsoft Windows Small Business Server 2003 (SBS 2003) has been sized to support companies with up to 75 simultaneously logged-on users or up to 75 operational client-access devices. Obviously, Microsoft would prefer that these client-access devices be personal computers running Microsoft Windows XP Professional, and in this case, I'm not going to disagree, because the Microsoft SBS 2003 product works best when used with Microsoft Windows XP and Microsoft Office Small Business Edition 2003.

This limit of 75 users/devices has increased from the previous version of the product; Small Business Server 2000 had a limit of 50 devices. Subsequently, the customer base for SBS 2003 has somewhat increased, without Microsoft compromising the sales of its enterprise server solutions, that is, the suite of products that make up the rest of the Microsoft Windows Server 2003 server family.

More realistically, SBS 2003 is a good solution for businesses with between 3 and 50 users. If you have any fewer than 3, it's better to at least consider cheaper options that still might offer a good range of IT capabilities; any more than 50 users, and your hardware platform might begin to struggle as individual capabilities compete for system resources (especially if you are running the Premium edition with additional features such as SQL Server 2000 and ISA Server 2004).

Note As soon as your business nears the limits of SBS 2003, it's worth considering the full Microsoft Windows Server 2003 product set to ensure that you don't limit yourself to a single server implementation that needs upgrading as soon as you outgrow SBS 2003's limits.

Putting all this aside for a moment, the facts are pretty straightforward to understand: SBS 2003 *will* support 75 users and *can* be stretched to this limit if you choose to do so; if you are positive you will not exceed the limitations, SBS 2003 is the right tool for the job.

This book is aimed primarily at the decision makers in small businesses, those visionaries who transformed the business from a dream to a fully-fledged profitable organization. So, hopefully by the time you have digested the knowledge in this book, you'll understand not only how to install and manage this intricate suite of software products, but also how to leverage its services for maximum business benefit—such as deploying Windows SharePoint Services to help deliver collaborative facilities to your staff, or employing ISA Server to deliver fresh, up-to-date web content right to your customers' desktops in as secure a manner as possible.

Challenges Faced by Today's Small Business

It's a hard fact of life that if a small business is to be expected to succeed in today's cutthroat marketplace, the plethora of daily, weekly, and monthly challenges that have to be met must be tackled head-on.

On the surface, it would seem not many of these trials are related to the business's use of information technology, but this is a misconception. By understanding the capabilities that a technology system can offer your business, it becomes possible to automate and streamline many aspects of your enterprise that you might once have considered beyond help.

From every conceivable point of view, a well-crafted technology system can help redefine your business. Take collaboration, for example: one of the primary factors elevating a mediocre business to a successful business is how effectively that business can bring together teams of people to deliver their services or products to their customers in as professional and cost-effective a way as possible. This applies to managers and desk clerks, consultants and suppliers, and even your customers, all being able to work together in the most effective way possible. The key is learning how to bring these guys together in effectual teams where they can deliver their contribution to the business as a first-rate service.

SBS 2003 comes complete with a set of collaboration tools that can be used to speed up product deployment, offer shared solutions for communication and brainstorming, as well as easily facilitate video and audio conferencing.

Take another example, that perennial problem facing nearly every product-based company: ordering and storing *stock* items. If a business needs a constant supply of parts or spares to ensure constant product availability to the customer base, it is vital to correctly forecast trends in demand, without under- or overordering. Too much stock leads to redundancy and unnecessary capital tied up in mountains of unused parts; too little stock can lead to long lead times in getting products to your customers, and subsequent customer dissatisfaction.

With careful implementation of a technology solution that looks after stock, it becomes possible to address these issues and integrate a Just in Time ordering solution (JIT for short). A JIT system allows you to order the most appropriate amount of stock, making it available at the best time, and ensuring that your cash doesn't end up inaccessible in unused stock. On a grander scale, even the biggest enterprises, such as Dell, which specializes in custom-made PC solutions, manages to keep as little as five days' worth of stock items in its warehouses at any one time. This means that when disaster strikes, maybe a fire razing a complete warehouse to the ground, they lose only five days of business, and not the whole year's worth. With careful planning and a detailed understanding of your business requirements, you can use SBS 2003 to create your very own centralized JIT supply chain system, even down to the automation of reordering when stock items are low.

This kind of technology implementation requires forethought and an intimate knowledge of what your business's current weaknesses might be. But the good thing is, by following the processes laid out in this chapter, it is possible to draw up a table of your business's requirements and map them directly against the capabilities offered by SBS 2003 technology.

Take the following examples as just some of the issues facing today's small business and see how an IT system, correctly engineered, can help in each case. This list is by no means exhaustive, but the important point is that SBS 2003 can be leveraged in every situation to help alleviate the problem.

Cash Flow

In the world of the small business, cash is the lifeblood keeping everything alive. The health of your business is directly linked to the health of your cash flow. It's vital to predict the tidal variants of available cash from month to month (see Figure 1-1), taking into account every nuance of credit and debt throughout each account period.

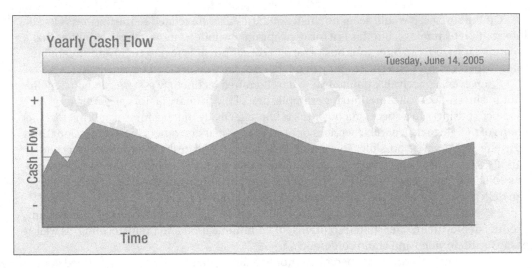

Figure 1-1. *Typical cash flow projection for a small business*

Cash flow is often predicted by using a paper-based accounting system, and in a lot of cases this is adequate. The main problem is that it can be extremely time-consuming. When parameters change, possibly through the employment of new staff or a change in tax law, then you are back to the drawing board for the next set of draft projections.

Using a combination of a simple spreadsheet software, such as Microsoft Office Excel 2003, and a good back-end server solution for maintaining records and securing this data (this is where SBS 2003 comes in), you can cut down on production time and ensure that the data is always at hand when you most need it—for example, when the bank manager needs to talk about the coming year's possibilities of paying back that loan.

Legal Stuff

Another daunting task for any business owner is keeping on top of all the regulations for running a small business. While larger companies employ specialist teams of accountants and legal beagles to address these issues, the small business owner takes on sole responsibility. It's tough to keep on top of everything: tax returns, payroll, employee benefits, indemnity insurances, and more. How can technology help?

Governments are becoming web enabled. Many governments around the world have started offering incentives to small businesses to file tax returns online, and in some places it is actively encouraged through generous discounts. Government departments are also offering much of their advice on the Internet, so instead of having to wade through countless pamphlets and advice sheets, a simple search on the IRS website will answer all your queries. By web-enabling your business and sharing your Internet connection with all staff, all this advice can be made readily available to the whole company. SBS 2003 can give you this flexibility to web-enable your business without compromising security or your system's integrity.

Automation

Ask small business employees what aggravates them the most, and they will almost certainly mention the dreaded word, *paperwork*. Some businesses are so engulfed by process and procedure that staff can be faced with over a dozen forms to fill out for nearly every task they might perform: annual leave, taking out the company van, customer orders, supplier orders, consultancy contracts, receipts, contacts, breathing.

Again, by adopting a clever approach to information technology, it's entirely possible to cut the number of forms down to an absolute bare minimum. Simple things like the leave calendar, for example, could be kept on the computer system so it's accessible to all but editable only by someone in charge. An email form can be used to request the leave, and a backup of the manager's email folder will ensure traceability over as many years as is deemed necessary for company records. A secondary benefit is cutting stationery costs—no more paper-based forms and less space needed in filing cabinets!

Marketing

Marketing is the key to a successful business. A business that can adapt and grow in a way that its customers demand will excel, and a business that ignores trends and current social requirements will certainly fail. And behind it all is the basic principle known as marketing. It's important to remember that marketing is not sales. *Sales* is specifically the action of selling your products or services to your customers. Obvious, I hear you say, but wait. Marketing is not advertising, although it plays a part. Instead, *marketing* is how you present your company and products as a whole.

Your company strategy is effectively a marketing strategy—where will you be in one year, three years, five years? How will you deliver your products through different media—from direct sales to Internet selling? All this is marketing, which is a subject in its own right, but behind any successful strategy, you'll find the ability for a business to rapidly react to new pressures.

This is why a business with a strong IT solution excels. Employing a solution that can rapidly transition from one way of working to another—allowing a business to swing from a product-driven company to a service-driven company within a few days, or from customer to customer—opens up possibilities that a non-IT-driven company simply could not cope with. By using SBS 2003's collaboration tools, and rapid deployment of team sites and Internet solutions using Microsoft FrontPage, you can churn out new company offerings in as little as a few hours—as long as it takes to type them up.

What Is Microsoft Windows SBS 2003?

Put simply, Microsoft Windows Small Business Server 2003 is a comprehensive IT solution optimized for use in the small businesses environment. It comprises an integrated suite of enterprise-capable applications, brought together as a low-cost solution that can be easily exploited by small business managers who demand the high-end capabilities only previously available to large organizations.

SBS 2003 offers the ideal opportunity for small business customers to introduce a server-centric IT solution and hence gain all the benefits of a centralized solution from a management, integrity, availability, and security point of view.

Note There are over 2 million Microsoft Windows NT Server 4.0 owners worldwide. All of these users need to think seriously about upgrading their infrastructure to cope with the ever-demanding business environment presented today—not to mention they are fast running out of people who are willing to support such antiquated (by today's standards) technology, including, most importantly, Microsoft.

Introducing the SBS 2003 Family Members

Microsoft decided the best way to offer big-business IT solutions to the cash-conscious small business community was to combine a number of key enterprise server products with essential client-side applications to enhance productivity. The SBS 2003 suite comes as two separate products, with a set of core applications common to both. These core products are what Microsoft calls the SBS 2003 Standard Edition. The SBS 2003 Premium Edition consists of the core products along with two extra server products and an extra client-side web-publishing product.

Both editions deliver an excellent set of core services that any small business could exploit. To decide which product is right for *your* business, you should read the rest of this chapter.

Small Business Server 2003 Standard Edition

The core products available to both versions of SBS 2003 are as follows:

- Microsoft Windows Server 2003 with Service Pack 1 (SP1)

- Microsoft Exchange Server 2003

- Windows SharePoint Services

- Shared Fax services

- Remote Web Workplace

- Microsoft Office Outlook 2003

Small Business Server 2003 Premium Edition

The Premium edition comes with all the features of the Standard edition and also contains the following:

- Microsoft SQL Server 2000

- Microsoft ISA Server 2004

- Microsoft Office FrontPage 2003

Throughout the rest of this section, I outline the key components that make up the server side of the SBS 2003 product set and then list the extra client-side tools you get with the Standard and Premium editions.

Server-Side Components in Detail—Standard Edition

The Standard edition server-side components form the core environment for your SBS 2003 network. These components are then augmented with further server and client applications to form the Premium edition. This section introduces the main components that comprise the SBS 2003 Standard edition package.

Microsoft Windows Server 2003 with SP1

Microsoft Windows Server 2003 is the underlying operating system powering SBS 2003. It is responsible for controlling access to files, the network, client computers, the Internet, and printers, and it hosts all the other server-side components listed here. This is by far the most robust server product Microsoft has ever produced, with the underlying Active Directory technology (covered in greater detail later in this book) being the foundation that all the other products are built upon.

Microsoft Windows Server 2003 comes complete with its very own web server, called Internet Information Services version 6.0, to allow you to host your own web content on an easy-to-administer, extremely secure system. Web pages can subsequently be made available internally on your company intranet, published externally via your ISP, or presented directly through your Internet gateway by using the Premium edition product called Internet Security and Acceleration Server.

Improvements in Microsoft Windows Server 2003 over previous editions are paramount, as the product offers greater availability and flexibility without compromising security. From a productivity point of view, Microsoft Windows Server 2003 offers simple file and print services that require very little administration or understanding of what goes on under the hood, which, for a small business, is critical to keep down the total cost of ownership. Control of clients and services through Group Policy allows a centralized model for all administrative tasks, and software can be deployed from a single source rather than someone having to go to each machine and install the software manually from a DVD.

Microsoft Exchange Server 2003

Microsoft Exchange Server 2003 is Microsoft's enterprise electronic messaging and collaboration platform. It is designed to seamlessly integrate with the Microsoft Windows Server 2003 Active Directory to offer all users a comprehensive set of electronic mail services, as well as an easy route for sending and receiving email externally to other systems such as the Internet. Email can either be sent from a standard client-access device, such as a Microsoft Windows XP workstation, or directed through a telecom provider's WAP gateway to mobile devices such as mobile phones and personal digital assistants (PDAs).

Another new feature to SBS 2003, bundled with Microsoft Exchange Server 2003, is Microsoft Office Outlook Web Access 2003. This provides a secure, browser-driven interface with the Microsoft Exchange Server 2003 environment, allowing remote access to all the services offered by Microsoft Exchange from any desktop with an Internet browser.

Windows SharePoint Services

Windows SharePoint Services is a relatively new product to Microsoft that has been around for only the last few years. It's quick to deploy and comes with prewritten web parts (pieces of computer software that run within web pages) that help automate certain common tasks associated with collaborative working—for example, shared file areas, document management, and team calendars. It's possible to customize Windows SharePoint Services (either directly or by using a development tool such as Microsoft Office FrontPage 2003) as specific business requirements emerge. As part of the package, you also get shared calendars, contact lists, announcement facilities, and discussion groups, as well as the ability to mount the system as a shared network place for applications to automatically save into by default.

Shared Fax Services

This facility provides a way to minimize the number of extra telephone lines you might require for corporate faxes, meaning you can route faxes going from your business through a limited number of devices. Faxes being transmitted from your business can be routed through Windows SharePoint Services, your email, or even directly to your printer. The tight integration with the other core components of SBS 2003 allows you to send faxes electronically from your desktop, use Microsoft Outlook contacts to distribute faxes, auto-archive faxes to secure storage locations for record keeping, automatically log faxes into collaborative workspaces within Windows SharePoint Services, automatically route faxes to specifically designated printers, and view faxes from a remote location because they can reside in your email inbox and are made available through a service such as Outlook Web Access. All in all, Shared Fax services have improved leaps and bounds since previous versions of SBS, and the product really is now the de facto small business solution.

Remote Web Workplace

This capability is an enhancement to the remote-access package supplied with SBS 2003. Remote Web Workplace allows you to connect any mobile device (from a tablet PC to a PDA) via a secure Internet link to your SBS 2003 system, granting your employees the right to access your business data from any remote location. Users can read their email, access the company intranet facilities (provided by Windows SharePoint Services), and even connect to their own personal computer to access files on their hard disks that might once have been totally inaccessible.

Connection Manager allows the remote machine to connect into your business environment after downloading a simple software add-on. With just a couple of mouse clicks, you can access company resources from anywhere on the planet (anywhere that is, where you can get to the Internet). As working from home is becoming increasingly popular, it's becoming less and less necessary for the entire workforce to be in the office from 9 a.m. to 5 p.m. A more-flexible approach to remote working enables your business premises to be limited only by the reach of the Internet.

Server-Side Components in Detail—Premium Edition

The Premium edition of SBS 2003 adds further functionality to the core set of application services delivered as part of the Standard edition package. This increased capability will allow Premium edition users to take advantage of the industrial-strength firewall, ISA Server 2004, and utilize the power of the scalable database solution, SQL Server 2000. The Premium edition upgrade is performed after an installation of the Standard edition.

Microsoft Internet Security and Acceleration (ISA) Server 2004

ISA Server is the first of the four Premium edition server products we will discuss. It provides an enterprise firewall solution that integrates well with the other products included with SBS 2003, as well as web-caching services for Internet browsing acceleration. The ISA firewall provides a comprehensive security barrier for your network connection to the Internet, capable of detecting attempts at intrusion and reacting on your behalf to isolate the threat. It also provides the building blocks for secure remote-access solutions via the Internet, such as virtual private network tunneling.

Microsoft SQL Server 2000

Microsoft SQL Server 2000 is Microsoft's relational database server product. Many applications require a database at the back end. These applications can leverage the power of SQL Server 2000 for enhanced resilience and querying as compared to the capabilities of smaller desktop products such as the Microsoft Desktop Engine (MSDE). SQL Server 2000 is a good server-side solution for your business's spreadsheets and line of business databases. It interfaces seamlessly with desktop products, such as Microsoft Office Excel 2003 and Microsoft Office Access 2003, to run queries against your business data.

Client-Side Components in Detail—Standard Edition

From a client point of view, SBS 2003 also delivers a number of useful features that integrate well with the server products already mentioned. The products are optimized to run their best on a Microsoft Windows XP desktop, although it is still possible to run them on older operating systems, such as Microsoft Windows 2000.

Microsoft Office Outlook 2003

The email client, Microsoft Outlook, provides the workstation side of SBS's messaging solution, interfacing with all the services provided by Microsoft Exchange Server 2003. Outlook is by no means a new product, but this latest iteration, Outlook 2003, is by far the best email client you could choose to leverage in a business environment.

Outlook is far from just a simple email client. It provides an interface to a long list of features delivered by Microsoft Exchange Server 2003, features such as the shared calendar (see Figure 1-2), where you can not only list appointments and create meetings, but also share your calendar with other users and create shared calendars that many users can access and update. The permissions to access the data, as for all Microsoft products discussed here, allow you to say who has access to what information, and at what level—you indicate whether they are information authors or simply information readers.

Outlook also interfaces with the Exchange global address list (GAL), which offers a complete list of email addresses and contacts for your business. You can also create customized address lists containing all your customer contacts and make these available to the business centrally. Outlook also contains a task tracker that allows you to create your own electronic to-do list, generating reminders for tasks when they approach their deadlines. Additional features such as public folders can be used to generate discussion groups, where subscribers can collaborate on discussion threads through the Outlook interface.

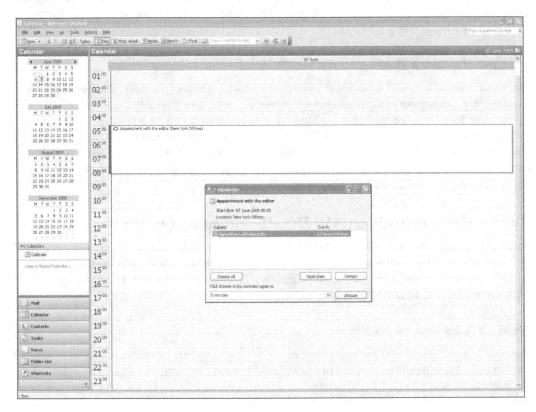

Figure 1-2. *Outlook can notify you when appointments are due.*

Client-Side Components in Detail—Premium Edition

Accompanying the extra server features included as part of the Premium edition comes FrontPage 2003, the website development package used to create your company website or intranet, or edit your SharePoint site. FrontPage comes on its own additional CD, and Premium edition users get one licence included in the price.

FrontPage 2003

FrontPage is part of the Microsoft Office 2003 suite and comes with SBS 2003 when you buy the Premium edition. FrontPage allows you to easily create elaborate websites, and comes with hundreds of premade web functions and special effects already coded up to make your life as easy as possible. In fact, you could probably get your company website up and running in as little as a couple of hours if you really put your mind to it.

The really great thing about FrontPage is that it's not designed for use by IT guys. Pretty much anyone (even a manager) could use the simple development interface to bolt together professional-looking web pages, but this is not the end of FrontPage's capabilities. If you want to take things further, you can really get down and dirty as you delve deep into the coding of HTML (HyperText Markup Language is the language of the web), DHTML (Dynamic Hyper-Text Markup Language is a modern data-driven language allowing dynamic objects that draw information from remote data sources), and XML (Extensible Markup Language is a much newer tool for advanced web development). FrontPage also integrates with both Windows SharePoint Services and SQL Server to allow you to create dynamic SQL-driven database sites.

If you're still unsure as to whether you want SBS 2003, you can always give it a try by ordering the 180-day free trail online on Microsoft's website (see Figure 1-3). The link is http://www.microsoft.com/windowsserver2003/sbs/evaluation/trial/default.mspx.

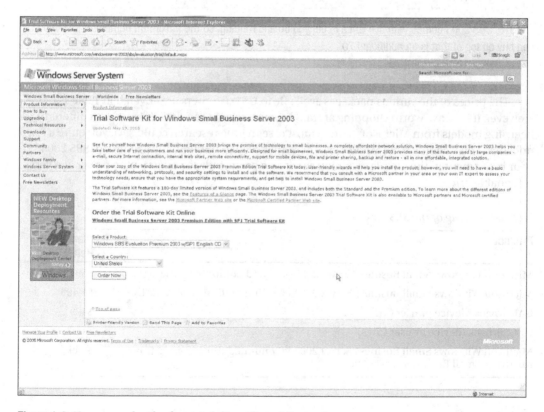

Figure 1-3. *You can order the free trial direct from Microsoft.*

When deciding which of the two products (SBS 2003 Standard or SBS 2003 Premium) would best suit your business, the best advice is to wait until you've identified your requirements before you purchase. Follow the rest of the advice in this chapter before you identify which way to go. You might find you are surprised by the result.

How Much Does It Cost?

The question on everyone's mind sooner or later is, how much will all this cost? With SBS 2003 there are two costs you need to consider:

- There is the initial cost of purchasing the SBS 2003 platform, be it the Standard edition or Premium edition.

- Then on top of that, you also have to purchase CALs (client access licenses) to allow your computers and users to access the network.

So, there are effectively two costs you must add together when you are planning to buy the SBS 2003 solution set.

Note SBS 2003 comes with five CALs to get you up and running, so the maximum number of CALs you can buy on top of that is an additional 70.

The prices of the various packages available to US customers are covered in Table 1-1. However, it's always worth shopping around because certain retailers operate with different licensing models from Microsoft, and in most cases a little research could save you quite a few dollars. If you upgrade from Small Business Server 2000 to the Premium edition of SBS 2003, your investment in the Standard edition services is protected, so you get more power at a very reasonable price.

Table 1-1. *Pricing of the SBS 2003 Platform*

Product	Standard Retail Price
Microsoft Windows Small Business Server 2003 Standard Edition + 5 CALs	$599
Microsoft Windows Small Business Server 2003 Premium Edition + 5 free CALs	$1,499
CAL 5-pack (device or user CALs)	$489
CAL 20-pack (device or user CALs)	$1,929
Microsoft Windows Small Business Server 2003 Premium Edition upgrade from Microsoft Small Business Server 2000	$599

As you can see in Table 1-1, the best value for your money is to upgrade a previous version of SBS to the latest Premium edition, giving you the entire product set at a mere $599.

Client access licenses are best purchased in bulk, so again, if you envision company growth in any way near the scale of 20 employees, or see the need for 20 extra computers, buy the 20-pack rather than four 5-packs.

SBS 2003 consultant David Pyke of Intanetworking explains the benefits of the SBS 2003 pricing model:

> *The cost model of SBS 2003 and its focus on tight integration and ease of configuration has enabled even the smallest organization to use the same enterprise-class software that the very largest ones use. We talk with many of these who are surprised at what is possible within their budget, particularly when it comes to enhancing the Internet experience or Internet-enabling the organization. With the cheap and widespread availability of Internet broadband connections and the SBS 2003 configuration wizards, it is simple and cost-effective to fully Internet-enable an organization, providing immediate email connections with Microsoft Exchange 2003. ISA 2004, included with the Premium edition and a very effective firewall and proxy server, can easily be configured to protect the organization yet still enable specific access into it—for example, for employee access to email from outside or for access to an SBS 2003-hosted public website.*

Restrictions of Small Business Server 2003

As well as knowing what SBS 2003 can bring to your business, it's also important that you know what it will *not* do.

First, the technical restrictions that govern whether to use SBS 2003 in your environment are fairly obvious:

- Do you exceed the client-access licensing threshold? You have an imposed limit of 75 user accounts accessing the network simultaneously, although the limit is imposed on the network access and not the management in Active Directory. The number of workstations that can access the network is also limited to 75, so in either case you cannot exceed these limits.

Note The restriction of 75 workstations and user accounts does not apply to peripherals such as printers and scanners.

- You end up with a single domain and a single forest. This means that the SBS 2003 environment cannot be extended by adding it to another Microsoft Windows Server 2003 infrastructure. There is a migration path from SBS 2003 to full-blown Microsoft Windows Server 2003, but this comes at extra cost. It's best to identify short-term growth in advance to see if it takes you over the limits, and invest in the most appropriate technology up front.

- How is your business distributed? Because all the components that come with SBS 2003 (Microsoft Windows Server 2003, Microsoft Exchange 2003, Windows SharePoint, and so on) must be installed on one server, with the exception of Outlook and FrontPage, you must position your business to access the location of this server. If you have multiple sites with low-bandwidth connections between them, and you don't want to upgrade these links because of ongoing costs, then you might be forced into a more distributed environment, using something like Microsoft Windows Server 2003 Standard Edition or SBS 2003 with a Microsoft Windows Server 2003 domain controller situated at the remote site.

On another level, SBS 2003 cannot fix your business if it is fundamentally flawed. If you don't have a marketable product, or the service you supply is no longer required by your customers, there is nothing SBS 2003 can do to help. In this case the only answer is to rethink your business plan.

SBS 2003 will not be able to do everything you need it to do straight out of the box. As with any critical system, you will need to work with the product set, configuring each of the internal components to make sure they work in the way that best suits the needs of your environment.

Basic configuration is carried out by using each separate component's configuration wizard (a helpful interface that takes high-level input and performs low-level configuration on your behalf). However, to get the extra mile from your investment, you'll still need to understand how to customize each component (don't worry, this book helps with exactly that).

Note Microsoft has gone to great lengths to automate as much of the SBS 2003 installation and basic configuration as possible. The introduction of task-based wizards allows you to perform most of the basic business configuration tasks very quickly.

You are also constrained by some other pricing point limitations that Microsoft has imposed on this product. You cannot expand to more than one forest/domain, and you cannot utilize a second SBS 2003 server in a consolidated environment. This forces users with a requirement to distribute services such as authentication and file services to move up to the full Microsoft Windows Server 2003 product set or add a Microsoft Windows Server 2003 domain controller to the SBS 2003 domain.

Another few points to consider when buying SBS 2003:

- SBS 2003 will not suggest ways to improve your business—that is *your* job.

- SBS 2003 will not fix staffing problems, such as having a team that is overworked and underpaid. This, again, is up to you.

- SBS 2003 will certainly not listen to you when you shout at it.

SBS 2003 consultant David Pyke of Intanetworking says:

The wizard-driven configuration in SBS 2003 is effective at delivering high functionality that would normally be prohibitively time-consuming (and so expensive), to deliver for small customers. One example: Windows SharePoint Services (WSS) is a powerful collaboration tool that provides tangible business benefit for all sizes of organizations, providing a central and searchable repository of knowledge. As it comes preinstalled and configured with SBS 2003, the only task is tweaking it for specific requirements, saving many man hours of installation and configuration. If a broadband Internet connection is available, providing secure access to WSS and to email from outside the organization's perimeter is another few mouse clicks, by using the Configure Email and Internet Connection Wizard (CEICW). This performs a whole range of steps that would normally take many hours if undertaken individually.

Building Blocks of a Successful IT System

Let's assume that you have a good idea about what your business is meant to be doing each day to earn your bread and butter. Let's even be so presumptuous as to assume that you know what you need to do over the next five years to ensure ongoing success. Speak to any small business owner about how to ensure that their business keeps afloat year after year and pretty much every time you'll hear them testify to *accurate measurement* of resources.

By this they mean measuring every one of the abundance of vital statistics that indicate how well (or how badly) the business is functioning. Looking at daily cash flow, trend forecasting, market analysis, business plan revision, payroll, and competition are just some of the dozens of metrics needing to analyzed on a regular basis, to make sure you know exactly what's going on. By keeping an eye on these metrics, you can make sure that you are prepared to react when problems arise.

But with all this careful measurement, have you ever thought about quantifying the value that your IT system brings to your company? A strange question, you might say. How is it possible to value something as intangible as a few PCs and a few cables splattered around the office? Is it really something that's worth worrying about? The answer, to be blunt, is simple: *yes*.

It is absolutely imperative to keep a close eye on every investment made by your business, and IT is no different. Ignoring the intrinsic worth that these facilities bring to your operations can become as much a revenue killer as any other factor.

The fact is, many small business owners perceive their need for an IT system as a necessary evil rather than as a solution to solve some of their business problems. They find themselves pumping hard-earned profits into hardware upgrades, complicated software that never seems to do what it says on the box, and expensive consultancy that brings them no nearer to their goals. The real key to understanding what an IT system brings to your business comes first from understanding what each aspect of the investment can be measured against. And to do this, you need to understand what the fundamental aspects of an IT system really are.

It's all a matter of logic. Break anything down to its fundamental component parts, map the functions of those parts to the roles they perform in your business, and then decide on the metrics that you can use to measure their performance.

Let's take one component most people are familiar with as an example: electronic mail.

Electronic mail is used to send messages back and forth between recipients, very much like the same service the post office performs for you with letters and parcels. So, what are the key driving factors for putting in an email system in your business? The key to determining why you need email is to understand its benefits. Look at the job it performs: it facilitates rapid communication. Using a robust email solution, you can replace some of those normal postal communications you have to make with customers and suppliers (the ones your secretary has to type out four times every month, put in envelopes, stick stamps on, and then rely on someone else not to misplace somewhere along the line) with something more efficient. Now put it in context. It can't replace the postal service completely—you still need tangible items such as spare parts to arrive in the traditional way—but electronic mail systems can automate many of your scheduled communications, making them easy to generate through the use of electronic forms (more later) and making them lightening fast to send, because the speed of the Internet is many times faster than any real-world service. But wait, there's more. What about the number of times you've been stuck on hold, trying to order some fax paper from your office supplier? Annoying, isn't it. But as other companies also move to an electronic-mail-based solution to support their business, there is a good chance they have adopted an email- or web-based system for placing orders.

The most important thing that this example illustrates is that we are measuring the success of the implementation of the electronic mail system against tangible business factors, such as the following:

- The actual amount of time saved by automating your supply chain communications

- Automation of mundane acquisition tasks that enables staffing resources to be used more effectively

- Scheduling of regular communications, making sure they are timely

- Lightning-fast customer feedback without the invasiveness or immediacy of direct telephone calls

- A central store for customer and supplier contacts accessible from the Outlook 2003 desktop

- A comprehensive audit trail of all electronic communications and business conversations

As you can see, these factors represent just one aspect of the overall IT solution. But it's this in-depth look at each fundamental IT component that enables you to successfully measure each component's worth and then give you the ability to measure the overall worth of your entire implementation.

So let's take a look at the primary components of a good enterprise IT system. Then in the next section we will match each of these IT capabilities with your business requirements.

IT from the Ground Up

To make your IT system as easy to understand as possible, try looking at it as a conceptual four-layer model. Then break down each layer into the component parts and match these components with the capabilities they might bring to your business.

Note All of the components we're going to examine over the next few pages will be expanded in more detail later in this book. The aim of the following discussion is to show you how to use the four-layer model to begin mapping the IT components' capabilities to their potential use in your business.

Network Layer

Underpinning everything is your network infrastructure. So, down at the very bottom of the stack is the *Network layer*, which defines the physical elements you require to enable the connection of devices, such as workstations, servers, printers, and fax machines, to each other (see Figure 1-4). This layer provides all the interconnectivity between devices as well as acts as the governance in enabling links between your network and external systems, such as the Internet.

A network comprises key components that work together to provide an infrastructure that enables systems to connect to whichever places they might need to connect to.

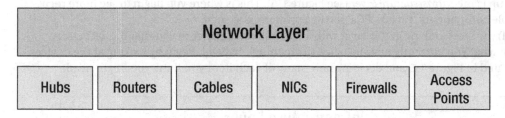

Figure 1-4. *The Network layer comprises physical network components.*

The key to understanding the capabilities provided in the Network layer is to ensure that you analyze each box shown in Figure 1-4. Each of the following items must be understood in the context of how it is used in your business and how it might be used in the future:

- Cables enable the interconnection of one device to another. They must be neat and discreet and as flexible as the business requires. If you are frequently moving offices or if workers need the flexibility to move desks frequently, the cabling infrastructure must accommodate this.

- Hubs, routers, and switches are intelligent electrical devices used to connect cables to each other and to connect cables to devices. You need to consider where they might be best positioned. Also, consider the number of ports they offer to the business. Routers connect networks, so a router would be used to connect your network to the Internet.

- Firewalls sit between one security domain and another, adding a layer of policing between these domains. For example, a firewall would sit between your network and the Internet.

- Wireless networks are becoming more widely used with the advent of more secure technologies appearing on the market. They replace your need for physical cables, instead using radio frequencies to communicate.

- Network interface cards (NICs) and modems provide the most common way of connecting servers and workstations to the network. A NIC is the component you connect network cables into, and a modem connects telephone lines to computers.

- Telephone lines are essential to all network designs. Broadband connections multiplex on existing telephone connections. Fax machines require telephone lines to transmit documents. Remote-access users dial into your business through telephone lines.

The main point to bear in mind when designing your network is, who needs to talk to what? Chapter 4 covers the Network layer in detail, discussing the nitty-gritty of hubs, routers, and switches as well as explaining how the electrical signals on the wires are converted into information that allows systems to communicate. It is important to at least have a basic grasp of this before you try to design your own network. The important thing for now is to understand the function that the Network layer performs.

Infrastructure Layer

Next up is the *Infrastructure layer* (see Figure 1-5). This is where you begin to see more recognizable components, such as PCs, servers, printers, and such.

Try to start looking at this layer with a blank sheet of paper in your hand. Don't worry about what you currently have installed (if anything). Instead, begin by looking at the devices indicated in Figure 1-5 and deciding how many of each item you think you might need.

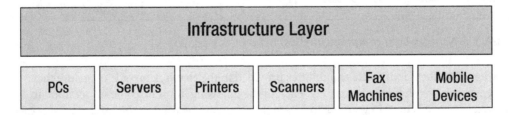

Figure 1-5. *The Infrastructure layer comprises physical devices.*

Ask yourself the following questions:

- How many PCs does your business require?

- If users will be accessing the system remotely, how many connections will be required?

- Is there a requirement for other kinds of mobile devices, such as PDAs and smart phones?

- How many hard-copy peripherals do you need?

- How many fax machines?

Note SBS 2003 comes with a Shared Fax services capability, so don't decide on the exact number until you've reviewed the "Faxing" section in Chapter 5.

After you have answered these questions, it's time to move up the stack to the next level: *operating systems.*

Operating System Layer

At the *Operating System layer*, the main things to consider are the operating system components that communicate to form the complete infrastructure. By taking a look at your infrastructure and making a list of all your current systems (see Figure 1-6), you'll probably find it's best to replace some older PCs with new ones running the latest client operating system (Microsoft Windows XP or Microsoft Vista).

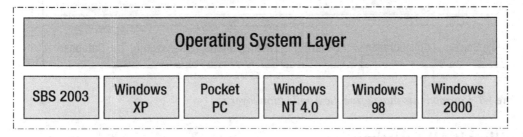

Figure 1-6. *The Operating System layer shows all your OS solutions.*

Note Bearing in mind that Microsoft Windows 9x and Microsoft Windows NT 4.0 clients do not talk to the Microsoft Windows Server 2003 server system without changes to the underlying Server Message Block (SMB) policies, an upgrade is always the preferred option. In support of the upgrade case, it's worth remembering that your systems will be more secure and supportable when they are up-to-date.

Let's say that one of your computers is running Microsoft Windows 98, one has Microsoft Windows NT 4.0, and the third has Microsoft Windows XP. This is typical of any small business, and this kind of mix and match setup must be catered to.

You also note that there are two possible access methods for getting to the Internet. Two home users are able to exploit the high-bandwidth offerings of broadband, probably achieving Internet connection speeds in excess of 1 Mbps, while the other poor fellow is subjected to the painfully slow speeds of dial-up (slow by today's standards), probably limited to a connection speed of around 56 Kbps.

Warning Be careful not to confuse *megabits* with *megabytes*. In the context of networking, *Mbps* stands for megabits per second. As 1 byte contains 8 bits, do the math and you'll see that 1 Mbps equals 128,000 bytes per second.

Application Layer

At the top of the pile, the *Application layer* defines your IT-to-business relationship (see Figure 1-7). Here you collate the business-oriented IT functions that will form the basis of your system and user functionality. Understanding the abstract concepts presented at the Application layer is vital to understanding what you need your SBS 2003 solution to do.

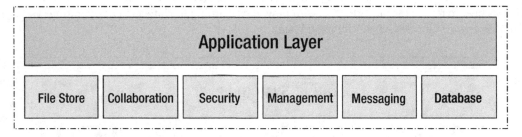

Figure 1-7. *Components that define the Application layer*

Pulling It All Together

After you have been through and analyzed the entire solution stack, you can sit down and evaluate what you've discovered. It's important to work systematically through each layer in turn, in each case evaluating the technology you have and what your future requirements might be. In summary, consider the following:

- Analyze the requirements at every level.

- Document your findings as you work through the levels.

- Produce logical diagrams that show how each layer of the solution stack adds an extra layer of complexity to the overall solution.

- Don't skip any of the building blocks, even if you don't yet see a use for it straight away.

- You can always revisit any aspect of your design if you decide you need to change something.

- Review your IT architecture each time you add new hardware, install new software, or reconfigure any of the components. This allows you to keep track of how your system is evolving, and in some cases it allows you to exploit some capabilities of new components in ways you might not have considered.

A Top-Down Approach to Business Requirements

After you've looked at the capabilities that the IT infrastructure can offer from the bottom up, the next stage is to look at your business requirements from the top down.

Purely from a business-centric point of view, it is vitally important to determine the real requirements of the business rather than trying to realize false requirements based solely on the vast array of services an IT system can provide.

Note Always remember, your business requirements should drive your IT solution rather than the other way around. To make sure you get the best value from SBS 2003, you must expose business requirements and IT capabilities and then marry the two together.

The High-Level View

This top-down approach allows the two sets of capabilities to be easily matched against each other, meaning the IT solution can be engineered in such a way as to meet as many of your business requirements as possible.

Start by asking yourself the following questions to get the high-level view of what your business is all about:

1. Which services do you provide? Write down an overview of the services you provide to your customers.

2. How do you provide these services? What processes and procedures do you use to enable you to deliver these services to your customers?

3. What products do you provide? List all the products your company sells (products are tangible items rather than services).

4. How do you manufacture or source these products? How are these products created, sourced from suppliers, and dispatched to customers?

5. Are there any additional factors that make your business unique? What else, at a high level, defines your business and sets your above the competition?

6. How do you measure success? What procedures do you have in place to measure the success of your service or product sales, and how do you measure overall company effectiveness?

7. What is your business strategy, if indeed you have one? What are your strategic goals over the next five years?

8. How do you manage your workforce with regard to pay and benefits?

Pay close attention to your processes and procedures, inputs and outputs, and all the staffing and management methodologies that you currently employ.

Table 1-2 shows a few examples of the types of services you might expect from a sample garage services company.

Table 1-2. *Top-Level Services for a Typical Garage*

Top-Level Service (Services and Products)	Customer (Internal and External)	Service/Product Description
Car servicing	Private vehicle owners	Provide scheduled car servicing for nonspecialty, privately owned vehicles
Routine maintenance	Private vehicle owners	Ad hoc maintenance on privately owned, nonspecialty cars
Bodywork repair	Private vehicle owners	Stone chip and extensive body shop repairs for privately owned, nonspecialty cars
24/7 emergency repairs	Private vehicle owners	An emergency call-out facility where mobile mechanics can attend to breakdowns on behalf of the customer
Car servicing	Fleet car services	Provide scheduled car servicing for nonspecialty fleet cars
Routine maintenance	Fleet car services	Ad hoc maintenance on nonspecialty fleet cars
AAA support	AAA	24/7 emergency support to AAA

Table 1-2 shows that this particular garage has answered the first question in relation to the services they provide.

You should go on to perform a similar exercise for each of the remaining high-level questions, creating a table for each one as you go. After you've completed this, it's time to proceed to the next level.

Break It All Down

The next step is to break down each of your high-level business functions into discrete components, looking closely at each of the entries in your tables.

Take the most fundamental question, for example: *Which services do you provide?* You've written down the high-level descriptions of the services your company provides, but now it's time to look even closer at each of these services and break them into component parts. Take, for example, Table 1-2: one of the key services provided is stone chip and bodywork repair for private customers with nonspecialty cars.

Try thinking a little deeper about the services covered by this top-level description. The sort of thing you'll come up with is as follows:

- Repairing stone chips

- Polishing paint

- Offering a complimentary car wash after the vehicle has been repaired

- Providing a vehicle collections and returns service

You see from this list that the services listed earlier at the high level can be broken down into more discrete components, each being as unique to your total business offering as any other, and each one defining your business as it stands today (see Table 1-3).

Table 1-3. *A Functional Breakdown of Just One High-Level Service*

Bodywork Repair

Subfunction	Customer	Description
Repairing stone chips	Private vehicle owners	Fixing the damage caused to paint from the effect of stones and gravel striking the car at speed
Polishing paint	Private vehicle owners	Cleaning the areas around the repair and working the new paint in such a way as to blend it into the surrounding panel
Car wash	Private vehicle owners	An external wash of the complete vehicle to finish off the job
Collections and returns service	Private vehicle owners	A service where the garage will collect and return a vehicle to a customer within defined limits with regard to the customer's location

After you've identified each subfunction, it's much easier to see where costs might be incurred—for example, the free wash after the repairs have been carried out costs in time, car wash detergent, and water. In your overall cost model, every single function should be factored into cash flow projections and profit modelling.

As you work your way through each of the high-level functional areas, expanding each from a business requirement perspective, you'll begin to see how these functions can be matched against the appropriate IT capability (if any) and where an IT facility would help with aspects of your business.

Take a look at another example: *How do you manage your workforce with regard to pay and benefits?*This one is great. Most small business managers pay their staff wages at the end of the week, and in return the manager expects a particular job function to be carried out to the best of the employee's ability. The thing is, as long as the job is being done and the return from the employee is seen, the details of how the activities are carried out is largely left to the staff in question. The job deliverables may be well defined, but what about the activities the staff member undertakes to deliver upon these requirements?

By analyzing the details of the daily, weekly, and monthly activities of each member of your staff, right down to the lowest level (for example, how the process of reordering paper for the A4 color laser printer is implemented), you will end up with a discrete set of processes and procedures that completely define how your business functions.

Matching SBS 2003 Capabilities to Your Business Requirements

The final and most important part of the whole exercise is to match the two sets of capabilities/ requirements together to ensure that you get the most from your SBS 2003 implementation.

But before you do that, there are a set of capabilities that any good IT system will deliver that must also be included. The following should be analyzed, each in their own right. When you draw up your final list of component-level business functions, each one of these facets must be also be considered.

All Good IT Solutions Should Do the Following...

The following capabilities are not vendor specific, but each has been put in context of SBS 2003 so you see how it is addressed within this solution set. Include all these capabilities in your requirements mapping, and feel free to break them down in whichever way best suits your needs.

Quick installation and rapid deployment is essential for reducing the initial cost of the system's implementation and reducing the effort in subsequent rollout of the infrastructure across your complete business network.

SBS 2003 comes with a number of easy-to-use setup wizards that configure and deploy the solution lightning fast. Installation of SBS 2003 is the easiest of all the Microsoft operating systems because the postinstallation configuration of all the extra SBS 2003 components is largely automated through the use of the Small Business Server Setup Wizard. This wizard runs the first time you log on to your system after the initial installation of Microsoft Windows Server 2003 and expertly guides you through the configuration of each of the SBS 2003 components (Microsoft Exchange 2003, Windows SharePoint Services, and so on).

Ease of management is vital for keeping the ongoing costs down for running an IT solution. There is no point putting in an IT solution that automates loads of business functions, cuts corners left, right, and center, and saves $50,000 every year, if the total cost of ownership of the whole solution is $75,000 per year.

SBS 2003 removes the burden placed on a business of providing a system administration team. Most small businesses (even the ones that have grown significantly to around 50 employees) can get away with a skeleton team of about two staff members running the whole system. This is a significant breakthrough for small businesses that have always seen IT as a necessary evil with exponential cost overheads removing any benefit they might receive. Microsoft has kindly addressed this by automating most of the common system administrative tasks by using wizards, hence freeing up your IT staff for more business effective work, such as streamlining client rollouts and upgrades, software deployment, and security auditing.

Instant intranet for collaboration is the ability to quickly enable your business to use the collaborative facilities offered by an intranet-style service. As with all benefits, they must be matched against deployment and running costs to see if they are effective and of real monetary value to your company.

SBS 2003's answer is Windows SharePoint Services. The installation of Windows Share-Point Services gives you a preconfigured intranet complete with a whole range of collaborative features you can link to real business requirements: meeting schedulers, shared calendars, and company announcements to name but a few.

■**Note** When you run the wizard, you change the operating system's security to allow some of the functionality that, out of the box, Microsoft Windows Server 2003 blocks. This is Windows 2003 by design, created to be as secure as possible, with little to no networking enabled.

Internet and email is another must-have requirement that any good IT system will provide. The network capabilities offered by having your business connected to the Internet will enable you to have those business-to-business (B2B) and business-to-consumer (B2C) solutions that you so dearly want. Leveraging the power of an email solution into your business environment is also key to exploiting the connected world of the Internet.

SBS 2003 provides these facilities with as little effort as possible. The Configure Email and Internet Connection Wizard (CEICW) is used to meet both these requirements, connecting SBS 2003 securely to your ISP and configuring Microsoft Exchange to direct mail through your ISP (or using DNS) to the Internet.

■**Note** The planning phase covered in Chapter 3 explains how to gather all the information needed by each of these setup wizards as you go through installation. Before you start the installation, you will (as long as you've followed the guidelines in this book) have all the details you need to hit the ground running the first time.

Flick of the switch security means security that is on with the touch of a button. Security is imperative (this is why there is a whole chapter dedicated to security later in this book) and must be considered in any IT solution as the fundamental factor that sets one IT solution above the rest.

SBS 2003 is built on the latest and greatest of Microsoft's operating system technologies, and with the latest service packs and hot fixes installed, coupled with the Microsoft Windows XP Service Pack 2 update that effectively reinvented the Microsoft Windows XP operating system, the combination is unique. No other small business solutions are so geared up to deliver a total security solution out of the box. This means that as soon as you install SBS 2003 and run through the Small Business Server Setup Wizard, you'll have a secure solution.

Note The running of a secure IT system involves a number of key elements looking at both the confidentiality and integrity of data. Although SBS 2003 is locked down in such a way as to grant access to only those who need it, it still has to be monitored to make sure your secure configuration has not been changed to open backdoor entrances into your corporate environment.

Remote access enables you to gain access to your business resources from places outside the scope of the immediate control of your networked environment. This might be through a dial-in service or an Internet service, but either way, both methods of gaining control must inherently be secure.

SBS 2003 offers two capabilities to expedite these connections. Remote Web Workplace provides Internet access to your resources, so that you effectively have a desktop environment served from your business network over the Internet, secured by some of the underlying SBS 2003 security services. Routing and remote access are the services providing secure dial-in to users, meaning you can access your business network by using a business laptop, extending the reach of your network out over the phone lines.

Matching Business Requirements to IT

So far you've used tables to capture your requirements and identify the functions that define your business. You've seen what constitutes an IT system, and you've seen the extra features an IT system can bring to your business from a functional perspective.

The approach to defining the IT capabilities was to work from the ground up. To define your business functions, you started at the top and then worked your way down. The final job to undertake in completely mapping your business to your IT solution is to map the two together. To do this, you will use yet another set of tables.

Expanding on the previous example, take a look at Table 1-4 to see the breakdown of the AAA support element of the garage services business described earlier. Here you see there are three subfunctions that can be decomposed from the high-level service, AAA support.

Table 1-4. *Three Low-Level Components That Compose AAA Support*

AAA Support		
Subfunction	**Customer**	**Description**
Communicate with AAA call center to receive 24/7 emergency call-outs	AAA	Receive calls from call center over the phone. Emergency number is routed to manager's cell phone.
Assign calls to appropriate mechanics	AAA	Manager passes call to on-call service mechanic.
Invoice AAA on a monthly basis	Self	Invoices are typed from paperwork records of jobs each month and posted to AAA headquarters.

Now take these three services and look at them from an IT perspective. With all the tools and capabilities you've seen so far, which aspects of your SBS 2003 system can be matched against these functions?

Look at Table 1-5. You'll see that all of these functions can be somewhat automated by the introduction of an IT system. They all benefit from the IT solution, but it is essential that you make sure to justify each of the matches before putting a plan in place to implement it.

Table 1-5. *Business Functions Mapped Against IT Capabilities*

AAA Support

Subfunction	Customer	Description	IT Capability	Justification
Communicate with AAA call center to receive 24/7 emergency call-outs.	AAA	Receive calls from call center over the phone. Emergency number is routed to manager's cell phone.	Email sent to mobile messaging system, routed directly to on-call mechanic but logged in Microsoft Exchange for auditing and billing.	No need for the manager to be the middleman, although all calls are still accounted for by the Microsoft Exchange logging system. Manager can trace all activity the following day.
Assign calls to appropriate mechanics.	AAA	Manager passes call to on-call service mechanic.	Automated, see previous.	All billing information is held in one place.
Invoice AAA on a monthly basis.	Self	Invoices are typed from paperwork records of jobs each month and posted to AAA headquarters.	Excel spreadsheet generates invoice.	A quick scan of the electronic mailbox shows the call activity. This data is fed into a preprogrammed spreadsheet, and an invoice is generated automatically.

After you have completed this task for all your business functions, you will have a clear understanding of exactly what you need Small Business Server 2003 to do for you.

A word of warning though: try not to let your IT system become driven by fabricated requirements. These are ones driven by that fatal flaw in most of us, to play with the latest gadgets. Try to look at every piece of technology in the context of its use in your environment. If there is a possibility it might be misused, look at ways of locking down its features or forcing a particular method of working.

Many of the technologies presented in this chapter have bells and whistles attached that might well be of no use at all to your business, but nevertheless their core capability is of paramount importance.

A good example is in identifying the need for secure Internet access, so ISA Server is essential, but do you really want everyone in your business surfing the Web whenever they like? Maybe you also don't want to be seen as a ruthless boss who denies privileges to the workforce, so instead you set a company security policy that permits access to the Internet between 12 p.m. and 2 p.m. for the general workers, and access at all times for management. You can even go so far as to still allow email to flow to and from the Internet while still barring access to the Web.

Requirements match capabilities. Capabilities are controlled by policy. Policy is administered though centralized control of your IT systems.

SBS 2003 can do all of this with as little overhead to your business as is possible.

The next part of this chapter takes a look at three real-world example companies. You'll get to see how three very different businesses captured their requirements, and in each case how they matched those requirements to the capabilities of their proposed IT infrastructure.

Case Study—Planthire

Planthire has been operating as a large machinery-leasing company for over 10 years and to date has never run into financial difficulty. Although they have been affected by market fluctuations over the years, revenue has, by and large, increased as the company has grown in reputation.

The manager, Philip Stanley, recently moved to acquire a better IT solution because he felt (as many managers do) that his company needed a kick in the backside to help take them into the next century.

The first thing Philip did was perform an audit of everything related to IT that the company might consider an asset. This is what he came up with:

- One Pentium 2 PC with Windows 98 on his own desk. He was using Microsoft Works for word processing and used an old version of Outlook Express to connect to AOL to pick up his email. There was also an old laser printer connected to his PC that was as old as his firstborn son (and he started school last year).

- Another PC running Windows 95 was placed on his secretary's desk, and she also used Microsoft Works and an inkjet printer for invoices, job sheets, contracts, and business letters.

- The last PC was stashed in a cupboard behind Philip's desk and was so old and unused that he considered trashing it as soon as he saw it.

So the audit was simple: three computers, two printers, no network.

Next, being the direct sort of person he was, Philip decided the best thing to do was pick up the phone and speak to Microsoft. So that's exactly what he did, and the resulting conversation introduced him to the idea that a great new suite of products, called Microsoft Small Business Server 2003, was available at a very low cost.

Now, Philip Stanley hadn't grown his business to where it was today by making rash decisions. He knew fine and well that Microsoft would tell him the product was "a great investment for the small enterprise" because, of course, Microsoft wanted him to buy it. So instead of jumping right in, he decided the best course of action was to do some research, and he subsequently requested some product information from Microsoft and picked up a good independent book from his local bookstore.

The more Philip looked into the details of SBS 2003, the more he became impressed by its list of capabilities. But there was a snag: he found it difficult to figure out how to match all these capabilities with his own business requirements. So, following the methodology of a top-down business requirement analysis and a bottom-up system analysis, Philip produced the information shown in Table 1-6.

Table 1-6. *Planthire's Two High-Level Business Functions*

Top-Level Service (Services and Products)	Customer (Internal and External)	Service/Product Description
Renting out heavy-duty commercial machinery	Many and varied, but mainly from the construction industry	Contract leasing of large machinery to customers who demand high-quality, well-maintained construction machinery, where appropriate delivered to and collected from the customer's site
Renting out lighter equipment for private use	Home owners, private builders, small companies	Contract leasing of high-quality, light machinery to anyone who needs this type of equipment

As you can immediately see in Table 1-6, Planthire is a relatively straightforward business, offering just two high-level services to its customers. The key to the ongoing success of this business has been Philip Stanley's tight control of all aspects of maintenance, customer relations, marketing, staff management, and contract management throughout the whole enterprise. But with added competition from other similar companies, now touting their business over the Internet, and the growth of his own business to the point where he can no longer control every aspect of operations he once could, he needs to figure out a way to do the following:

- Maintain current customers and win new business

- Make sure customers are completely satisfied

- Streamline cumbersome processes, allowing Philip to maintain the tight control that he so enjoys over his enterprise

- Ensure that all business-critical information is secure

- Automate ordering over a simple web interface

- Implement a resilient system-backup solution

- Launch an enhanced marketing campaign through a web presence

- Manage inventory

- Provide remote access for working from home—mainly for managers

- Manage suppliers

Small Business Server 2003 in Planthire

After going though the complete business analysis, Philip Stanley decided that SBS 2003 was indeed a worthwhile investment. As he reduced each of his business requirements down to basic component-level functions, nearly every one of them benefited from a server-based IT infrastructure with a connection to the Internet.

The main concerns Philip had in acquiring an IT solution were that he didn't want to employ a technology that would only add to the daily woes of managing his business. He wanted something that would free up some of his and his staff's time to concentrate on other areas of business growth, such as marketing and sales.

The capabilities that he focused on when he looked at SBS 2003 were the collaborative capabilities of Windows SharePoint Services, which would enable him to create a centralized view of the state of all the machines he had to offer. Windows SharePoint could also be used to deliver job sheets electronically to his staff. The integration with a centralized email system meant his staff could communicate with all arms of the business in an instant.

He also decided that the best course of action regarding his existing IT equipment was to simply scrap what he had and start again. He got a good deal with a local computer company to supply a server with the Original Equipment Manufacturer (OEM) version of SBS 2003 Standard Edition already installed, and he procured 10 low-specification PCs for the general workforce, each one running Windows XP Professional and Microsoft Office 2003. He also bought two high-specification PCs running Windows XP Professional and Microsoft Office 2003 for his desk clerks, and two top-of-the-line PCs with Windows XP and Microsoft Office 2003 for himself and his secretary.

Most of the goals Philip Stanley exposed for his company's adoption of a modern IT infrastructure appeal to every small business owner. Indeed, who wouldn't want to streamline cumbersome processes to allow staff to make better use their time? Who wouldn't want to find better ways of satisfying their customers when a good business model always seeks ways of securing repeat business?

When Philip Stanley fully analyzed his requirements, he was able to easily determine which aspects of his business were congruent with the capabilities of SBS 2003, and in doing so he was able to effectively plan the next phase of the implementation.

Case Study—Servideal

Husband and wife team Henry and Maria O'Leary decided after many years of working at the big corporations that they needed to strike out on their own, to build a better life for themselves.

Maria had previously worked as a buyer for a large importer and had many contacts across the globe, while Henry had been in the IT business, albeit as a technical project manager type, for practically half his life.

Both of them knew the power of direct B2C and B2B selling models, in which the business effectively acts only as the middleman for the end consumer. They agreed that this model was the one they should adopt to get their vision off the ground, and a subset of the products Marie used to buy for her company was identified as having a tactical demand for the international market. On paper this sounded like a success story just waiting to happen, but then they hit a snag. Neither of them knew how to go about implementing a successful system to meet their aspirations.

Using his contacts, Henry rang up some of his old techie buddies from his previous company for advice. It was at this stage he learned of a great Microsoft bundle called Small Business Server that was so cost-effective that it made no sense to choose anything else.

Being originally from an IT background, many of the capabilities he learned about were ones he knew of in one way or another, but the real shock came for him when he reviewed the pricing model. The product set that came as part of the bundle got him really excited. With SBS 2003 he could do everything Servideal needed to do to get trading, delivering products straight to customers with a comprehensive B2C business model.

The ease of management of SBS 2003 really impressed Henry. With the plethora of configuration wizards for setting up the network, remote access, a messaging system, an intranet, plus the added security features of ISA Server and the data warehousing and data management solutions supplied by SQL Server, he knew the business would benefit from SBS 2003 more than any other consolidated package. Henry rushed straight out and struck a deal with his local computer systems supplier for the complete package: brand new server, SBS 2003 Premium Edition, and two brand new laptops for himself and his wife.

Case Study—Country Estates

Managing director Alan Smith was worried. At night he would lie awake, cold beads of sweat resting on his forehead as he considered data loss, virus attacks, hackers, and disk crashes. He was a proud man, proud of his company ethics, proud of his reputation, and most of all, proud to serve his customers; but his pride was the primary source of his anxiety. He'd recently been shown a diagram of his internal IT system, and the sprawling spider's web that was scrawled across the page by his IT staff sent shivers down his spine. No one knew where all his data was. There was no central place where anyone (including him) could look at the entire customer base. None of the data was backed up. There were countless connections to the Internet, installed by whomever needed them, and the network was exposed to all sorts of attacks with no consolidated protection via antivirus or firewalls.

After consulting with an outside agency, Alan saw light at the end of the tunnel: migration to a brand new, server-centric network solution that would "fix" all his problems. By drawing all his staff into a centralized collaborative work space, offering them better lines of communication to each other, strengthening the boundary network protection, and employing a rigorous backup methodology, he saw his business start to make better use of resources right across the organization and the ability to create virtual teams across the branches that were simply not possible using the old IT system.

Summary

This chapter has covered the basics of making good use of an IT system in your small business, looking primarily at how the technologies included in SBS 2003 can be used to grow and manage your business, and where appropriate, transition it into something new and competitive. You've seen the importance of understanding your fundamental business processes and how those processes must be accurately mapped to the IT capabilities to make sure you are streamlining your business by introducing technology, rather than adding a burden.

The rest of this book is more focused on introducing the technology you have identified in this chapter. However, as you proceed with your SBS 2003 installation and configuration, you must always question your use of technology functions to make sure they are justified and are increasing your performance.

CHAPTER 2

■ ■ ■

Getting Connected

Computer networks have been around for a lot longer than most people realize. The first concepts of what could be likened to the networks of today emerged from the mind of a German aircraft engineer named Konrad Zuse in 1938.

Zuse had been trying to solve an engineering problem: lengthy and extremely complicated calculations used in designing aircraft would often result in weeks of wasted effort. And in most cases, this was largely due to human error. Being the resourceful type, Zuse pondered the problem, and in a blinding epiphany, he came up with a design for the world's first mechanical calculator, cryptically named the Z1. It wasn't long before Zuse turned his concept into reality and finally had a working model of the Z1 to help solve his problem.

By the beginning of the 1950s, a vast number of computer companies had emerged from the haze, all sporting tangible products rather than the scientific prototypes of the previous decade. With the worldwide reach many of these electronic giants possessed, the possibilities and power that computer systems could bring to big business were beginning to make the company CEOs sit up and smell the coffee.

Development of computer systems shifted up a gear during the 1960s, when most of today's biggest and most well-known IT companies jumped on this new and exciting bandwagon. The computer revolution was definitely in full swing.

Running in parallel to the massive private sector push to get computer products to market was an initiative run by the US government's research agency, the Defense Advanced Research Projects Agency (DARPA), which was looking at ways to enhance and exploit telecommunications networks for the purposes of the defense sector. In 1969, the very first internetwork (a network of networks) appeared in the dark recesses of their research labs, and probably should be considered as the birth of what today is called the Internet. These developments allowed computing systems to communicate over previously unobtainable distances by using standard, already installed telecommunication lines.

At this point, the two industries of computers and networks, spawned from two very different industry sectors, set off on a collision course that would eventually take the shape of today's connected workplace.

No one believed back then that the technologies would change the face of the world so dramatically, but some visionaries certainly saw the potential back in the 1980s. A new start-up company, run by a techno-geek programmer named Bill Gates, created the world's first IBM-compatible PC-based operating system that made PCs accessible to the general public. This company was called Microsoft, and the product was MS-DOS. By 1985 the first Microsoft Windows system environment was being rolled out across the US, and people had been bitten with the network bug.

The academic community also jumped on the bandwagon, networking up their campuses to enable students both to work and to socialize. Students used facilities such as the old bulletin board systems, which have grown into the Internet-available service now known as newsgroups.

As the Internet developed and everyone accepted that it was here to stay, Bill Gates announced an unprecedented change of focus for Microsoft, whereby all future development would be geared toward the connected world of the Internet.

And no one has looked back since.

Nowadays, the Internet is available at high speed and low cost to anyone who wants to use it. Public libraries offer free services for their members, allowing anyone access to Internet resources. Broadband solutions multiplexing telephone calls and Internet connections over a single telephone line allow telecom companies to exploit the infrastructure they have already deployed to every home in the US. This means that the Internet is readily available with little to no installation time required.

With the latest client and workstation products exploiting all these network capabilities, and operating systems such as Microsoft Windows Small Business Server 2003 and Microsoft Windows XP being the most network-ready components available on the market, you can get simple access to a wealth of information and services that can really change the way your world works.

It's important to get a basic understanding of what a network is and how it works, and that's exactly what this chapter is all about. You'll learn about local area networks (LANs), such as the one in your office, and wide area networks (WANs), such as the Internet. You'll see the benefits and gain an understanding of what server-centric networked systems can offer and you'll get to look under the hood at how the bits and bytes of a network communicate with each other.

Next we'll look at the features of wireless networking, a new standard in cable-free networking that can help position computer systems in awkward or extremely mobile environments (for example, using a laptop or PDA in a warehouse). Then we'll take a look at remote-access devices to see how home workers and mobile workers can communicate with your business securely.

Finally we'll take an in-depth look at exactly what network security is all about. You'll learn about firewalls and content checkers, as well as the installation of your networking solutions from an engineering perspective. We'll then concentrate on the Microsoft server-based networking environment known as the domain.

The OSI Model

There is no doubt in anybody's mind that networks can be difficult to comprehend, especially if you try to figure out exactly how those tiny electrical voltages passing down your cables can let you securely purchase products from Amazon.com.

To make life easier, back in 1984, the International Organization for Standardization (ISO) created a conceptual framework for defining network architectures, splitting the total solution into seven discrete layers. This model is known as the Open Systems Interconnection (OSI) model and is nowadays the most widely used method for describing network architectures.

From your point of view, the OSI model can be used as a teaching aid, helping you visualize how networks function and reflecting each layer as a logical function in the seven-tier hierarchy. Each layer can be analyzed in its own right without the need to look above or below, but when the whole stack is put together, you have yourself a network.

In relation to the Internet, the OSI model was the framework used by the clever people who invented the internetworking protocol known as TCP/IP. Today, most people have heard of TCP/IP even if they don't know much about it, but for now it's sufficient to say TCP/IP is the underlying technology that makes everything you're about to read about in this book possible. The "TCP/IP" section later in this chapter goes into a lot more detail on setting up and configuring TCP/IP in the small business environment.

Without further ado, let's take a look at the OSI model from the ground up (see Figure 2-1).

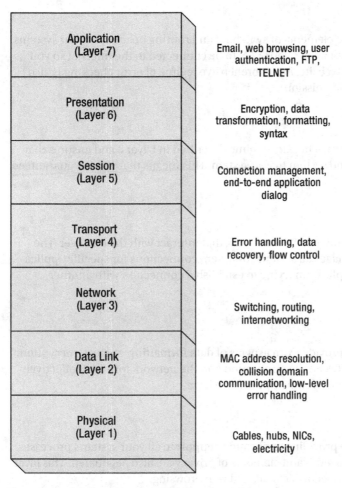

Application (Layer 7)	Email, web browsing, user authentication, FTP, TELNET
Presentation (Layer 6)	Encryption, data transformation, formatting, syntax
Session (Layer 5)	Connection management, end-to-end application dialog
Transport (Layer 4)	Error handling, data recovery, flow control
Network (Layer 3)	Switching, routing, internetworking
Data Link (Layer 2)	MAC address resolution, collision domain communication, low-level error handling
Physical (Layer 1)	Cables, hubs, NICs, electricity

Figure 2-1. *The seven-layer OSI network model*

Physical (Layer 1)

The *Physical layer*, right at the bottom of the stack, represents all aspects of your network that might be considered physical. It defines all electrical and mechanical characteristics of the devices and fully describes the voltages used on the cables, the cables themselves, all your cable connectors, and your network interface cards (NICs). From an information perspective, all this layer is capable of understanding are the voltages transmitted on the wire. At this point there is no concept of data, just electricity.

Data Link (Layer 2)

The *Data Link layer* takes you one stage further toward a connected system. It relies on the components provided in Layer 1 to begin interpreting the voltages passed through your cables into some form of communication. This layer is where the MAC address (see the section later in this chapter the MAC address) is used to identify each system trying to communicate. Some rudimentary error checking takes place in this part of the stack.

Network (Layer 3)

The *Network layer* provides all the elements of switching and routing needed for your systems to talk to other networks. This layer allows your LAN to be connected to the Internet so you can send email and publish your website. A comprehensive regime of error checking is also mandated at this stage of data transmission.

Transport (Layer 4)

The *Transport layer* adds to the error-checking regime described in Layer 3 and ensures that all data is sent seamlessly from end system to end system. This means that you are guaranteed complete data transfer.

Session (Layer 5)

Here you are beginning to see elements of the network that interact with the end user. The *Session layer* establishes and manages all system-to-system connections for specific applications. Specific aspects of each application trying to establish a connection with another application are handled here.

Presentation (Layer 6)

The *Presentation layer* is used to provide extra aspects of data formatting, such as encryption, by negotiating the data syntax between the application and the network format. It effectively transforms data into the correct form for the Application layer.

Application (Layer 7)

The *Application layer* is the key to providing application support to all your system's processes. User authentication is done at this level, and elements of privacy are also negotiated. This layer provides services for file transfers, electronic mail, and web browsing.

Components of a Network

To put it simply, the term *network* describes all the hardware and software needed to enable two or more computer systems to communicate with each other.

After you understand how the basic principles of building, configuring, and running a network are applied to create a total solution, you'll be surprised at how easy it is to share information resources within your business environment. In no time at all, you'll be able to leverage the power of collaborative features, such as electronic mail and instant messenger, and access the wealth of information resources presented on the Internet. Your network will connect all your peripheral services, such as your printers and scanners, making them securely available to any authorized user on your network.

Network Interface Cards

A *network interface card*, or NIC for short, is the hardware component used to connect devices such as workstations, servers, and printers, together on your network.

Today nearly all NICs come with a telephone-style connector, making connection of cables as simple as connecting a telephone to the wall socket; but many other network interface types are also available: coaxial, fiber-optic, and USB to name but a few.

Older computer systems used a coaxial cable strung from computer to computer, but this technology could transmit data at speeds up to only 10 Mbps, which over the last 10 years became extremely limiting as the power of end computer systems increased exponentially.

■**Note** The speed a network communicates at is written in bits per second, or *bps*. This figure is the number of individual 1s and 0s the network is capable of transmitting to other computer systems every second. The prefixes commonly in front of bps are M (for *mega*), when the speed of the network is shown as a million bits per second, or G (for *giga*), when the speed of the network is a billion bits per second. The abbreviations are usually written as Mbps and Gbps.

A modern cabling solution was required and subsequently the unshielded twisted pair (UTP) cable was born. With its easy-to-use telephone-style connector at each end, it's effectively plug and play, meaning the stringing together of networks is no longer a black art. These cables are capable of interoperating with networks running at 10 Mbps or can be pushed to much faster transmission speeds of 100 Mbps or even 1 Gbps.

■**Note** To see if a NIC is compatible with your computer system, check the Microsoft Hardware Compatibility List (HCL) on Microsoft's website: http://www.microsoft.com/whdc/hcl/default.mspx. The HCL also covers approved software items that have been tested on Microsoft platforms.

You should remember the following points about NICs:

- Always check the NIC's compatibility before proceeding with a purchase. When in doubt, consult either the Microsoft Hardware Compatibility List (see Figure 2-2) or the manufacturer's documentation.

- There are four kinds of interfaces available for connecting your NIC to your computer device: USB, PCI-X, PCI, and PCMCIA. Make sure you get the right one for your system.

- After you've installed the hardware device driver, check that it's working properly by clicking Start ➤ Control Panel and then double-clicking Network Connections. Right-click on the device icon and select Properties. Then click the Configure button. The Device status is displayed in this window.

- It's possible to have multiple NICs installed in a single computer, depending on how many networks you require.

- Modems and NICs can coexist, so your computer can access a dial-up network as well as a LAN.

Note PCI, and more recently PCI-X, NICs are most commonly installed in desktop machines and servers, whereas PCMCIA NICs are most commonly targeted at the laptop community. USB devices are normally available for both laptop and desktop computers, so long as your machine has a compatible USB port.

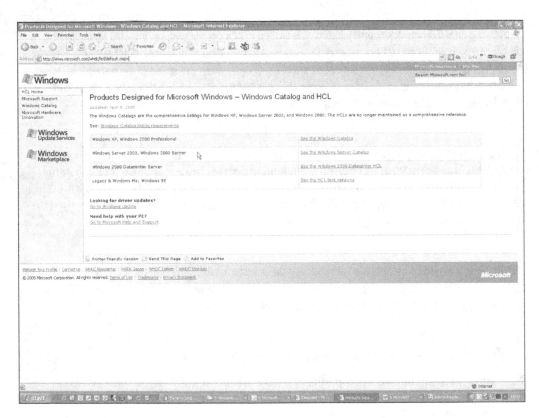

Figure 2-2. *The Hardware Compatibility List at Microsoft.com*

Hubs

The next question you need answering is, how do you go about connecting all your systems together? The answer is simple: use a device known as a hub.

A *hub* is a hardware component that provides the interconnection between as many networked devices as you need. The device is called a hub because it acts as the central part of the network that connects all the spokes. On the end of these spokes are your computers and peripherals (see Figure 2-3).

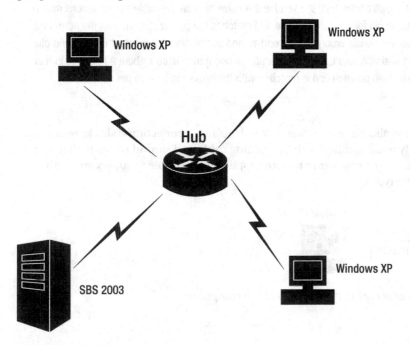

Figure 2-3. *A simple hub-and-spoke network*

Connecting devices to your hub is easy. All you need is the correct number of standard UTP cables (any PC store can supply these) properly measured to span the distance from each PC's location to the hub.

Note When measuring cable runs, make sure you measure the route the cable will take rather than the straight line distance from PC to hub. You may wish to hide cables in conduit in the same way power cables are hidden. Make sure to take all aspects of the run length into consideration. To make doubly sure, add 15 percent to the final figure. Excess cable can be hidden in the conduit. *Do not exceed 225 feet in any UTP cable runs.*

Deciding whether to use a hub is one of the easiest decisions you'll ever have to make. If you have only two computers to connect and you're not planning to expand your network beyond two machines, try using the direct-connect cable technology known as a crossover, as shown in Figure 2-4.

Note The standard anatomy of a cable used to connect your computer equipment to a hub provides what's termed a *straight-through* connection; the send and receive pins on the cable's terminations match each other. In other words, the pin for receiving on one end matches the pin for receiving on the other end. In this case, the hub swaps the signals around so the end-to-end connection still means that the send pin connects to the receive pin and vice versa. A *crossover cable* is one that is used without a hub—so in this cable's construction, the send pin on each end is matched with the opposing receive pin.

Crossover cables can also be used to facilitate hub-to-hub connections (also known as uplinks) and are usually manufactured with contrasting cable and shroud colors to that of the straight-through cable. Most computer hardware suppliers will be able to supply you with either of these two cable types.

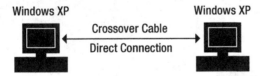

Figure 2-4. *Use a crossover cable to directly connect two computers.*

Switches

A *switch* is an improved version of a hub, usually retailing at a slightly higher cost because it has an element of built-in intelligence that a hub does not. Switches are also markedly faster than hubs, and instead of offering a shared network on effectively a single wire, a switch separates the network into individually controlled segments, each with its own dedicated bandwidth.

A switch automatically decides which segments should be linked so that each time a device tries to communicate with another device, the connection is not affected by other systems on the network.

It is worth paying the extra money for a switch these days because the prices have come down dramatically since they were first introduced.

Modems

A *modem* is a device used to convert the digital signals generated by a computer into the appropriate analog signals needed for signal transmission over traditional telephone lines.

Note The word *modem* comes from the literary contraction of the two terms *modulate/demodulate*.

Modems are probably the oldest of all IT communications devices; at one time long-distance connections were possible only by using the already available and widely distributed telecommunications networks. The quality of the cabling that was used to provide these networks was suitable only for the analog signals needed in telephone calls, so some method of sending the 1s and 0s necessary for computer communication was necessary.

The speed at which a modem is capable of transmitting data is measured in bps, and most modern modems are capable of connecting at speeds of up to 56,000 bps. It should be noted, though, that this maximum capacity is rarely achieved and a number of slower speeds below this are more commonly used.

Note Although network connection speeds are measured in bits per second, virtually all connection devices (of which modems tend to be the slowest) work in thousands if not millions of bits per second. You will see modem speeds written, for example, as 56 Kbps (56 kilobits per second = 56,000 bits per second) and network speeds written as 100 Mbps (100 megabits per second = 100,000,000 bits per second).

In operation, the two corresponding ends of the connection negotiate the data transfer speed when the connection is first established. Quite often this connection speed is not under the control of the client system but is more commonly controlled at the server end by the Internet Service Provider (ISP).

Routers

A *router* is a device used to create a path between two networks. A router might be configured, for example, to allow your business network to send and receive email from the Internet (see Figure 2-5).

By using a set of rules, typically defined by the network administrators at either end of the connection, the factors that limit the connection of the two networks can be established. These rules govern the format and transmission characteristics of the information that can pass between the networks, as well as providing an extra layer of security so that the traffic on one local area network is self-contained except for what is positively permitted to be sent.

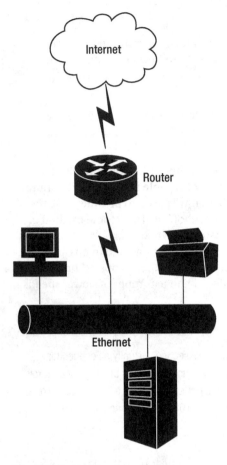

Figure 2-5. *A router is used to connect networks.*

Firewalls

You've probably heard the term *firewall* used many times before, and if you're a Windows XP user with Service Pack 2 installed, you probably have firsthand experience of using one—even if what you can configure and manipulate with this particular software system is limited.

The origin of the term *firewall* is just as you might expect: it comes from the building trade, where a firewall is used to prevent the spread of fire from one room to another. By taking this analogy into a networking environment, you can see that the "fire" is any malicious attempt from external sources to attack your systems and that the firewall is the defenses built up to stop the fire from coming in. See how the firewall is positioned in Figure 2-6 between the Internet and the internal business network.

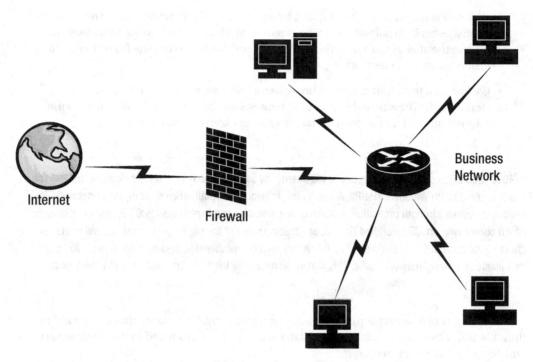

Figure 2-6. *Firewalls protect your systems from external threats.*

In many ways, firewalls act in the same way as routers, but the difference is in the *extra features* they provide, from a security perspective, to help bolster your business's defenses.

Firewalls work by analyzing and filtering all data that flows in and out of your network and can be configured to perform a variety of duties. Different firewalls will have varying numbers of the following facilities, but remember, good ones will have them all:

- *Packet filtering* describes how a firewall will look at each element of information being sent into your network and match the data against a list of authorized types. If it's on the "allowed" list, the data is passed on to the appropriate recipient; if it's not on the list, it's junked.

- *Stateful inspection* is another method of data analysis, but this time instead of looking at the complete data packet, it looks only at certain signature parts—parts that commonly identify threats.

- *Proxying* enables the firewall to act as a go-between, passing information to and from systems on the internal network that wish to connect externally. In this way, external systems never connect directly to your internal network; instead, all traffic passes via the firewall. A proxy effectively protects the identity of your internal systems.

- *Web publishing* can also be provided by using state-of-the-art firewalls. The firewall publishes an internal website on an external interface and allows external users to browse the site, even though the authorship and control of the site is still maintained inside the internal network.

- *Caching* is a term that describes how external web pages from the Internet can be stored on the firewall and subsequent requests for those pages are served from the internal network rather than initiating a slower external connection.

Note SBS 2003 can connect directly to the Internet by using the built-in Windows Firewall, just like the one that comes with Windows XP SP2. Although this is ideal for a small office system, larger networks in need of industrial-strength protection because of valuable data can exploit SBS 2003 Premium Edition, which comes with an ICSA-certified firewall as capable as any of the big players in the firewall world. ISA offers all the capabilities in the preceding list as well as a comprehensive logging system that allows you to look inside all flowing network traffic. This feature alone makes the Premium edition worth every cent.

Thresholds can be set for many networking parameters. You'll learn much more about firewalls and setting up a secure network later, when you're introduced to the Internet Security and Acceleration Server in Chapter 8.

Local Area Networks

A *local area network*, or LAN, is a group of well-connected computer systems, all sharing a common communications infrastructure. The reason for using a LAN is to permit the sharing of information and resources over a local geographic area, for example, within a warehouse or office.

LANs can be created as server-centric networks, in which all governance of the communications activity is controlled through a central server. Alternatively, they can be set up in a peer-to-peer configuration, in which each system manages its own resources with no central governance. You can liken these two methods of control to their political counterparts:

- A server-centric network is akin to a dictatorship, whereby the control of all activity of minions (the computers participating in the network) is centrally enforced.

- A peer-to-peer network is more akin to a federation, in which control is distributed to many different authorities, and each one is responsible for its own resources.

- On a grand scale, networks such as the Internet are a mixture of both styles of governance. Many aspects of the Internet's security and administration are distributed to end systems, but there is still a centrally controlled aspect ensuring that the end systems all abide by the rules.

■**Note** If you use SBS 2003, you will automatically place network governance on your server. This means you will control your information sharing, security policy, and collaborative capabilities from this central system.

Ethernet

Nowadays, virtually every LAN environment you might encounter will use a standard known as *Ethernet* for PC to PC communications. This standard first emerged from the Xerox Corporation's Palo Alto Research Center (PARC) as a method of connecting a computer system to one of Xerox's printers, but the possibilities exposed by this early implementation of Ethernet had far-reaching effects into the world of computer networks.

The Ethernet standard defines exactly how electrical signals are used to transmit digital information from one computer system to another by using an underlying method known as Carrier Sense Multiple Access/Collision Detection (CSMA/CD). In OSI model terms, the Ethernet standard applies to the Data Link layer.

Carrier sense, multiple access, with collision detection, sounds a bit more like some MIT graduate's finest work, but it's actually not that complicated to grasp the basics—and for your purposes, that's all you really need to know.

In a nutshell: CSMA/CD is a protocol, and like any protocol, it ensures all devices respect each other's manners when it comes to sending data.

So what happens when one computer wants to talk to another? Down at the wire, the sending computer listens to see whether any other machines are busy chatting to each other. This is *carrier sense*. If there is another conversation happening between another two computers (*multiple access*), the sender waits and listens until there is a break. When the line becomes free, the sender tries to send its information. If all goes well, a communication channel is established and everyone is happy. But what if another machine attempts to speak at exactly the same time? Simple, this is where *collision detection* comes into its own. Both systems trying to send information back off for a random amount of time. This random amount of time is crucial to make this system work. Think about it this way: If you were having a telephone conversation with someone, and you both tried to speak at the same time, you would probably pause and wait to see what happens. If the other person didn't speak, you could say your piece. This random element means both computers won't try to restart the process again at exactly the same time, so the chances are, next time either one tries, they will succeed.

■**Note** The CSMA/CD Ethernet protocol is the same underlying principle that applies in both cabled and wireless networks.

As cable technology has advanced significantly over the years, allowing Ethernet systems to operate at higher and higher speeds, cabled solutions can be driven to transmit data at rates up to a staggering 1 million bits per second. Most networking infrastructures end up using a combination of transmission speeds, with some devices limited to 10 Mbps, while others might operate at 100 Mbps or even 1 Gbps.

All networks default to communicate at the speed of the lowest common factor for each connection. If a 10 Mbps–capable device wishes to communicate with a 1 Gbps server, for example, the server network will synchronize the connection at the lower speed of 10 Mbps. To gain maximum advantage from any new equipment, try to upgrade any old 10 Mbps NICs, hubs, and switches to match the fastest speeds capable of your total solution.

Note Most modern PC systems come already supplied with an Ethernet-compatible NIC in the chassis. If you purchased a brand new server or workstation, especially as a package deal from a retailer, it's unlikely that it would come without a modern LAN device capable of at least 100 Mbps connection speeds.

The MAC Address

Every Ethernet device has a unique code that identifies it from all other Ethernet devices. This allows it to maintain its own globally understood identity. This code is known as the *Media Access Control address*, or MAC address. No two MAC addresses are the same.

You might remember that I introduced the concept of the MAC address earlier in this chapter when we examined the OSI seven-layer networking model. In this case, the MAC address is the Ethernet implementation of the MAC components mentioned in the Data Link layer, and it is used to identify local LAN systems to each other. It's always worth remembering that the OSI model is purely a reference model, whereas Ethernet is a real implementation of part of that stack, similar to the way that TCP/IP as a transmission protocol is also a real implementation of the Network and Transport layers.

Note There are ways of copying and spoofing MAC addresses for a whole range of reasons, some legitimate and others downright malicious. Legitimate manufacturers of Ethernet devices are allocated a range of MAC addresses to engineer into their products, ensuring all devices remain unique, but cases have been reported of unauthorized companies shipping duplicate batches of Ethernet-cloned addresses.

If you want to see what MAC addresses are used on your computer systems, sometimes they are printed on the NIC itself (this is common if you bought the NIC separately from your PC or server). Alternatively, you can boot Windows, click Start ➤ Run, and then type **cmd.exe** and press Enter. At the command prompt, type **ipconfig/all** and hit Enter. The MAC address is displayed next to Physical Address and appears as a 48-bit hexadecimal number (12 characters).

You can also see the MAC address and lots of other useful networking information by clicking Start ➤ All Programs ➤ Accessories ➤ System Tools and selecting System Information. Expand the Components category, expand the subcategory Network, and highlight Adapter as in Figure 2-7.

Figure 2-7. *The MAC address is the physical address of the NIC.*

Client vs. Server Networking

Two very different paradigms of computer networking exist, both with their merits and both with their uses. A distributed, client-controlled principle known as *peer-to-peer networking* provides an environment in which every machine controls access to its own resources, with no central server in charge. A more controlled environment, known as a *server-centric network*, uses a network operating system such as Microsoft Windows 2003 to control all security and resource access from the central server.

Peer-to-Peer Networks

Peer-to-peer networks can grow to be as elaborate and complicated as required. The main problem comes from the distribution of the control. On a small scale, managing data-access permissions on three PCs is relatively simple. However, even when you have three machines, administrative tasks such as backup and recovery of data, and finding valuable corporate information, can begin to pose serious problems.

In a Windows environment, the peer-to-peer network is known as a workgroup. A *workgroup* simply describes one of these loosely coupled networks in which security control is devolved to each participating machine in the federation. Although workgroups do still provide a few aspects of management from a low-level system-networking perspective, they pose a much greater nightmare for systems managers once they grow larger than a couple of PCs.

Note You will not be using a peer-to-peer network for your business once you buy into SBS 2003 because it comes complete with the sophisticated network operating system capabilities of Windows 2003.

Take a look at Figure 2-8. You'll see here that the network comprises a number of PC devices, a printer, and access to the Internet through a firewall. All the information on this network must be made available to everyone else, with each machine needing to be managed independently. With no central control over security policy, you'll probably end up devolving full responsibility for the security of each computer to the end user, giving them administrative accounts. Next thing you know—anarchy.

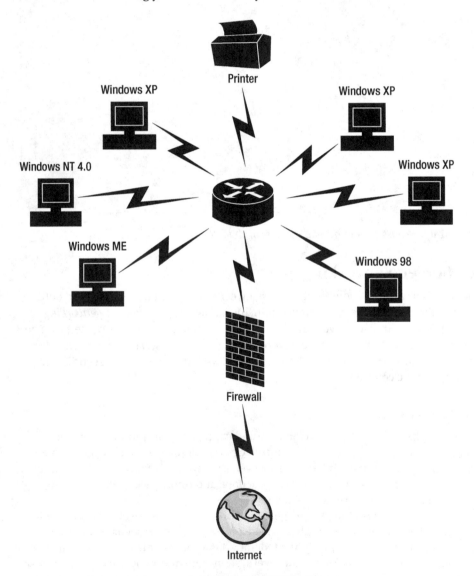

Figure 2-8. *A peer-to-peer network devolves administration.*

Server-Centric Networks

In a Microsoft Windows Server 2003 environment, the server assumes control of the security and administration of all aspects of the network, including all workstations, printers, and file permissions.

The grouping of clients under the control of a Windows 2003 server is known in Windows terms as a *domain*. In your SBS 2003 network, the SBS server will be your *domain controller*. See Figure 2-9.

At the heart of the Windows Server 2003 operating system is a service known as *Active Directory*. This is effectively a database of all objects under the direct supervision and control of the SBS 2003 domain controller. Active Directory can be probed for information resources on your network and stores all your user names, group names, share names, and printers; in fact, it can be manipulated to store any data you want.

Changing permissions on data or granting access for new users to websites is a lot more straightforward in a networked domain environment. No need to visit each machine and create users and access rights on each—all this configuration can be accomplished by using a policy from the domain controller.

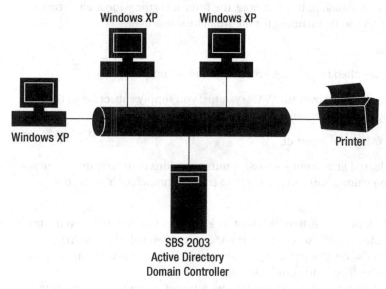

Figure 2-9. *A Windows 2003 Active Directory domain*

Note The best choice for any small business is to opt for the server-centric network. SBS 2003 gives you exactly that, and with the Active Directory at its core, your systems administration and security will be tightly controlled with the overall cost greatly reduced.

Wide Area Networks

Wiring systems up on a local scale is one thing, but the real power of networking comes from being able to span long distances and share information with remote networks that are not under your control. Collaborating with suppliers or customers who might be situated on the far side of the planet is now commonplace, and to make this all possible, you'll need to exploit the services offered by the world's largest wide area network: *the Internet*.

A *wide area network (WAN)* is used to connect systems over a wide geographical displacement, acting primarily as a method of connecting distributed local area networks.

To put this in context, if you are using SBS 2003 in your business and decide to send an email to a colleague, the chances are you'll be using the Microsoft Exchange 2003 component of SBS 2003 to do this. The email is processed on your local server, and all the network traffic is contained within your business environment. You have exploited the facilities of your LAN to send the email. If you subsequently need to send an email to a supplier who happens to have his business in Peru, your email is first passed from your LAN, out to the Internet, and then posted through many, many email relay systems until it finally reaches the end client system that knows about your supplier. Your supplier's server is probably on its own LAN, where the supplier logs in and reads your email. In this example, the Internet is the wide area network.

A few points about WANs should be noted for the small business user:

- WANs connect LANs.

- WANs are normally supplied by your telecommunications company.

- You will have no direct control over the WAN systems; you simply subscribe to the services provided by the telecommunications company.

- The most popular WAN is the Internet.

- It's possible to hire leased lines from your telecommunications company that offer dedicated WAN connections. You can use these to connect branch offices to your headquarters.

Another kind of WAN connection is that provided by a modem. When you dial in to your SBS 2003 server to get remote network access to your LAN, you are effectively creating your own mini WAN. On a grander scale, you can use point-to-point dial-up connections to span the distance between branch offices and your headquarters.

Security can be added to connections that exploit the Internet, using technology known as virtual private networks (VPNs). These are covered in more detail later in this chapter, but for now it's sufficient to say they provide a safe-enough medium to connect distributed LANs together, meaning every business can exploit the Internet for B2B and B2C connectivity without the worry of hackers easily gaining access.

To get an idea of how distributed the Internet is, have a look at The Internet Mapping Project (see Figure 2-10). Started by Bell Labs and now run by Lumeta, this project has been running since the summer of 1998. The project's goal is to analyze the layout of the Internet over a long period of time to help with long-term trending problems of sizing and distribution. To date, their data has helped fix routing problems and helped track down the source of distributed denial of service (DDoS) attacks. For more information, see `http://research.lumeta.com/ches/map/index.html`.

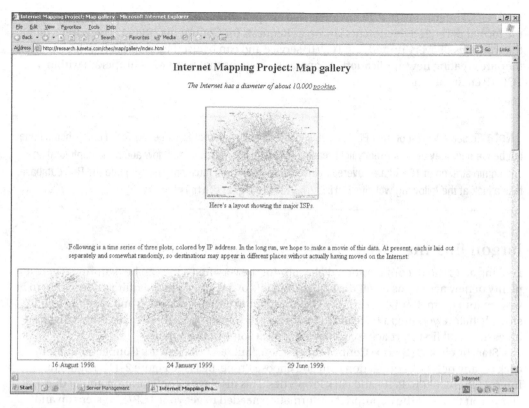

Figure 2-10. *The Lumeta Internet mapping project*

TCP/IP

You've heard a lot about it, but what is TCP/IP? It stands for *Transmission Control Protocol/Internet Protocol* and is the industry networking standard used most widely today. Other networking standards also exist, but with the advent of the Internet (which is solely based on the services provided by TCP/IP) and industry giants such as Microsoft standardizing platform development on the paradigm of "Internet readiness," then it's little wonder that TCP/IP is removing all the competition.

The protocol itself was designed as a global player, capable of routing many diverse networks together over a number of different connection types (from slow dial-up to the staggering speeds of some of the modern SDSL connections, which can carry data up to 24 Mbps—for example, ADSL 2).

Microsoft Windows platforms rely heavily on the underlying principles of TCP/IP to create the networked environment known as the domain. Many of the services and applications you have come to rely on in the modern world, such as email and the Internet, would not be possible without TCP/IP.

The standards for TCP/IP are published as open source documents on the Internet, all in the format of ratified documents known as Requests for Comments (RFCs). These RFCs detail the workings of every underlying TCP/IP service and can be used by systems developers when they are creating new applications or operating systems that need to interoperate within a TCP/IP environment.

Note To see a full list of the RFCs available today, go to the Internet Engineering Task Force's home page, but be warned, they are not exactly light reading. All the things you need to know about the configuration and administration of TCP/IP are covered in this chapter, but if you must start digging into the RFC database, take a look at the following website: http://www.ietf.org/rfc.html.

Jargon Busting

Looking at a TCP/IP configuration dialog box for the very first time can be daunting. There are plenty of new acronyms to get the hang of and lots of data fields that require information to be written into them. It might seem like you are about to embark on a long and grueling uphill struggle before you might be ready to set up a whole network. To try to make things that little bit easier, we'll first start at base camp and look at some of the jargon.

Start by clicking Start ➤ Control Panel. Then double-click Network Connections. Right-click on any network connection icon and choose Properties (see Figure 2-11). Highlight Internet Protocol (TCP/IP) and click Properties. This displays a configuration applet that allows you to set all the appropriate information needed to get your TCP/IP system up and running, and more important, chatting on the network. Start at the top and work your way down:

- Dynamic Host Configuration Protocol (DHCP) is a method of address allocation used by network clients to obtain an IP address from an authoritative server, such as your SBS 2003 server. In the case of a Microsoft Windows XP system connection to the Internet, the DHCP address is allocated by the ISP.

- The IP address is the unique address used by your computer to communicate within the TCP/IP networking environment. There must never be two systems configured with the same IP address on your network.

- The subnet mask is associated with your IP address to help identify which network the computer is participating in. This can also be assigned by using DHCP.

- The Domain Name System (DNS) is used to translate meaningful names such as www.microsoft.com into a reachable IP address. DNS servers operate all over the Internet, helping worldwide clients resolve names. The DNS service is key in operating your SBS 2003 domain because Active Directory services also rely on this form of name resolution.

- The Advanced tab takes you further into the depths of TCP/IP, allowing you to configure other methods of name resolution or add additional IP addresses on your NIC interfaces.

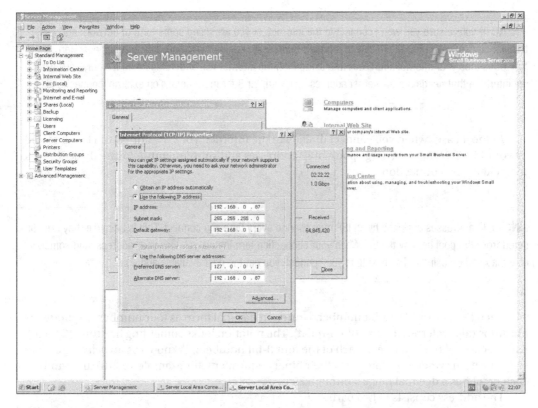

Figure 2-11. *View the TCP/IP configuration properties of a connection through the GUI.*

The IP Address

Every system in a TCP/IP networking environment must have a unique address allocated to it. This address allows all the systems to find and talk to each other and is universally known as the IP address.

The *IP address* is a network layer address, having no direct dependence your system's MAC address. The MAC address, if you remember, functions lower down the OSI model at the Data Link layer.

Note Systems that participate in a TCP/IP network are known as *hosts*. This applies to servers, workstations, printers, and any other device that requires an IP address.

An old analogy (but a good one) likens an IP address to a street address. The street address uniquely identifies the house, allowing mail to almost always be delivered correctly from anywhere in the world. The same follows suit in a networked world: every system must be uniquely identifiable from every other; otherwise, data wouldn't get to where it's supposed to go.

The conventions for formatting host addresses must be followed closely, especially if the host system is to be connecting to the Internet.

Note If you're sure you won't connect to the Internet, or you are using some form of network address translation (NAT), it's possible to use an arbitrary addressing scheme internally in your business. Here, the NAT translates your internal addresses into something the Internet will understand, and it's only your external interface that needs a real Internet address. See Chapter 8 for more details on external connections.

In most cases when you connect directly to the Internet, your IP address will be allocated by your ISP. ISPs maintain large pools of IP addresses and subsequently allocate these down to their clients on connection.

Note IP addresses assigned by an ISP may change every time you connect. This is because they are allocated from the pool held by the ISP. When your connection terminates, you lose your address, and someone else may end up using it. The next time you connect, you get the next available address.

Each IP address is a 32-bit number, written in decimal form as four numbers separated by full stops (also referred to as a dotted-quad). The notation looks something like this: 127.0.0.1. Each section of the IP address (each of the four 8-bit numbers) is known as an *octet*. There are eight positions when translated into their binary equivalent, for example 100010101—and each octet has a decimal range 0 through 255.

The address consists of two parts:

- The *network ID*, used to create a pool of addresses that can be allocated to hosts

- The *host ID*, identifying each individual host

Because this numbering system theoretically can support 4.3 billion combinations of IP addresses, a system had to be devised to control their allocation. To accomplish this, a system for grouping IP addresses into varying sized networks was created, known as the class system.

There are five address classes you need to know about, each having a different number of hosts per network ratio:

- *Class A*: These addresses are assigned to extremely large networks, such as international companies, which need to connect a large number of host systems. IP addresses with the first octet from 1 to 126 are part of this class. The other three octets are free to be used internally by the owner in whatever way they see fit. This means each of the 126 allocated Class A networks can have a total number of 16,777,214 hosts.

Note In reality, most Class A network addresses have been allocated, farmed off to network providers such as AT&T and Sprint. Many Class A addresses have been allocated at a regional level through national agencies for each Internet-enabled country (such as the United Kingdom, Australia, and Canada) and in each case the Class A network would be further partitioned to allocate smaller network portions to controlling bodies such as ISPs.

- *Class B*: Class B addresses are allocated to medium-sized networks, such as university campuses. IP addresses with a first octet from 128 to 191 are part of this class. Class B addresses also include the second octet as part of their assigned identifier. The other two octets identify the host. Class B networks (of which there are a total number of 16,384 possible) allow for 65,534 hosts.

- *Class C*: These addresses are commonly assigned to small/midsize businesses with the IP addresses from 192 to 223 in the first octet. Class C addresses also include the second and third octets. There are a total of 2,097,152 Class C networks, each allowing 254 hosts to connect.

- *Class D*: Class D addresses are special addresses used exclusively for network multicasts. Multicasting is used for broadcast-style communications, such as that of streaming video or audio.

- *Class E*: Class E addresses are reserved for experimental purposes and should be of no consequence to a small business environment.

Small network allocations, such as Class C networks, are relatively easy to manage, but just imagine trying to keep 16 million hosts under control if you owned one of those Class A networks. Not an easy task. For this very reason, a system known as subnetting was introduced to allow people to split large networks into smaller, more manageable ones. A *subnet* is a defined portion of a network that allows systems with that subnet to directly communicate. To communicate with systems outside the subnet, information must be passed through a device that knows about the existence of the other network, with an interface on both networks. This device is known as a router.

Configuring Your IP Address

As soon as you've come to grips with the basic principles of IP addressing, it's easy to set up large, seemingly complicated networks in no time at all. First you need to understand three important aspects of configuration and how each relates to each other.

Note There are ranges of addresses that are reserved for private network use, starting with the first two octets, such as 192.168.x.x. These can be used within your business, and the SBS 2003 server can act as the router connecting your private network to the public Internet. All your hosts can be configured with addresses beginning with 192.168.x.x and subnet masks of 255.255.255.0. The default gateway is set to the inward-facing address on the SBS 2003 server. Other ranges also exist, such as 10.x.x.x and 172.x.x.x, but these are less commonly used.

- The *IP address*, to recap, is the unique address assigned to each host on your network. This network might be a private network or an Internet-allocated one from one of the address classes A through C. This IP address contains all the information needed by your computer to allow it to recognize both the network ID and the host ID.

- The *subnet mask* is used to determine which portion of the network your host is communicating on. (A complicated algorithm is used to mask the IP address against the subnet number.)

- The *default gateway* is effectively the doorway from your network to the outside world. In the SBS environment, the default gateway is usually the SBS 2003 server itself.

Three inseparable chums: the IP address, the subnet mask, and the default gateway. Without the first two, nothing would work. Without the third, you'd never find anyone outside your own network.

Note When you install SBS 2003, you will use a system of address allocation called DHCP. This system allocates from a private stash of its own IP addresses, automatically configuring all client computers with their IP address, subnet mask, and default gateway.

The Domain Name System

Question: If IP addresses identify each host on the Internet, why do you not type in an IP address when you want to connect to Amazon.com?

Answer: Because it's a pain in the neck. So, to get around this problem, you will be exploiting the system known as the Domain Name System (DNS).

Note If you wanted to, you could connect to Amazon.com by IP address only, but remembering these addresses would be nearly impossible. Humans need human-readable names, and that's what DNS is for!

When you surf the Web, you tend to type in the Universal Resource Locator (URL) for the address of the system, the first part of which is the DNS name of the server you are trying to contact.

Domain names consist of two or more parts separated by dots, with the piece on the left being the most specific and the piece on the right being the most general—for example, Microsoft.com. Because IP addresses are numbers but humans work better with "real" names, some method was required to translate the numerical IP address into a more easily recognizable name—the domain name. And DNS was born.

The sole purpose of DNS is to turn readable names into IP addresses so network systems can contact each other using the correct address. The deluge of computers that flood the Internet use a distributed database of domain names mapping all names to corresponding IP addresses. This database is available to all computers and users of the Internet, allowing your local business systems to perform DNS lookups anytime they need to.

In an SBS 2003 environment, the DNS server plays a vital role in helping all your systems talk to each other. The SBS 2003 server itself hosts its own DNS service to aid the Active Directory. All your clients, servers, and services register in DNS automatically so they can all find each other with little to no overhead.

The DNS server on your SBS 2003 server manages all DNS information internally to your business (see Figure 2-12). When clients need to resolve names of external, Internet-based hosts, the DNS server forwards the client request to an Internet DNS server and then awaits the response. When the response comes back, the reply is forwarded to the client and the connection is established.

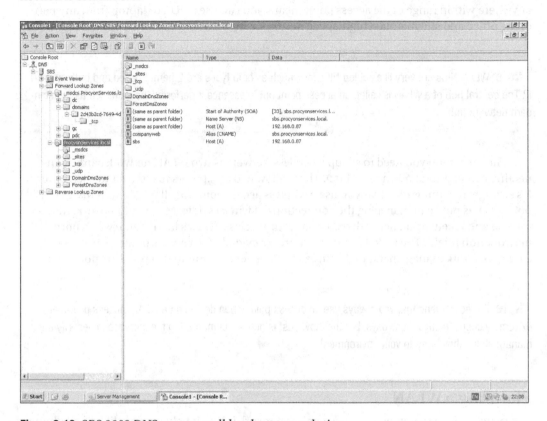

Figure 2-12. *SBS 2003 DNS manages all local name resolution.*

Going Wireless

Not that long ago, wireless networks where not an option for small businesses. Hardware components were so expensive that an average IT budget couldn't be stretched to accommodate them. Coupled with the fact that the technology was so complicated you would need a degree from MIT to understand it, wireless technology was reluctantly confined to the drawing board of university labs.

That was five years ago; today things are very different. After significant research and development by the Institute of Electrical and Electronics Engineers (IEEE), a global standard for wireless networking was ratified in 1999, known in the industry as IEEE 802.11. Since then, fierce competition has resulted in simplification of the technology, leading to radical price drops. Today, wireless local area networks (WLANs) are a useful alternative to copper cabling when copper cabling is not possible (environmental issues may restrict the running of cables) and should always be a consideration during the planning phase of a new system.

Microsoft has made the wire-free environment much more attractive by integrating wireless LAN drivers into the latest Windows operating systems. WLAN network cards automatically configure themselves in Windows 2003 Server and Windows XP, making it possible to install and configure a WLAN in a matter of minutes.

WLAN technology brings with it many benefits: the flexibility to access your network from anywhere within range of the access point means you can use a PDA or laptop from any part of the office and still maintain high-speed network connectivity.

Note WLAN NICs are very like cabled NICs insomuch as both types are Ethernet based and both support IP. The central hub of a WLAN is called an access point but in essence it performs the same job as the standard network hub.

The minimum you need to set up a wireless network is two WLAN network cards (connecting in a manner known as ad hoc). These allow two computers to connect to each other. It's strongly recommended that you use a wireless access point for all WLAN systems. Access points act as police in managing the connections of wireless devices to your network, transmitting and receiving all network data from your wireless devices in the same way a normal network hub might. The added security features provided by an access point, as well as the ease of network management, make this a much better solution than a point-to-point setup.

Note I'd recommend that you always use an access point when designing a WLAN. Access points are extremely cost-effective these days, but their low cost is nothing compared to the increase in security and manageability they bring to your environment.

Planning a WLAN

The main thing to remember about a wireless network is that it behaves very like a cell phone network. Wireless access points have a set range, as do cell phone repeater stations; hence devices within coverage can connect to the network while machines outside drop signals and lose connectivity.

Note WLAN access points have a variable range depending on the environment they are installed in. Most will happily cover 40 to 60 feet in even the most hostile (to wireless) environment, but like cell phone systems, the more interference around, the less likely you'll be able to stretch your access point to its full 100-foot diametric span. Microwave ovens, overhead power cables, metal factory walls, heavy-duty machinery, and Bluetooth headsets are all sources of interference that can disrupt your wireless network, so if your office is prone to all of the above, consider a cabled environment if at all practicable.

When deciding where to place your wireless access points, opt for the position that is most central to all your business activity. Get a building blueprint and find the center as accurately as possible. Then, using a compass, draw a circle measuring about 60 feet out from this center of activity. This should be the limit of any single access point. If all is well, and all your systems fall within the circle, you will need only one access point.

Note Access points also have a limit on the maximum number of users: 10 users would be the absolute maximum for a single access point, so if you have more than 10 users needing connection inside your designated area, you'll need to install additional access points.

If you find you need to extend coverage, you can link access points to give you wider coverage (again, much like the cell phone network), and systems can roam between them without losing connectivity. The thing to watch for is that you might introduce black spots (places where there is no signal), so be careful to measure your installation accurately (see Figure 2-13). A few feet either way won't matter, but if you are wildly out in your calculations, black spots may well creep into places where you need connectivity. This would mean a redesign of your network and the possible purchase of more access points.

Realistically, you should not load access points to more than about 10 connections because bandwidth is limited just as in any other hub-based network. A simple way of resolving this is to use multiple access points all wired into a central switch. This means you segment your network traffic and give yourself the ability to expand as much as you need to.

Also make sure you place access points in an elevated position so as many devices that need connection have line-of-sight access. (If you have to put a shelf up high on a wall, do it. It's worth it.) Finally, try to keep the access point away from any localized interference culprits such as power cables, microwave ovens, or televisions.

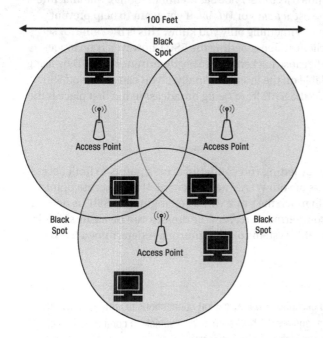

Figure 2-13. *Access points combine to offer greater network coverage.*

> ■**Note** Another name for wireless networking is *Wi-Fi*. Products that are Wi-Fi certified are interoperable with each other even if they are from different manufacturers. A Wi-Fi product can use any brand of access point and brand of network card displaying the Wi-Fi stamp. Within the technology groups of Wi-Fi-certified products, the most interoperable of the standards is 802.11g, so this is the most advisable standard to adopt. 802.11b Wi-Fi equipment will be recognized by and interoperate with a 802.11b system (by dropping the speed of connection to match the older technology).

Wireless Security

We've not really delved into computer security yet because there is a whole chapter dedicated to this subject later in the book. At this stage, I thought I'd best summarize some of the security features included with today's wireless product set to try to set your mind at rest.

Radio frequencies, unlike copper cabling, can be difficult to secure. Anyone who has a computer with a WLAN network card within range of your access point (possibly sitting in a car outside your office) can potentially access your system. With only limited expertise, an attacker could compromise the security of your network in as little as four minutes.

Okay, I was scaremongering somewhat, but when you take a look at the following technologies, you'll see why. Not one of these methods of securing a wireless network are considered secure anymore, although when they were introduced they were seen as the first and last lines of defense.

SSID

The name you assign to your WLAN is known as the Service Set Identifier (SSID). Manufacturers use a default SSID for their devices; some use *wireless* or *WLAN*. If you want to help prevent someone from guessing your SSID, set it to something only you know. This is the same for setting secure passwords for logging in to client systems. Setting the SSID, however, is no longer considered much of a security measure because hackers can easily determine the SSID by using one of the many wireless "sniffers" available on the Internet. Finally, if you can switch off SSID broadcasting altogether, do this. Stopping the SSID from being broadcast in the first place is the best course of action.

MAC Authorization

Vendors have increased security further by letting you configure access points to limit access by MAC address. This is the MAC address of your WLAN network card. If your access point offers this feature, make sure to use it. In much the same way as changing the SSID is no longer considered much of a security countermeasure, MAC addresses can be easily sniffed out and mimicked by using readily available systems on the Internet. A determined hacker will not be fazed by this approach.

> ■**Note** Hackers use the term *war driving* to describe how they exploit connections to wireless networks while driving around in their cars. War driving requires the hacker to have a vehicle, a computer, a wireless network card, and some kind of antenna, typically mounted on top of the car.

WEP

The Wired Equivalency Protocol (WEP) was designed as an optional extra, bolted on top of the 802.11 standard to heighten the security of targeted WLAN systems. It acts by encrypting all data transmissions between devices and associated access points. The problem with WEP is that most manufacturers' hardware uses a shared encryption key. It is this design flaw that makes WEP somewhat dangerous: you could rely too much on it and consider your systems secure, when in fact, they're not. A determined attacker could acquire this key and penetrate your network very quickly, leaving you wide open to data theft.

What you have to remember is that WEP is an *extra* measure of defense, not your only measure. Using a unique SSID, MAC address authorization, and WEP together, you're building walls that should keep out your average drive-by snooper. It's recommended that you change your WEP encryption keys at least once a month. This might seem an annoying overhead, but if it stops your data from being stolen or corrupted, it's worth it.

■**Warning** Using even the strongest combination of this technology, there is still a great threat that a determined hacker could compromise your network security. By using the right tools, a hacker could break WEP, have your SSID, and spoof your MAC address in around four minutes. Not very promising, is it? If you think you can rely on any of the previously mentioned technologies, you are kidding yourself and will be leaving yourself open to attack.

The Best of the Rest

Recent developments in more high-grade commercial wireless products have brought about new protocols and standards such as 802.11i or WPA encryption that can help secure your systems to industrial strength. If you feel you need to investigate these enhanced encryption standards, take a look at http://www.windowsecurity.com/articles/80211i-WPA-RSN-Wi-Fi-Security.html.

A much better alternative to WEP is a newer authentication protocol known as 802.1x. To exploit 802.1x, you'll need to install a system known as Remote Authentication Dial-In User Service (RADIUS) to authenticate client devices as they attempt to access your network.

To get a much better understanding of Wi-Fi security and how it affects you, take a look at http://www.wi-fi.org/OpenSection/secure.asp?TID=2.

Case Study—Planthire

When Philip Stanley looked at the networking requirements for Planthire, it was clear that he needed not only to connect the machines in the offices and shop floor, but also to provide remote access for himself and a few others (mainly administrative staff).

Wireless or Wired?

An interesting dilemma faced by Philip when deciding which way to go on the connectivity was to choose between the flexibility of wireless systems and the more traditional cabled solution.

Analysis of the environment and user requirements for all 14 staff members revealed that his business would benefit most from a split wireless and wired solution. The server and local computers for himself, his secretary, and his two desk clerks would remain wired, using desk-top PCs. For the rest of the 10 work positions on the shop floor, he decided laptop computers with wireless cards would better suit this working environment, with a laptop PC assigned to each user, and access points strategically placed around the environment. This allowed his workforce to take their system with them as they worked in different parts of the yard, allow-ing them immediate access to maintenance schedules, and so on.

Philip decided to buy three wireless access points to cover his shop floor, and the server and four workstations were on a 100 Mb hub in the main office.

Remote Access

Philip decided, because of cost, that initially he would permit remote access from home only for himself and his secretary. This would allow him to catch up on business matters that he didn't have time for during normal working hours, without having to spend many long and tedious hours away from his family. He decided on a brand new desktop computer to be installed in his office at home, and he used his broadband system to access his business networks via a VPN connection to his ISA Server.

Case Study—Servideal

The networking system for Servideal is probably the simplest model possible. Two computers need access to the internal business network, and the users (Henry and Marie O'Leary) wanted access to the system to be from any room in their house. The server's connectivity to the Internet needed to be as slick as possible because their core business is supplying prod-ucts to their customers over the Internet.

ISP Connectivity

To give Servideal the fastest connection to the Internet that its owners could afford, Henry opted to set up an ADSL service with his local telecommunications company, giving him a 2 Mbps connection to the Internet. At this stage of business development, this was more than enough for Servideal because they didn't yet have a stable customer base. Although the ADSL connection is not dedicated and can sometimes be unavailable, this was by far the most prac-ticable and cost-effective choice for a start-up business such as this. This always-on Internet connection also allowed the O'Learys to access their server (and hence their business) remotely to answer customer queries, update the catalog, and check on sales.

Wireless Flexibility

Marie wanted their home to be their main place of work, and she forecasted that both she and her husband would be working many late hours during the start-up phase of the busi-ness. To facilitate a more comfortable solution in the home, she installed a wireless system that allowed them to access their business network from any room in the house. They could comfortably sit in front of the television, retire to an office, or even sit in bed and do updates.

Case Study—Country Estates

To analyze a business as large as Country Estates, Alan needed to go back to first principles. He started with a top-level (practically geographic) diagram of his business, showing where the main office and branch offices were in respect to each other and how they were connected. It was clear even at this stage that he needed to do something extra to his network connectivity to allow him to put into practice the aspirations he developed with the consultant. He subsequently ordered 1 Mbps leased lines between his sites and adopted a new IP addressing policy that allowed all his machines to be on the same network.

On each of the sites, the majority of staff worked at designated desks, assigned to the individual for the duration of their employment with Country Estates. This was fine for most staff, but he also saw a need for managers and some team leaders to be able to plug in at remote sites when travelling between branches and the main office. For these staff, he decided a laptop computer better suited these travelling users, and in each branch he created a contingent of "hot desks," where visiting users could arrive on the premises, plug in, and continue working.

Remote Access

Alan decided, in an anxiety-free moment, that he also needed to offer some of his part-time staff more flexibility. People with family needs (for example, having to leave to pick up the kids from school) should be given the option to work in a more flexible way. He introduced the concept of home workers: these staff members received a company laptop, and he paid for a broadband connection so they could access the company network. Home workers were given the option of coming into the office or not, depending on what suited them. When they came in, they would use the hot desk facilities provided on the site. Using the remote access capabilities of SBS 2003, the home workers had exactly the same experience of using the system as locally connected full-time staff.

Summary

A well-planned, efficient network infrastructure will be the foundation for the rest of your SBS 2003 technology platform. Understanding the networking principles outlined in this chapter will not only help you understand how each technology layer interoperates with the next, but it will also give you a good grounding in the theory to take your learning further if you desire. Knowing the fundamental principles of TCP/IP, such as how DNS and DHCP work, as well as seeing the difference between the different physical components, will allow you to plan and implement a network that will be successful now, last into the future, and be as extensible as you need for an expanding business.

CHAPTER 3

■ ■ ■

The Planning Phase

Installing a suite of back-office server applications has never been so easy. After receiving a tirade of bad press over previous versions of the SBS product, Microsoft decided it was time to start afresh, completely redesigning SBS 2003 to be as user-friendly as possible. This new version offers a much better "out-of-the-box" experience, allowing you to easily install, configure, administer, and troubleshoot each of the included products.

SBS 2003 installation and configuration is driven through a simple, yet highly versatile wizard interface. Each wizard configures the underlying operating system on your behalf, abstracting the bits and bytes far enough into plain English as to make the setup much less of a black art than it used to be.

This is great news for both technical consultants and business managers who consider the time spent in product installation (especially the installation of an operating system) a waste of time and money, money that's better spent delivering value into the business.

Installing SBS 2003 will take you no longer than six hours, and as long as you have the best hardware available, the Premium suite could well be operational in fewer than four. Although you also need to subsequently configure each of the individual products, tailoring them to your specific needs, there's also a wizard for each of these.

Note Many SBS 2000 clients complained that the installation and initial setup of the product suite was by far its worst feature. Reports of installations taking three, maybe even five, days to complete were not unheard of. This became overly expensive for some small businesses because SBS 2000 required a lot of detailed, low-level configuration and possibly having a consultant on-site for the duration.

It's easy to be wowed by the improvements in SBS 2003, thinking your whole business can be reshaped in a matter of hours, but this would be a misconception. I'd like to get one thing straight before we proceed: you don't stop work as soon as the system is installed. A successful solution relies not only on the implementation of the software suite—you'll also need to consider several other factors to ensure that it's as powerful as it can be.

In this chapter you'll learn how to identify the information you need before setting off to install SBS 2003. The result: a configuration plan that will guide you through the installation and setup routine so you don't have to stop and think, "So, what do I type for the computer name?" or "What's the IP address of my server?"

I've included an example planning guide for each of the three real-world example companies that contains configuration information for each solution.

A Brief Word on SBS 2003 Licensing

You've already looked at the licensing model in Chapter 1, so all I'll do at this stage is reiterate the importance of making sure you've bought enough licenses, in advance of starting the installation process, especially if you are migrating an existing network infrastructure to SBS 2003 and expect all your users to have access to their systems and data come Monday morning.

Note Remember that SBS 2003 comes with five client access licenses included in the price of the product. This applies to both Standard and Premium editions. License packs can be added from the To Do List immediately after installation (see Chapter 4), or at any time in the future via the Server Management console.

Planning Hardware

When planning to install a small business network solution, you must consider the hardware requirements of all components that make up the solution. This includes the hardware you select for your server, your workstations, your network, and your printing and faxing needs.

The Server

Choosing the right hardware for your SBS 2003 server is a good place to start. You might decide to use a server you already have in the office. If you're already running SBS 2000 and decide to follow the upgrade path, then it's best to make sure your hardware at least meets the minimum requirements. Table 3-1 shows the minimum requirements of the all hardware components you'll need to have before you can think about installing SBS 2003.

Table 3-1. *Microsoft-Recommended SBS 2003 Hardware Configuration*

Hardware Component	Minimum Configuration
Processor	Pentium 4, 300 MHz
RAM	256 MB
Hard disk	4 GB
Ethernet NIC	10/100 Mbps (× 2 if you want to run Microsoft ISA Server from the Premium edition as your firewall device)
Backup device	An external FireWire- or USB-connected hard disk, or alternatively an internal tape drive
Optical drive	CD-ROM
Display	Monitor capable of 800 × 600 pixel resolution

It's worth noting, however, that minimum requirements are just that: an absolute minimum. It's far better to spend the money upgrading your system to the best specifications you can afford, or if you're starting afresh, make sure to maximize the capacity and processing capability.

If you can afford to buy hardware components that exceed the minimum requirements shown in Table 3-1, you will considerably benefit. The following list explains the significance of upgrading each hardware component in your SBS 2003 server to better-than-minimum specification:

- *Memory*: If you can afford to put some extra memory in your server, you should. Memory is cheap. However, there is no need to go overboard. Not many SBS users have more than 2 GB RAM in their servers and this would, in most cases, be considered excessive. Aim for around the 1 GB level unless you are running some memory-hungry line of business applications or large database systems.

- *Hard disk capacity*: Using much the same justification as with RAM, think about increasing hard disk capacity to as much as you can realistically afford. Take a look at the files your workforce currently stores on their workstations. You might have 10 workstations scattered around your office, each with 100 GB disks in them. Even if the business-related information on each machine is 10 percent of total usage, it totals 100 GB. If you are prepared to spend more money on your disks, think also about redundancy. Remember that choosing Redundant Array of Inexpensive Disks (RAID) (where you build in some extra fault tolerance to your hardware) will save your data if a hard disk crashes, giving you better business continuity. You should also consider the context of the files your workforce generates: spreadsheets and documents take up much less space than massive graphical computer-aided design (CAD) files. In a typical office generating invoices and spreadsheet files, 200 GB might be enough for 20 users. However, an architect's office of 5 users might need three times as much disk space to accommodate their enormous CAD files.

Note Think about the cost of your backup media as compared to the cost of disk storage. When you consider that all data you store on the server should be backed up as "business critical," you might well reconsider how you allocate server storage space.

- *Optical drive*: On a new machine it would be unlikely not to get at least a DVD player with CD-RW capabilities built right in. If you are upgrading, consider an internal DVD-RW because this will allow you to use the DVD writer (in the event of a tape drive breaking down) to also cut your backups. Often businesses use DVDs to transfer large amounts of data to clients by mail, as these are normally readable by most computer users.

Note Remember that burning CDs or DVDs can be hard on computer systems, so if you must burn disks on your server, try to do it at noncritical times.

- *Network interface card*: 10/100 Mbps network cards should be more than enough for your business environment in the office, but if you are considering a wireless system as part of your plan, still keep the server hard-wired into a Wi-Fi bridge.

- *CPU*: You might think it odd that I put the processor at number 4 in the list, but to be honest, unless you are doing highly complicated floating-point calculations or running extremely processor-hungry server-side database applications, then I stand by what I say and keep it low on the priority list. If you have a choice, go for the best processor you can, but if you are running a tight ship, consider last year's best processor on this year's best motherboard.

- *Display and backup*: Finally, the display and listed tape backup systems will suffice. As long as they work and do their job in the time you require, they'll do just fine. Fast tape systems are available, but they are expensive, and if your backups run okay in the time you've allocated to do them, don't fret. You could always opt for a removable hard disk to store backups because they are cheap and extremely fast. Similarly, you should consider the monitor interface only as a console for administration to the server components, and even here you will be performing a proportion of administration from workstations connected to terminal services, so use your money wisely and buy a little more RAM or disk space.

Tip Make sure all the components you have selected for your server are compatible with SBS 2003. If you are unsure, check the Windows Server Catalog (also known as the Hardware Compatibility List): http://www.microsoft.com/windows/catalog/server.

Future Upgrades

Needless to say, unless you go out and spend a small fortune, you'll have a system that could do with an upgrade at some time in the future. If more users come online, for example, or you start running memory-sapping applications, such as Microsoft SQL Server, you most certainly will have to change or augment your current hardware profile.

When the system is running, it becomes much easier to keep an eye on performance. SBS 2003 contains many useful tools such as Performance Monitor (see Figure 3-1) to show what's really happening over a long period of time.

You should plan an upgrade when you see a trend that might take you over the operating capabilities of your current system. Use the following three categories as a rule of thumb when scaling your system's growth:

- *Microbusiness*: This business might well need the power of the SBS 2003 platform but it won't have a large number of users (up to about five), or a great deal of storage and processing requirements. In this case, the minimum hardware configuration would suffice. If you will not grow beyond a microbusiness, you probably won't need to upgrade for some time.

- *Minibusiness*: These businesses are larger and might have up to approximately 20 users logging on simultaneously. If you are moving from a microbusiness to a minibusiness, consider adding RAM and disk space accordingly, and if possible consider a CPU upgrade.

- *Small business*: A small business in this context is anything with up to about 50 users. In this case, consider scaling up your system's RAM, hard disk capacity, network adapter speed, CPU, and possibly even offloading some application functionality onto separate servers. You will have to pay an upgrade fee for a stand-alone application, but the performance enhancement is significant in the case of intense SQL database applications or high-end web services. Multiple processors are also a possibility and would make a significant difference to your server's performance when running these sorts of intense applications.

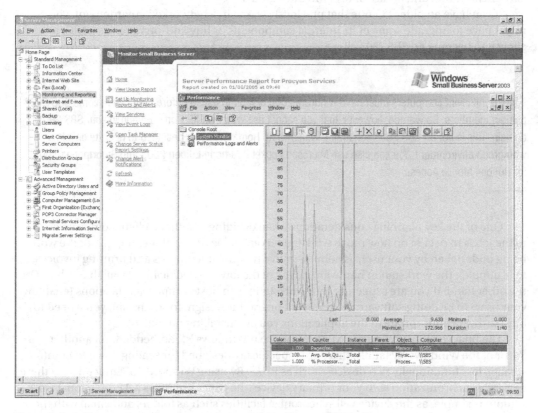

Figure 3-1. *Collect and analyze server data with Performance Monitor.*

Note that I've limited the small business to 50 users (rather than the SBS 2003 limit of 75 users) simply because, from a capacity-planning perspective, if you've already reached 50 users and the number is still climbing, you will probably have to come to terms with the fact that you're destined for bigger things. As your business grows beyond the threshold of what makes it a small business, the Microsoft products in the SBS 2003 suite (Microsoft Exchange Server, Windows SharePoint Services, Microsoft SQL Server, Microsoft ISA Server, and so on) work better as individual products, each one installed on its own server.

Client Workstations

The term *client* is a general name for any PC system that connects to and uses the services of a server. In the SBS 2003 environment, client computers commonly run the Windows XP Professional operating system, but there's no reason why you can't use Windows 2000 Professional.

If you're buying a brand new PC with Windows XP Professional already installed, it should be of high-enough specification to plug straight into your network. Most modern PCs are shipped with onboard NICs, modems, high-quality graphics cards, huge hard disks (100 GB isn't uncommon), and oodles of RAM (in the region of 512 MB).

If you have an older PC, one that previously wasn't in a networked environment, you might have to upgrade some of its internal components or buy add-ons such as a NIC, to allow it to become an SBS 2003 client.

Note All client computers must have Windows 2000 or later installed before they can become SBS 2003 domain members. Be warned, however, that you cannot use Windows XP Home Edition in your SBS 2003 domain. This is not an SBS 2003 constraint; Windows XP Home Edition is designed to operate only in a workgroup environment. You can also use Microsoft Pocket PC Phone Edition 2003 and Smartphone 2003 for Outlook Mobile Access.

One of the key planning considerations when deciding whether a client computer is up to the job is to decide on how much work the server will be doing. If the majority of the work being undertaken by your users is administrative (writing documents and printing invoices, for example), the workstation hardware can be of the lowest specification available to buy. On the other hand, if you are expecting your workstations to host complex applications (enabling your users to be doing software development or graphic design, for example), you'll need to buy hardware appropriate to the applications you are installing on top.

The final version of Windows XP to introduce is Windows XP Embedded. Yet another flavor of the Windows XP family, this one is specifically designed for scaling down to fit into smaller, less functionally rich devices, such as PDAs. By using Windows XP Embedded in these devices, synchronization with your primary device (the user's Windows XP Professional workstation) is simple, as the device will synchronize facilities such as folders and email with the mother operating system. Windows XP Embedded comes in a modular construction, and OEM hardware manufacturers use the parts they need to make their devices work.

Peripheral Hardware

In addition to the core components that make up your server and workstation community, you'll need to consider all the extraneous devices, such as printers, scanners, and fax machines.

Printers

When deciding on your future printing needs, take a look at what you do now and rationalize it. What output do you really need? Don't take your business's current hard-copy regime and accept it as your future requirement; instead, look to see where this function can be streamlined. A paperless office should be your ultimate goal.

When you select a printer, look at the price of the replacement cartridges and try to find a system that uses toner as efficiently as possible. Some printers may look cheap when you first buy them, but you'll be shocked when the replacement toner systems come in at almost three-quarters of the price of the hardware.

Fax Machines

The fax-to-desktop facilities built into SBS 2003 are good enough that you can do away with any previously direct-connect model that sits monitoring a dedicated telephone line. When you specify to your hardware vendor the components that you want installed in your SBS 2003 server, make sure to request the installation of a fax-capable modem.

Warning The best type of modem to request is still the old favorite, the external V.90 fax modem. Modern V.92 systems and USB-connected modems have been reported to cause major problems with SBS 2003 systems.

SBS 2003 can then be configured to route faxes to an email address, a SharePoint website, or even directly to one of your network printers. Users cans send faxes directly from their desktops. Each fax is sent through the server fax queue, where it can be appended with the company cover sheet (see Figure 3-2), and each transaction is logged and archived for future auditing.

Figure 3-2. *A cover sheet can be automatically appended to each fax.*

And the Rest…

As with any new device you are considering adding to your environment, ask yourself, *is it really necessary?* Do you really have to scan documents, or is a scanner just a corporate toy? If you do have a genuine requirement, you might want to consider a three-in-one device (printer, scanner, and photocopier) instead of a standard printer.

Note Three-in-one devices are becoming increasingly popular. As more businesses buy into the concept of using these three-in-one devices to provide a consolidated approach to these services, hardware manufacturers are looking closely at product ranges and releasing devices capable of handling much higher throughput and being more robust in a business environment. Three-in-ones initially were targeted at the home market, so they might fare well enough on a small scale, but you'll need separate devices for really high-volume work.

Planning Internet Connectivity

You'll need to speak to an Internet Service Provider (ISP) to get your internal network connected to the Internet. The ISP will be able to provide the following:

- Physical Internet connectivity

- Connection device, such as an ADSL modem

- Email accounts

- Domain names and websites

- Advice on configuring the interconnectivity between your network and the Internet

When you approach an ISP, check how wide-ranging and versatile their service portfolio is. You don't want to be tied into a year-long contract that prohibits you from upgrading dial-up to ADSL access. Also check with the ISP what level of devolution of services they offer—you might want email delivered directly to your SBS 2003 server rather than having it stored on the ISP server to be retrieved.

Physical Internet Connectivity

Ask your ISP what methods of connecting to the Internet are available. Also check the cost against what you budgeted to spend monthly on connectivity. Table 3-2 lists connectivity methods offered by a typical ISP.

Table 3-2. *Typical ISP Internet-Connection Methods*

Connection Type	Download Speed	Upload Speed	Service Description
Dial-up	V.90 = 36 Kbps V.92 = 48 Kbps	56 Kbps	Traditional dial-up connections have been around for some time. Although the top connection speed is 56 Kbps, this is rarely achieved and more than likely the modem connects at speeds of around 40 Kbps.
ISDN	128 Kbps in blocks of 64 Kbps	128 Kbps in blocks of 64 Kbps	ISDN is very similar to dial-up but offers higher connection speeds. Can be costly if you use the Internet a lot.
ADSL	Up to 8 Mbps	Up to 1 Mbps	A much faster connection than ISDN, provided through your existing telephone lines. The level of service available is determined by your distance from the local telephone exchange.
ADSL 2/2+	Up to 24 Mbps	3.5 Mbps	These are the latest generation of DSL services and are proving to be extremely cost-effective for the small business community to get really fast Internet access.
Microwave	Up to 10 Mbps	Up to 10 Mbps	Your system's receiver dish must have line-of-sight to the ISP, similar to that of satellite Internet connectivity. Higher bandwidth is extremely costly.
T1	Up to 1.54 Mbps	Up to 1.54 Mbps	T1 lines offer the highest availability, so are by far the best for a business with a high dependence on the Internet for its customers. The high availability comes at high cost, so this must be weighed against cheaper ADSL services.
Satellite	Up to 3 Mbps	Up to 128 Kbps	Line-of-site to satellite required, and the high latency means they are virtually unusable for real-time broadcasting or multimedia. Expensive, last resort option.

As you can see in Table 3-2, there are a lot of ways to connect to the Internet. The best value for your money is by far ADSL 2/2+, giving you an always-on connection for roughly the price of the dial-up service you'd have used of old. Only under certain circumstances would you need to choose a microwave or satellite solution, and in these cases you will have exhausted all other routes of inquiry. Sometimes, if the service you are after is not available, it's worth asking the ISP or telecommunications company what criteria they would use to consider installation worthwhile. For example, some telecommunications companies will wait until they have enough general queries from a particular area code before upgrading the local exchange to cope with the digital signals of ADSL or ADSL 2/2+ (depending on availability).

Connection Devices

After you've established which ISP you're going to use and chosen the connection type you're going to subscribe to, you'll need to work with your ISP to decide on the best equipment to employ within your business's networking environment.

The choice of equipment completely depends on which type of service you've chosen—for example, a dial-up connection requires a traditional modem and telephone line, whereas a microwave service requires a router, specialized cables, and a microwave receiver. The choice also depends on the product set available through your ISP, so if you opt for ADSL, for example, you'll need a suitable (digital-capable) telephone line, a broadband modem, and a set of microfilters. Depending on the package you select and the complexity of the connection type, you'll either get a DIY installation kit (for dial-up and ADSL), or you'll get an engineer out to set it up.

■**Note** ADSL microfilters are in-line devices that allow you to connect your modem or router directly into your telephone line. They are cheap and normally come as standard when you order your ADSL package. The filters are there only as a way of removing the audible signal from the telephone line.

Email

When you order your Internet package, be sure to decide how you want to handle email. Do you want a single email address for the business or do you need an individual email address for each user? Do you want email delivered directly to your SBS 2003 server or should it be stored on the ISP's server and pulled down when your server connects to the Internet?

If you decide to collect email from the ISP in the same way as you would when you dial up from a home machine, you'll be using the POP3 connector that Microsoft Exchange 2003 provides, and email will be downloaded on a schedule (see Figure 3-3) into the appropriate Exchange message store. This is useful for slow or intermittent Internet connections because you can schedule the POP3 activity to happen when the server loading is low.

Alternatively, if your connection is always on, such as with a T1 or ADSL, you might consider asking your ISP to route email directly to your server's Internet IP address. In this case your Internet domain name for email will be resolved to the IP address of the Internet-facing NIC on your server. Internet email routing uses a DNS record called an MX record. Your ISP sets up an MX record to point to your SBS 2003 server, allowing other email systems on the Internet to route email directly to you.

■**Note** An *MX record* (Mail Exchange) is an entry in the Internet DNS database that helps resolve a domain name to an IP address. Normally an ISP will have the domain name registered with one of the ISP's servers, so email sent to your domain name is stored for later collection. If you request that the MX record points to your server, you'll need to be able to receive the email when it's sent; otherwise, email may be delayed or lost.

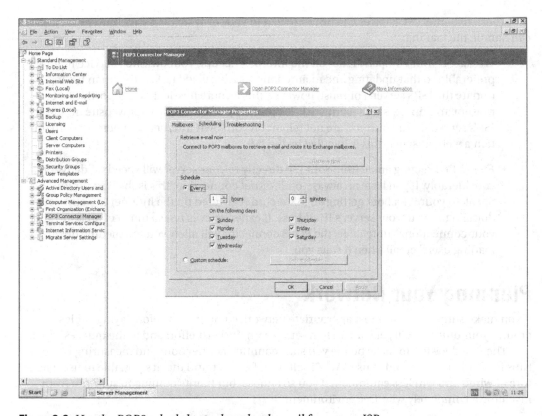

Figure 3-3. *Use the POP3 scheduler to download email from your ISP.*

Domain Names and Web Space

Say, for example, you own a company called *My Company*. You decide the best way for your company to succeed is to start trading online, so you decide to set up an ISP account to connect your SBS 2003 network to the rest of the world. You need a website, email, and access to the World Wide Web to gather customer and competitor information.

To get your company known, and to make sure your web presence is akin to your physical embodiment, it's best to get yourself a .com address. This means your domain name—the name that defines your entire capability on the Web—becomes mycompany.com. You register this domain name with your ISP, and in turn the ISP makes sure that anyone accessing a web address suffixed with mycompany.com is accessing your site. Any email sent to a user@mycompany.com will be stored in the appropriate mailbox on their server, and you are allocated some space on their web server so that anyone accessing the website www.mycompany.com is directed to the appropriate directory on their server.

These two Internet services can be redirected to your own server if you think your system can handle the loading:

- *Website*: If your company relies on the Internet, hosting your own web service might be preferable so that updating and maintenance is a localized task, rather than having to update the ISP's server. For most, however, this is more hassle than it's worth and can present an unnecessary security risk. It's probably best to leave your website on the ISP's server. In this case you are not reliant on your own Internet connectivity to maintain a web presence; this is handled by the ISP.

- *Email*: Redirecting email from your ISP directly to your server will speed up delivery considerably. If you have an always-on Internet connection, this is the best option. Speak to your ISP about getting an MX record registered on the Internet to point your domain name to your server's IP address. If expediency is not so much of an issue and your connection is unreliable, the POP3 connector will allow you to schedule downloading users' email when it suits you.

Planning Your Network

If you make sure to buy the most appropriate network components before laying cables around your office, you'll get your system set up with the least effort and in the quickest time.

The first decision to make before you start counting connections and measuring cable runs is whether you intend to use a Wi-Fi solution. Bear in mind that it's possible to use a mixture of wired and wireless equipment if you so choose, but there's nothing to stop you from installing a completely wire-free environment.

Note A total Wi-Fi solution is preferable if you rent an office where you are constrained in what you can do to the building's infrastructure. If you cannot hide cables in discreet cable ducting, you might have to string cables over the floor or ceiling. Aside from the obvious dangers of tripping and lawsuits, a poor installation looks unprofessional and may cast your business in a bad light with any visiting customers.

Because the details of the components needed to set up a network have already been covered in Chapter 2, I'll move on to helping you decide how many, where they go, and how to connect them.

Wired Networks

A typical small-scale Ethernet network comprises a number of computers (with network interface cards) connected via Ethernet cables to ports on a hub or a switch.

The following list of questions should be asked when deciding what to buy:

- *What speed is the network?* Ethernet networking components can operate at a variety of different data transmission rates, as discussed in Chapter 2, but the speed the entire network performs at is determined by the lowest common denominator on each connection. If you require a high-speed network, choose modern components capable of transmission speeds of at least 100 Mbps and make sure you buy good-quality Cat5e or Cat6 patch cables.

- *Hub or switch?* As I've already said, a switch divides a network into LAN segments, allowing traffic to any individual port to be isolated from the rest of the network. In the small business environment, however, the majority of network traffic is directed at the server, so for a small business it makes no sense to choose a switch over a less-expensive hub. In networks that have many clients connecting to many servers, switch technology comes into its own. Saying this, however, you might find that switch technology has become so competitive that if you really have to fork out to buy new equipment, a switch might be the only sensible option.

Note A *LAN segment* is any piece of a network not separated by a bridge. This means that all traffic on a LAN segment is inspected by every NIC. A switch will provide a discrete LAN segment from each port, while a hub joins the ports together, creating a single LAN segment.

- *How many host systems do you have?* Count the number of network devices you intend to connect into your network infrastructure: this includes workstations, servers, network print servers, wireless uplinks, or any other Ethernet device. The total number of host systems will equate to the minimum number of ports you'll need on your network hub. To facilitate expansion and to make sure you haven't missed a couple of devices, add 20 percent to the port count.

- *How many cables and how long?* Measuring the length of a cable is not as straightforward as it sounds. A common mistake people make is to judge the length of the cable based on the computer's proximity to the network hub. When you come to feed the cable through the cable ducting, under a false floor, through the roof void, or through some integrated cable management solution in the desks, you suddenly find you are 6 inches short. This wastes a lot of time and money, and commonly the cable ends up in the spares box, never to be used. Make sure you measure every aspect of the cable run, and to be safe add 15 percent to the length. If you are running cables through a cable management system, any excess can be lost in the cable duct.

Wireless Networks

Wireless networks also use hubs, known as access points (as discussed in Chapter 2), but in this case the major planning concern is deciding on the best location for radio broadcasting.

Devices such as microwave ovens, cell phones, DECT home telephone systems, and even electrical cables can disrupt the performance of the most commonly used Wi-Fi equipment (based on the 802.11b and 802.11g standards), both of which broadcast around the 2.4 GHz frequency range. The most-effective location to place an access point is high up on a stand, where as many computers have an unblocked, line-of-sight view of the access point antenna. Try to make sure that the access point is as central to all your computers as possible, but if this means putting it in the kitchen above the microwave, you might want to reconsider.

All of the security measures used on a wireless network should be preplanned. You will need to decide on a passphrase for WEP encryption—the primary encryption protocol used on medium-security Wi-Fi networks—and if you have the option to assign a private SSID number, do so and document your decision.

Note Security experts recommend you implement WPA because most recent Wi-Fi cards support this more-secure technology.

It pays to read the manufacturer's instructions for Wi-Fi equipment before you start the installation because various security regimes are available, depending on the amount of money your spend on your equipment, and each has its own requirements. Make sure to document this in the appropriate section of your planning guide.

TCP/IP

Your IP addressing model will depend on whether you're using a set of public Internet addresses or a private network from behind a NAT device. For details on how private networks connect to the Internet, see Chapter 2. From a planning perspective, it's important at this stage that you decide which way you intend to go.

Both addressing models are viable in a small business environment, and both have their benefits and limitations. When you opt for using public Internet addresses, each host is a legitimate Internet entity that can be directly addressed. This means you can communicate with that host from anywhere on the Internet without any form of translation or intermediary. If you use a private network, connecting the Internet through the NAT device, connections can be initiated only from the internal network going out. In most cases this is fine; because the SBS 2003 server acts as the NAT device, all internal resource access is facilitated through the server via the server's public network interface.

Note Many SBS users connect their network to the Internet by using a separate stand-alone firewall product such as one from the Firebox range by Watchguard. See http://www.watchguard.com/products/appliances.asp.

If you are using an Internet addressing model, your ISP will allocate the IP addresses to use for each of your clients. This address will be in the form of a subnet, allowing you to still use DHCP to allocate the addresses to your workstations.

If you decide to use a private network, the recommended IP address is in the 192.168.xxxx.xxx range, and the subnet mask will be 255.255.255.0.

Note You can also use addresses in the ranges of 10.xxx.xxx.xxxx and 172.xxx.xxx.xxxx.

To allocate private IP addresses to your network, use the following guidelines:

1. Allocate a static IP address to your server. It's best to allocate the first IP address in the range for this device—for example, 192.168.0.1.

2. Allocate the next 20 addresses to peripheral devices, such as network printers, because many of these devices should have hard-coded addresses.

3. A DHCP reservation will be used to secure the fixed addresses from being allocated dynamically.

4. Assignment of the remaining addresses will be dynamic. This means all your workstations and other DHCP-aware client systems will receive a new IP address from your server when they request connection to the network.

5. The DHCP scope (the range of addresses and associated configuration data for each assignment) will contain the IP addresses, the local DNS server name (your SBS 2003 server), and the IP address of the Internet gateway. If you've followed these guidelines, the gateway device will be 192.168.0.1.

6. In each case, the subnet mask should be the same, set to 255.255.255.0.

DNS Naming

The DNS name of your network should remain private even though you are planning to connect to the Internet and maintain an Internet web presence. When you install SBS 2003, you are asked to enter a DNS name for your local installation. By default, SBS 2003 selects a default DNS name appended with the *.local* suffix. Your external Internet address will be something like mycompany.com, so the complete name for your internal system will be mycompany.local. Stick to this standard because the DNS suffix .local is not used on the Internet. This means the DNS name will remain private, with all extraneous naming requests being passed out of your network and onto the Internet.

The external DNS name you select should first be registered with your ISP for the following reasons:

- To make sure it's available

- To make sure you don't have to reconfigure SBS 2003 later if the name is not available

- To allow your POP3 connector to access your company email service at the ISP

Remote Access

Remote access is one of those concepts we know we need, but it's often hard to quantify in terms of real user experience. In SBS 2003 terms, remote access can take on many forms, from simple web-based email using Outlook Web Access, right through to a VPN solution extending the boundary of your network to mobile users needing all services provided on your infrastructure.

To set up remote access, you'll need to plan how many users will require these rights. You'll need to decide whether your users are truly mobile, or rather have home-based access. Last you'll need to decide on the best connectivity method for providing remote access in each case: dial-up, VPN, or direct-connect.

Often remote-access solutions are overengineered, providing more capability than the user needs—and this leads to a less-secure solution as a whole.

Questions to ask yourself before embarking on a remote-access solution design are as follows:

- How many users need remote access?

- What services do each of these users require?

- What forms of connection are available for each user?

When you set up remote access, having thought about these questions in advance will undoubtedly speed up the installation.

If you are unsure as to how you might connect users to the network, speak to your ISP to see what options are available. If, for example, you decide to let some of your knowledge workers do their job primarily at home (this can be advantageous because productivity can increase when workers are happy), you might be able to make a deal with your ISP to install low-cost ASDL connections that provide a VPN tunnel over the Internet into your business network. In this case, using ISA 2004 as your Internet gateway (requiring you to purchase SBS 2003 Premium Edition with Service Pack 1) would be preferable.

Planning Consistent Nomenclature

It's important with all naming conventions that you decide in advance the most appropriate nomenclature and stick to the rules for name generation. The names of computers, users, and peripherals should all be meaningful and unique, and your scheme should be scalable to grow with your business. There's no point in calling your computers by the users' names, for example; if a user leaves, you'll have to rename the computer for the new staff member who joins and inherits the equipment.

Computer Naming

Every computer on your network must have a name that individually identifies it to the other computer systems, including your server. Each of these names is registered in your local DNS system as a prefix to your network DNS domain name. This means that the complete address of any system on your network is in the format *mycomputer.mycompany.local*.

Note The complete name of a system, consisting of the host name and the domain name, is known as the fully qualified domain name (FQDN).

The thing about computer names is that they can be set to anything you like—similar to that of user names—but if you're smart in how you name your systems, the name can become more useful than simply a random set of characters. You should come up with a convention that is scalable and information laden, without tying the name to information that changes, such as a user name or a physical location.

You should split up your computer systems into pools of resources based on how they are used, where they are situated, and what their function is.

When deciding on a naming convention, the following guidelines will help you come up with something sustainable as your business grows:

1. On paper, split your systems into groups of PCs, ordered by equipment type (that is, desktop, laptop, and tablet). Then split each group further based on the installed operating system (for example, four desktop PCs running Windows XP, two desktop PCs running Windows 2000, and two laptop PCs running Windows XP).

2. For each subgroup, decide on an alphabetic code that designates the attributes of the subgroup. For example, if you are looking at desktop PCs with Windows XP, your designator might be DESKXP.

3. Append a four-digit number to the end of the alphabetic code to individualize each member computer.

4. Each new computer added to the group will take the next available number. You should always work in sequence.

5. Servers installed on your network should also follow an alphanumeric naming convention. The server's function, for example, could be written as a three-digit alphabetic code, such as SBS or SQL, with a numeric suffix individualizing every instance of that server type when multiple servers with the same function exist.

By following this convention, the first Windows XP desktop PC installed on your network will have the name DESKXP0001. In the same vein, the 16th laptop running Windows 2000 Professional to be added to your SBS 2003 domain will assume the name LAPT2P0016. Your SBS 2003 would become SBS0001, and the third SQL server on your network would become SQL0003.

As your business expands, as users change jobs, or even if you move premises, your computer names will *always* identify the computer for what it is.

User Account Naming

For the same reason that you need a consistent approach to computer naming, it's also good practice to have a standard for your users' account names. The main reason for standardizing this naming convention is to ensure that there is a consistent look and feel to facilities provided for your users when they interact with the system.

By looking at an account name, it should immediately become apparent who the user is, and this will nominally be the prefix to their fully qualified email address.

Take, for example, a Wi-Fi networking company called TechSynch. TechSynch recently hired a new secretary named Brenda Taylor. As part of her induction, she is allocated a building pass and a new starters guide, and the IT support team is tasked with creating her identity on TechSynch's SBS 2003 infrastructure.

TechSynch's user-naming convention is to take the first letter of the employee's first name, append it to their last name, and then suffix it with a two-digit numerical code, beginning at 01 for the first person with that name to join the company.

■ **Note** Putting a two-digit numerical code on the end of the user name might sound like overkill, but I kid you not, I've worked in an establishment with nine users named John King.

So Brenda's account is created on the system and her username is *btaylor01* (see Figure 3-4). Her email address, by default, will become btaylor01@techsynch.com, and she will have a network share created for her user called *btaylor01*.

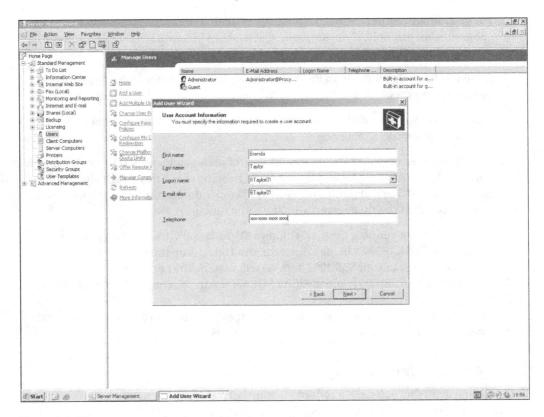

Figure 3-4. *The user name also determines the email alias.*

Share Naming

Shares are the places on your server where you share information with groups of users. These shares should also be given relevant names, ones that users can easily identify and connect to, as long as they have permission. Access to the data behind a share is controlled by using file permissions, so the knowledge of a share does not cause a security concern. Shares should be given names appropriate to the data they contain; then Security Groups are created and applied to these shares to control access to the underlying resources.

If you have a shared file store for invoices, call it *company invoices*. If you have a share containing personnel records, call it *personnel records*.

Security Group Naming

As with shares, Security Groups (the method used in Windows systems for granting access to objects in either the file system or in Active Directory) are easiest to administer when they have meaningful names. A Security Group granting access to a set of documents in the *invoices* file share should be called *Access Invoices*. If you need a Security Group to explicitly deny access to a set of files, prefix the meaningful name describing the data with the word *Deny*.

Now, when administrators need to grant access for a user to the *invoices* area, they add the user into the Security Group *Access Invoices*. Hey, presto, the user has a new set of rights and can access the controlled data.

Planning for Security and Safety

Information security is covered in detail in Chapter 11, so I'll not reiterate what's covered there, except for one thing: get yourself a good-quality antivirus software solution to cover your workstations, servers, and Exchange 2003 server. Follow the guidelines laid out in Chapter 11 and you should be safe from electronic and social engineering attacks.

In the rest of this section, I'll concentrate on another piece of the security puzzle—that of physical security. *Physical security* is any countermeasure employed by your business to protect your physical assets from tampering, espionage, or theft.

Warning If you don't have good physical security, a hacker could simply steal your server and then have much more chance of getting into it while he's working on the system directly in his basement. This would be preferable to trying to breach the more conventional network defenses, such as getting through your firewall.

The following list of potential threats and countermeasures can be applied to both home and office, and should, if nothing else, reduce your insurance premiums:

- *Outer doors (home or office)*: Make sure any outer doors are secured, if possible, with two five-lever deadlocks. Alternatively, if your doors don't permit this level of locking (due to the build of the frame or door panels), a built-in deadlock with chain and bar would work just as well.

- *Internal doors*: Make sure all doors leading to business-related data (whether hard copy or the physical locations of computer equipment) are fitted with a key-operated security bolt, if possible at the top and bottom of the door.

- *Windows*: All ground-floor windows, or any easily accessible window (accessible via a drainpipe, climbing on the garage, and so on) should be lockable. Alternatively, you can fix these windows shut by using internally fitted nonreturn screws, screwed through the frame into the window surround, as long as you are not compromising any fire regulations.

- *Workstations*: Use case locks on all computer equipment. Make sure all case lock keys are secured in a safe, somewhere away from the computer's location. Laptops left on the premises should be stored in a secure cabinet or in a safe if space permits.

- *Laptops*: Use Windows XP file encryption (known as the Encrypting File System, or EFS) to encrypt the contents of the hard disk.

- *Servers*: Servers are the heart of your solution. If you can, lock the server to a secure floor ringlet by using a chain lock and also use a case lock to secure access to the server internals. Case lock keys and chain lock keys should be stored in the secure safe.

- *Card key access*: Secure the office environment by using controlled card key access systems. This provides an audit of who's where in the building, and when they were in.

- *Burglar alarm*: Use a burglar alarm system that connects to the local police force. These systems can be expensive, but the installation cost can be offset against the price of your yearly insurance reduction for the use of a system like this. Often modern burglar alarms can notify the owner of security breaches, and surveillance systems can also allow remote camera operation via the Internet.

- *Position*: Consider where the best place in your building would be to house your server and networking equipment. Don't put it in the reception area, next to the secretary's desk, or in the kitchen area (where coffee might inadvertently get spilled through the cooling vents) and please, please, please, don't leave your backup tapes anywhere they might be swiped because these contain *all* your business's private and confidential information. Who needs to struggle with a server when a tape the size of a cigarette packet would suffice?

As any good IT consultant will tell you, it is essential to capture the requirements of the business, and to agree on them, before designing a solution to meet those requirements. This is true from the very smallest to the very largest of IT solutions. This comprehension also leads to a dialogue in how the business could operate with greater efficiency, within the expanded margins of an effective IT solution. There are several areas where a solution like SBS 2003 can provide efficiency savings in a business, once you understand that business. One customer, a medium-sized light engineering firm, was handling 75 percent of its orders via incoming faxes that were photocopied, filed, and then a confirmation printed out and separately cranked through the fax back to their customer. SBS 2003 fax services was an obvious enabler for early efficiency savings here—incoming faxes are now automatically filed to a Windows SharePoint Services document library, an email alert automatically sent to the Accounts department, whereby a confirmation is sent from the desktop, via the SBS 2003 server.

—David Pyke, SBS 2003 consultant, Intanetworking

Case Study—Planthire

When planning the implementation of his IT system, Philip Stanley devised the requirements shown in Table 3-3. This table shows the high-level choices he made when planning what to buy and what services to contract from his ISP.

Table 3-3. *Planthire's Business Requirements*

Topic	Requirement	Notes
Licensing	SBS 2003 Standard	Philip decided that he didn't need the Premium edition features, so Standard would suffice.
Client workstations	14 new Windows XP systems	The machines already used by Planthire were old and beginning to fail. The best course of action was to buy new systems running Windows XP. This gained maximum advantage from compatibility with SBS 2003.
Peripherals	Two modern color laser printers 1 Scanner 1 Fax card in the server to offer faxing services to all IT users	The two color laser printers will be centrally controlled while the scanner will connect to the manager's workstation. Incoming faxes will be automatically routed to the color printer in the secretary's office.
Internet connectivity	ADSL 1 MB	This was the minimum cost option with the local telecommunications firm for acquiring an always-on Internet connection.
Domain name	www.planthire.com	Philip decided a .com domain name best suited his image.
Email addresses	14 independent POP3 addresses on the ISP	He decided to use the Exchange POP3 connector and download email from the ISP into Exchange.
Web space	50 MB	Philip will be contacting a friend to develop his website. The friend advised Philip to get the minimum hosting package his ISP offered. In this case he ended up with 50 MB.

Case Study—Servideal

When the Servideal owners looked at their server requirements, it was apparent that they needed a medium-range server but lots of disk space. They decided SBS 2003 Premium was better for them because the ISA Server product was a more robust firewall—essential in this environment for protecting confidential customer information and credit card details. The specifications shown in Table 3-4 show the rationale for each component's selection.

Table 3-4. *Server Specification for Servideal*

Hardware Component	Purchased Configuration	Notes
Processor	Pentium 4, 2.8 MHz	The majority of compute power used in this system is in access to the e-commerce facility. In comparison with running complicated applications or servicing lots of users, this is a minimum requirement.
RAM	2 GB	As with all server specifications, buy as much memory as you can comfortably afford.
Hard disk	2 × 400 GB	Lots of disk space is required for the catalog and customer databases.
Ethernet NIC	100 Mbps	This connectivity came as part of the server hardware package and is more than enough to connect into the wireless system they installed in their house.
Backup device	An internal tape drive	A tape device offers the maximum flexibility and maximum storage capacity for each component tape. This, on such a large disk volume, is essential.
Optical drive	DVD-R and CD-RW	Standard with the server hardware. DVD offers maximum flexibility with today's software media.
Display	Server console capable of 800 × 600 pixel resolution	Only a basic screen is required for direct server management.

Case Study—Country Estates

Security planning for the Country Estates system was one of the most important things Alan Smith was interested in. He was concerned about virtually every aspect of IT security, from viruses to hackers, burglars to earthquakes. He needed to know that his data, his operations, and his business were safe. Table 3-5 shows the security features Alan has built into his IT system.

Table 3-5. *Security Components Considered by Country Estates.*

Security Feature	Purchased Configuration	Notes
Antivirus	McAfee GroupShield and VirusScan	This system will protect the email system from email worms and malware in attachments, as well as protecting the NTFS file store on both the server and the workstations from similar threats.
Firewall	SBS 2003 Premium Edition with ISA Server 2004	The industrial strength of the ISA Server firewall offers in-depth content filtering and inspection.
Delegation of administration (DoA)	A comprehensive DoA model should be adopted	The DoA will delegate system permissions and rights to only the appropriate level of users. This means that users can access only what they *should* access and no more.
Physical security	Computer room lock Workstation tagging	The SBS 2003 server is to be located in a secured room within the head office facility. This room will have limited access, and the security guard will hold the key. Only CEO-authorized staff can access the room.
Data loss	Comprehensive backup policy	All user data is held on the server, and all data is backed up every day. The backup tapes are stored off-site.

Summary

The basic process of planning your IT system is no different from planning a household DIY job. When you install a new radiator, for example, you will check the flooring to determine whether there are obstacles beneath the surface that may thwart your running of pipes. Networks pose the same sort of problems. If the network is to be hidden within the walls, you need to understand the wall construction and how to make good on any installation work that affects the wall's finish.

The key to success is making sure you avoid the most obvious problems, trying to eliminate any complications that might occur at this early stage rather than facing them when time becomes critical. Plan each cable run meticulously, and each software installation and backup with enough time and tolerance to not upset normal business. Where you might find difficulties (for example, in the wired cable approach), consider using an alternative (such as Wi-Fi).

CHAPTER 4

■ ■ ■

Installation and Configuration

This chapter guides you through the installation and postinstallation configuration of SBS 2003. I cover all aspects of the different installation methods, including fresh installations and system upgrades, and I've also gone into the typical postinstallation configuration requirements for most small business customers: features such as connecting to the Internet, activating user accounts within the Active Directory, creating policies for controlling users, adding workstations and printers to the network, and setting up all the security and management features.

In some cases, you might be upgrading your system from a previous version (such as SBS 2000), while in other cases you might be using a preconfigured hardware platform sourced from a Microsoft SBS 2003 OEM system builder. In the case of the former, you'll get to see the best method for upgrading from a legacy system. In the case of the latter, if you're using an OEM-sourced SBS 2003 system, you'll not be required to perform the Windows Server 2003 software installation, going straight to the Windows Small Business Server Setup Wizard 2003. However, for reference, it's still worth reading through the server setup routine to see exactly how your SBS 2003 ends up in its final state.

Note *OEM* stands for *Original Equipment Manufacturer* and refers to hardware vendors who sell computers with preinstalled Microsoft products on the hard disk at a reduced cost through an agreement between the vendor and Microsoft. An element of configuration will have already been done by the vendor on these computer systems, and all you need to do when you get it back to the office is to personalize the software to your environment.

Whatever you're doing—starting afresh, upgrading, or migrating—you'll need to allocate about half a day to complete the job properly, and I'd recommend that you do try to do the job as one continuous piece of work. Installation of the underlying Windows 2003 operating system is fairly boring, requiring just the occasional input from the installer, but this occasional input is required to confirm aspects of the installation before you can proceed with the rest of the SBS 2003 product installations. For this reason, hitting an OK button and then heading off for the night might well delay you further, because the next morning you might not have progressed that far.

After you've installed SBS 2003, and before you move on to tailoring the applications (such as Windows SharePoint Services) to your specific business requirements, you'll need to run through a standard set of configuration wizards to perform tasks such as creating your networking environment, connecting SBS 2003 to the Internet (as your shared connection), setting up your system-monitoring and security-auditing infrastructure, and a whole heap of other items necessary to create the basic underlying infrastructure.

A Word on Upgrading

Upgrading an already-running Windows server system to SBS 2003 is, at first glance, the easiest way to get the software installed, but, as with anything that makes life easier, there must also be a downside.

When you perform an upgrade, the SBS 2003 installation program looks at your current system's configuration and then reuses that configuration to set the parameters of SBS 2003 components. This means that your upgraded SBS 2003 server will inherit any configuration problems you might have been encountering on the previous system.

For this reason alone, I strongly recommend that you *don't* perform an upgrade unless you are left with no viable alternative. Even if the legacy hardware will easily support SBS 2003 and you feel the system doesn't have any real configuration issues, problems might be just waiting to strike, and all the upgrade will do is move them into SBS 2003.

Instead of doing an in-situ upgrade of the operating system, try migrating your users and data from the old solution onto a clean build of SBS 2003.

Note This whole procedure will take some time to complete, so it might be best to do the work over a weekend. That way you at least have time to recover your old system from a backup if you run into problems.

Migrating To SBS 2003

The following four steps should be followed to migrate your old system to the new SBS 2003 environment:

1. Take a complete backup of the legacy system and put it in a safe place—preferably off-site.

2. Back up all your business-related data: record user and group names, as well as all roles defined on your system; save files owned by your users, including websites, onto a separate device. Keep all this data close at hand.

3. Perform a clean installation of SBS 2003, removing all traces of the old software system from the server.

4. Finally, using the backup of your business-related data that you created in step 2, run the backup and restore utility on SBS 2003 to import this data into the fresh SBS 2003 environment.

Warning Make sure you choose to restore only the user-related data and not any system data. You don't want to spoil all your hard work by overwriting the fresh operating system configuration with old data.

Migrations are by far the best approach to updating your solution, aside from completely starting again (but there are not many businesses that can completely start again). You might have systems that cannot be upgraded (systems simply not on the upgrade list), but you'll still need to maintain old company data that resides on your computer workstations, and so on.

For this reason, I'd feel entirely comfortable in saying that in nearly every instance you'll be performing a migration of some kind or another. Whether this is simply copying files from a floppy disk or CD to the new server, or something as elaborate as moving a 40-strong peer-to-peer network into an SBS 2003 server-centric environment, they are all migrations, and all need a strategy.

The key to making your strategy a success is to plan it well in advance:

- Allocate plenty of time to recover the system in the event of a failed migration—preferably do the work over a weekend or public holiday.

- Take backups of all your critical systems to allow you to regress in the event of a catastrophe. Record all licenses and software keys used for later reference and make sure any hardware authorization devices, such as dongles, are protected.

- Keep backups safe and off-site.

- Make sure backups of user and business data can be restored on SBS 2003. If you're unsure, check the backup system's help files.

- Keep a log of your progress, taking account of IP addresses, system names, users, data volumes, and so on.

- If you are unsure about the migration, seek guidance from a Microsoft Small Business Specialist or Microsoft Most Valuable Professional with experience in Small Business Server 2003 migrations.

Which Legacy Systems Can Be Upgraded?

For completeness, here is a list of the server platforms that can be directly upgraded to SBS 2003 by using the SBS 2003 installation and upgrade program:

- Microsoft Windows Small Business Server 2000

- Microsoft Windows 2000 Server

- Microsoft Windows Server 2003

Note If you really *must* do an upgrade, the best advice I can offer is that after you've completed the upgrade procedure, go to each of your workstations and take stock of everything you have installed. Next, log on to the server and audit your security configuration, disk layouts, NTFS permissions, and virtually every other aspect of configuration that you think might be relevant in the event of fixing a bug. On workstations, make sure you uninstall all old proxy software or ISA Server clients and take note of any other software your users might have installed. A complete system audit will benefit you greatly later.

For more information on migration strategies, see http://www.sbsmigration.com.

Backing Up Windows Clients

It's worth putting the time aside to back up not only your server systems, but your workstation client systems as well (the My Documents folder on most modern Windows clients will suffice), because they may well contain much of your users' business-related data. Even if these backups are never used, it would not do any harm to keep them safe for at least a year after your system is upgraded.

Note After you install SBS 2003, users' data will generally be stored on the server. The backup regime you undertake for the server will ensure that all business-related information is safe. Users' My Documents folders can be redirected to a file share on the server.

After you've completed the upgrade, you'll probably not have to think about backing up your workstations again, but just in case you do, there are tools on the latest Windows clients to help you do this.

It's a misconception that backups can be taken only on specialized devices. You can just as easily use a device such as a USB hard drive or a DVD-RW drive to store data.

Warning Be sure to size your selected backup media accurately. You might find that a DVD-RW is okay for backing up a single workstation's My Documents folder, but it probably won't be the best choice for your server.

Windows XP Professional comes with a simple-to-use backup facility, offering a wizard interface that makes the whole process as painless as possible.

To start the Backup Wizard (see Figure 4-1) from Windows XP, click Start ➤ All Programs ➤ Accessories ➤ System Tools ➤ Backup.

For more information on using the Windows XP backup software, have a look at www.microsoft.com/windowsxp/using/setup/getstarted/backup.mspx.

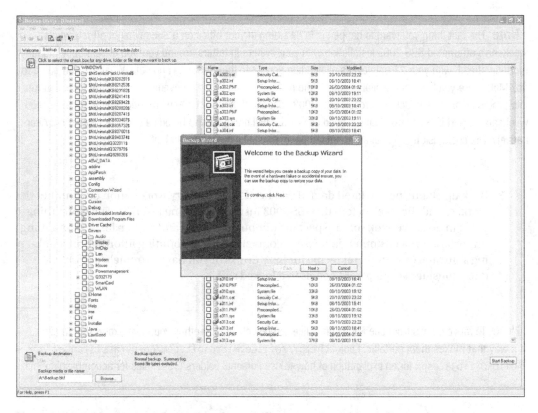

Figure 4-1. *Windows XP Backup Wizard can utilize any removable media.*

Preinstallation Tasks

At this stage, you will have already decided the best approach for your needs regarding upgrading, migrating, or performing a clean installation. But before you jump in and unsheathe your SBS 2003 installation media, there are a few things you should do to make sure it all goes as smoothly as possible:

1. Make sure you are prepared to write everything down. Have a notepad and pen available for scribbling down every little detail about the installation and configuration of your SBS 2003 server. These details will be essential for further configuration at a later date and for troubleshooting if you run into problems. During the installation of SBS 2003, and most commonly from the last screen of each configuration wizard, there are options to print your settings. I'd advise you do this on each occasion and keep the copy safe for future reference and troubleshooting.

2. Create a plan for the software installation (see Chapter 3). Decide exactly how you will approach the installation, how much time you will allow for it, and any cutoff points where you might consider calling in the experts if things go wrong.

■**Note** The last thing you want to happen is to be sitting in your office on a Sunday night after a whole weekend's attempted SBS 2003 installation with your system in tatters around you. You have a busy Monday morning ahead, with your 27 employees all needing access to their systems and data. What are you going to do? Make sure you have a reasonable cutoff time planned, say a Saturday evening, and just in case you run into problems, try to contact a Microsoft SBS 2003 consultant in advance to warn them that you might need weekend support if things go wrong. A good consultant will make sure to be on call over the weekend. Alternatively, you could ask the consultant to undertake the installation on your behalf.

3. Back up all business-related data. If you need to go to every workstation on your network, spend the week before the SBS 2003 installation doing just that. The worst thing you can do is overlook some aspect of your business data and end up losing something important like a customer database, a contacts sheet, accounting information, banking software, or your secret recipe for fizzy drinks. If you have extremely important data, consider keeping hard copies in a locked safe.

■**Note** To move emails from one Microsoft Office Outlook client to another, you must export the emails in a way that makes them portable. Look at `http://office.microsoft.com/en-us/assistance/` `HA011030811033.aspx` for an explanation of how to use Personal Folders (`.pst`) files for accomplishing this.

4. Perform a last check of your SBS 2003 server's hardware against the Hardware Compatibility List on Microsoft's website, the Windows Catalog (`http://www.microsoft.com/` `whdc/hcl/default.mspx`). If you discover any discrepancies, fix them now before you attempt an installation. This could save you many hours because the SBS 2003 installation may halt if the server hardware is not acceptable.

■**Note** To migrate mailboxes from your legacy Microsoft Exchange systems, you can use a free download utility called ExMerge, available from `http://www.microsoft.com/downloads/details.aspx?`➥ `FamilyID=429163EC-DCDF-47DC-96DA-1C12D67327D5&displaylang=en`. ExMerge (Exchange Mailbox Merge) will extract data from mailboxes on one Microsoft Exchange system and merge it into mailboxes on another Microsoft Exchange system, via whichever method you use for transporting the data (magnetic tape, DVD-RW, and so on). It copies mailbox data by using `.pst` files and merges it back into the target server by using an automated import.

Is Your Server Ready?

Before you get going installing SBS 2003, give your server hardware the final once-over, looking at the settings defined in the system Basic Input/Output System (BIOS). The manual for your server will explain how to access the server's BIOS configuration settings.

The BIOS is effectively the low-level hardware operating system that interfaces the physical hardware components to your Windows operating system. The configuration settings selected within the BIOS interface directly affect the server system as represented to the Windows system—for example, you can set the hard disk size, memory allocation, and system boot order from the BIOS interface.

After you've accessed the BIOS, make a note of the current configuration, paying close attention to the wording that describes the disk configuration, memory sizes, network information, and BIOS version number.

■**Note** Check with your hardware manufacturer that your server's BIOS is up-to-date. If not, obtain an update and apply it by using the manufacturer's guidelines. If you are unsure, or wary, about doing something of this nature, contact a professional who will guide you through the process. Before doing any hardware BIOS upgrade, always make sure that you have a complete, up to date, and verified full system backup.

Take note of the physical size of your hard disks. This will help you later when you need to decide how to set up your SBS 2003 partitions.

Finally, take a look at the boot order. Make sure the device first in the list is the CD/DVD drive. This means that you will be able to start the installation directly from the SBS 2003 source media. This is by far the easiest way to start an SBS 2003 installation.

Creating Disk Partitions

When you install the SBS 2003 operating system, one of the very first things you have to do is split your available physical disk space into chunks that will be addressed by the operating system; these chunks of addressable space are called *disk partitions*.

There are countless combinations of ways physical disk space can map to logical space, but the principle is always the same. The partition layout should best match the way you intend to use it from a business perspective.

When designing your disk partition layout, the following rules should be applied:

- Physical disks can be split into four partitions.

- Only one of these four partitions can be made active. This partition will become your C: drive.

Note The *active partition* is the partition that the operating system uses to boot from. It holds some special information, such as the boot sector, allowing the boot process to pass control from the hardware initialization to the Windows operating system kernel.

- The C: drive should be allocated at least 8 GB of disk space, but most installations run into double figures. Start with around 20 GB if you can. This will allow you to grow your system over time and leave enough room for service packs and hotfixes. If you intend to also install applications on the C: drive, consider allocating much more space. You also need to take into account the amount of RAM you have installed, because a crash dump writes the contents of memory to the hard disk (so that it can be analyzed by an expert). Augment your disk allocation to the system by the amount of memory you have and add another 50 percent to allow for system updates, service packs, and patches, and swap space for use by the operating system.

- You can create a separate partition (for example, D:) for your applications to be installed on, and again, subsequent partitions for your data.

- Don't make things too complicated. Configuring three partitions is probably as far as you'll need to go: one for the operating system, one for applications, and one for data.

- Consider the size of each partition. If you are configuring the system drive for SBS 2003 files only, 10 to 15 GB would be sufficient. If you want to add some hefty server applications into the SBS 2003 partition, you'll have to scale it accordingly. Use all spare space as your data partition.

Using RAID

The final consideration you'll need to address before beginning the installation is whether you intend to use the software resilience capabilities offered through the SBS 2003 operating system.

Note Hardware RAID is much better than software RAID. If you have the option, always choose to use hardware RAID.

Redundant Array of Inexpensive Disks, or RAID (also known as Redundant Array of Independent Disks), is a way of using a collection of physical disks as a single logical disk. The data is spread across the physical disks to increase performance and enhance resilience. There are seven possible RAID capabilities using hardware devices (with combinations of the capabilities leading to even greater possibilities, known as multiple RAID levels). SBS 2003, in software, provides only the following three:

- RAID 0

- RAID 1

- RAID 5

RAID 0

When you use a RAID 0 solution, portions of your data are simultaneously written across multiple physical disks, meaning you get better performance when you read and write to the logical disk. You would address this through Windows as, say, your D: drive, but this would be implemented in hardware as two separate disks. This system is also known as a *striped set*. RAID 0 offers no fault tolerance to your data, and in the event of a disk crash, your data would need to be recovered from your backups.

Note The best performance from RAID 0 is achieved if you spread the load across multiple hard disk controllers as well as across separate physical disks. This means the controller is no longer the bottleneck in I/O requests to and from the physical disks. The same thing applies in a RAID 5 configuration.

RAID 1

Unlike RAID 0, RAID 1 does increase your system's resilience. Also known as a *mirrored set*, RAID 1 makes exact copies of all data written to both physical disks. You would still address the disk as a single entity, copying your Microsoft Office Word document to the D: data drive, but the underlying disk controller would write the data twice, to two physical disk drives. From the perspective of the disk subsystem, this is slower (negligible), but the added resilience means your tape backup solution is the last resort for data recovery. In the event of a disk crash, rebuilding the mirror set consists of putting a new, similarly sized disk in the hardware chassis and letting SBS 2003 re-create the previous configuration. It copies all data from the one remaining disk to the new disk and then allows you to continue working.

RAID 5

Another name for RAID 5 is a *striped set with parity*. The difference between RAID 5 and RAID 0 is that the data is recoverable if one of the disks fails. You need at least three physical disks allocated to the set to implement RAID 5, and if more than a single drive fails, the system will fail completely. The upside is that if just one of the drives fails, the system will remain available and useable. All an administrator needs to do is replace the broken drive with a new one of similar size and characteristics, and the system will rebuild itself.

If you do intend to use a RAID solution in your SBS 2003 server implementation, remember the following:

- Hard disks should all be identical in size and specification.

- Accessible disk space is less than the physical space and depends on the RAID level chosen:

    - RAID 0 gives you full disk capacity, but unlike the others, it offers no redundancy.

    - RAID 1 halves your available disk space because all data written has a mirrored copy.

    - RAID 5 removes, depending on the number of hard disk drives you are implementing in the solution, a percentage of your overall disk capacity for the use of the parity stripe.

> **Note** If you want to perform a quick check to see how much of your disk space will be lost when you implement your resilience option, have a look at `http://www.ibeast.com/content/tools/RaidCalc/RaidCAlc.asp`.

Recommendation for SBS 2003

RAID 0 offers no redundancy at all (so possibly should not be called RAID), and although the speed increase for high-capacity file servers is worth having if your disk subsystem is being hammered by hundreds of users accessing thousands of files, SBS 2003 has its own capacity limitations that prevent your business from being this size anyway. If you did want a RAID 0 solution, you'd have to consider multiple disk controllers as well to make the system in any way useful, and there are many hardware solutions that do the job so much better than SBS 2003.

For the same reason, RAID 5 is much better if implemented as a hardware-level solution rather than relying on it being performed by the SBS 2003 operating system. If you can use hardware RAID, opt for RAID 5 because this is by far the best solution for the small business.

> **Note** If you have hardware RAID capabilities on your server, configure the RAID solution before you start the SBS 2003 installation. Better still, if you ask the hardware supplier to configure it for you before it arrives, this could save you hours of low-level disk formatting.

So this leaves you with only one viable choice, in my opinion. If you must use one of the software RAID features provided by SBS 2003, use the *mirrored set*, RAID 1.

Make sure to decide on your RAID layout before you start the SBS 2003 installation. This allows you to correctly specify the partitions you need to create during the initial phase of the procedure.

Anything Else Before You Start?

You will already have compiled a list in Chapter 3 of all the information you need for the installation of the SBS 2003 software.

You should have a detailed understanding of the following:

- IP addressing scheme

- Domain-naming convention

- DHCP configuration parameters

- Time zone

- ISP account details

- Email addresses

- Number of users

- User-naming convention

- Number of computers

- Computer-naming convention

- Wireless security configuration information, such as WPA configuration, and documentation of SSID numbers

You should ensure that you also have the CDs and DVDs needed to install every application you intend to install on your server, including any SCSI drivers or other specific hardware drivers for low-level system operation. This is not limited to the SBS 2003 installation disks for Standard and Premium editions. You might also require the following software:

- Antivirus software

- Antispyware software on workstations

- Server device driver media

- Peripheral software and device drivers for printers, scanners, and fax machines

- Line-of-business applications, such as accountancy packages, ready for distribution to appropriate workstations

Finally you're ready. The time has come to start the installation, so brew some coffee, find a comfortable chair, and crack open the SBS 2003 installation media pack.

Note Hotfixes and service packs are coming out all the time for Microsoft products. At the time of writing this book, the latest service pack for SBS 2003 was Service Pack 1, containing many patches and functionality enhancements for both Standard and Premium editions. Check the Microsoft product website before starting installation to see whether you can download or order the latest service pack: http://www.microsoft.com/sbs.

Detailed Installation Walk-Through

Installation of the SBS 2003 product suite is performed in three main phases:

1. Installing the base Windows Server 2003 operating system

2. Running the Windows Small Business Server Setup Wizard to install the Active Directory

3. Installing infrastructure services, such as Exchange 2003, Windows SharePoint Services, and Shared Fax services

After you complete this procedure, you'll have a fully installed (but not yet configured) SBS 2003 Standard Edition server.

If you've opted to purchase SBS 2003 Premium Edition, you'll need to perform subsequent installations of the Premium edition extras, such as ISA Server or SQL Server. These products are not installed automatically. Installation of each of the Premium edition extras is covered later, in the appropriate chapter for each component.

Phase 1—Installing the Windows Server 2003 Platform

If the media you acquired from your SBS 2003 reseller came on DVD, all the SBS 2003 components are on just one disk. If the media came on CD, you should have four CDs for the Standard edition or five CDs for the Premium edition. The Premium edition will more than likely have two separate license keys included with the package: one for the Standard edition components, and an extra key for the extra features of the Premium edition.

The following procedure should be used to install the basic Microsoft Windows Server 2003 operating system (the core of the SBS 2003 technology). So, on with the show:

1. After physically installing all your server peripherals, such as modems, tape drives, and fax cards, turn your system on and put your media in the CD or DVD drive.

2. After you see the option to boot from CD/DVD, press the appropriate key (generally any key will do, but make sure to read the instructions on the screen).

3. The system will begin the boot sequence from the Windows media, starting by installing a text-based installer in the system memory (see Figure 4-2). If you need to install a third-party RAID controller or SCSI system driver, remember to press F6 during the start-up sequence.

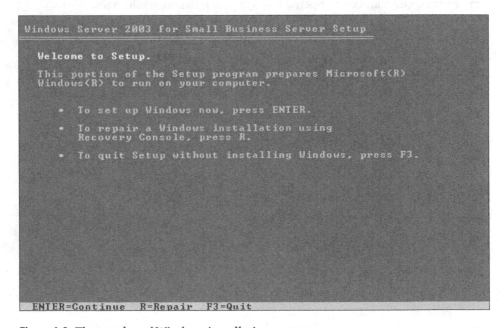

Figure 4-2. *The text-based Windows installation system*

4. You will see a screen announcing Welcome to Setup. Press Enter to continue setting up Windows. The Repair option is used for troubleshooting and is covered later in this book. At this stage, you can also press F3 to quit if you have decided not to proceed for any reason.

Note If all is well, the Windows 2003 setup will recognize your server's hardware and proceed. If it doesn't, follow the instructions on-screen to use the hardware drivers you received with the server. This part of the setup routine will include those drivers in the list of devices it loads into memory.

---

5. The next screen displays the Windows License Agreement. You must press F8 to agree to the terms of the license before you can continue with the SBS 2003 installation. Not agreeing (pressing Esc) will cancel the installation.

6. You are now presented with a view of your available disk partitions. This screen lists all the disks available to the operating system as presented by the system or RAID controller BIOS. Before you can install the Windows operating system, you must create your partitions. Using your preplanned disk layout as a model for the way you want to split up your disk, press C to create the first partition.

7. You will see the full amount of space available on your selected disk displayed on the screen (see Figure 4-3). To create a smaller partition than the full amount, simply type in the number of megabytes you wish allocated. This will be your C: drive. Press Enter to create the partition.

8. Repeat the process until you are happy that you've created the disk layout you decided upon earlier.

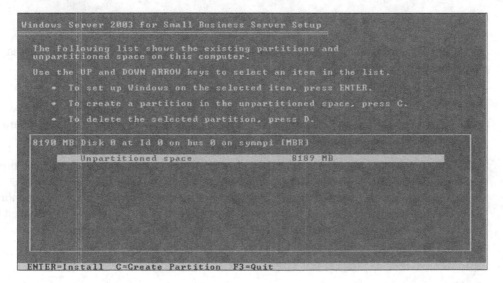

Figure 4-3. *Create disk partitions from unpartitioned space.*

9. To Install Windows, highlight the C: partition and press Enter.

10. You can now select the file system to use on your C: drive when the drive is formatted. The best file system to select is NTFS. It is the most secure file system available for use on SBS 2003 and should always be used in preference to FAT32. (Microsoft ISA Server, for example, requires NTFS to function, so it should be a given rather than an option.) Press Enter. Depending on the size of your disk, this may take some time. Refill your coffee cup at this stage. Avoid using NTFS Quick Formatting the first time you install the server. If you have started again, having previously formatted the hard disk, Quick Formatting could be used.

Note The only exception to performing an NTFS Quick Format is when you are using a hardware RAID system. In this case, low-level formatting is carried out by the controller, and a quick format using Microsoft Windows Server 2003 will suffice.

Warning Some hardware manufacturers preinstall disk utilities on a small partition (usually no more than a few hundred megabytes) on your disk, accessible by some hook into the BIOS system. Do not delete this because it may be useful later. This might appear as the first partition on your system disk, but it is normally not set to be bootable and will not appear to the operating system as the C: drive.

11. When the disk is finally formatted, the operating system installation files will automatically be copied from the installation media. You will then need to follow the instructions for installing Windows Server 2003 into the default directory (C:\Windows).

Warning Reports of wizards not working properly when the default directory has not been selected suggest that you should always select C:\Windows.

12. When you are happy, press Enter, and the Windows files will be copied to your hard drive. Windows automatically reboots.

13. When your system restarts, the setup program will have changed to a graphical interface (see Figure 4-4). The whole process so far should not have taken more than 60 minutes. In this time, the display may flicker or momentarily turn blank. This is normal and is related to the Plug and Play system detecting which devices are plugged in to your system and determining the best drivers to choose for your screen.

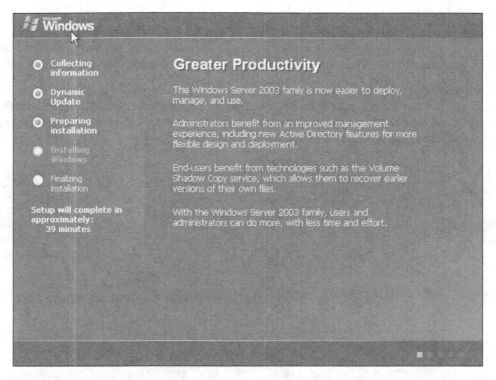

Figure 4-4. *The graphical installation interface*

14. Next you are offered the option to change the language your system will display—the default is English (United States). Be careful if you are in the UK, for example, as there are settings specifically for the UK that you should take care to select. To change the settings, click Customize. When you are happy you have selected the appropriate language and regional settings and applied them as the system's default, press Next to continue.

Note Make sure you change the standards and formats to suit your situation. It's important that you select the appropriate location, language, and so on from the menu.

15. Enter your name and the name of your business in the appropriate boxes. Click the Next button.

16. Now enter your product key exactly as it is shown on your media. There should be five sets of five characters. Press Next to continue.

17. In some installations (depending on how you obtained the software), you are required to select the licensing mode you have bought into. To remind you, SBS 2003 comes with five client access licenses included. If you need more than five, you should have bought them when you approached your SBS 2003 reseller. When ready, click Next.

18. Now it's time to bring out the planning material you compiled in Chapter 3. You have to enter the computer name you designated for your server as well as the password to be used by the administrator's account (see Figure 4-5). Rules for creating strong passwords can be found in Chapter 11. Click Next.

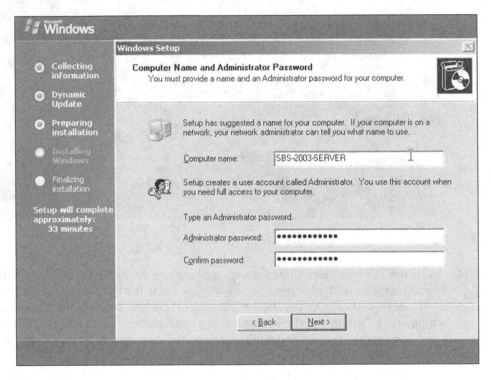

Figure 4-5. *Make sure to enter a strong administrator password.*

Note The password you choose at this point will be used later to perform some very advanced troubleshooting, such as logging in to the system in Active Directory restore mode. This account is different from the one you would normally use to manage the system.

19. Next you have the opportunity to adjust the time zone to suite your locality. Also make sure the date and local time are correctly set. Click Next.

Warning It's vitally important that you get the time zone settings right at this stage. Changing them later might result in extensive authentication problems that are best avoided at all costs.

---

20. You should already have installed your modem/fax modem at this stage. After the installation program detects your modem, it will ask you to select your dialing location. Select your country, type in your area code, and then type the digits (if any) you need to dial to get an outside line. Click Next.

Note Modem dialing settings can be modified at a later date, so don't worry if your dialing prefix changes or you get something wrong. You can use the Control Panel applet Phone and Modem Options to modify them later.

---

21. You are now returned to the graphical installation interface, where more files are copied to your hard drive and the rest of the underlying operating system is finally configured for use as the base of SBS 2003. This part of the installation could take up to an hour to complete, with no user input required.

At this stage, the first phase of the installation is complete.

If there are any issues detected by the SBS 2003 installation program, you will be presented with a dialog box explaining exactly what these issues are. You also might be offered advice on where your server configuration falls short of the minimum specification. You can still continue the installation, although the levels of service might be reduced. Take note of any issues highlighted and consider an upgrade to your hardware at a later date.

If all is well, the system will reboot. When it starts up, you are presented with a standard login dialog box. Press Alt+Ctrl+Del to start the login process. You can access your server by using the Administrator account and password entered in step 18.

Note Before moving on to phase 2 of the installation, take the time to check in Device Manager to see whether all the hardware and drivers you'd expect to be installed have actually been installed. If not, you can rectify this at this point before proceeding to set up the rest of the SBS 2003 product set.

Phase 2—Running the SBS Setup Wizard

As soon as you log in to your Windows 2003 server, the Windows Small Business Server Setup Wizard will launch (see Figure 4-6).

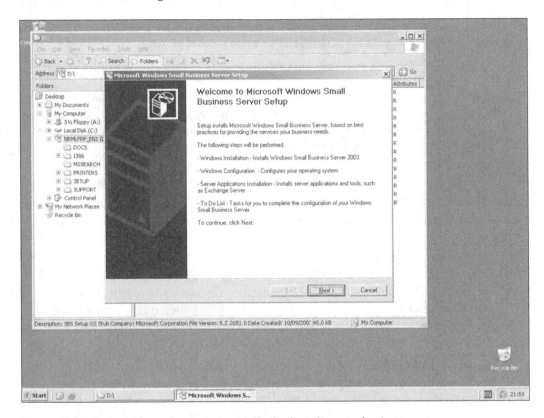

Figure 4-6. *The wizard launches automatically the first time you log in.*

If for any reason the Windows Small Business Server Setup Wizard does not start automatically, place Disk 1 of the your CD set (or DVD) into your optical drive and launch the wizard manually from the root of the disk. The file to launch is setup.exe, and you should click the option to Set Up Windows Small Business Server.

Note The Windows Small Business Server Setup Wizard is a program designed to streamline the installation of the separate components of the SBS 2003 suite. If you have not already done so, this would be a good time to create your application and data disks (D: and E:). You will be able to specify these hard disk locations to the Setup Wizard so you don't have to do this manually later.

The wizard starts by scanning your hardware to check once again that your system is prepared to accept all the components of the SBS 2003 software suite. You will be presented with the results in the form of a list of informational warnings, and in some cases, if you have overlooked some essential prerequisite of the SBS 2003 software suite, the installation will be blocked.

It might seem very late in the day to be stopping the installation from proceeding, but as long as you've done your homework and followed all the advice laid out in this book, you won't come across any problems.

The most common warning message you'll see when installing SBS 2003 is that there is only a single network interface card installed in the system. Many customers will already have a secure Internet interface on their network and won't be using SBS 2003 as their Internet gateway device. In this case a single network card might be sufficient.

Note If you are intending to use ISA Server as your Internet gateway, you will be required to have two network cards: one for the internal network and one for accessing the Internet. If you have only one network card at this time, you'll need to install one later. Having two NICS is the recommended approach, and this is upheld throughout the existing SBS 2003 user community.

If you have not added the minimum amount of memory or disk space to your server, the installation routine will halt. You will not be able to proceed until you have rectified this problem.

Note If you can purchase more memory and install it at this point, you could try running the Windows Small Business Server Setup Wizard again from the root of the installation media. This will stop you from having to go right back to the start of the Windows 2003 installation.

Use the following guidelines when running through the Windows Small Business Server Setup Wizard:

1. After the system scan completes and the wizard starts properly, you are presented with the Company Information dialog box. Type in your contact phone number, fax number, and business address, and select the region where your business is located. Make sure you get this right the first time because this information is inherited into the Active Directory. Click Next to continue.

2. The following screen is the Internal Domain Information screen (see Figure 4-7), where you enter the domain name assigned internally to your business. This might be the domain name as represented on the Internet (although this is not recommended for various reasons, including security), or might simply be the naming system used internally to define users and computer resources. The best domain name is something meaningful to your business, such as the business name itself, and it will be suffixed with .local to keep it separate from any external naming conventions.

Note If you are planning to connect any Macintosh OS 10.x clients into your network, the .local convention should be avoided.

3. The NetBIOS name (used for communicating with legacy clients, such as Windows NT 4.0 and Windows 9x) should be the same as the first part of your domain name (as long as it is fewer than 15 characters) or a truncated version of the DNS name if the domain name is too long. In the example shown in Figure 4-7, the domain name is ProcyonServices.local and the NetBIOS name is PROCYONSERVICES.

Note The .local extension to your DNS name keeps your system logically separate from any external names. The .local extension is added to the DNS name automatically by the Setup Wizard. *Do not remove it.* You can subsequently connect to the Internet and register a .com address for your business at a later date. This .com address can be used as your email domain name (this is covered in more detail in Chapter 7).

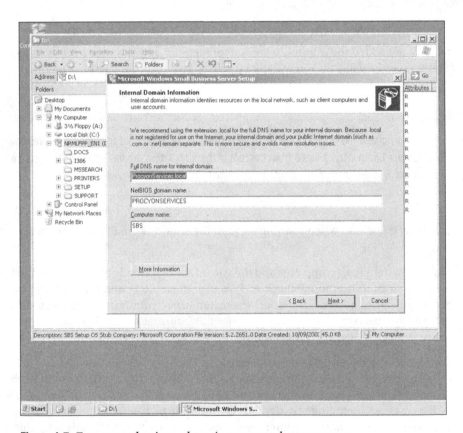

Figure 4-7. *Enter your business domain name and server name.*

Finally, you enter the computer name. If you've followed the guidelines in Chapter 3, you should have already decided on your computer-naming convention, so this should be no problem. In my case I've stuck to a simple, no-nonsense naming convention and opted for using the purpose of the server to allocate its name: SBS. Click Next to continue.

4. You are now presented with the Local Network Adapter Configuration dialog box (see Figure 4-8). If you are using more than one network card, make sure to highlight the network interface you are using for your local network connectivity. Then click Next to continue. At this stage, you should rename your NICs (as long as you have two) Internal and External. This will help you identify them easier in the future when you set up your Internet connection.

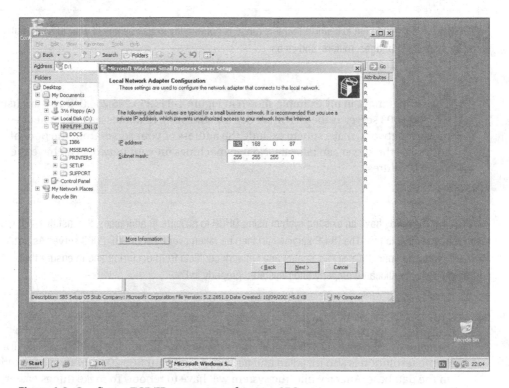

Figure 4-8. *Configure TCP/IP parameters for your SBS server.*

■**Warning** Selecting the wrong NIC as your internal network card will cause you serious problems and should be avoided at all cost. Double-check that you have selected the correct card before clicking Next. Start a command prompt by clicking the Start menu, selecting Run, and then typing **cmd.exe** in the data entry box. At the prompt, type **ipconfig/all** and press Enter. This information will help you identify the NICs installed in your system.

---

5. The next screen is used to configure your internal network interface card's TCP/IP parameters. You should have already decided on the best IP addressing regime for your business during the planning phase, so simply enter the IP address and subnet mask you are using for this server. You will probably (as I have) use a private IP address range, in the 192.168.x.x address space.

Warning It's a good idea to confirm that this range is not already in use by any of your existing equipment, such as Wi-Fi bridges, routers, and so on.

---

6. The subnet mask in my example shown in Figure 4-8 is 255.255.255.0. If you are using the SBS 2003 server as the DHCP service for allocating IP addresses to the clients on your network, make sure to exclude the address of your server from the pool of addresses the server can allocate. No two machines on your network can have the same IP address.

Note If you already have an existing system using DHCP to allocate IP addresses, the installer will recommend that you disable this. The DHCP service can then be taken over by your SBS 2003 server. As a rule, SBS 2003 must be your DHCP server to stop any network conflicts from occurring and to ensure that addresses are both allocated properly and registered properly in DNS.

---

7. The next stage of the installation is automatic. The installer configures the Active Directory based on the DNS domain name you chose in step 2. The DNS service for name resolution is also installed and activated, and your SBS 2003 server is registered in the database. After a while, the system will have to reboot. To make things easier, you can instruct the installation program to remember your password for the duration of the setup so you don't have to keep logging in each time the system power cycles.

Phase 3—Installing the Infrastructure Components

Transition into the third phase of the installation is seamless. You won't really notice the transition except that you are offered the Component Selection screen, which enables you to move from configuring Windows 2003 to configuring the extra infrastructure components supplied as part of SBS 2003.

You should complete the following steps to install the rest of the infrastructure components that make up the SBS 2003 Standard Edition suite:

1. Setup displays the Component Selection screen, as shown in Figure 4-9. This is used to select the components you need to install for your SBS 2003 infrastructure, allowing you to customize aspects of each component. As a default, all the components are selected, and in most cases this default should be accepted. To see what each of the components actually gives you, try highlighting a component such as Fax Services and then clicking the More Information button. If you don't want to install any of the components, click the down arrow in the Action column next to the word Install. When you are satisfied you have finished selecting the components to install, click Next to continue.

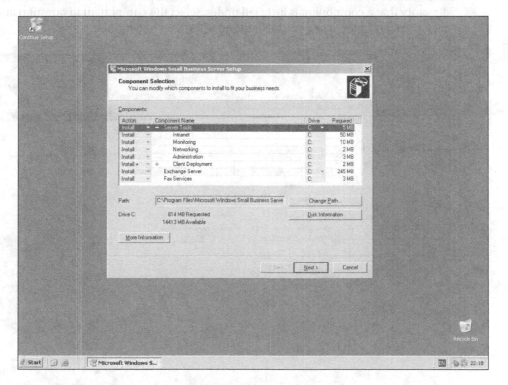

Figure 4-9. *The Component Selection interface*

■**Note** It is strongly recommended at this stage that you move your CD-ROM drive to the G: drive, install all Windows server components to drive C:, all application components (such as Microsoft Exchange 2003) to the D: drive, and leave E: for user data.

---

2. The next screen to be displayed is the Data Folders screen, as shown in Figure 4-10. You can modify the location of the folders containing data, such as Exchange 2003 transaction logs, your Exchange message store, MSDE database files, and users' shared folders. All these data folders would benefit from being installed on different partitions, all of which would benefit from being on separate disks. This should already have been taken into account when designing your partition structure, and if you decided then to have a separate application drive and user data drive, relocate each folder accordingly. This means, in the case of a three-disk system, that your system files (Windows 2003, Exchange 2003, and so on) are installed on the C: drive; your application data files (Exchange message store, SQL databases, and so on) are installed on the D: drive; and your users' data files will be stored on the E: drive. To change the directory that a component is installed under, select the component in question and click Change Folder. When you are finished, click Next to continue.

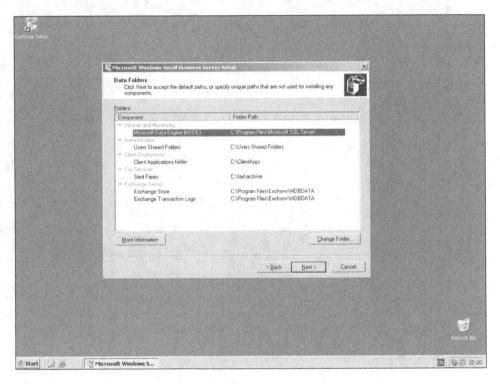

Figure 4-10. *Configuration of component data folders*

3. You are now presented with a summary of the components you have selected for installation. If you are happy with everything you see, click Next to start the final part of the installation process.

4. From now on you'll not be required to provide any input to the installation process. All you'll have to do is change the CD as the process continues (unless you are a DVD user, and in this case you can put your feet up and be happy with a job well done).

5. Finally, SBS 2003 will reboot one last time. This marks the completion of the installation process.

Well done—you have successfully installed SBS 2003 Standard Edition on your server hardware. If you are a Premium edition customer, each of the Premium edition components are installed separately, and the installation of each is covered later in Chapters 8, 9, and 10.

■**Note** Before proceeding, it would be a good idea to connect your modem to the Internet.

Product Activation

After you've bought a retail copy of the SBS 2003 software, you'll have to activate it over the Internet within 30 days of installation. This is Microsoft's latest piracy countermeasure, ensuring that every copy of any Microsoft product is individually accounted for.

To activate the product, you will be required to have Internet access from the server. If you already have this, follow the on-screen instructions to connect to the Microsoft website. If you have to wait until later when your Internet connection is activated from your SBS 2003 server, you can follow the instructions to activate the server from the icon in the system tray. If you have a problem activating your product, contact Microsoft on their local customer support help line, available through the Microsoft website, http://www.microsoft.com.

Postinstallation Configuration

After the final reboot of the installation routine, SBS 2003 starts the postinstallation configuration phase.

■**Note** Before you proceed, a useful tip for making working with the system easier is to modify your server's desktop to include the most commonly used desktop icons: My Computer, My Network Places, and Internet Explorer. To do this, right-click anywhere on the Desktop, select the Desktop tab from the Display Properties dialog box, click Customize Desktop, and select the check boxes next to the Desktop icons you wish to display. Click OK and then click Apply.

Configuration is carried out by using an easy-to-understand list, known as the To Do List (see Figure 4-11). It's important to complete all items on the To Do List because this will ensure that you end up with a well-configured and secure system.

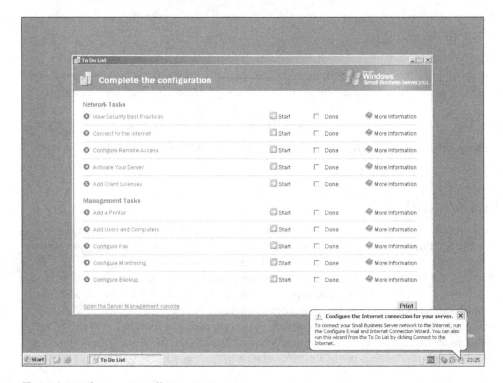

Figure 4-11. *The postinstallation To Do List*

The best (and Microsoft recommended) way of approaching the To Do List is to start at the top and work your way down through each of the items. Click on each of the items in turn to launch the appropriate configuration wizard for each task.

Note Even if you have installed a third-party backup solution, you should still run through the Configure Backup item at the end of the To Do List because it configures specific SBS 2003 attributes, such as Exchange item retention.

As you complete each wizard, you can mark it as complete by selecting the Done check box.

If for any reason the To Do List is not displayed, or you wish to come back and work on it some time in the future, you can do the following to access the interface:

1. Click the Start menu.

2. Select Server Management.

3. Highlight the To Do List in the left window, and the list is displayed on the right.

View Security Best Practices

Starting at the top of the list, View Security Best Practices opens a help file (see Figure 4-12) that illustrates the security features of SBS 2003 and explains how they would be best implemented.

As you work through the rest of the To Do List, it will become apparent that many of the strategic decisions referenced in the Security Best Practices help file are carried out automatically when you use a configuration wizard.

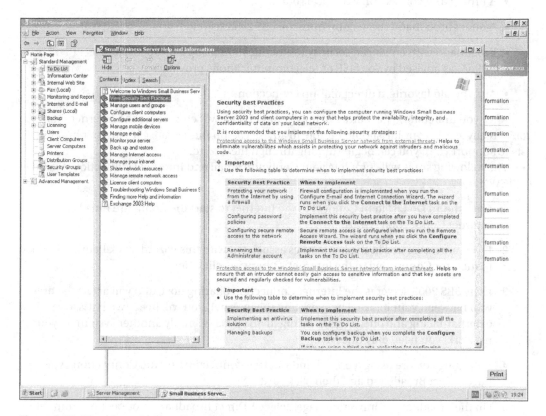

Figure 4-12. *View Security Best Practices*

It's a good idea to come back to the Security Best Practices after each configuration item has been completed, allowing you to see exactly how that aspect of your system is delivered from a security perspective.

Microsoft has undertaken a massive security initiative, pushing security awareness material to every customer: users, integrators, and consultants alike. This is just another example of their determined effort to make their products as robust as possible, opening their market to customers who require such stringent levels of security. For more information on the Secure Coding Initiative, see http://www.infoworld.com/article/05/11/11/460Psecadvise_1.html.

Connect to the Internet

Before you run the wizard that creates the connection between your business network and the Internet, grab all the information you have about your ISP: account details, IP addresses, telephone support numbers, and so on.

Before you start, check with your ISP to determine the type of Internet connection they are providing. The options are as follows:

- A broadband connection with local router

- A direct broadband connection from the SBS 2003 server

- Broadband with enhanced security (authentication using a protocol such as PPPoE or PPPoA, as advised by your ISP or telecommunications provider)

- And the old favorite, a direct dial-up connection

After you understand the nature of how your network will connect to the Internet (and if you're really stuck, your ISP should be able to advise you on this because it's in their best interests to support you), you can begin running through the wizard.

The following steps will complete your Configure Email and Internet Connection Wizard (CEICW):

1. Click the To Do List item Connect to the Internet to start the Configure Email and Internet Connection Wizard.

2. If you are interested in the help topics associated with this wizard, click Required Information for Connecting to the Internet. Otherwise, click Next.

3. If the SBS 2003 server is the Internet Connection Sharing host, and will act as the firewall between your internal network and the Internet, you will need two NICs, one external-facing and one internal-facing. If SBS 2003 is simply another system on your network, you need only one NIC.

4. Assuming you are using a broadband Internet connection, on the Connection Type page, select Broadband and then click Next.

5. On the Broadband Connection page, select A Direct Broadband Connection from the list and click Next.

6. Make sure ISP and local network connection details are correct on the Network Connections Page. Then click Next.

7. Now you need to type your gateway IP addresses and the addresses of your ISP's primary and secondary DNS servers (these can be obtained from your ISP). Click Next to continue.

8. If you are using the ISA Server firewall product that comes with SBS 2003 Premium Edition, or you are using some other third-party firewall product, such as the Symantec Enterprise Firewall (see http://www.symantec.com), you won't need to configure the SBS 2003 firewall service (although you should still run through the wizard to set up other aspects of your Internet connection, such as email).

If your SBS 2003 system is the Internet gateway and you have no other firewall product, continue with the following steps to set up the SBS 2003 firewall.

9. When the Firewall configuration page appears, click Enable Firewall and then click Next.

10. On the next page, select the services you need enabled through your firewall. If you are intending to use Remote Web Workplace, you'll need to enable terminal services. You'll also need to enable virtual private networking (VPN) to allow remote access over the Internet using the virtual private network service. Email is essential to send externally to the Internet. Click Next after you've selected the appropriate services for your business.

Note Selecting VPN before running the Routing and Remote Access Service (RRAS) setup can sometimes fail. To get around this problem, you can run the RRAS setup first and then proceed to run the VPN setup.

---

11. The next screen, Web Services Configuration (shown in Figure 4-13), is where you configure the specific web services that your SBS 2003 network can use.

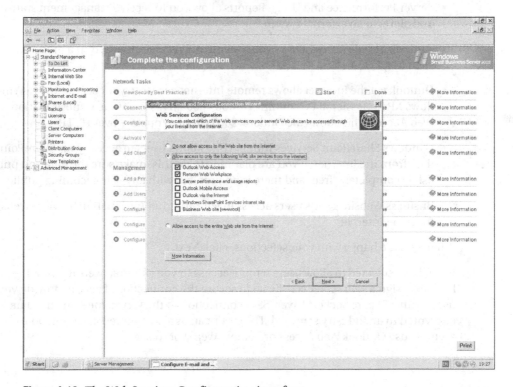

Figure 4-13. *The Web Services Configuration interface*

Make sure you select the web services appropriate to your requirements. Selecting too many web services will open up potential security holes in your firewall and is detrimental to your total security solution. Consider the following information before selecting a web service:

- Outlook Web Access lets you access your Exchange 2003 mailbox from a web client (such as Internet Explorer) from anywhere on the Internet.

- Remote Web Workplace allows users to use all the resources of your internal network from afar. You can also enable Outlook Web Access, SharePoint Services, and Server Performance and Usage Reports by selecting the appropriate check boxes.

Note If you intend to use Remote Web Workplace to gain network access to your systems from another location, you'll need to ensure that there is a free Windows XP workstation to act as the host on your business network.

- Server Performance and Usage Reports allow you to receive management statistics and alerts to an external system.

- Outlook Mobile Access allows you to send and receive emails from a mobile device such as a PDA.

- Outlook via the Internet allows remote Internet access to your server from a Windows XP Professional PC running Outlook 2003. This is not the same as Outlook Web Access. This allows the Outlook 2003 client to operate over HTTP.

- Windows SharePoint Services Intranet Site allows users to access your SharePoint data from the Internet. If you are planning to do this, make sure the data you publish is completely "free" and there is no problem with any of it becoming public.

- Business Website grants users access to your Internet Information Services website from the Internet.

When you are happy with your selections, click Next.

12. If you have selected to allow users remote access to your internal website, you'll have to assign a web server certificate to secure the connection. This will provide your users with a Secure Sockets Layer (SSL) connection to the server, meaning the data is encrypted to an industry standard. The certificate is also required if you intend to securely use Outlook Web Access or Remote Web Workplace.

Note It's best to use the certificate generated by SBS 2003, although you can opt to use one from a secure online certificate authority such as VeriSign for a little more insurance (around $300 a year). To learn more about certificates or to obtain one online, see http://www.verisign.com.

---

13. Select Enable Internet Email to configure Exchange to use Internet email. Click Next to continue.

14. When you see the E-mail Delivery Method screen (see Figure 4-14), you can choose to forward email directly to the Internet, or send all email to your ISP email server first. Select the Use DNS to route email check box to route all email directly to the recipient—this is the most efficient method of email transfer. The only drawback would be if your systems used dynamically allocated IP addresses and you were sending email to servers using Domain Name System Blackhole Lists (DNSBLs). Some of these DNSBL servers (such as AOL) don't permit email to be received from dynamic IP addresses.

■**Note** A DNSBL is an extension of the Domain Name System that allows the server to check a list of known spam originators and block email coming from any host on that list. The system is intelligent enough to block based on various criteria, one of which is the originating IP address being dynamic. This DNSBL policing can be troublesome for legitimate business users who rely on dynamic addresses. However, the plague of spam currently proliferating on the Internet has driven many IPSs to implement this kind of filter. For more information on DNSBLs and a list of current DNSBL databases, see http://www.declude.com/Articles.asp?ID=97.

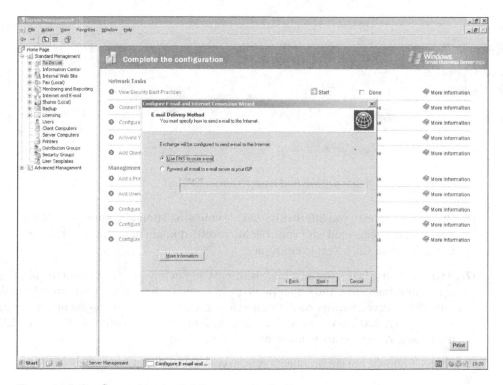

Figure 4-14. *Configure the email delivery method.*

15. On the next screen, select Use the Microsoft Connector for POP3 Mailboxes if you have email accounts held at your ISP. Otherwise, if you instructed your ISP to have email directly routed to your server's Internet-facing IP address (the same as is specified by the MX record), select the Use Exchange check box and select Email is delivered directly to my server (see Figure 4-15). The final option of using a signal to pull email should be used only if this was originally specified by your ISP when you set up the account.

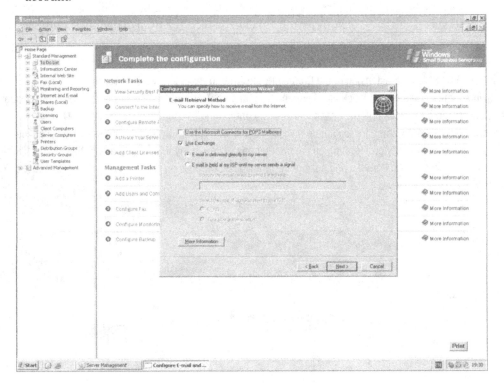

Figure 4-15. *Configure the method used to retrieve email.*

16. On the next screen, you inform SBS 2003 of your email domain name—the official one you have registered with your ISP. Microsoft's domain name, for example, is microsoft.com. Click Next to continue.

17. If you are using POP3, the next page is where you put in your ISP account details, the user name, password, and server name details used to draw down your email from the ISP's POP3 server. Further configuration is necessary later when you set up and configure Exchange 2003; here you will be mapping internal user accounts to ISP-held POP3 mailboxes. When you are ready to proceed, click Next.

18. Set the frequency of email collection from your ISP and click Next.

19. The next screen allows you to adjust the list of attachments you will allow to be transmitted into your network by using email (anything in the list is blocked and removed). This is a useful security feature and should be properly understood if you are to make the best decision on how to configure it. Attachments are files "attached" to emails and can be any type of file you would find anywhere else on your system. Although useful in transmitting company deliverables, such as Microsoft Word documents, invoices, and photographs, you might decide that executable files with extensions such as .exe must be blocked. Who would be sending executable code to your users over email? If the answer is no one, you can block all .exe attachments, keeping .exe-bound viruses from ever being transmitted into your server. This facility gives you the first line of defense against email-borne viruses, and your Microsoft Outlook 2003 client offers a similar barrier at the desktop. If you want to add a new extension not already on the list, click Add, input the extension and description (as shown in Figure 4-16), and then click OK. After you've finished selecting the attachments you want to block, click Next. To change anything on this list in the future, you will have to revisit this wizard.

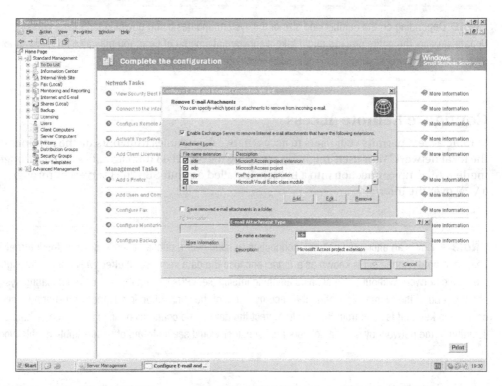

Figure 4-16. *Configure a file extension to be blocked.*

20. The last page of the wizard allows you to view your configuration choices in the order you selected them. Try clicking on the word *here* to see a complete listing of your system's configuration. You should print this and keep it as a record of your installation choices. When you are happy with your choices, click Finish.

Note As soon as the wizard exits, you are asked whether you'd like to configure password policies. Password policies allow you to enforce security measures on your users related to the strength of their passwords. I'd advise doing this later, because there are many other configuration tasks to do first before you start locking down the user environment.

As long as all goes well and you now have a fully functional and secure Internet connection, you should scan the Microsoft Update site for critical software patches. An approach to keeping your system up-to-date with all security- and functionality-related patches is outlined in Chapter 11, but for now, your server automatically attaches to the Windows Update service and downloads all critical updates. Allow this procedure to complete before moving on to the next section.

Note Depending on the number and size of the system updates being downloaded by the Windows Update service, the entire process might take a substantial amount of time. You may also be required to perform various server reboots to complete the installation of the patches.

Configure Remote Access

Remote access permits your users to access network resources from outside the confines of the local network. Your users might be accessing the SBS 2003 infrastructure either through a modem (dial-up connection into a modem installed on your SBS 2003 server) or through a VPN over the Internet.

Note A *VPN* is an encrypted network connection running over a public network, such as the Internet. This encrypted connection is known as a *tunnel* because the data sent over it effectively passes through the public network without being seen as anything intelligible. VPNs rely on the two communicating systems at either end of the tunnel negotiating the security terms of the connection in advance and sharing a secret encryption key that is used from then on to protect the data in the connection. Anyone (such as a hacker) listening to the network by using a network packet sniffer would see a stream of unintelligible gobbledygook.

The important thing to remember when you set up remote access is that you should grant access only to users who need it. Sounds obvious, but a carte blanche approach to turning on this capability would punch holes in your network defenses, potentially giving unauthorized users an easy route into your environment.

Warning The services and facilities you'll be enabling to grant remote access to your workforce are the same services that would be targeted by hackers. Keep user passwords safe, enforce strong password policies whereby the passwords are changed often, and ensure that your firewall is always switched on and working correctly.

To set up SBS 2003 remote access, click Configure Remote Access from the To Do List. This launches the Remote Access Wizard. Follow these steps to configure remote access:

1. Click Next on the Welcome screen.

2. On the next screen, click Enable remote access. You are presented with two options: VPN access and Dial-in access (see Figure 4-17). If users dial in to your SBS 2003 server by using a modem, select the Dial-in Access check box. If users access your systems via the Internet, select the VPN access check box. Click the Next button. Dial-in access will be grayed out if no modem was detected during setup.

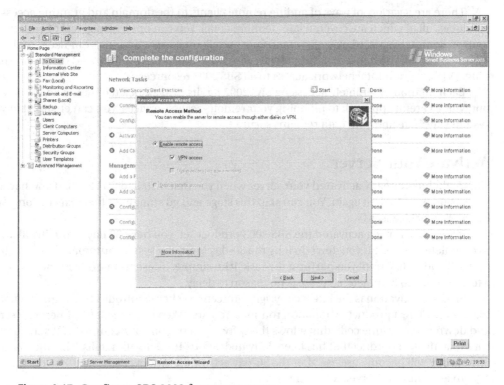

Figure 4-17. *Configure SBS 2003 for remote access.*

3. On the Client Addressing Page, select DHCP to supply TCP/IP details to client computers. This means that your remote-access users will automatically have their settings configured for the duration of the connection. When the client closes the connection, the IP address will be released into the DHCP pool for further allocation at a later date. This is by far the easiest way to configure remote-access clients. Click Next.

4. On the next screen, you'll either see the Modem Selection page (if using dial-up access) or you'll be asked to select the Internet domain name of the server for VPN connections. This is the name registered with your ISP that clients will access when they come in using a VPN and it is the same name as the one on your remote-access certificate. Click Next.

5. The next screen is used only when configuring a dial-up connection. You are required to enter the phone numbers where remote clients will be calling from. When you have typed these in, click Next.

6. Finally you are presented with a summary of your remote-access settings. If you are happy, click Finish.

There are a variety of ways of adding remote clients to the domain and granting access to resources, all of which are covered later in more detail. You can open up aspects of your system via Remote Web Workplace for email and SharePoint access, limiting your users' ability to do much else on the network. Alternatively, you can use a domain-authorized computer running a VPN to grant total network access to all SBS 2003 resources.

Each method of remotely accessing SBS 2003 has its own associated merits and problems, but with a careful approach to planning your remote-access services, you can ensure that your system stays safe and your data remains secure.

Activate Your Server

You might have already activated your server when you first installed SBS 2003. If you have, there is no need to do it again. You can skip this stage and go straight to the next section, "Add Client Access Licenses."

If you have not yet activated the SBS 2003 product set, you have 30 days from installation to complete this task. If you don't do it by the 30-day limit, the system automatically switches off DNS and DHCP until you perform the task. It's a simple, Internet-based task and takes only a few minutes to complete, so there is no reason to delay.

Product activation is the latest copyright protection scheme introduced by Microsoft into many of the latest product installation routines. You are asked to connect to a Microsoft server and download a unique code that allows the software to run on your computer. If someone tries to activate a product that has been activated before, the activation fails. This means the pirate copy will become useless after the 30-day activation window passes.

To activate your server, follow these steps:

1. Click the Start to Activate Your Server option.

2. You'll see the Let's Activate Windows screen. As long as your Internet connection is working, select the option that says Let's Activate Windows over the Internet. If you don't have an Internet connection yet, you can telephone the Microsoft customer support desk to activate the product manually. Click Next when you're ready to proceed.

Note Phone numbers can be found on the Microsoft website: http://www.microsoft.com/licensing/ resources/vol/numbers.mspx.

3. You can register your company details at the same time as activating the product.

4. If you want to check whether your server is activated already, again navigate to the To Do List and click the Start arrow next to the Activate Your Server option. If the server is already activated, you'll see the screen shown in Figure 4-18.

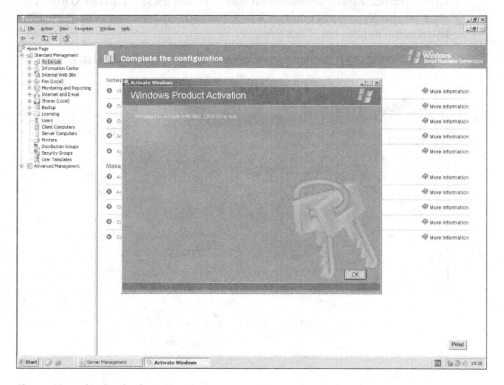

Figure 4-18. *Check whether your SBS 2003 server has already been activated.*

Add Client Licenses

When you purchased your copy of SBS 2003 from your software reseller, you had to buy the appropriate number of client access licenses that allow your users to access your server. Out of the box, SBS 2003 allows you to add five Windows clients into your domain, but any excess must be manually added through this interface. You will have been given a license key (much like the product key you typed in during the first part of the Windows 2003 installation), which will add the licenses you bought into the interface.

To add new licenses, use these steps:

1. On the To Do List, click Start next to the Add Client Licenses option.

2. Click Next on the Welcome page of the Add License Wizard.

3. On the License Agreement page, select I Agree. Click Next.

4. On the Contact Method page, select Internet or Telephone, depending on which you want to use. Click Next.

5. On the next screen (see Figure 4-19), you'll see a row of blank boxes where you can type in the license key associated with the license pack you purchased from your software vendor. Type the key and click Add. The code and number of licenses will be listed in the bottom box. Click Next.

6. Follow the steps to complete the wizard and return to the To Do List.

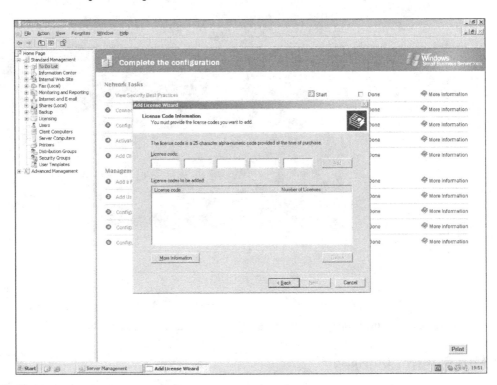

Figure 4-19. *Type in the license key for your client access package.*

Add a Printer

There are two kinds of printing architectures you need to understand before you can decide how to set up your business's printing capability:

- Printing to a locally connected printer

- Printing to a network-attached printer

A local printer is attached to the machine you are trying to print from. In this case, you might have a printer attached via the USB or parallel ports to your Windows XP Professional workstation, and all print jobs would be sent to this computer. This is the way a home user might set up a printer when there is only a single computer and no network.

One of the benefits that a network can bring to your business (and to a home user, for that matter) is the ability to share resources. A printer, like a scanner or any other peripheral device, should be considered a network resource and so made available to all users of the network. To do this, the printer is shared over the network. One of the networked computers is designated the print server, in charge of all print jobs being sent to that device.

The Add a Printer item on the To Do List on your SBS 2003 server allows you to set up either of the two kinds of printer in the SBS 2003 system (local or networked).

Note Any Windows system can act as a print server. If you have three printers already attached to Windows XP Professional workstations, they can all be shared on the network and used by anyone you grant permissions to. Sharing printers is much like sharing any other resource in the network, be it file store, access to websites, or email. All shared resources are controlled by using permissions to restrict access to authorized users. More information on sharing printers is covered in Chapter 5.

To add a printer to your SBS 2003 server, do the following:

1. On the To Do List, click Start next to Add a Printer.

2. You'll see the Welcome page of the Add Printer Wizard. Click Next.

3. On the next page (see Figure 4-20), you can choose to add a local or a network-connected printer. If the printer is already installed on another machine and all you are doing is making it available to your SBS 2003 server, choose the second radio button. If you are installing a new printer on this machine to be locally connected (to the USB or parallel port), select the top radio button and select the check box to instruct SBS 2003 to automatically detect and install your Plug and Play printer.

4. Windows now searches for your local printer. After it finds the device, it tries to install any drivers it might already have installed. If it does not find the drivers, you get a message saying the wizard was unable to detect any Plug and Play printers. You will need to have the driver disks on hand if you want to proceed beyond this stage. Insert your printer driver CD in your optical drive and click Next.

5. Select the port that the printer is connected to. Your printer documentation will tell you which port to use.

Note Most modern printers will be connected to the network, so there is no need for USB or parallel cables and no direct connection to a computer. Printers connected directly to workstations might come with a USB cable for connecting them; then the printer can be shared on that system. Older models come with parallel or serial connections and have 25-pin or 9-pin connectors.

Figure 4-20. *Select either a locally connected or network printer.*

6. Next you'll be asked to specify the printer manufacturer and model number of the device. If you have a disk with your printer, put it in the drive and click Have Disk. Follow the instructions to locate the printer driver on the disk and install the appropriate files. When you're happy, highlight your printer manufacturer and model and then click Next.

7. Type the name your printer will be called on your system. This should be a recognizable name possibly offering some indication of what the printer does—for example, Color Laser Printer (Main Office). If this printer will be the one your system will always use by default, select Yes. Click Next.

8. If you want to share this printer with other network users, click the Share Name radio button and type the name it will be known as to other users. Again, choose something meaningful. Click Next.

9. Type in the exact physical location of this printer and then comment on all the capabilities this printer has. This information is useful if you have many devices with many features. Click Next.

10. If you want to print a test page to see whether the printer has installed correctly, select Yes and press Next.

11. The last page, Completing the Add Printer Wizard, summarizes your installation choices and allows you to go back and change any aspect of the printer installation before completing the wizard. If you are happy with all your choices, click Finish.

The subject of printing is huge. Whole books have been dedicated to installing, managing, and troubleshooting the plethora of devices you can connect in a networked environment, and there is much too much to try to cover in this book. In Chapter 5, you'll get to see the most common tasks associated with managing and troubleshooting a typical small business printing environment, but for more detailed information on each device type, or any special features your software might have, check your device documentation and speak with the manufacturer.

Add Users

Adding users to your SBS 2003 domain allows those users to be granted access to your system's resources. By completing the wizard, you will create a complete user environment for each user you run through the wizard for. This gives users the following attributes:

- A user account. This is the Active Directory object that defines the user, allowing that user to log on and gain a security token that grants access to Windows 2003–controlled resources.

- A mailbox and email address. This is the Exchange 2003 mailbox that the user sends and receives email from.

- A home folder. This is the place where the user's files will be stored. It will be on the E: drive on the SBS 2003 server (that is, if you've configured a user data drive called E:) and should be backed up as part of the SBS 2003 backup strategy.

- Security group memberships. The user account is given the appropriate access to system resources by placing it in security groups that control the user account's capability, for example the difference between Administrators and standard Users.

- Distribution group memberships. These are the distribution lists for sending broadcast-style emails to groups rather than individuals (used for company notifications, for example).

- Access to SharePoint Services and Remote Web Workplace. The wizard also grants access to SharePoint Services and Remote Web Workplace as part of the initial user setup.

- Disk quotas, which are turned on by default. If you've decided to use a disk quota regime within your network, the user will be allocated the appropriate disk quotas (more covered in Chapter 5). If you don't want to use disk quotas, the administrator must explicitly switch them off.

- Client computers set up for users.

- Configuration changes to the Windows XP client to make sure the environment is optimized for accessing SBS 2003.

To add a user to the system, do the following:

1. On the To Do List, click Start next to Add a User. This launches the Add User Wizard.

2. On the Welcome page, click Next.

3. On the next page, add the appropriate user details. You'll remember in the planning phase you decided on your user-naming convention, so use this convention here. You'll see the logon name and email address created automatically. Click Next.

4. Provide the password the user will use when first logging in to the domain. Click Next.

5. The next page allows you to select the template (or create a new one) to be used to configure this user account (see Figure 4-21). User templates are covered in more detail in Chapter 5. Click Next.

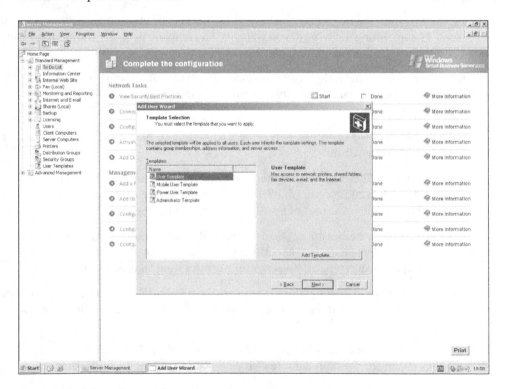

Figure 4-21. *Select the template appropriate to the user you're creating.*

6. On the next page, you get to assign your new user account to the appropriate security groups. The default groups required for each user type are automatically allocated based on the User Template. If your user is a mobile user, he/she is automatically granted permissions such as logging on to the system from a remote location. The default allocations should not be changed if you want the user to do the functions he or she was designated in the template. You can add extra privileges to user accounts by adding the user to further groups. Click Next when finished.

7. Next you have to add the user to appropriate distribution groups. Click Next.

8. SharePoint access is granted on the next page. Specify the user's SharePoint roles to have those roles applied to your intranet site. SharePoint roles are covered later, in Chapter 6. Click Next.

9. Supply the user's address information and click Next.

10. If you are using disk quotas, specify here the amount of space allocated to this user. Click Next.

Warning Because quotas are switched on by default, you will need to ensure that users have the appropriate quota assigned to them. Otherwise, they might run out of usable space and not be able to save their work on the server.

---

11. If you decide not to set up a computer account by using the Set Up Client Computer page, the wizard summarizes your user's details and completes. Click Finish to create all the attributes of this account. If you decide to set up the client computer, use the computer-naming convention you planned previously and click Next.

12. Select the applications you intend to install on the user's PC. More details on assigning applications to workstations are covered in Chapter 5. Click Next.

13. If the computer is to be used as a mobile system (for example, a laptop), select the check box that allows you to install the Connection Manager (an easy way to install a VPN connection on a client computer). If you have a PDA to connect to the system, select the check box to install ActiveSync. Click Next.

14. The last page is the summary screen, where you can look at the settings you've selected and possibly go back and change any before committing to them. If you are happy with everything you've selected, click Finish.

Configure a Fax

If you are setting up a fax service for your business users, you'll need to have the hardware installed before you run the Fax Configuration Wizard.

The beauty of integrating the SBS 2003 fax services into your network solution is that you will be able to move away from fax hard copies and do it all on the screen. A fax modem integrates with the SBS 2003 server to route faxes to email recipients and log them into SharePoint

Services websites. It allows you to send faxes from a workstation via the fax service running on the server. This system can also be used to archive faxes, and SharePoint Services can be used to notify users (subscribers) when a new fax arrives in the fax container. Faxes can be automatically routed to a printer, where they will be printed on reception.

To run the Fax Configuration Wizard, do the following:

1. On the To Do List, click Start next to Configure Fax. Click Next on the Welcome page of the Fax Configuration Wizard.

2. The next screen should already have most of the information filled in (entered earlier during phase 2 of your SBS 2003 installation). If any fields are blank, fill them in and click Next.

3. On the next screen, any fax modems installed in your server are listed. To get more information on the Outbound Fax Device selection page, click More Information (see Figure 4-22). When you are ready, make sure the device you are selecting is suitable, highlight it as your preferred fax device, and then click Next.

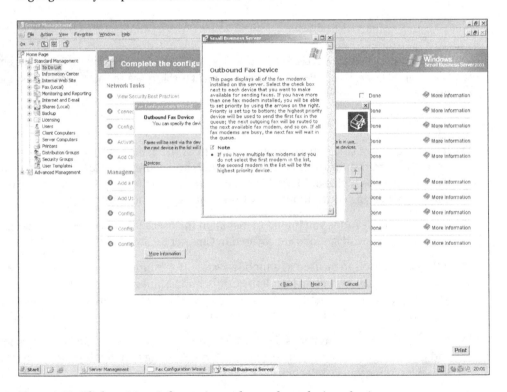

Figure 4-22. *Click on More Information to learn about device selection.*

4. Select the device to use as your inbound fax device—this could be a second modem if you have a lot of fax traffic or service a lot of dial-in users. Click Next.

5. Now you'll need to determine where your faxes should be sent. As you work through the options you want to configure, selecting the appropriate check boxes, you'll be presented with a Configure dialog box that allows you to set the destination for each incoming fax. You can send faxes to email addresses (or distribution lists), shared folders, SharePoint libraries, or even directly to a designated printer. When you're finished, click Next.

6. Finally, you'll see the last page of the wizard, where the choices you've made are summarized and you have the option to go back and change any that might be incorrect. When you are content you've finished, click Finish.

Further configuration of the fax service is possible, and this is covered later in Chapter 5. There you will learn how to configure standard company cover sheets, obtain transmission receipts, and reconfigure fax routing to best suit your needs.

Configure Monitoring

The reporting facilities not only provide the ability to monitor and regulate staff mail and Internet usage, but also allow efficient management of data costs. Valuable information contained in the reports about our usage helps us maximize our savings and get the best possible prices for Internet and data connections that are suited to our specific needs.

—Sam Trenerry, accountant, Copyworld

It's important to keep a close eye on the running of your server and look for degradations in any of the services your system offers your users. To set up the best monitoring configuration of SBS 2003, use the Monitoring Configuration Wizard.

To run the Monitoring Configuration Wizard, do the following:

1. Click Start next to Configure Monitoring on the To Do List. This starts the Monitoring Configuration Wizard.

2. Click Next on the Welcome page.

3. It's advised that you collect both Performance and Usage statistics from your server because these two sources of data serve two very different purposes. A performance report can be used to see how your system is running, how the network is coping with the load, and how SBS 2003 is possibly suffering from a shortage of disk space or memory. A usage report concentrates on how the system is being utilized by the users, and offers you a good idea of why certain user functions might not be considered as good as they could be. For diagnostic information and how these reports can help you in troubleshooting, see Chapter 12. Click Next.

Warning A lot of reports are generated and sent to the mailbox chosen in this step. If the administrator's mailbox is not used very often (if at all), consider carefully where these reports are sent. Some SBS 2003 system managers outsource their system maintenance so you might consider in this case sending the reports to your IT service provider.

---

4. When you see the dialog box to select where to send the reports to, choose to send the reports to the administrator's email address (see Figure 4-23). Click Next.

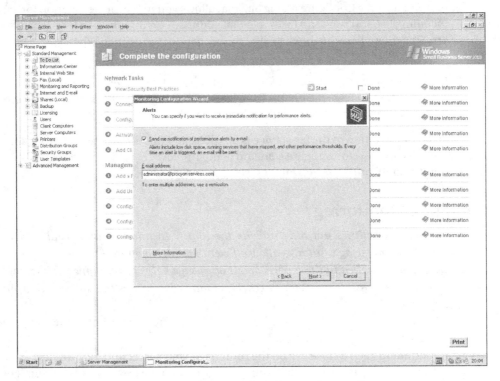

Figure 4-23. *Reports should be sent to your administrator by email.*

5. Complete the wizard and click Finish.

We have many sites to maintain and many users. Previously we could only react after the fact, if a fault occurred. We needed to make phone calls, disturb people, and do live maintenance. The new SBS monitoring has helped us be alerted to issues, faults, and users or workstations misbehaving.

We religiously read the reports every morning and can stop issues from causing system downtime for users. We can react before the faults are widely known.

Because we can monitor mailbox size and email usage, Internet usage (through ISA), and many other features, we have been able to save resources and money.

—Michael Jenkin, IT manager, Copyworld

Configure Backup

Backing up the contents of your server is by far the most important aspect of systems management you'll have to get right. If you intend to sustain a good level of service to your users and customers, you will need to be able to recover quickly and efficiently in the event of a disaster.

When I say *disaster*, I mean anything that causes your server to stop working: a hard disk crash, a fire, a flood, a virus attack, or someone switching the power off. Whatever the cause, you'll need a recovery plan.

Note Even if you intend to use a third-party tool for backing up your system, you should always run the Backup Configuration Wizard as part of an SBS 2003 setup.

To run the Backup Configuration Wizard, do the following:

1. Click Start next to Configure Backup on the To Do List. This starts the Backup Configuration Wizard.

2. On the Welcome page, click Next.

3. The next page lets you configure your backup location. A tape drive is by far the best option for your backups, but if you don't have a tape drive, you can use some other kind of removable media such as a USB or FireWire hard drive. If you decide to back up to a hard drive, you can select the location the backup should be written to (see Figure 4-24). If you don't have a tape drive installed in your server, the option will be grayed out. To select the location of a disk-based backup, click Browse. Click Next when you're ready to continue.

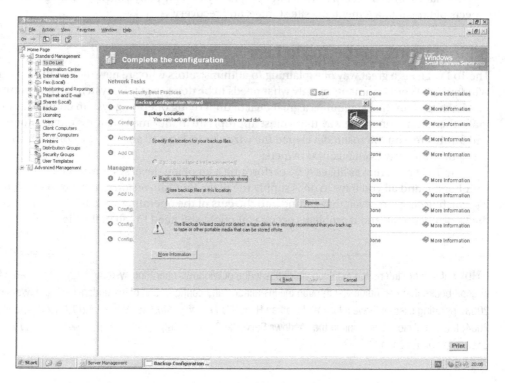

Figure 4-24. *Select the location your backup will be sent to.*

4. On the Backup Data Summary Page, you'll see that the default backup is configured to store everything on your system. If you want to block a folder from being backed up, you can click Exclude Folders and select the appropriate block. To exclude a particular folder from the backup, highlight the folder and click Add Folder. Click OK when you're finished. You can click Calculate Folder Sizes to see exactly how much data you've excluded. When you are ready to proceed, click Next.

5. Now you have to define your backup schedule. You will learn more about backup schedules later, but for now accept the default. Click Next.

6. If you are backing up to a removable disk drive, the next screen is entitled Storage Allocation for Deleted Files and Email. On this screen, select the defaults and click Next. If you are using a tape backup device, you'll see the Onsite Tape Changer page appear. Nominate the appropriate person who will be changing the backup tapes and select the time they should be notified of their impending task. If you select the check box to Send a Monthly Tape Drive Cleaning Reminder (opt to clean roughly every 35 hours of tape time), your nominated backup administrator will receive an email with instructions to perform the monthly maintenance on the selected drive. Click Next.

7. The last page of the Backup Configuration Wizard summarizes your settings and gives you a final chance to go back and change anything that you're not happy with. When content, click Finish.

In Chapter 5, you'll learn how to put into place your company's backup strategy, covering aspects of tape management, off-site storage, and recovery.

A Final Word on the To Do List

The To Do List is a great way of explaining to administrators who are new to the SBS 2003 and Windows 2003 environments exactly what needs to be done to get the system up and running.

Each task on the list requires a great deal of underlying operating system configuration to make them function in the way that's most appropriate to the small business environment, and for this reason Microsoft developed the wizard interfaces to abstract the complicated configuration away from business owners.

The To Do List makes life easy by performing a lot of low-level system configuration on your behalf, and all you have to do is supply the plain-English version of the configuration. It's worth noting, however, that getting into the guts of the operating system is still a job for the IT professional, and if problems occur, you might still need to call in the big guns.

Note If you are interested in taking your knowledge of Windows operating systems further, there are plenty of good books that can guide you through the installation and configuration of the underlying Windows Server 2003 operating system. Have a look at Jonathan Hassell's *Learning Windows Server 2003* (O'Reilly Media, 2004) for a really low-level look at the Windows Server 2003 operating system: http://www.oreilly.com/catalog/lwinsvr2003/.

If you want to come back to the To Do List at any time in the future, you can click on the Start menu and select Server Management. In the left-hand menu, click To Do List to display the list in the Server Management window.

The remaining sections in this chapter deal with aspects of initial installation that are not explicitly covered by the operations of the To Do List. Although your system is probably up and running quite happily now, you still need to look in more detail at server security and server management.

■**Warning** Do not install any end-user applications on the server. Retain the server for server-side functions and infrastructure applications such as Microsoft Exchange Server 2003. If you need to install a system-hungry line-of-business application, put it on its own server hardware.

Server Security

The items already covered in the To Do List have given your infrastructure a solid security baseline that you can now manage and build upon. The most common tasks associated with securing your infrastructure have already been completed, and this has happened most importantly before any users begin using the system.

The problem you face, however, is that as your system's usage ramps up, with applications being installed on client workstations, users connecting to the Internet, and email beginning to flow between you and your customers, your security baseline will start to change.

Later in this book, Chapter 11 introduces a wide range of subjects that should be considered in your environment, topics such as the following:

- Patch management

- Physical security

- Social engineering

- SBS 2003 configuration

- Hacking, viruses, and Trojans

- Privacy

All aspects of IT security must be considered when you design your ongoing service management methodology. You need to make sure you impose strict security countermeasures, such as regularly sweeping your systems for viruses and spyware, ensuring that server backup tapes are safely and securely stored, and making sure that your users are aware of security issues.

Security should become a way of life rather than a hindrance, and when it finally becomes second nature, you'll feel confident that your business is safe. Every time you schedule a change to your system's configuration, ask yourself the question, *how does this affect my system's security?* If it does, consider and document the consequences.

Server Management

As you've already seen, you can access the To Do List again at any time from the Server Management console, simply by clicking Start and selecting Server Management. This brings up an easy-to-use interface offering access to all the most common systems management features you'll need to use as you administer SBS 2003.

A total of 17 administrative capabilities are accessible from the Server Management console, each with its own associated wizard, walk-through, and links to good-quality help files (see Figure 4-25).

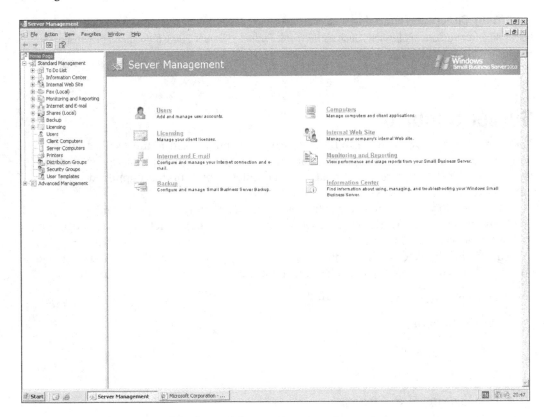

Figure 4-25. *Top-level view of the Server Management console*

In this section, I'll briefly outline the capabilities that you can access through the Server Management console. Chapter 5 goes into the detail of each administrative and management task you'll need to undertake to keep your system running smoothly.

The Server Management console is split into two categories:

- Standard Management

- Advanced Management

The Standard Management tree, contained within the Server Management console, contains links to the most commonly used administration facilities you'll need to access to run your server. These utilities will be used 90 percent of the time you'll spend administering your system. As you highlight each facility, you'll see help and guidance on the topic before you proceed to perform any actions.

The Advanced Management tree simply offers a direct route into the native toolsets in SBS 2003 for managing your system. These tools are the same underlying tools exploited by the wizard interfaces accessed through Standard Management, although you'll need to be much more fluent with the low-level Windows operating system to understand exactly what you're doing. With experience, these facilities will become quicker for you to use, but for now, stick with the Standard Management interface.

Here are the server management utilities available through the Standard Management interface:

- *To Do List*: We've already covered this in great detail, but just to recap, the To Do List is a comprehensive walk-through of management tasks required after your first installation of your SBS 2003 server.

- *Information Center*: This provides a list of websites and useful guidance on all aspects of running SBS 2003. There are many links to useful Microsoft sites as well as a link to start a Microsoft support request.

- *Internal Website*: Windows SharePoint Services is managed through this interface. This is covered in more detail in Chapter 6.

- *Fax (Local)*: From this menu item, you can reconfigure your fax services, including reconfiguring fax devices and routing. You can also access further management interfaces for creating cover sheets and standard receipts.

- *Monitoring and Reporting*: Configure your systems diagnostics reporting capability so that you get feedback on how SBS 2003 is performing and where problems might be arising.

- *Internet and Email*: Through this interface, you can manage all aspects of your Exchange email solution as well as configuring other aspects of Internet connectivity such as remote access and ISP connectivity.

- *Shares (Local)*: Shares are server folders used by multiple users to store data. From this interface, you can manage the permissions to SBS 2003 shared folders as well as viewing which users are currently connected to which shares.

- *Backup*: This feature launches the SBS 2003 backup utility, offering a simple interface to all features of the server backup and restore facilities.

- *Licensing*: You can access your currently installed licenses and introduce new ones as well as get an idea of how your current server load compares to the licenses you have purchased.

- *Users*: This interface shows you the users you've created in your Active Directory and offers you the ability to create new users, delete users, and change group memberships.

- *Client Computers*: From here you can manage all client computers (such as Microsoft Windows XP Professional computers) that are members of your SBS 2003 domain. You can set up new computers by using the Setup Computer Wizard and install applications to already functioning domain members.

- *Server Computers*: Any additional servers you've added to your network are displayed here. You might have off-loaded a SQL function to a separate member server (and bought the appropriate license upgrade for the product); you can manage that server from this interface.

- *Printers*: Your printer configuration, printer sharing, and queue management can be done easily from this interface.

- *Distribution Groups*: These are email-enabled groups for distribution of electronic mail. Email can be sent to a distribution group, and all members of the group receive the email in their own inbox. From this interface you can create, delete, and manage the membership of distribution groups.

- *Security Groups*: Security groups are used to apply permissions to system resources. This interface allows you to create, delete, or manage the membership of SBS 2003 security groups.

- *User Templates*: By using this interface, you can define new user templates for assigning specific rights and permissions as a new user is created. User templates can be created, deleted, or modified from here.

Case Study—Planthire

Installation of the SBS 2003 server was indeed an onerous task for someone of Philip Stanley's limited IT experience, so he decided to put a ready-built OEM version of the software on his new server hardware. This gave him the head start that he needed, meaning the underlying Windows 2003 server platform was already installed and configured and all he had to do was jump in at the personalization stage of the SBS 2003 installation.

At the point when Philip was asked to provide input into the installation of the software, the GUI was running and the intuitive Small Business Server Wizard offered him plain-English advice on the most appropriate answers to the questions posed during setup.

Philip decided, to be on the safe side, to stage the installation, bringing the server platform up early in the week, but not moving the users over to use it until later. When he was satisfied that the server was stable, he started by adding his own workstation to the domain and deploying his business software to that system.

Next he connected to the ISP and made sure he could access the Internet and email systems from his own computer before beginning the user migration. The existing computers in the office were backed up, and the relevant data that he needed to keep moved onto an SBS 2003 share, where eventually it would be input into WSS.

All in all, the entire process, playing it as safe as possible throughout the transition, took a little under three weeks. This was by far the least risky way of approaching the introduction of the new system and gave Philip the chance to set up the WSS sites as needed and soak test the entire system before letting his users loose.

Case Study—Servideal

As with Planthire, Henry decided to buy the server equipment with a preinstalled OEM version of SBS 2003. He requested from his supplier that he have the media just in case he needed to do a subsequent rebuild in the future, and he also got the Premium edition software components as extras with the deal.

The installation and setup of the SBS 2003 Standard edition components were easy for Henry because he's had plenty of experience with IT systems in the past, but the difficulty came with the installation of the Premium edition components.

ISA Server (as with most elements of IT security to "normal" people) is a black art, so for this aspect of his business he decided "better to be safe than sorry" and called in a consultant. The IT security consultant configured his ISA Server to screen all external traffic, protecting his business from malicious attack. The key to the consultant's expertise (and the justification for his inflated rate) came from his ability to weigh business functionality against risk and configure the system appropriately.

Henry and Maria are happy that their system (although not yet populated with business material) is safe, secure, flexible, and functionally rich, and should give them a great foundation for building the Servideal reputation.

Case Study—Country Estates

The installation of the new system into Country Estates was as straightforward as for everyone else. The bigger, yet easily managed, problem came from the migration of the business's current data from many users' individual workstations into the new environment.

Alan wanted all company-related data to be controlled centrally, accessible by the right people and protected from eyes that are not authorized to see it. This meant a rigorous migration strategy for moving data from Windows NT 4.0 workstations to the SBS 2003 server needed to be devised. To do this, Alan instructed his IT people to create a shared folder on the server for every user to copy the entire contents of documents and settings from their NT 4.0 computers. By copying their Internet favorites, documents, Outlook .pst mail storage files, and any other specific information from their workstations that they might need when they moved, it was a simple process then to swap the old computer out and put the new desktop on the desk. The data collection and migration was completed over a three-day period. Users' data was copied off the systems on a Friday night by using a batch script and then on Saturday and Sunday the offices were visited and the new PCs installed on the users' desks.

Summary

This chapter has stepped you through, in minute detail, every aspect of installing and configuring your SBS 2003 server. You've gone from a bare-metal computer system with little to no software installed on the hard disk to a fully operational network solution providing user connectivity. Subsequent configuration of your server, provided by the wizard interfaces accessed through the To Do List, has enabled many business capabilities (such as shared file store, email, remote access, Internet connectivity, and many facets of system management) to be set up and scheduled to operate on a regular cycle.

The next section of the book moves away from the initial installation and configuration of SBS 2003 and concentrates more on the day-to-day running of your service.

You've done a good job so far, and hopefully it's not been too painful, but you should remember that this is only the beginning.

■ ■ ■

CHAPTER 5

Running Small Business Server

Now that you've successfully installed SBS 2003 and run through the tasks covered in the To Do List, it's time to shift focus from initial setup to ongoing management functions. System administrators have to be aware of these functions to keep SBS 2003 running smoothly and securely.

Organizing Your Workforce

By gaining a proper understanding of how your workers interact with the network, you'll be better placed to manage your system resources and apply the appropriate access control to each object residing on your infrastructure.

To make life as easy as possible for SBS 2003 administrators, SBS 2003 leverages the existing Microsoft Windows Server 2003 operating system features. By using the underlying operating system tools and a combination of policies and permissions, you can control your users, computers, file shares, databases, and applications.

The Active Directory

The concept of applying policies to control objects on your network (users and computers) has been around for a long time—ever since the early days of NT 4.0. The only difference with the latest Microsoft Windows Server 2000 and 2003 technology over previous operating systems is the sheer scale of what it can achieve. To better understand what's possible with system policies, it's important to understand exactly what this new capability does to your systems.

On every computer system under the direct control of your Windows Server 2003 domain, there is a configuration database known as *the Registry*. This Registry came about as a direct result of the difficulty that network administrators had in controlling the disparate set of configuration files they needed to tamper with in the old days of Windows 3.11. In this legacy environment, every application and operating system nuance had a specific .ini file that contained all information about its function in your environment. As systems became more complex, the number of .ini files grew exponentially, and the size of specific .ini files (such as system.ini and win.ini) were outgrowing the maximum size limit of 64 KB. Keeping tabs on all that was going on with every computer became extremely difficult, and the administration of such a distributed system was virtually impossible. To make things easier, Microsoft introduced a new way of centralizing the control of application and operating system configuration when they moved to the Windows NT technology, collapsing these .ini files down into a central store known as the Registry. This meant that administrators had only one place to look when they needed to check or modify some aspect of system functionality.

At the same time as the Registry appearing, the concept of the domain emerged. A *domain* is a logical container holding all devices and users within a predetermined security boundary.

Note Windows NT version 3.51 was the first system to pioneer the domain model, but this system was without the new innovative Registry database.

Within a domain are users, workstations, and servers, all of which are controlled by the overarching policies defined at the domain level by the company. To influence change in the domain environment, Microsoft introduced a centralized version of the Registry used to override the local settings, meaning systems in the domain could have change affected by an administrator who had the appropriate domain-level permissions, without the administrator having to make a trip to each individual computer.

It's these two concepts—the domain and the Registry—that still underpin the control aspects of today's Windows Server 2003 network environment. Although the centralized database used to contain all aspects of the infrastructure has evolved into the much more scalable Active Directory, the concept of change being affected from a central location to a local system registry is still exactly the same. All policy changes deployed by the Active Directory to the computers within the domain environment will modify local system settings in each computer's Registry, and it's these settings that dictate exactly how the system will operate.

The *Active Directory (AD)* is an integral part of the Windows Server 2003 domain and is Microsoft's name for the database used to hold every user and computer object on your SBS 2003 infrastructure. The concept of the Active Directory has been around for a few years, since the days of Windows 2000, and is based on an industry standard directory technology known as Lightweight Directory Access Protocol (LDAP).

Because access to every object in the Active Directory is strictly controlled by using permissions, it's easy to see how administration capabilities can be delegated to users through simple group control. You'll learn more about group membership and user rights delegation later in this chapter.

Organizational Units and Group Policies

Every object stored in the Active Directory must be placed inside a container known as an *organizational unit (OU)*, in much the same way that all files on your system are held inside folders. OUs are the most fundamental components of the Active Directory for assigning policy, so all policy-level decisions must be made in the context of the OU they apply to. For example, you might create an OU specifically to control the company policy applied to the use of all laptop computers. Your laptop computer objects would be placed in this OU and as a result, the computers would receive the appropriate policy control from the Windows Server 2003 environment to permit or deny certain facilities.

Every policy you create to control the objects in an OU are known, in Windows terms, as *group policies*. Each specific group policy defining the rules for particular sets of users or computers is referred to as a *Group Policy Object (GPO)*.

■**Note** *Group policy* is a term describing a method of applying a set of policies or rules to containers of objects. For example, you would use a user group policy to set attributes particular to your user accounts, such as the password length and complexity rules, logon schedules, and password periodicity. There is more detail on group policy later in this chapter.

Some of the more typical configuration functions administrators can enforce through the use of group policy are as follows:

- *Standardization*: It's possible to create templates that define the functionality of particular types of resources (users or computers). Through automatic application of these templates as standard policies, you can easily manage the resultant policy and any individual OU.

- *Application and functionality enablement*: Through the use of well-defined GPOs, it's possible to assign applications and functionality to groups of resources. In some cases, GPOs can even be used to deliver software to workstations and users.

- *User profile management*: Using GPOs, administrators can redirect users' folders to server file-store locations, meaning there is no need to write cumbersome logon scripts or visit workstations to set up file shares. Folders can therefore be redirected on the fly by the administrator, and the user will not be affected.

Control over the user environment, on a per-domain basis (there is only one domain in an SBS 2003 environment), is achieved by using GPOs applied at the domain level. These allow administrators to adopt a company-level approach to users' passwords (setting the length and periodicity of each user's password centrally), as well as implementing the standards applied to other operating system services such as software restriction policies.

■**Note** A *software restriction policy* is a special security countermeasure, available only for Windows XP clients, that allows administrators to define exactly which applications can run in their environment. Enforcement of such a policy will prevent users from introducing their own software onto their workstations, hence preventing problems such as inadvertent virus infection or malicious hacking. Software restriction policies can be difficult and cumbersome to manage and so should be used with caution if at all.

SBS 2003 Organizational Unit Structure

When you first install SBS 2003, a default OU structure consisting of six containers is created (see Figure 5-1).

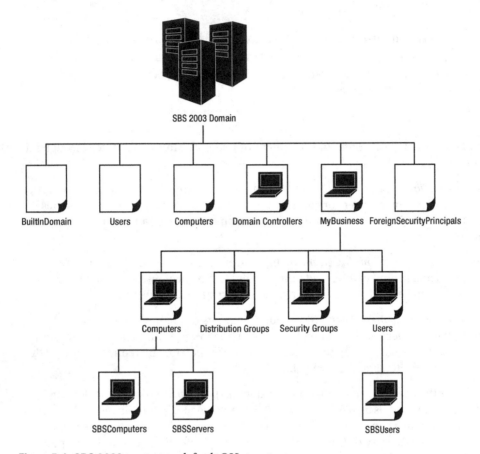

Figure 5-1. *SBS 2003 postsetup default OU structure*

During the first phase of the Windows Server 2003 installation, the top tier of the OU structure is created (as it would be with any Windows Server 2003 installation). It's the next phase, during the SBS 2003 setup, that the *MyBusiness* hierarchy is created and populated with relevant information about your SBS 2003 infrastructure. Much of the information in the default containers is repeated under the MyBusiness hierarchy because this logical view of your system's resources facilitates administration and ongoing application management of the resources held within your SBS 2003 Active Directory.

To view the OU structure shown in Figure 5-1, do the following:

1. Click the Start menu and select Server Management.

2. Under the Advanced Management section, expand the Active Directory Users and Computers subtree and highlight the container showing your system's DNS name.

3. The window on the right-hand side shows the six default containers from Figure 5-1: BuiltinDomain, Computers, DomainControllers, ForeignSecurityPrincipals, MyBusiness, and Users.

4. You can double-click the MyBusiness OU to drill into the hierarchy as shown in Figure 5-1.

Each of the OUs under the MyBusiness container holds information related to its purpose—for example, look in the SBSUsers OU to see all the users configured to access the SBS 2003 server. By default, this OU contains user templates—used as a basis for creating new users through the Add User Wizard (which is available through the Server Management Users interface).

Warning You should not, under any circumstances, move the MyBusiness OU to any other location in the Active Directory tree because this will seriously affect the ability of SBS 2003 to function properly. Much of the automation and wizard functionality relies on the OU structure being as it is when SBS 2003 is installed. You can add to the OU structure safely; just don't modify the default one.

Most of the time, you won't need to worry about the underlying Active Directory, but it's worth understanding what each of the high-level wizards actually does in case you run into problems and have to troubleshoot issues that cannot be resolved through the normal methods.

Setting Rights and Permissions

Two important concepts you need to understand before heading into the depths of user management are those of rights and permissions.

In Windows terms, when I say *rights*, I mean the attributes associated with a user account that allow that user to perform certain functions when interacting with the system. For example, the Administrator account has many more rights over the domain than a standard user, allowing the administrator to create new users, add new hardware, take ownership of files, and log on to the SBS 2003 server locally. A standard user account will have none of these capabilities.

User rights are assigned to user accounts through the use of a security policy applied either to the individual account, or in most cases the security group that contains a set of similarly authorized users (more on security groups in a moment).

The term *permissions* applies to the level of access a user has over the file system, normally delegated within the bounds of the NTFS. Again, similar to user rights, access permissions are attributed by using either direct authorization of the user to access a file or folder, or more commonly a security group will be used to assign the permissions and the user's membership of that security group inherently grants access to the information.

When a user logs in to the domain, a security token is generated for her containing all the rights and permissions she has been allocated through her group membership.

Using Security Groups

A *security group* is an Active Directory object that contains users or other security groups/ distribution groups. There are three kinds of security groups you can configure in the Active Directory—domain local groups, global groups, and universal groups—and each one serves a slightly different purpose in the Windows networking environment.

Security groups are used as a way of collecting together user accounts that require equal-access permissions to resources under the direct control of the Windows domain. If a user account were to be allocated explicit permissions to access individual resources, such as files and folders, every user on the system would need to be added individually to every controlled aspect of the file system. This is entirely possible to achieve using Windows NTFS permissions, but the administrative overhead of such as model would be wholly unworkable. To address this, security groups are nested in such a way as to minimize the administration overhead and maintain an overall control of the underlying file store's security.

To see a list of the security groups configured by default on your SBS 2003 server, it's best to use the Advanced Management interface rather than the Standard Management interface because the MMC snap-in for Active Directory Users and Groups offers more information and an immediate view of the security group type and its description.

Note The *Microsoft Management Console (MMC)* is a convenient management interface that uses items known as snap-ins. *Snap-ins* perform a variety of system management functions and come as discrete management interfaces that have been written to a standard. This allows them to be snapped in to the MMC. Using this facility, you can add as many snap-ins as you need to do your most commonly encountered tasks, creating your own tailored management toolbox.

To see the security groups installed in SBS 2003:

1. Click Start ➤ Server Management.

2. In the left-hand menu, expand Advanced Management.

3. Expand Active Directory Users and Computers.

4. Expand the subtree pertaining to your system's DNS name.

5. Highlight the Users container.

If you order the list in the right-hand window by clicking Type, you'll see all the users and security groups listed in order of type.

To understand security groups in the context of SBS 2003, you must remember that SBS 2003 always uses the facilities of Windows Server 2003 as the underlying operating system—so in this case, all user management, group management, permissions, and rights are handled by Windows Server 2003. This means that the Windows Server 2003 domain architecture (which applies to enterprise systems that have multiple domains and multiple forests) is used here to supply a single SBS 2003 domain in a single Active Directory forest. Okay, so you've got that: *one domain, one forest.*

Now I'll explain exactly what each security group is used for, and you'll see from each description that the concepts shown here apply more to large systems with many domains and forests rather than the 1/1 architecture of SBS 2003:

- *Domain local groups*: Domain local groups are used to directly apply permissions to objects within a domain. Following the best practice for assigning permissions, a domain local group would contain global groups either from the local domain or connected domains and it's this security group that would be directly applied to a network object such as a printer, folder, file, or Active Directory object. Domain local groups cannot be added to security groups in other domains or other security groups within the local domain. They can be applied only directly to objects.

- *Global groups*: Global groups are domain-wide security groups that normally contain users or other global groups from the local domain. This means a user account might be added to a global group called Domain Users, and then that global group might in turn be added to a domain local group called Printer Users. Permissions are inherited from the resultant set of permissions derived from all security group memberships.

- *Universal groups*: Universal groups are only really of any use in a multidomain environment, but in the case of SBS 2003 they are of little consequence. Many of the default security groups created during the SBS 2003 installation are universal groups, but these should be treated exactly as you would a domain global group.

When you are assigning permissions to objects on your network, you would use security groups—for example, when you want only a select few of your users to access the color laser printer, because most users don't need color hard copies and the color cartridges are too expensive to grant everyone full access.

As a more general example, take a look at Figure 5-2. In this case, User A is a member of the built-in global security group Domain Users, which is in turn a member of the domain local group Printer Access. The access control list for the printer has an entry that grants the Print permission to the Printer Access domain local group. From now on, any user who is a member of Domain Users is, by inference, allowed to use the printer.

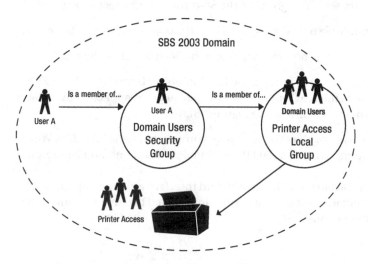

Figure 5-2. *Nested security groups ease the management burden.*

Granting NTFS Permissions

The file store that resides on your SBS 2003 server is managed by the services provided by Windows Server 2003. In turn, this is controlled directly by the underlying file system services, providing capabilities such as access control, encryption, and compression. This file system is known as *NTFS*—from the New Technology File System Windows NT 4.0 days—and from now on when you see *NTFS*, assume I am referring to the file system or the permissions and attributes associated with it.

Permission to access a file is granted by the NTFS service after checking the user's credentials against an *access control list (ACL)* for that object. To put this in context: Say a user tries to access an invoice in your invoices folder. The NTFS service checks the user's access token (the culmination of all permissions granted to that user through security group membership) against the invoice's ACL, and if it finds an *access control entry (ACE)* that permits that user to access the file, permission is granted and the user proceeds.

The control doesn't stop here, however. The real control comes not from deciding whether the user can have access to an object, but exactly what *type* of access that user can have. You might want some of your users to have Read access to certain files on the network, while others have Full Control (which allows the user to update or even delete the file).

There are two levels of permissions you'll need to understand, both of which are covered here in detail. In most cases, however, you shouldn't need to apply the latter. These permission types are Standard and Advanced.

Standard NTFS Permissions

Granting permission to files and folders on your network can be tedious, and there's no doubt in my mind that the Standard model for applying permissions is by far the easiest and quickest. In a small business environment, there is little call to modify this standard set of permissions, but just for completeness, and to aid with troubleshooting, the Advanced model is also covered in detail.

To see the ACL for a particular file or folder, do the following:

1. Open a Windows Explorer session (right-click the Start menu and select Explore).

2. Navigate to the appropriate file or folder, right-click on the object, and select Properties.

3. The file/folder properties dialog box appears. Select the Security tab at the top.

4. The ACE for each user and security group added to that object is shown in the top box. If you highlight any one of those ACEs, you'll see the permissions applied to that object in the bottom section of the dialog box (see Figure 5-3).

You can do this for any file system object on a domain computer system: SBS 2003, Windows XP Professional workstations, Windows 2000 Professional workstations, and Windows NT 4.0 workstations.

Each of the permissions available through this standard interface are general permissions, comprising the fundamental access control permissions added together to form a more useful whole. The standard permissions available on your system are listed in Table 5-1.

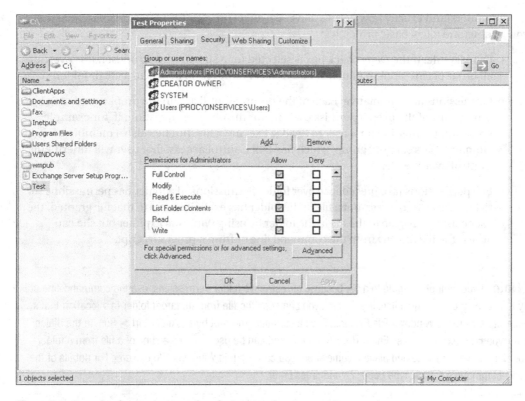

Figure 5-3. *Standard permissions are obvious and easy to assign.*

Table 5-1. *Standard Permissions Available Through Using NTFS*

Standard Permission	Description
Full Control	A user with Full Control over a file or folder can read, write, execute, and delete the file system objects in question as well as take ownership of objects for which no explicit permission has been added. Full Control also offers the user the ability to change the permissions set as desired.
Modify	Modify is almost as powerful as Full Control, but stops the user from being able to take ownership of files and folders. The explicit abilities granted to someone with Modify permissions are to read, write, execute, and delete file system objects.
Read & Execute	This permission grants the user the ability to read files or the contents of a folder as well as execute files inside the folder that have executable content.
List Folder Contents	This permission allows users to list the contents of a folder without those files being able to be executed. However, any new files created in the folder will automatically inherit the Read & Execute permission and be executable.
Read	This allows users to only read a file, not to execute files or traverse folders.
Write	Assigning this permission to a user allows that user to write to the contents of a file or folder and also create new files and folders.

To understand exactly how permissions take effect on your file system, it's essential that you understand a few basic principles:

- Denials rule. If the Deny check box is selected for a specific group or user, this overrides all other permissions. A denial of Full Control removes all access to a file or folder.

- Permissions are cumulative. Each of the permissions listed in the properties dialog box is only part of the overall permission story for the object in question. If, for example, you grant permission for a user to Read & Execute a file, but he's also a member of the Domain Users security group, which has Full Control access, that user will inherit Full Control over the file.

- File permissions take precedence over folder permissions. If a folder has permissions set to block access to a user, but a file in the folder has explicit access to that file granted, the user cannot navigate to the file in the folder by using Windows Explorer but she can access the file directly from the command line or from a program script.

Note If you cannot navigate to a file because of restrictive folder permissions, use the command-line utility to access the file in question. If you want, you can copy the file from its target folder to a location that's accessible by using Windows File Explorer. Start a command prompt by clicking Start ➤ Run. In the dialog box, type `cmd.exe` and press Enter. The `copy` command can be used to take a copy of a file from a folder you don't have access to and place it somewhere you can see it in Windows File Explorer. For details of the `copy` command's syntax, type `copy /?` and press Enter.

Advanced Access Control

The standard permissions covered in the previous section are each made up of lower-level file system permissions. There are 13 of these low-level permissions, and by assigning collections of these, you can create the appropriate access permissions for individual requirements.

To give you an idea of how these fundamental privileges group together to create the permissions outlined in Table 5-1, have a look at Table 5-2. The standard permissions are listed across the top of the table, and the lower-level permissions are listed down the left side. By assigning the standard permissions, this table gives you an idea of the advanced permissions required to give that level of access.

Table 5-2. *Advanced Permissions Used for More Granular Control*

Permission	Full Control	Modify	Read & Execute	List Folder Contents	Read	Write	Description
Traverse Folder/ Execute File	Yes	Yes	Yes	Yes			Access a folder within a tree even if you don't have permission to see the folder contents.
List Folder/ Read Data	Yes	Yes	Yes	Yes	Yes		View files within a folder, open the files, and read the file contents.

Permission	Full Control	Modify	Read & Execute	List Folder Contents	Read	Write	Description
Read Attributes	Yes	Yes	Yes	Yes	Yes		View the special attributes of a file (archive, hidden, system, and read-only).
Read Extended Attributes	Yes	Yes	Yes	Yes	Yes		View the extended attributes (or metadata) of a file, each application generating its own specific set.
Create Files/ Write Data	Yes	Yes				Yes	Create new files or folders within a folder or overwrite existing files and folders.
Create Folders/ Append Data	Yes	Yes				Yes	Create subfolders inside a parent folder or append data to a file.
Write Attributes	Yes	Yes				Yes	Change the attributes of a file (archive, hidden, system, and read-only).
Write Extended Attributes	Yes	Yes				Yes	Change the extended attributes (metadata) of a file, such as those created by Microsoft Office 2003 products.
Delete Subfolders and Files	Yes						Delete all files and folders beneath a selected folder. These are special permissions that apply only to folders.
Delete	Yes	Yes					Delete a single file or folder but no others within or beneath the selected folder.
Read Permissions	Yes	Yes	Yes	Yes	Yes		View the permissions of a file or folder.
Change Permissions	Yes						View and change permissions on a file or folder.
Take Ownership	Yes						Assume control of a file or folder not explicitly named as your own.

To manipulate the advanced permissions ACL for a file or folder, do the following:

1. Open an Explorer session (right-click the Start menu and select Explore).

2. Navigate to the appropriate file or folder and right-click on the object.

3. Select Properties. The file/folder properties dialog box appears.

4. Select the Security tab at the top of the dialog box.

5. Highlight any one of the object's ACEs and then click Advanced.

6. Click the Add button to create a custom set of advanced permissions for the selected user or group.

7. Select the means by which the selected permissions become effective, that is, should they affect all subfolders and files, or only the files and folders in question (see Figure 5-4).

8. Click OK.

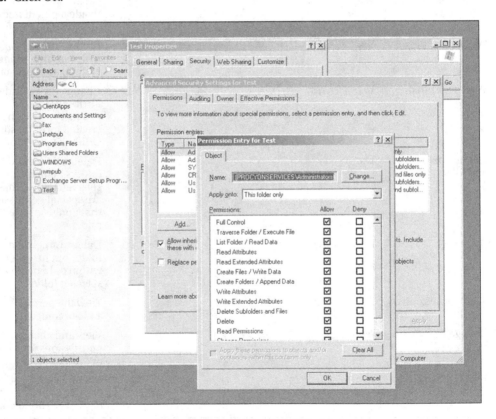

Figure 5-4. *Advanced permissions can be set for all NTFS objects.*

If you want to modify any of the ACEs already set up for a file or folder, simply click the Edit button in the advanced permissions menu to access the properties dialog box and change any of the entries listed in Table 5-2 (see Figure 5-3). If you want to see how a combination of advanced permissions might affect a user's abilities to use a particular file or folder, match your choices against the Table 5-2 entries and see how they map to the standard permissions. You'll probably find that under most circumstances you always end up assigning a standard set of permissions for most normal users and objects.

File and Folder Ownership

The concept of file and folder ownership is worth expanding on. If a user has the permission to create a file or folder, that user will inevitably be the owner of that file or folder and maintain Full Control permission over that object. In some cases, when one user does not have specific access to a file or folder and a second user has Full Control, the first user would be given access by an administrator or by the owner of the object. However, this is not always possible. Say, for example, a user leaves the company and has explicitly denied access to his data files to all users of the network. Your administrator can take ownership of the files and effectively assume the role of the original owner. The administrator can modify the permissions assigned to the data and make it again available to the rest of the business.

To take ownership of files that you don't have explicit permissions to access, follow these steps:

1. Log in with a domain administrator account (by default the administrator account can perform this operation).

2. Open Windows File Explorer (right-click the Start menu and select Explore).

3. Navigate to the appropriate file or folder you need to take ownership of and right-click on the object.

4. Select Properties. The file/folder properties dialog box appears.

5. Select the Security tab at the top of the dialog box.

6. Click the Advanced button.

7. Select the Owner tab at the top of the screen.

8. From the list at the bottom of the screen, select the user who will assume ownership of the file.

9. If you want this ownership to percolate through the list of subfolders beneath this folder object, select the check box at the bottom of the screen. Click OK.

■**Warning** Care should be taken if you think you need to take ownership of system folders or users' profile folders. These types of folders have special NTFS permissions attached to them and may not work properly if ownership is modified.

Inheritance

As new folders and files are created beneath a folder, the permissions on the parent folder, by default, are passed along to the child container and its contents.

You can choose to block inheritance if this perpetuation of permissions does not suit your purposes by doing the following:

1. Open a Windows File Explorer session (right-click the Start menu and select Explore).

2. Navigate to the appropriate file or folder and right-click on the object.

3. Select Properties. The file/folder Properties dialog box appears.

4. Select the Security tab at the top of the dialog box.

5. If you need to modify permissions, do so and then click the Advanced button.

6. Uncheck the check box for inheriting permissions and click OK (Allow Inheritable Permissions from Parent to Propagate to This Object).

Note You may also see (for previously created folders) another dialog box asking whether you wish to copy previously inherited permissions or whether you wish to start afresh with a blank ACL.

From now on, all files and folders created beneath this folder will require explicit permissions to be added by the user or administrator before access can be achieved.

The Cumulative Effect

The final word I have to say about the file system is really about troubleshooting. A useful way of determining the effective permissions that a user has over a file system object is to use the Effective Permissions tab in the object properties box.

Because a user can be a member of many security groups, and many security groups can be nested inside many other security groups, sometimes finding exactly where certain permissions have come from is somewhat complicated. You might be expecting a user to have Read & Execute permission on a specific customer folder only to find that because of some obscure group nesting, that user ends up with Full Control.

To see exactly what permissions a user has as a culmination of all permissions derived from group and explicit ACEs, do the following:

1. Open an Explorer session (right-click the Start menu and select Explore).

2. Navigate to the appropriate file or folder and right-click on the object.

3. Select Properties. The file/folder Properties dialog box appears.

4. Select the Security tab at the top of the dialog box.

5. If you need to modify permissions, do so and then click the Advanced button.

6. Click the Effective Permissions tab and then click Select. You can choose the user or group you'd like to check. Then click OK. The effective permissions are listed in the lower dialog box.

Managing User Accounts

Every user on your system must have a user account created within the Active Directory. All information defining a user is stored within the Active Directory database, and the account is housed within the appropriate OU. Account information is made available to all operating system functions and applications that have the appropriate permission to access it.

■**Note** As with every aspect of running your SBS 2003 system, there are many ways to access information and perform administrative tasks: through intuitive wizards that do the hard work for you; through direct Active Directory access by using the native Windows Server 2003 tools; or via the command-line interface, where advanced users can create scripts that access the tools and facilities that streamline the day-to-day running of the system.

To view the attributes of a user account, do the following:

1. Click Start ➤ Server Management.

2. In the left-hand menu, highlight Users.

3. In the Manage Users interface, in the right-hand pane, you'll see a list of all the interactive user accounts held in your Active Directory.

4. To obtain the details of a specific user account, double-click on the account name.

5. Navigate to any of the account properties by using the appropriate tab at the top of the account properties dialog box.

■**Warning** This interface does not show all accounts created on the system; instead it shows the accounts used for interactive login by real users. Other user accounts exist on your system, known as service accounts, and are used for applications needing the extended privileges of these accounts rather than the privileges of the logged-in user. To see a complete list of all users on your system, you'll need to use the Advanced Management interface. Open the Server Management tool, expand Advanced Management, expand Active Directory Users and Computers, and then expand the container equating to your system's DNS name. Highlight the Users container to get a full list of all user accounts on your system. You'll notice a couple of extra accounts listed in this container for running Internet Information Services and Help and Support. All the security groups configured on your system will also be displayed here.

You can see from the example shown in Figure 5-5 that every piece of information associated with a user account is available through this interface. The beauty of this consolidated view of the information is that all aspects of user configuration can be carried out from this single interface. Your administrative rights determine which of the functions you can configure.

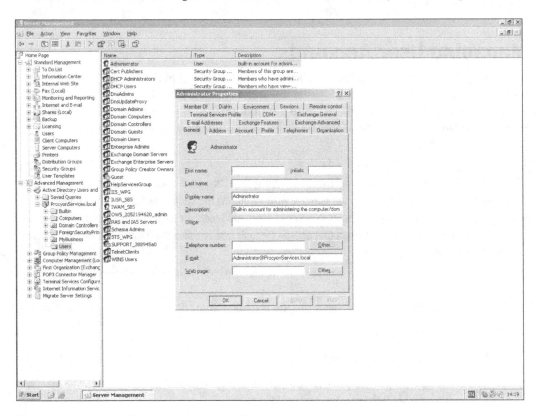

Figure 5-5. *The Active Directory contains all user information.*

Creating a New Account

Using the SBS 2003 Server Management console, the basic job of adding new users to your system is easy.

Note As with many aspects of SBS 2003 management, there is also an option to create users from the To Do List.

To create an account by using the Server Management console, do the following:

1. Click Start ➤ Server Management. In the left window pane, highlight Users to open the Manage Users interface.

2. Click Add a User to start the Add User Wizard. When the wizard starts, click Next to begin.

3. Type the user's first and last name in the dialog box and make sure the automatic data fill fields are adhering to your company's user-naming standards (see Chapter 3). When you are content that the login name and email alias are correct, click Next.

4. Type in the password the user will use when first logging in to the domain. Repeat the password and select the User Can Change Password at Any Time radio button. Click Next.

5. Select the appropriate template to set the new user account with the appropriate level of administrative rights over the SBS 2003 server and your infrastructure. Table 5-3 explains the rights associated with each of the default templates. When you're happy with your choice, click Next. Creating your own custom templates is covered later in this chapter.

6. Now you have the option to set up a client computer for this user. Select Do Not Set Up a Computer. You will cover setting up computers and assigning software to users later in this chapter. For now, this is all you need to do to create the user's basic account. Click Next.

7. You are presented with the wizard summary. If you are satisfied with your choices, click Finish.

8. The wizard creates the account, adds it to the appropriate security groups, and returns you to the Manage Users Server Management interface. The wizard has added your user to the appropriate SharePoint Services groups, Remote Web Workplace access groups, and much, much more.

Table 5-3. *Default User Templates*

Template Name	Description
User	The standard User template offers typical network access to printers, shared folders, email, and other network resources. Users created with this template have no administrative rights and will require administrative intervention to reset passwords, install software, and perform many other low-level system functions such as adding devices to workstations and changing permissions on folders.
Mobile User	The Mobile User template inherits all the permissions of the standard User template but in addition provides the user with the ability to dial-up to the SBS 2003 server or connect via the Internet by using a virtual private network circuit. This template should be used to create the users you decided would be based at home, or workers who travel with laptops and access the system remotely.
Power User	The Power User template inherits all the attributes of the previous two templates, User and Mobile, but in addition has the ability to manage users, groups, and shared file store areas as well as to log on to the server from the network. A power user could access the server directly by using the Remote Desktop Connection client. It's worth noting, however, that the limit of two simultaneous connections is imposed because of the terminal services working in administrative mode rather than application mode. This is a limit imposed from the underlying Microsoft Windows Server 2003 system rather than an SBS 2003 restriction.
Administrator	Administrators have total control over the server operation. Make sure you limit the availability of administrative accounts to a select few, and in each case assign an individual account to these users rather than giving them access to the Administrator account you created during setup. This means that your administrators, even when acting in the context of their jobs, are individually accountable for their actions on your system.

User templates are simply user accounts that have not had all the personalization of a discrete account applied to them. This means that straight copies of template accounts can be modified to create individual users with little configuration necessary other than the personal information about that user.

You can assign all the attributes of an account manually by accessing the Active Directory and dropping users into the appropriate security groups that delegate rights to the user objects they contain (security groups are next).

To see the user accounts in the Active Directory, use the following steps:

1. Click Start ➤ Server Management.

2. Under the Advanced Management section, expand the Active Directory Users and Computers subtree and highlight the container showing your system's DNS name.

3. The window on the right side shows the six default containers. Double-click Users.

4. Double-click on the user you are interested in. Click the Member Of tab to see the groups that that user is a member of.

5. The user account is added to these groups as a result of selecting a user template.

Note It is possible to use the command-line interface to add a user account quickly to the Active Directory by clicking Start ➤ Run. Type `cmd.exe` in the dialog box and click OK. To see a full list of all the facilities available for adding users, type `dsadd user /?` and then press Enter. A word of warning, however: although there are many ways to do things with the SBS 2003 product set, you're best sticking to the preferred SBS 2003 way because many wizards and functions specially configure aspects of SBS 2003 that you would need to otherwise do manually.

Removing a User

Deleting an unwanted user account is even easier than creating one. From the Server Management interface, highlight the user you want to remove and click Remove User. You will have to also delete the user's email account, and this interface allows you to do just that. If you also want to remove the user's home file store, select the check box next to the user's home folder and then click Yes. This process will delete all mailbox and user information. If you need to keep any of this information for your records, make sure you back it up or print it first.

Warning If a user has left your company or is suspended, it's a good idea to not delete the account. Instead, disable the account so that the user can no longer access his resources. You can later decide to take administrative control of his file store, email inbox, and any other resources he had access to. The account can also be reactivated if you decide the user can return to his post. One thing to note, however, is that email accounts that have been disabled will force any incoming email to bounce. An alternative might be to change the user's password and then point the email to another account before finally disabling the original account.

Enabling/Disabling a User Account

To toggle the status of a user account between enabled and disabled:

1. Click Start ➤ Server Management.

2. In the left window pane, highlight Users to open the Manage Users interface.

3. Highlight the appropriate user account you intend to toggle and then click Disable Account or Enable Account, depending on the current state. Click OK. Disabled accounts are shown in the list as having a red circle with a white cross inside it emblazoned on the user name.

Adding Multiple Users

It's possible to add a group of users all at once by using the Add Multiple Users function of the Manage Users Server Management console:

1. Click Start ➤ Server Management.

2. In the left window pane, highlight Users to open the Manage Users interface.

3. Click Add Multiple Users.

4. Click Next to start the wizard.

5. Choose the appropriate user template from the list. Click Next.

6. On the User Information page, click Add. Click OK after you add each user.

7. After you've added all your users to the list, click Next.

8. On the Set Up Client Computers page, select Do Not Set Up a Computer. The wizard finishes off by creating all the user accounts you entered information for in step 4.

Using Custom User Templates

If you need to create many users with similar rights and permissions, but these users don't fit into any of the standard, predefined user templates, it's easy to create your own user templates to meet your own business requirements.

To illustrate the process of creating a new user template, the following example explains the process well.

GerriCan, a medium-sized gas station in Colorado, is an established SBS 2003 customer. The owner of GerriCan, Gerald Langdon, has recently reviewed his profits, and after seeing a good increase in productivity and much better cash-flow management over the last 12 months, has decided to take a risk. A small car-servicing company, Benton's, in his town is struggling and might go under without intervention, but Gerald sees the potential in streamlining a business such as this. He decides to put up the cash to buy half the business for himself, taking on co-ownership with Benton's manager, Fred Benton.

Gerald is keen to push the streamlined business model he's developed with SBS 2003 into the failing servicing company, and to do this he'll be assuming total control of Benton's IT infrastructure. To ease the transition for Fred's staff into Gerald's new working environment, Gerald has instructed his IT administrator to create user accounts on his SBS 2003 system that are more akin to the way Fred's staff currently works. This means a deviation from the standard User template supplied with SBS 2003. The administrator decides to create a brand new custom user template for creating new users from Benton's (this is more than value for money because there are 30 staff to create accounts for), offering the appropriate permissions to both the legacy business data he'll be migrating into the SBS 2003 environment, as well as access to GerriCan's corporate data.

The GerriCan administrator logs in to the SBS 2003 server and opens the Server Management console by clicking Start ➤ Server Management. He then proceeds to do the following:

1. He clicks User Templates.

2. He clicks Add a Template to access the Add Template Wizard.

3. He clicks Next to start the wizard.

4. On the Template Account Information page, the administrator types in the name of the new user template, in this case, **Benton Users**. He chooses not to make this the default template because he still wants the default to be the standard User template for Gerri-Can staff. He clicks Next.

5. The wizard proceeds to the Security Groups page. Various security groups have been created to grant access to both the imported corporate data from Benton's and a subset of GerriCan's corporate data. The appropriate security groups are now added to this template. He clicks Next.

6. On the Distribution Groups page, the administrator selects the appropriate distribution groups being assigned to the new Benton users. This will allow Benton only email broadcasts to be sent, as well as global email broadcasts to all users from both companies. The administrator clicks Next.

7. On the SharePoint Access page (see Figure 5-6), the administrator decides which roles Benton Users will have over the corporate intranet. When completed, he clicks Next.

8. On the Address Information page, the company location should be entered for these users. In this case, the address is the servicing yard rather than GerriCan's address. Any aspects of the address that will vary from user to user should be left blank and explicitly typed as the user account is created from the template later. When complete, he clicks Next.

9. Finally, the template is configured to provide the appropriate disk space quota for Benton users. In this case, disk quotas are not being used. The administrator clicks Next to proceed to the final page.

10. He checks the choices he's made for the Benton Users template, and when happy with his choices, clicks Finish.

The GerriCan administrator can now create Benton User accounts from this template, meaning all information supplied in the template is already configured. The creation of the initial 30 user accounts should not take too long and should be mistake-free, and any new Benton users can be created with the same level of access permissions and rights as the other Benton users.

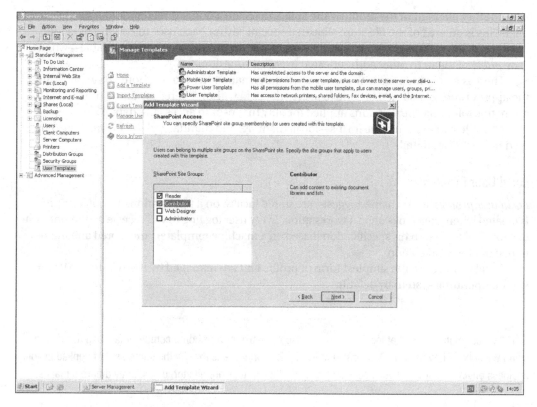

Figure 5-6. *You can allocate SharePoint roles to your custom user templates.*

Creating User Profiles

One of the most powerful features a Windows Server 2003 infrastructure brings to your business is the ability to create a flexible working environment that totally suits the way your business and users need to function.

It's entirely possible, and not too difficult, to create an environment in which any user can log on at any office position. In doing so, the Windows Server 2003 infrastructure creates the user's personalized desktop environment, with all of the user's Internet links, desktop icons, and screen savers, as well as the relevant rights and permissions that that user has within the domain. If another user logs on to that computer, the server redirects that user's personal environment to the desktop.

This redirection and personalization of a user's personal environment is known in Windows Server 2003 terms as a user's *profile*. This means it is possible to have many users configured to use a small number of workstations; for example, if you run a shift roster, you can supply a single workstation for 10 users, and each user still gets a personalized desktop environment.

Note Profiles that follow the user around the network are known as *roaming profiles*.

Another element of the profile is the ability to create a home directory folder for the user's data. This is an area of the file store allocated specifically for each user to contain personal documents or work-in-progress that the user does not want to be publicly available—when I say *public*, I mean to other authenticated users on your domain.

There is an obvious security concern with information held in this home directory: only the appropriate user should be able to access the data within. Therefore, at the time of creation, this folder has permissions applied for only that user to access the data.

A profile can exist in three forms—local, roaming, and mandatory—all of which are covered here in more detail.

Local User Profiles

Local user profiles, as the name suggests, are stored locally, on a workstation. A local user profile is created when a user logs on to a workstation. Every user logging in will receive a different local user profile tailored to his specification (based on a machine template), and stored and maintained on that workstation.

Local profiles are the simplest form of profile and are managed by the Windows XP workstation operating system by default.

Note You might notice that local profiles are also available on your home computer (as long as you are using Windows NT, Windows 2000, or Windows XP). This principle is exactly the same as that applied in your business environment when you use local profiles, although they are all stored in slightly different places.

Whether the user account is a domain account (one that is authenticated against your Windows Server 2003 server) or a local workstation account (one that is authenticated on the local workstation), both will store all profile data on the user's workstation.

The downside to local user profiles is that because users are allowed to be authenticated from any networked computer in your domain, users can "hot-desk" and sit where they like when they come into the office. Each time a user logs on to a workstation she has not logged on to before, she'll get a brand new profile copied from the default local profile on that computer. This means that each time she will have a new My Documents folder and that her desktop settings will have to be set up from scratch to suit the way she works.

Local user profiles are created and managed automatically, so there is no setting up involved for this method of operation.

Roaming Profiles

A *roaming user profile* has many advantages over a local user profile because the user's profile travels with him to each workstation he logs on at, except for a few key files (such as temporary files). Authenticating on the domain notifies the domain controller that you wish to start working, and the domain controller sends all your profile details to the computer you log on at. By doing this, your settings are maintained and your My Documents folder will be stored centrally on the server.

■Warning Although the concept of your profile following you wherever you go is great, try not to allow users to store too much data in My Documents. If a user's My Documents folder grows too big, it may adversely affect logon and logoff times.

Now, it doesn't matter where you log on from; your workstation experience will be maintained exactly the way you like it.

■Note Each profile contains application data specific to that user's environment. Many Internet Explorer elements, such as cookies and favorites, are also stored so that each position you log on at gives you a consistent look and feel through the operating system and the applications that sit on top. Desktop shortcuts, network mapped drives, default printing devices, and the Start menu components are also stored in the user's profile. All of these setting are transient as the user moves from one workstation to another when you employ roaming user profiles on your network. This is a very desirable end result because security is still as strong with a roaming user profile as it is with a local user profile.

To set up roaming user profiles, you'll need to create a new folder on the server to contain all the user profile data. This profile will be copied to the user's workstation when he authenticates to the server and it will appear, for all intents and purposes, that the data is local to the workstation.

■Note A technology known as folder redirection can also be employed (albeit not necessary for roaming profiles) to redirect the local My Documents folder on the user's desktop to a directory on the server. Folder redirection is covered in more detail later in this chapter.

To create a roaming profile area on the server:

1. Using Windows Explorer on the server, navigate to the root of your user data disk and create a new folder called **User Profiles**.

2. Right-click on the new folder and share it by using the hidden share name **Profiles$**.

3. Click Start ➤ Server Management to open the Server Management console.

4. In the left window, highlight Users to display the Manage Users interface on the right.

5. Highlight the user's name you are creating a roaming profile for in the left window, right-click, and select Properties.

6. Click the Profile tab.

7. Next to the Profile path, type **\\yourservername\Profiles$\%username%**.

Note By using the convention %username%, you've told the Windows login session to use a system variable rather than a specific name. You could easily have used an explicit account name, such as TCampbell, but this means that as each user account was created, you'd have to perform this configuration job manually. If you build the template accounts by using the %username% system variable, the variable is translated into the user's account name as the user logs on, and the template path will be replaced by the literal translation, allowing the access to the correct part of the file store.

8. You can also map a drive for the user's home file store, effectively creating a network drive that the user can use to store files on the server (see Figure 5-7). Type the folder path in as you did for the profile path, including the %username% variable to make sure each user's path is unique. You can share the folder as Users$ and each individual user's file store will be beneath this share.

Note Where possible, add this sort of information to your user templates. By doing so, you will not have to explicitly type this information into each of your user's account properties.

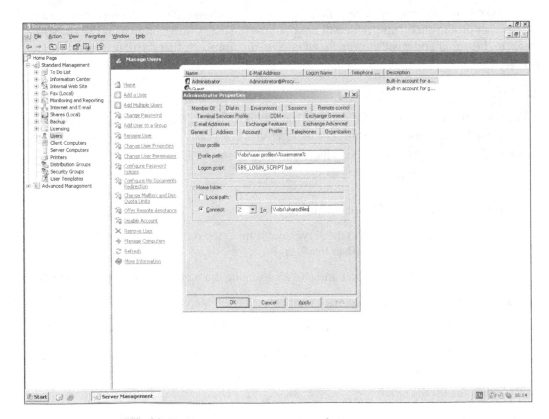

Figure 5-7. *Use the variable* %username% *in your user template.*

■**Warning** When a user logs in, the network drive for the user's home drive will be mapped by using the letter chosen in the properties dialog box. Always make sure that you are using a free drive letter for this drive, as you might already have various mapped network drives on a user's workstation. The default letter is Z for the user's home drive and should be left as the default because this is the last one selected for use automatically when you use Explorer to map a drive.

Mandatory User Profiles

The final, and less used, method of assigning profiles is the most restrictive: that of *mandatory user profiles*. A mandatory profile allows an administrator to effectively assign the settings he wants imposed on all users using the mandatory profile and to not permit any deviation. All settings normally stored in the user's personal folder will be overwritten with the mandatory settings assigned centrally.

Although this sounds like it has its benefits, every user is different, and your hardware and software sets assigned to each workstation and user might vary so significantly that managing a mandatory profile across every user and workstation becomes too much of a burden. There is no harm in users having the freedom to modify elements of their profile; it enhances their ability to customize the environment to best suit their needs, and by letting users have an element of freedom, you also imply an element of trust—and trust is the most important part of any employee/employer relationship.

Redirecting My Documents to the Server

It is possible to redirect a user's My Documents folder to a network folder on your server. Then, instead of data being stored locally on that user's workstation, all files and folders under the My Documents folder in the user's profile are stored on the server—without that being obvious to the user. This is in addition to the user's home directory being mapped through the account properties dialog box and means that you can back it up and use Volume Shadow Copy rollback.

■**Warning** Users could store gigabytes of data under their local My Documents folder, because applications such as Windows Media Player automatically store MP3s and video files in this location. If you use folder redirection for My Documents, you'll need to ensure that you have enough disk space to accommodate the data your users will be storing there (or have strict policies in place with staff). If you are in any way uncertain as to whether your server can cope with the potential load, leave the user's home directory on the server as the one mapped using the account properties dialog box, and My Documents should remain on the local workstation. The downside is that My Documents will not travel with the user if you have a hot-desk policy. Another alternative is to consider laptops for your users so the computer they log on with is always the same, even if they change desk positions. If you do this, you'll need to inform your users that they will still need to copy any business-critical files to the server to ensure that they are backed up.

If you decide to redirect the My Documents folder to the SBS 2003 server, do the following:

1. Click Start ➤ Server Management.

2. In the left window pane, highlight Users to open the Manage Users interface.

3. In the right-hand window, click Configure My Documents Redirection.

4. On the Client Documents Redirection page, select Redirect All My Documents Folders to the Default Shared Folder for Users on the Small Business Server.

5. Click OK.

To reverse this operation, all you need to do is select the option Do Not Redirect My Documents Folders from the same menu. A copy of the My Documents folder is always held locally on the workstation, and when the user logs on to or off the domain, the local copy is synchronized with the networked copy. In this way, when a user logs on to his normal workstation position, the only files copied over the network (except for the very first time folder redirection is initialized) are the updates. This greatly reduces the user's logon and logoff time.

Performing Ongoing User Management

Generally, it's worth auditing your user base once a month. As people leave the company or as users' roles change, you should react with the appropriate action in the IT system. For example, your user policy for employee resignation should be that on the day a member of staff leaves your employment, you disable the account. The account cannot be used but can be reactivated in case you need to assign it to someone else or to audit what the user has been up to.

Note Always check what local legislation requires about company record keeping and auditing requirements. Because email now falls under such legislation, you're better being safe than sorry.

When you audit your system every month, make sure that the accounts you have disabled have remained disabled. This might sound obvious, but your security could be breached, and if someone with access to your business is using an account you believed to be disabled, you might be inadvertently hosting someone else's illegal activities. If the user happened to be an administrator, make sure that you change the password immediately and that there are no other "backdoor" accounts created on your system that the user might still use to gain unauthorized access after he leaves.

Accessing Networked Data

You've already seen how files and folders have NTFS permissions applied to them, determining exactly who has access to the data within. When you directly access the file system on either a workstation or a server, you are actually accessing the local hard drive, controlled by the local operating system.

This is fine until you consider the network. How do you get to the file system on another machine to allow NTFS to start authorizing your access to the files? You need some sort of portal to gain access to the local file system that governs each file and folder you need access to. Similarly, there are other resources on your infrastructure you need to consider access to over the network, such as network printers, scanners, shared fax systems, and remote applications.

Network Shares

On virtually every Windows-based computer system on your network (workstations and servers), some default network shares will already be created for administrative purposes.

There are two kinds of network shares you can create—normal and hidden—both of which you'll need to understand to get the whole picture:

- *Normal network shares*: When a folder is shared on your network, on any computer, by default it is a normal network share. Its existence is known to the Windows network operating system and can be browsed by using standard network browsing tools, such as My Network Places and Windows Explorer.

- *Hidden network shares*: It is possible to hide the identity of a share from the network so that only explicit connections can be made to the share by clients who know the share exists. This is useful in stopping users from browsing for shares you don't want them having access to—remember the old adage: out of sight, out of mind. Hidden shares are identified on the system by the $ suffix. Windows automatically creates a variety of these on installation for administration purposes.

To view the shares already created by default on either a workstation or server, the quickest way is to run the command shell and use the Net Share utility:

1. Click Start ➤ Run.

2. In the dialog box, type cmd.exe and press Enter.

3. At the command prompt, type net share and press Enter.

The default list of shares on an SBS 2003 server is shown in Figure 5-8. Each is covered in detail in Table 5-4.

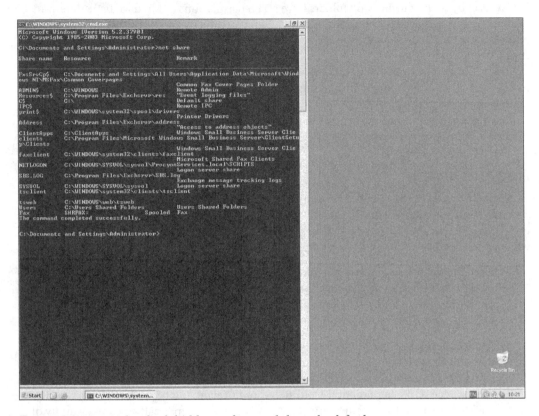

Figure 5-8. *SBS 2003 has both hidden and normal shares by default.*

Table 5-4. *Default Shares Created on an SBS 2003 Server*

Share Name	Description
FxsSrvCp$	This hidden share is used by the operating system to pick up commonly used cover pages for the Shared Fax service.
ADMIN$	This is a Windows Server default hidden share used by the operating system for administrative access to Windows Server resources.
Resources$	Another default Windows Server hidden share used by the operating system to access and write information to the Windows event logs.
C$	This hidden share is created by default on the root of the system drive on the workstation (Windows NT, Windows 2000, and Windows XP) or server.
IPC$	An essential operating system hidden share used for remote administration by users to authenticate using an administrative account on a remote server.
Print$	Printer drivers are held on the system under this hidden share. When a printer driver is requested by a system connecting to the server or workstation, this is where the driver is retrieved.
Address	All Exchange addressing information is disseminated via this network share.

Share Name	Description
ClientApps	Client applications assigned to client workstations are distributed via this network share. This share is particular to SBS 2003 servers.
clients	This share is used for the setup of SBS 2003 network client systems, as instigated through the Manage Users interface in Server Management.
faxclient	This share is used to distribute the Shared Fax client software.
NETLOGON	This share is the primary network logon share for all domain-based or local-based logons, depending on whether the request is against a workstation or server.
<servername>.LOG	This share offers network access to the Exchange message tracking logs. These logs are used in troubleshooting your email system, containing a comprehensive list of who did what and when with Exchange.
SYSVOL	This is another logon server share specifically for use when connecting to the Active Directory.
tsclient	This share is for use with Windows Terminal Server, allowing access to the back-end software repository from the RDP client.
tsweb	Another administrative share for terminal services web access and Internet Information Services.
Users	This is the default SBS 2003 share for User network shares.
Fax	This system share is used by the Shared Fax service to spool faxes to the external fax device.

To create a network share, either on a workstation or server, it's best to decide who on the network will need access to the data beneath. Do you want the share to be hidden from users when they browse the network, or should the share be readily available to all authenticated users?

Network Share Permissions

The best way to secure access to a network share is to create a domain local security group for each level of access to that share. Call each security group by the name of the share, and add a descriptor word at the end of the name, defining the level of access. For example, to create a network share on your SBS 2003 server to store all company invoices, the folder is created on the server and called Invoices. You will then share the folder on the network (using the procedure detailed below) and give it a name such as Invoices. There will be two levels of access you need to grant to the Invoices share: half your staff needs to be able to fully access the data on the share, while the other half should be blocked. To achieve this, two domain local security groups are created: Invoices_PermitAccess and Invoices_DenyAccess. Two domain global groups should also be defined (using the methodology described earlier for assigning users into global groups and global groups into local groups): Invoices_PermitAccessGlobal and Invoices_DenyAccessGlobal. Assign the two domain local groups to the share, giving the Invoices_PermitAccess group Full Control and the Invoices_DenyAccess group Deny access. The users should now be added to the appropriate global groups, and the appropriate global groups added to the appropriate domain local groups. Now, when a new user is needed to access the Invoices folder on the server, he is added to the domain global group, Invoices_PermitAccessGlobal and he's in.

A detailed walk-through of the procedure is needed to ensure that you know exactly what's going on:

1. Click Start ➤ Server Management.

2. On the left side, expand Advanced Management.

3. Expand Active Directory Users and Computers.

4. Expand your domain name and then highlight the Users container.

5. Right-click on an area of blank space on the right-hand side and then select New ➤ Group.

6. Type the name of the group, Invoices_PermitAccess, and make sure you've selected the Domain Local and Security Group radio buttons. Click Next.

7. Do not create an Exchange Email Address for this group. On the next page, click Next and then click Finish.

8. Follow the procedure from step 5 onward to create the other three groups for this example: Invoices_DenyAccess domain local group, and two global groups, Invoices_PermitAccessGlobal and Invoices_DenyAccessGlobal.

9. Double-click the Invoices_DenyAccess local group and select the Members tab. Click Add.

10. Type Invoices_DenyAccessGlobal and click OK. Click OK again to go back to the list of users and groups.

11. Double-click the Invoices_PermitAccess local group and select the Members tab. Click Add.

12. Type Invoices_PermitAccessGlobal and click OK. Click OK again to go back to the list of users and groups.

13. Open Windows Explorer and create the folder called Invoices.

14. Right-click on the folder name and select Properties.

15. Click the Sharing tab at the top of the properties dialog box.

16. Click Share This Folder.

17. Keep the name Invoices as the share name and add a meaningful description.

18. To make the share a hidden share, simply add a $ to the end of the share name.

19. Click Permissions.

20. Click Add.

21. In the dialog box, type Invoices_PermitAccess and click OK. Highlight Invoices_PermitAccess and click OK.

22. Under the Allow column, click Full Control.

23. Click Add again. This time add the Invoices_DenyAccess group and instead of granting Full Control Allow, select the Full Control Deny column and click OK.

24. Accept the warning about denying access.

25. Click OK twice to exit from the folder permissions. You'll see the folder now has a small hand underneath the folder icon in Windows Explorer. This means the folder has been successfully shared.

You might have noticed during this exercise that the level of control over a network share is much less granular than that of NTFS files and folders. As you've already seen, the NTFS system provides 14 low-level permissions that can be grouped to create fairly complex rules for accessing data, but in the world of the network share, you are limited to just three high-level permissions: Full Control, Change, and Read.

Warning Remember that network shares have no control over users who log on locally to a computer and directly access the file system. Never consider a network share as a way of totally securing data. You must always bolster the security provided by network share permissions by assigning appropriate NTFS permissions to information beneath.

When considering network shares and how you'll be using them, try to think of them as simply portals on your network, offering access to the data held on the target server or workstation. The share is basically an entry point onto the networked computer, where the user then accesses files and folders controlled by NTFS.

When both share and NTFS permissions have been defined for a file or folder, the most restrictive permissions apply. Therefore, it's worth making sure that the cumulative effect of both sets of permissions gives the right result.

Note One way system administrators get around the problem of determining the effective permissions granted from a combination of NTFS and share permissions is to open up the share as Full Control for Everyone and then limit access to the data by using NTFS (although some viruses have been to known to exploit this, so make sure your NTFS permissions are tight). In this way, you never need to concern yourself with the permissions on the share itself, and all control is applied using NTFS. NTFS is more granular, and having the tools for troubleshooting effective permissions means you can troubleshoot any problems much quicker.

Performing Computer Management

Much in the same way as your users need a user account to log on to the SBS 2003 domain, all computers being used in your domain environment must also have an associated computer account that allows the computer to be authenticated by the domain controller.

SBS 2003 has many additional tools over and above those provided by the underlying Windows Server 2003 operating system to aid in streamlining the addition of computers into your Active Directory, as well as making the distribution of software to these computers a trivial task.

The underlying technology for deploying client computers and their associated applications has been around since the days of Windows 2000—mainly using Group Policy Objects to assign software to these end systems. The added value in SBS 2003 is the Set Up Computer Wizard interface that creates the computer account and assigns the software, all through the same simple interface.

Many of the additional software applications you'll be assigning to your workstations come as part of the SBS 2003 software bundle. Packages such as Microsoft Office Outlook 2003 and Microsoft Office FrontPage 2003 for Premium edition customers can be deployed to your clients by using this method of GPO assignment. It's worth noting that the Microsoft Office FrontPage 2003 license that comes with SBS 2003 Premium Edition is for a single installation only, so this would be worth setting up for deployment only if you intend to augment your license pool with more Microsoft Office FrontPage 2003 licenses.

Note Every workstation you wish to log on from should be added to the SBS 2003 domain by using the Set Up Computer Wizard.

Adding a Computer to Your Network

To add a new computer to your network and assign some software to that system, do the following:

1. Click Start ➤ Server Management.

2. In the left window pane, highlight Client Computers.

3. In the right-hand window, click Set Up Client Computers. This starts the Set Up Computer Wizard.

4. On the Welcome screen, click Next.

5. Type in the name of the client computer and then click Add (use standard characters and no spaces in the computer name).

6. Repeat this procedure for as many computers as you intend to add at this time.

7. When you're ready to proceed, click Next.

8. On the Client Applications page (see Figure 5-9), select the check boxes next to the applications you want installed on each of your selected computers when they join the domain. If you want your users to interact with the product installation tasks, select the top check box, During Client Setup, Allow the Selected Applications to Be Modified. This means the user can redirect data and installation files and potentially install additional components for the software you don't normally install by default. It's also a good idea to select the bottom check box, After Client Setup Is Finished, Log Off the Client Computer, because a reboot will ensure that the workstation goes back to the logon prompt (more secure) and any changes introduced by the application will be applied. If you want to add new applications to the list, see the next section for a walk-through of the procedure. Click Next.

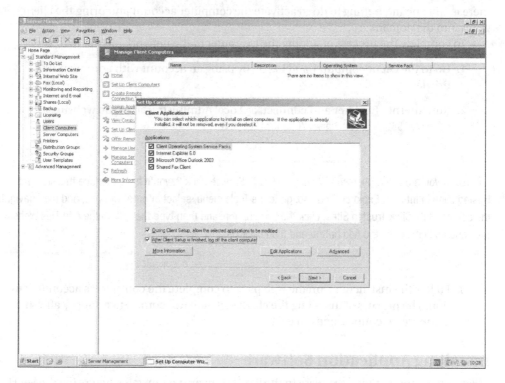

Figure 5-9. *Assigning applications to new client computers is easy.*

9. The next page allows you to set up components of the operating system that will allow users with mobility requirements to access the various resources mobile users need, such as dial-up and VPN access and Pocket PC connectivity. On the Mobile Client and Offline Use page, select the Install Connection Manager check box to enable computers to access your network by using a dial-up link or over the Internet using a VPN. If the computer will connect to a PDA running Windows Mobile, select the check box to install ActiveSync. Click Next. (If you skipped the remote-access part of the To Do List, you'll be warned and offered the option to run through this now.)

■**Warning** The SBS 2003 version of ActiveSync is special for SBS 2003. It has additional capabilities for handing certificates, as well as various other SBS 2003 server-related features. Do not use the version of ActiveSync that came with your mobile device or any you might download from the Internet because you will reduce your capability.

---

10. On the last page, check that all the details are correct, and when you're satisfied, click Finish.

You've now completed the part of the process that needs to be done on the server, but there is still one more thing to do to activate the computer account and bring the client computer into the domain.

To complete the process of adding the computer to the network, do the following:

1. Go to the client computer and log on by using an account with administrative privileges.

2. Run Internet Explorer and connect, as Local Administrator, to the website `http://<SBS Server Name>/ConnectComputer`.

■**Note** If you are using Microsoft Windows XP with Service Pack 2, you'll have to place this site in the trusted zone in Internet Explorer. To do so, go to the Tools menu, select Internet Options, and then navigate to the Security tab. Click Trusted Sites, click the Sites button, and then type the URL in the Add This Website to the Zone text box. Click the Add button and then click OK.

---

3. Follow the instructions on the web page to complete the computer's account activation. The process of installing the client software will commence shortly after the computer account is activated.

Installing Application Software

Assigning new application software to the list of software you install when using the Set Up Computer Wizard is fairly straightforward. To allow the SBS 2003 server to deliver the installation routine for the application to the client computer, you'll need to copy the entire contents of the installation media to a shared folder on the network. In most cases, this should be underneath the preexisting `ClientApps` default share. This folder can be found on the SBS 2003 server under the `C:\ClientApps` folder (unless you shifted it during SBS 2003 setup).

Note The key to understanding application installation is to know that every application is different. Many applications autorun when you pop the CD in your optical drive, so you don't get to see what goes on under the hood. This is great for normal usage, but to automate the task in this way, you need to know the command being executed by the operating system to install the software. In many cases, the software will have a setup.exe program that must be run, and many applications have command-line switches for silent installations, logged installations, and so on. The user manual for the software will tell you what needs to be done for each unique application. It's also worth noting that some applications (mainly Microsoft ones) can perform what's called an administrative installation: all the setup files are copied to the network share to make sure any subsequent installation from this point can access all the necessary files. To perform an administrative setup, consult the product guide for the relevant software to see if it's possible. If you cannot perform an administrative installation, simply copy the entire contents of the installation media to the network share being used on your server.

The following procedure can be applied to any software that has the ability to be installed by using a command-line procedure:

1. Click Start ➤ Server Management.

2. In the left window pane, highlight Client Computers.

3. In the right-hand window, click Set Up Client Applications. This starts the Set Up Client Applications Wizard.

4. On the Welcome screen, click Next.

5. On the Available Applications page, click Add.

6. In the Application Name field, type the name of the application as it will be identified in the list of available applications. This should be in plain English and understandable to your users.

7. In the Location of Setup Executable for this application file, type the full network path of the setup file, including any switches that apply to the application's installation routine. Click OK. (This also applies to Microsoft Installer files that come with their own installation description database file with the extension .msi).

8. The application is added to your list of available applications. If you want to remove an application installation, highlight it and click Remove. When finished, click Next.

9. On the last page of the wizard, review your choices and click Finish.

If you remove an application from your available applications list, don't forget to remove the installation files from the server. The application installation files can take up a lot of disk space, and if you are short of space, you might still consider using the original installation media and taking a trip to the user's desk. Although automation of management tasks is always preferable over slower manual intervention, automation always comes at a cost.

Note Make sure you remove all old versions of applications from your users' systems because these can take up loads of disk space and add no value at all to the workstation.

Removing a Computer Account

If you decide a computer should no longer have a computer account on your network, it's good practice to delete the computer account, leaving the computer unable to participate in domain activities. It's recommended that the client should always remove itself from the network by using the network wizard on the workstation, but if this is not possible, you can use the following procedure:

1. Click Start ➤ Server Management.

2. In the left window pane, highlight Client Computers.

3. Highlight the computer for which you want to remove the account. Then click Remove Computer from Network.

4. Click OK.

Adding a Server Account

Server computers can also be easily added or removed from the network, just in case you have expanded to a multiple-server environment since the initial installation of your system.

Note Remember, you can add as many member servers as you like to the SBS 2003 domain. You can even add further domain controllers as long as they hold none of the Flexible Single Master Objects (FSMO) roles for the forest. They can still be set up as Global Catalog servers and still perform authentication, which can be useful in a more distributed environment.

To add a server account to the Active Directory, do the following:

1. Click Start ➤ Server Management.

2. In the left window pane, highlight Server Computers.

3. In the right-hand window, click Set Up Server Computers. This starts the Set Up Server Wizard.

4. On the Welcome screen, click Next.

5. Type in the name of the server computer and then click Next.

6. It's good practice to assign a static address to your servers, so click the Use the Following Static IP Address radio button and type in the IP address and subnet you've set aside for this system. Click Next.

7. If the system prompts you that the DHCP server could assign an address to the server, ignore this and click OK.

8. You will now need to log in to the server with an Administrative account, as with the client, and visit the `http://<sbs server name>/ConnectComputer` website address to complete the server account creation process.

Managing Active Directory and GPOs

The Active Directory is the core data service, holding information on everything to do with your network, your users, and your computers, and acting as the governor over absolutely everything that goes on with your SBS 2003 infrastructure. For this reason, it's a good idea to understand at least a little about what it does under the hood.

The key things a directory service brings to a networking environment are the following:

- *Security*: The AD contains every one of the infrastructure's user accounts, computer accounts, shares, and peripherals. Each of these items is securely stored on the domain controller, where only authorized users can gain access to the data. The AD acts as the data store for all security-related functions happening on your infrastructure and manages discrete security technologies such as Public Key Infrastructure, Kerberos (for user, computer, and certificate authentication), and delegation of administration capabilities. The AD also manages the authentication services provided by the primary AD server-type, known as a domain controller.

Note The AD contains some objects in their own right, such as users and security groups, as well as containing information about other types of objects, such as printers.

- *Directory service*: Because the AD contains an abundance of data related to the SBS 2003 infrastructure, it seems only sensible that this "directory" is used by users and applications to look up information that they are allowed to view. The AD can be used to store and search for email contacts, users' names, printers, and network shares. Think of it as an electronic version of the phone book.

- *Delegation of administration*: The security model of the AD allows it to be partitioned by using NTFS-like permissions to delegate access to directory objects. Certain users can have more permissions than others, meaning they have more control over what happens to the objects stored in the AD. By inference, this method of applying permissions to AD objects allows us to delegate the authority for managing certain AD attributes to individual users or groups of users deemed responsible for management practices.

As you've already seen earlier in this chapter, the AD is split into various organizational units, and these OUs contain objects that can have policies applied to them for controlling their behavior. This is just part of the whole AD story, and I'll go into more detail soon on how to create OUs, how to create GPOs, and how to connect them so that you can start asserting control over your directory objects.

First, however, we'll take a walk through the different interfaces you can use to manage your AD, starting with the standard Windows Server 2003 tools for looking at your AD and how it's configured.

Note Remember that the SBS 2003 platform is based on Windows Server 2003, and although there are constraints on the number of users, computers, domains, and trusts you can have within an SBS 2003 domain, the underlying Windows Server 2003 operating system remains the same.

To see exactly how the AD is configured, we'll be stepping away from the SBS 2003 Server Management tools, and into the tool used by system administrators running large-scale Windows Server 2003 infrastructures.

Creating a Custom Management Console

Nearly every aspect of the operating system is managed through a highly customizable interface called the *Microsoft Management Console (MMC)*. This is effectively an empty toolbox that tools can be added to, offering a consistent interface to all aspects of the operating system. As many tools as you need can be snapped into a single interface. You can also create subsets of individual tools to delegate certain management tasks to users who don't require total control over that aspect of the operating system.

To create a customized MMC for looking at your AD, do the following:

1. Click Start ➤ Run.

2. Type mmc and press Enter.

3. Click File ➤ Add/Remove Snap-in.

4. Click the Add button. This brings up the complete list of all MMC-compatible tools on your server (this also works on Windows 2000 and Windows XP workstations).

5. There are three primary AD management tools you can select from the list. Highlight each one in turn and click Add. The three tools are Active Directory Domains and Trusts, Active Directory Sites and Services, and Active Directory Users and Computers.

6. After you've added all three, click Close.

7. Click OK.

8. Click File ➤ Options.

9. At the top of the screen, change the name of the console to **AD Management**.

10. Drop down the Console Mode menu and select User Mode—Limited Access, Multiple Window.

11. Click OK.

12. Click File ➤ Save. Rename the file **AD Management** and save it on the Desktop.

13. Close the console and open it again.

Note You'll notice that the only management console available directly from the Server Management console is the Active Directory Users and Computers, and even this is available only through the Advanced Management node of the console. This is because the rest of these AD functions are largely related to multidomain, multidomain-controller environments, where you need to manage server replication and authentication services from other domains. These facilities are all available from the Control Panel ➤ Administrative Tools menu.

This AD Management console can be used to view and manage all aspects of the AD. If you want a tool to manage any of the other tasks related to the SBS 2003 infrastructure (available as a snap-in through the MMC interface), you can create another console dedicated to the feature. This means that you can create a customized toolbox that suits the work you do on your system, rather than having to use individual tools and interfaces. It's possible to have an MMC snap-in with all the tools installed at once, but in this case the interface would be impossible to navigate around. Make useful tools, and if you don't require them anymore, delete them—it's no hardship to create them again when needed.

For informational purposes only, expand the Active Directory Domains and Trusts node. You'll see that the only domain listed is your SBS 2003 domain. If you were using a standard Windows Server 2003 infrastructure, all of your domains and the trusts between them would be shown here. If you right-click on your domain name and select Raise Domain Functional Level, you'll see this is by default set to Windows Server 2003. The Domain Functional Level is set to allow no interworking with down-level Windows domain controllers from either Windows 2000 networks or Windows NT networks. I realize this is largely irrelevant for you as an SBS 2003 user, but I think it's important that you understand where you sit within the Windows Server 2003 family of servers, and what the differences are. If you outgrow SBS 2003 and intend to move to a full Windows Server 2003 infrastructure, all these items will become of paramount importance.

Try expanding the Active Directory Sites and Services node and then expand Sites and take a look around. Many of these features are irrelevant in a single-domain, single-server infrastructure (like many SBS 2003 installations) because replication between domain controllers is not a consideration and site links are not relevant. However, for more-advanced users with an SBS 2003 infrastructure that has been expanded to include backup domain controllers and to span multiple Active Directory sites, these tools become a valuable interface exposing how things are really working. Look at Figure 5-10 to see a test environment's Sites and Services node.

Note An SBS 2003 installation can have as many domain controllers as you like so long as you remember to have all the FSMO roles located on the SBS 2003 server. For more information on FSMO roles and how they are manipulated, see `http://support.microsoft.com/default.aspx?scid=kb;en-us;324801`.

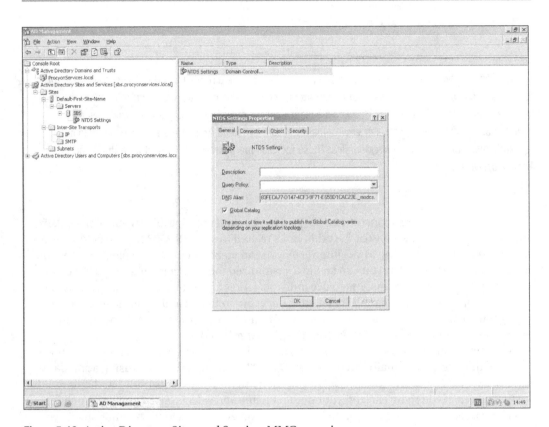

Figure 5-10. *Active Directory Sites and Services MMC snap-in*

Managing Users

Practically all management tasks carried out in an SBS 2003 infrastructure are concentrated on manipulating elements of the AD through the Active Directory Users and Computers MMC snap-in. This snap-in (available through the Server Management/Advanced Management console) allows you to perform important management tasks, without having to run the individual (and in many cases more-limited) management interfaces available through the Standard Management components of the Server Management console.

The following AD management tasks can be performed through the Active Directory Users and Computers snap-in or from the tool on the Control Panel ➤ Administrative Tools menu:

- *Account management*: Users' account information can be updated and new users created inside any OU or default container. Users can also be added to security groups and deleted from security groups by using this interface.

- *Delegation of control*: Users and security groups can be delegated elements of the AD to have control over. Delegation can be assigned to the top-level domain container or any lower-level OU.

- *Security groups*: Security groups can be created inside any OU and can be nested in other security groups if necessary.

- *OUs*: Using this facility, you can create or delete OUs, nest OUs, and delegate rights and permissions to the management of OUs. GPOs can also be assigned to OUs by using this facility.

Managing your users is important, and it's useful to get to know your way around the user account properties dialog box to get a feel for exactly what information can be stored for a user in the AD. Take the Administrator's account, for example (see Figure 5-11). The following list explains what each tab under the user properties page is used for, and how the information in there is used elsewhere by the AD or other applications. The impact of modifying information in each tab is also covered as follows:

- *General*: Here you enter the user's name, description, and some general information about who the user is, their telephone number, and contact email address. All this information is indexed and searchable from the AD.

- *Address*: On the Address tab, you can enter a complete postal address for the user's location. This could either be a business or personal address and is also indexed and searchable from the AD.

- *Account*: The information configurable via the Account tab is important in deciding how a user logs on. When a user authenticates on the system, by default she uses the pre-Windows 2000 logon name (the short name) identified when the administrator created her account. This can be modified to a user name in email format by giving the user a logon name (top of the screen), and then clicking the drop-down list and selecting the email suffix for the domain. Through this interface, you can limit the hours a user is permitted to log on to the system, as well as limiting which machines she can log on to. You can also force a user to change her password the next time she logs in, set a few other password-specific security measures, and unlock locked accounts.

Note Limiting the user's ability to log on only during normal office hours is a great security enhancement. Any unauthorized attempt to access company resources during the less-supervised hours of the evening and night are denied, as is any attempt the user might make to log in from home.

- *Profile*: As discussed earlier in this chapter, this tab is used to configure the location of the user's profile and can be used also to map a network drive automatically to a server location for the user to store personal documents.

- *Telephones*: As with the other user information pages, the Telephones tab can contain a list of all the user's telephone numbers, including his fax number and IP telephone number if applicable.

- *Organization*: The Organization tab allows you to store details about the user's position in your company. Again, this information is indexed and searchable through the AD.

- *Terminal Services Profile*: When a user is accessing the server by using terminal services rather than a direct connection from a workstation, you should always set up a different profile for that kind of connection. Applications work differently in a terminal server environment, so it's essential that this profile is in a different place and maintained as a separate entity.

Note Terminal services allows you to connect to a Windows server (and hence domain) from a client computer that is not itself necessarily a domain member (possibly from a home computer or a system in an Internet café). The workstation is sent a replica desktop so that it mimics a Windows desktop (provided from the server) from within the domain. You log in through this interface as if your system were on the SBS 2003 network, and the desktop will appear similar to that of your fixed office machine (with all the same access rights you'd have if you logged on to a workstation on the domain). It's highly recommended that if you are going to use a terminal services style of connection for your workforce, it's best to farm out the responsibility to a member server. The load on your SBS 2003 server would be too great, and the end result would degrade both the server functions and the user's acquired desktop.

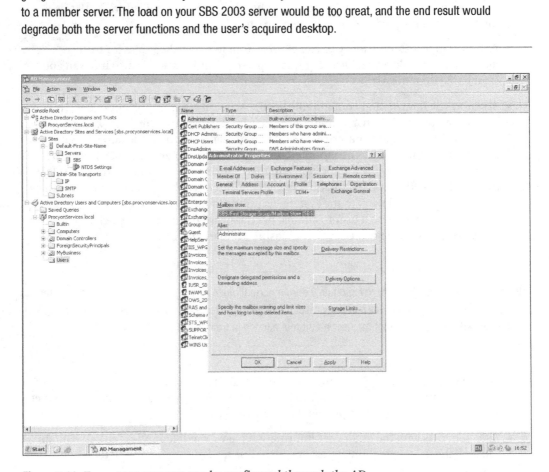

Figure 5-11. *Every user account can be configured through the AD.*

- *COM+*: This tab is used to configure the "COM+ partition set" the user is a member of. This is an application setting and should be of little consequence to you as a standard SBS 2003 administrator.

- *Exchange General*: Much of the user-related Exchange email administration can be done from the user account properties dialog. Through the various Exchange-related tabs, you can configure mailboxes, limits, mail forwarding, and messaging services, and modify your users' email addresses. In Chapter 7, you'll learn more about Exchange and messaging.

- *Email Addresses*: This tab displays the default email addresses assigned to the user account as well as offering the ability to add new email addresses for that user. The kinds of addresses you can add will depend on the message formats you have installed to support. By default there is an SMTP address and an X.400 address. You can also add in Microsoft Mail addresses, cc:Mail addresses, Lotus Notes addresses, and Novell GroupWise addresses. If you need to connect to any of these systems, you'll understand their significance; otherwise, they should remain unimportant to you. You can also add further email aliases so, for example, `psmith`, `paulsmith`, `pauls`, and `ps` could all be email aliases used by the user Paul Smith.

- *Exchange Features*: From this tab you can switch off certain Exchange services to the user in question. For example, you might decide to disable the user's Outlook Web Access capability.

- *Exchange Advanced*: This tab allows you to modify user accounts associated with Exchange mailboxes to do various advanced configuration tasks, such as hiding the user from the contact list and modifying mailbox permissions (say, for example, you wanted multiple users to access a single email account).

- *Member Of*: This tab displays a list of all the security groups the user is a member of. You can also add the user to new security groups if desired and remove the user account from any that are no longer required.

- *Dial-in*: All the elements of remote dial-up and VPN access are configured from this tab. After the user has the connectivity enabled on his workstation, this tab can be used to set callback options, assign IP addresses, and add in a static network route for the user in case assigning the IP address was not enough to gain access to the back-end server resources.

- *Environment*: This tab is used to define an advanced desktop configuration for terminal server users, such as running a particular application on the remote desktop and mapping various remote devices and drives.

- *Sessions*: Another terminal server tab used to manage the individual session when the user connects to the terminal server session. Even if a user disconnects from a terminal server session, the session remains active (and can be reestablished) until disconnected at the server. You can set an automatic time-out of up to two days as well as managing other session characteristics, such as where the client can reconnect from and the number of permitted active sessions on the server.

- *Remote Control*: Remote control is the ability granted to an authorized user (such as the administrator) to remotely access or monitor what's happening on a user's workstation. The capability can be limited to simply viewing the user's session or alternatively the administrator can interact with it, moving the mouse and executing commands.

Delegating Administration

A useful feature provided by the combination of Active Directory, organizational units, and group policy is the ability to delegate administrative capabilities to certain users over the objects contained in specified OUs. You can assign control of certain facets of your infrastructure to individual users without having to give them an administrative account. This is a key point in maintaining control over your assets as well as keeping the security of your system intact—users with delegated rights can do only what you let them, whereas legitimate administrators have free reign to do whatever they like. Certain key users, for example, a team leader, might be given the rights to reset users' passwords within his own team. By doing this, you've devolved the responsibility of password management to lower-ranking users (in an administrative context) and left the domain-wide administrative functions to members of your IT team.

Administrative control can be delegated to any level of the OU structure by using the Delegation of Control Wizard (see Figure 5-12).

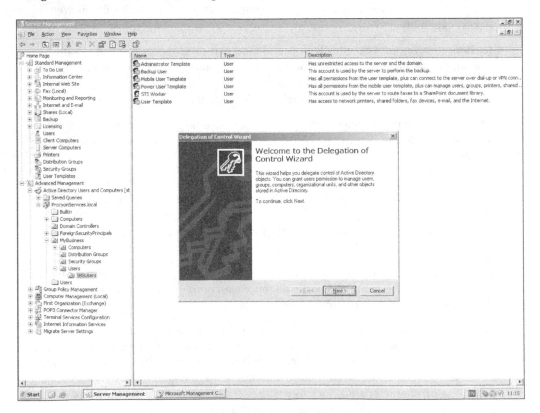

Figure 5-12. *The Delegation of Control Wizard devolves responsibility.*

To run the wizard:

1. Right-click on the OU container holding the users or groups you wish to delegate rights to. Select Delegate Control and then click Next.

2. Click Add to select users or groups you wish to delegate responsibility to.

3. Click Advanced to search the Active Directory for users and groups.

4. Highlight the appropriate user or group and click OK.

5. Click OK again to add this user or group to the list. Click Next.

6. You can now select from a set of typical tasks, the ones you'd like to delegate to your selected user or group. Click Next.

7. Read the summary and then click Finish to complete the wizard.

Note It's a good idea to document all delegation of control to make sure you have a total picture of who can do what on your system. When you are delegating control of certain tasks to users, make sure those users are fully briefed on their responsibilities and understand how to use the tools to perform their duties.

Using Group Policies

The final piece of the Active Directory puzzle is learning how group policies work to control the objects you've placed inside your infrastructure's organizational units. The combination of shares, permissions, rights, and GPOs will give you total control over everything that occurs on your network. It's this level of total control over your system that ensures your computers, users, and resources remain stable, your users get access to only the information they require, and your network remains secure.

Note In case you're wondering about the difference between an OU and a security group, it's quite straightforward. A user account can exist in only a single OU (also referred to as a container) but can be a member of as many security groups as required. Policies applied to OUs affect all the objects inside that OU. Security groups are used to control the permissions a user has to individual objects, such as files and folders. OUs are primarily there for administrative purposes to divide the high-level resources you need to control within your domain. To fully understand how they work in relation to each other, it is best to not even try to decide which should be used. You will always need both technologies, configured correctly, to ensure that you are in total control of your network. You should try to associate security groups with permissions, while OUs should be thought of as administrative partitions.

GPOs should be considered as basically a collection of configuration settings that are applied to objects in your Active Directory. The most fundamental level of control over objects in your Active Directory is the application of GPOs to the organizational unit, so you need to create an OU structure that reflects how you want the business managed.

For SBS 2003 users, Microsoft has attempted to do all the hard work for you, creating a set of OUs and GPOs that will control the infrastructure well enough for most small business users. GPO management is an advanced topic and is extremely complicated when you get right down to looking at every setting—there are highly paid consultants who do this sort of thing for a living—so it's impossible in the context of this book to really go into too much detail. What we will do is look inside one of the default GPOs supplied as standard with the product and look at how some of those settings might be modified to suit your needs, such as delegating the Internet Explorer default home page for all your users to be on your company's intranet site.

All members of an OU will assume the settings delivered to it by every single GPO that has governance over that OU. Lower-level OUs will inherit the settings of parent containers unless you specifically block inheritance at that level.

There are three settings that any item in a GPO can assume—enabled, disabled, and not configured—and as you learned earlier in this chapter, GPOs can be configured to be applied either on a user basis or a computer as follows:

- GPOs that are configured to modify the settings of the user accounts in the OUs that the GPO has been applied to, modify the Registry on the user's machine under the `HKEY_CURRENT_USER` Registry key.

- GPOs that are configured to modify the settings of any computer in the OU that the GPO has been applied to, modify the Registry on the user's machine under the `HKEY_LOCAL_MACHINE` Registry key.

Group policies are not only inherited through the OU tree structure, but are also cumulative as you progress down through the tree. This means that policies applied to the lowest container in the tree are only part of the overall policy picture for that container. You have to take the sum of all GPOs cascading down from above unless you've specifically blocked inheritance at some point in the hierarchy.

Warning The more GPOs you create and assign to your OU infrastructure, the harder job you'll have keeping track of who has access to what resources and what policies are causing certain functions to work or not work. Troubleshooting GPOs is the bane of most Windows Server 2003 administrators' lives, and although there are now tools available with the operating system to help, such as Resultant Set of Policy (RSoP), many administrators still turn to expensive management tools when the business is large enough to merit. In your case, with SBS 2003, the trick is, keep it simple. Always remember to give your GPOs relevant names so you understand their purpose in the Active Directory.

SBS 2003 comes with its usual Server Management interface to help manage this aspect of your infrastructure, removing the need to get under the hood. In this case, GPOs are most definitely best managed from this interface.

So, without further ado, let's take a look at the Group Policy Management console:

1. Click Start ➤ Server Management.

2. Expand the Advanced Management node and then click Group Policy Management.

3. In the Contents pane on the right side of the screen, double-click your domain name.

4. Double-click Domains and again double-click on your domain name.

5. You will now see the five default GPOs created especially for SBS 2003.

6. Right-click the GPO called Small Business Server Domain Password Policy and select Edit.

7. You'll now see the Group Policy Object Editor. Under Computer Configuration, expand Windows Settings and then expand Security Settings.

8. Now expand Account Policies and highlight Password Policy (see Figure 5-13).

9. In the right-hand window, you'll see the Password Policy settings being applied to your SBS users.

The settings you see in the right-hand window define the policy set for this particular aspect of system control; in this case, your password policy. Six settings can be configured for your users in this case:

- Enforce Password History

- Maximum Password Age

- Minimum Password Age

- Minimum Password Length

- Password Must Meet Complexity Requirements

- Store Passwords Using Reversible Encryption

The great thing about GPOs, and one of the finest features delivered with Windows Server 2003 (in my opinion), is the amazing help facilities built into the operating system for creating and understanding what each setting within a policy actually does. Pick any setting, such as Enforce Password History, and right-click on it. Select Help from the context menu and you'll be presented with a detailed description of exactly what that setting does and how it should be configured.

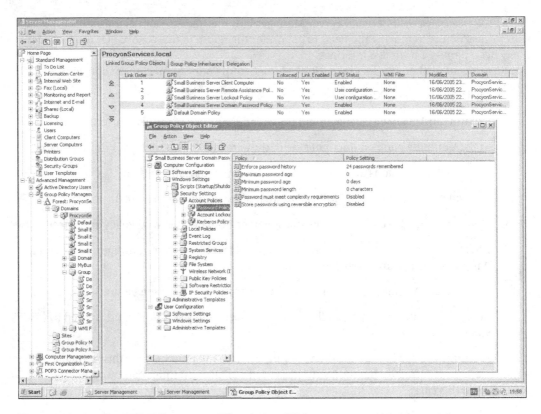

Figure 5-13. *Use the GPO Editor to modify existing GPOs.*

There is no point in this book reiterating the description of each of these settings and how they each affect the user, but as an overview of this example, it's sufficient to say the following:

- The system will remember the last 24 passwords used by your users and prohibit their reuse until the 25th occasion of changing the password.

- There is no minimum or maximum age for a password, and there is no minimum length a password has to be.

- There is no enforcement of complex passwords, and the system is not required to store the passwords in any manner other than in the standard Windows Server 2003 fashion.

If you close the Group Policy Object Editor and double-click on the Small Business Server Domain Password Policy GPO, you're taken to a new screen where you can view the details of that GPO in a summary format. Now, click the Settings tab at the top of the screen and you'll be presented with a cut-down list of only the policy settings that have been configured within this GPO (see Figure 5-14).

Warning The main drawback of using this interface is that you have no access to the help facility that you have when using the GPO Editor. I'd always recommend using the GPO Editor unless you are sure that you know what the settings mean. You cannot edit the GPO from here, only view the setting that will apply.

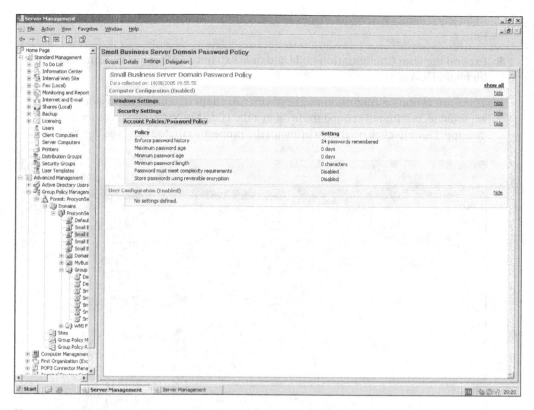

Figure 5-14. *Effective settings for a GPO through Server Management*

Creating a Brand New GPO

So, you've decided you want to try your hand at creating a new GPO, one that stops users from having the My Network Places icon on their workstation desktop. This might be to simplify the users' experience of your system, removing options that they might only misuse and waste time experimenting with, and alleviate any security concerns caused by exposing this capability to the user.

The following procedure will help you understand the entire process for creating and linking GPOs, as well as look at Resultant Set of Policy (RSoP) and inheritance:

1. Click Start ➤ Server Management.

2. Expand the Advanced Management node and then click Group Policy Management.

3. Expand the domain name node and then expand Domains.

4. Again, expand your domain name. Underneath the five default GPOs for SBS 2003, you'll see a node called Group Policy Objects. Right-click on it and select New.

5. Give your new GPO a meaningful name, such as **Remove Network Places**, and then click OK.

6. Remove Network Places is added to the list of available GPOs. You'll notice that it's enabled by default. At this point, the GPO will do nothing because it has not yet been assigned.

7. Right-click Remove Network Places and select Edit. This starts the Group Policy Object Editor.

8. Expand the User Configuration node and then expand Administrative Templates and highlight Desktop.

9. There are various configuration settings you can adapt to control the users' desktop experience, but for now concentrate on just the Hide My Network Places icon on the desktop. Double-click on this to bring up the properties dialog box (see Figure 5-15).

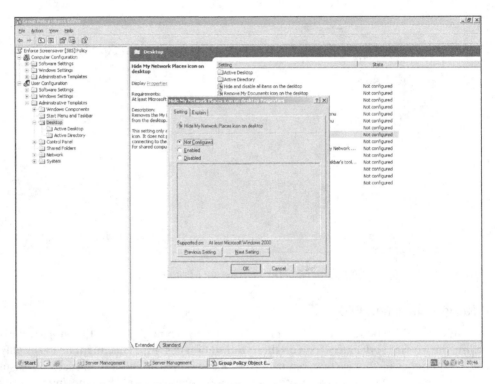

Figure 5-15. *Configure the GPO properties box for each setting.*

10. Click the Enabled radio button and then click Apply.

Warning Make sure to carefully read each GPO setting's description before you decide to modify it. You should pay especially close attention to the tense of the phrasing. It's easy to misinterpret what is intended and end up turning something off rather than on.

---

11. Click OK.

12. Close the Group Policy Object Editor.

13. On the left-hand side of the screen, right-click on your domain name (beneath the Domains container) and click Link an Existing GPO.

14. Select your new GPO name from the list of available policies and click OK. Your new GPO now appears in the list of applied, active GPOs on your server.

Deleting a Group Policy Object

Deleting a GPO from the list is as easy as right-clicking that GPO and selecting Delete.

Policy Modeling

We've talked about the RSoP capability for looking at which settings apply to a user. Now it's time to put this into practice. The tool we'll be looking at to see the cumulative effect of all the policies in your domain is called the Group Policy Modeling Wizard and is available through the Server Management console. Follow these steps:

1. Click Start ➤ Server Management.

2. Expand the Advanced Management node and then click Group Policy Management.

3. Expand the domain name and highlight Group Policy Modeling.

4. Right-click on the object and select Group Policy Modeling Wizard.

5. On the Welcome screen, click Next.

6. Click Next on the following screen, because you have only one domain and one forest.

7. Select either the computer or user container, and if you want some-lower level OU, click Browse and select the one you are interested in. When ready, click Next.

8. On the following page, click Next.

9. On the User Security Groups page, select Everyone and click Next.

10. On the WMI Filters for Users page, select All Linked Filters and then click Next.

11. On the Summary of Selections page, click Next.

12. On the final page, click Finish.

You are now presented with the Group Policy Modeling screen, where the results of the model you just ran can be analyzed. Click the Settings tab to see exactly which policy settings have been configured for the criteria you selected during the setting up of the model. If you expand User Configuration and then click Administrative Templates ➤ Desktop, you'll see the policy setting you created in the previous walk-though: Hide My Network Places icon on the desktop.

Managing Your Network

As with your users and computers, your network also requires a certain amount of ongoing management, although SBS 2003 is fairly good at managing all of this for you. In this section, you'll learn how to manage the following aspects of your network infrastructure:

- DHCP

- DNS

- Remote Web Workplace

- Remote control of servers and workstations

DHCP

DHCP is used to assign IP addresses and other important network configurations to client systems on your network that don't have a static address. This is a great way of controlling your IP address allocations because there is no need to visit each client computer and type in the same details over and over again. DHCP gives you the following benefits:

- It automatically assigns IP addresses to client computers from a predefined pool.

- It configures clients with the appropriate subnet mask, default gateway/router, DNS server addresses, WINS server address, and other specialized network options appropriate for your environment.

- It can be used to partition the network so that some machines have a fixed address while others have a dynamic address assigned from the pool.

- It centralizes control of IP addressing and IP configuration.

By default, SBS 2003 sets you up with a private network using the 192.168.x.x address range, so in essence you don't need to worry about running out of addresses (you have way more than SBS 2003 will allow you to connect anyway) and the default gateway is automatically assigned to your clients, as are the subnet mask and DNS servers.

However, it's still worth having a look at DHCP, just to explore the interface and see how some of the key components of the service function:

1. Click Start ➤ Server Management.

2. Expand the Advanced Management node and then expand Computer Management (Local).

3. Expand Services and Applications and then highlight DHCP.

4. In the right-hand window, you'll see the active scope (the set of IP addresses available to the DHCP service). Double-click Scope.

5. Double-click Address Pool. Here you will see the list of any IP addresses excluded from the DHCP pool, as well as the subnet the server has available to assign addresses from.

6. On the left side of the screen, highlight Address Leases. You are presented with a list of all active IP addresses currently assigned to client computers.

Note To see how these addresses are assigned on a workstation, log on as the administrator and click Start ➤ Run. Open a command prompt by typing `cmd` and pressing Enter. At the command prompt, type `ipconfig/all` and press Enter. This command displays the IP addressing details of that workstation and informs you of whether the address is assigned from a DHCP server or is fixed on that machine.

---

7. On the left side again, highlight Reservations. From this screen, you can exclude certain addresses from ever being allocated to your network clients. If any of your other network systems require a fixed IP address (for instance, a printer), you should add a reservation into this list. To add a reservation, right-click on the Reservations node on the left side of the screen and select New Reservation. Fill in the details of the reservation, along with a meaningful description (see Figure 5-16), to ensure that this address remains unallocated by the DHCP service. It's a recommended good practice to reserve the first 10 addresses in your address space for servers, printers, and other such hardwired IP clients.

8. After you've added a reservation, click OK to continue.

9. On the left side of the screen, highlight Scope Options. This displays a default list of optional extra pieces of information that DHCP can configure on your system, as well as the IP address and subnet mask. The options preconfigured on an SBS 2003 server are the default gateway (003 Router), a list of DNS servers (006 DNS Servers), the DNS domain name of your network (015 DNS Domain Name), and two further options for a network system known as the Windows Internet Naming Service (WINS), which is required to support aspects of the Exchange 2003 messaging system.

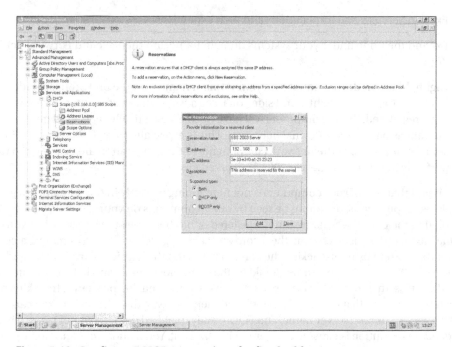

Figure 5-16. *Configure DHCP reservations for fixed addresses.*

10. Further options can be added to your DHCP server if needed. To add an extra option, highlight Server Options on the left side, right-click, and select Configure Options.

11. On the Server Options screen, you'll see a list of approximately 60 server options that can be configured to be sent with the IP address to your network clients. More than likely you'll never need to set any of these options during your running of an SBS 2003 system, but it's worth knowing about the interface, just in case.

If your client computer is having problems with its IP address for any reason, it's worth flushing the old IP address from it and telling it to ask the server for a new one. From the command prompt on a workstation, do the following:

1. Type **ipconfig /release** and then press Enter. This releases the workstation's hold over the address and effectively returns it to the pool for reuse by the DHCP server.

2. To obtain a new address, type **ipconfig /renew** and then press Enter.

3. To see what the newly assigned IP address is, type **ipconfig /all** and then press Enter.

DNS

As with DHCP, the SBS 2003 server manages this for you, but it's still worth knowing where the interface is and what you're looking at when there's a problem. To open the DNS management interface, do the following:

1. Click Start ➤ Server Management.

2. Expand the Advanced Management node and then expand Computer Management (Local).

3. Expand Services and Applications and then expand DNS.

4. Expand the node under your system's domain name and then expand Forward Lookup Zones.

5. Highlight the node that equates to your domain name (not the one prefixed with _msdcs). Then on the right-hand side you'll see a list of all the computers that have been registered. These computers will have been automatically registered on the domain as part of their normal operation. This is especially true of Windows XP Professional computers, as the network components of the workstation are designed to work perfectly in a Windows Server 2003 networked environment.

If you find that one of your computers is not functioning properly in the domain, not getting deployed applications, or cannot be seen by other computers on your network, look in DNS. If you find that the computer's name is not registered or has been registered incorrectly, you can delete the old record by right-clicking the record and selecting Delete. Then try creating a new record for that system by right-clicking the domain name (on the left side of the screen) and selecting New Host (A). The hostname should be the computer's name, and if the computer has a static IP address, this should be registered here. If you are still having problems, try taking out a DHCP reservation for that client's IP address, and then re-create the DNS record. You can also try pinging the IP address, server name, and FQDN (fully qualified domain name) to see which aspect of name resolution is causing problems with this host. You'll find a reference to pinging in Chapter 12.

Remote Web Workplace

Telecommuting was never an option for us. We needed to be at work to accomplish any work. Off-line folders and the like helped immensely but could not fill in some of the gaps. Since we have had the new SBS server, working from home has been a breeze. I can work from a web café, a client's site, or home. I can remote in and do administration from my PDA or a remote office. I can add or remove users and then RWW in and check that their profile worked. It has drastically slashed downtime and travel.

—Michael Jenkin, IT manager, Copyworld

The Remote Web Workplace (RWW) is simply a website on your server that offers browser-compatible interfaces for accessing email (Outlook Web Access) and your intranet SharePoint website, and allows you to activate fully fledged remote desktop connections by using a terminal services client.

Accessing the Remote Web Workplace is as easy as a user authenticating on the normal LAN. He simply navigates to the website (using Internet Explorer): `https://<fqdn of the server>/Remote`.

Note FQDN is the full DNS name of the server, including the server's own name prefixed on the domain name for your infrastructure—for example, `sbsserver.procyon-services.co.uk`.

The logon page looks very like a standard Windows Server 2003 logon page, so all a user needs to do is use his domain credentials to gain access to the primary Remote Web Workplace interface. Here he will see links to email, intranet, and various other features he has been authorized to access.

Note It's good to know that the RWW is extremely secure and you will be introducing no further vulnerabilities by implementing it in your network infrastructure. It uses a certificate-based access system for authorizing connections, and along with the underlying port translation service that masks the internal network's identity from the Internet, you can rest assured that the RWW gives great benefit without the risk.

Remote Control of Servers and Workstations

From any workstation or server where a Remote Desktop Protocol (RDP) client has been installed (most Windows Server 2003 servers and Windows XP Professional workstations come with these as standard), you can connect to the Remote Desktop capability on any other machine and take control of that system.

■**Note** If you want to use the RDP client via the RWW, it will require the use of client-side ActiveX to be permitted, and you'll also have to open port 4125 on your firewall/router. You can do this by using ISA Server (see Chapter 8), or on the router supplied by your ISP. RWW is *not* the same as Remote Desktop and should not be confused with this technology.

The terminal services (RDP) client can be found under the Start menu on Windows XP workstations, by clicking Start ➤ All Programs ➤ Accessories ➤ Communications ➤ Remote Desktop Connection. To access any machine on your network, type in the computer's name and click OK. This will present you with a dialog box for logging on to that computer. If you are planning to perform administrative tasks on that computer, log in by using the Administrator account.

Auditing and Accounting

In an SBS 2003 business environment, security policies are used to govern what is allowed to happen on the computers on your network. The application of these security policies is controlled centrally (from your SBS 2003 server) and delivered to both servers and client computers by using GPOs.

When client computers boot, a series of actions occur as the system identifies itself to the server, authenticating itself and receiving security policies before any users are allowed to log on.

The term *auditing* refers to the collection of pertinent events that are recorded in the *Windows event logs*. It's these logs that are used to diagnose hardware faults, track security breaches, and locate software errors and database corruptions.

By using the Server Management interface, it's possible to configure a high-level diagnostic facility called Monitoring and Reporting that records information from many sources and creates reports about your server's health. These reports can then be forwarded to a responsible person (or persons) by email to make sure any serious notifications are followed up before any significant problem occurs.

To configure your system to collect and report server health information, do the following:

1. Click Start ➤ Server Management.

2. Under Standard Management, highlight Monitoring and Reporting.

3. On the right-hand side of the screen, click Set Up Monitoring Reports and Alerts.

4. On the Welcome page of the Monitoring Configuration Wizard, click Next.

5. Select both of the available check boxes: Performance Report and Usage Report. Also select to have a usage report sent to you by email every other week. This automatically sends you the report, reminding you to keep an eye on what's really happening on your server. (These would have already been set up when you ran through the To Do List). Click Next.

6. On the next page, type the email address of the system administrator. Click Next.

7. The next page, Business Owner Usage Report, asks you to select the users who are allowed to see the usage report. An email notification will be sent to these users when the report is available. Click Next.

8. On the Alerts page, select the check box to be sent email notifications of alerts generated on your system. This should always be selected because alerts can warn of potentially critical problems building up on your server. Type the appropriate email address for your administrator and then click Next.

9. On the final page of the wizard, review your selections and then click Finish.

You won't have any data to look at when you first configure Monitoring and Reporting, and, as the system warns you, you might have to wait until the following day to see how your system is really performing (see Figure 5-17).

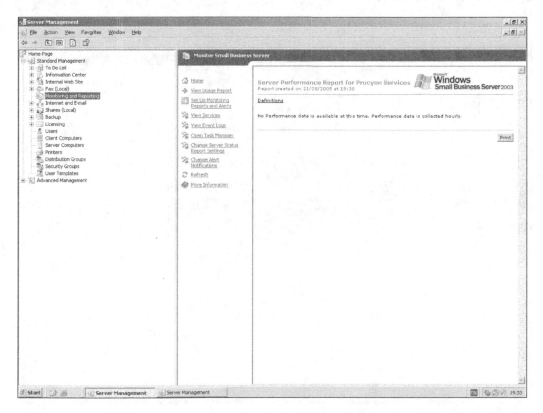

Figure 5-17. *You'll have to wait 24 hours to receive your first report.*

As with all SBS 2003 application defaults, Microsoft has tried to make as best a guess as possible at determining how the average small business would configure its auditing capability, but you need to bear in mind that the underlying auditing engine of Windows Server 2003 is capable of a whole lot more.

Windows Server 2003 is in use across the globe in many high-security establishments, protecting the secrets of governments, banks, the military, and giant commercial conglomerates as well as your own business information. The secret to getting the level of auditing right for your own business is to value your data appropriately. You might not demand the secrecy of the National Security Agency, but you sure don't want your data stolen by your competitors or staff, and you definitely don't want users with stolen passwords breaking into your network.

There are two elements to consider when designing your auditing capability:

- Which machine should you audit?

- How much data do you want to collect?

It's easiest to address both questions together, but first you need to know what's possible. You can collect data on any Windows-based workstation and server on your network. This data is stored in the local computer's event logs, and each audit record is stored in the form of an event (see Figure 5-18).

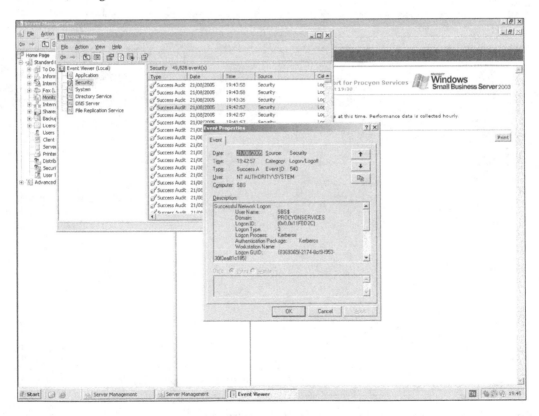

Figure 5-18. *Audit data is stored as events in the event logs.*

First, we'll look at your networked client computers. It's possible to switch on a comprehensive auditing regime across all computers on your network. To view the data, you connect remotely (from the server or another workstation) to the event log of the machine you are interested in looking at. The event logs that contain this information can be set to have a maximum size, and when that size is reached, the oldest event is overwritten, then the next one, then the next one...and so on.

By determining how much auditing information is appearing each day and multiplying that by the number of days you need to store, you can set the cyclic log size to be that value plus 20 percent for good measure. In this way, you have peace of mind that you can go in at any time to that computer's event logs and trace patterns of unusual behavior over whatever period of time you need.

The same philosophy stands for the server, but in this case it's worth holding as much audit information as possible because the server is the heart of your business network.

To switch on comprehensive security auditing on your SBS 2003 server, do the following:

1. Click Start ➤ Server Management.

2. Under Advanced Management, expand the Group Policy Management node.

3. Expand the child node with your domain name and then expand Domains.

4. Again expand the node with your business's domain name and then highlight Group Policy Objects.

5. Right-click Default Domain Controllers Policy and select Edit to start the Group Policy Object Editor.

6. In the GPO Editor, expand Computer Configuration, expand Windows Settings, and then expand Security Settings.

7. Now expand Local Polices. Highlight Audit Policy. On the right-hand side of the screen, you'll see the list of possible event types you can configure.

8. By double-clicking any of the events listed on the right, you'll get a dialog box that allows you to configure whether you collect successes or failures for each event type.

9. By default, many of these settings are set to Success. To change the events collected, simply select the appropriate check box and click OK.

Note In my experience, it's much better to record both successes and failures for events such as account logons. In this way, you can catch the user who's trying to guess someone else's password. If she's doing it here and failing, is it possible she succeeded somewhere else?

To configure the audit policy for all computer systems on your network, do the following:

1. Click Start ➤ Server Management.

2. Under Advanced Management, expand the Group Policy Management node.

3. Expand the child node with your domain name and then expand Domains.

4. Again expand the node with your business's domain name and then highlight Group Policy Objects.

5. Right-click Small Business Server Client Computer policy and select Edit to start the Group Policy Object Editor.

6. In the GPO Editor, expand Computer Configuration, expand Windows Settings, and then expand Security Settings.

7. Now expand Local Polices. Highlight Audit Policy. On the right-hand side of the screen, you'll see the list of possible event types you can configure. In the case of client computers, you will notice that none of the events are collected by default.

8. Double-click any event you want to collect. Select successes, failures, or both for all concerned.

Warning Remember, setting auditing on your client machines will potentially, depending on the policy settings you choose, cause those machines to collect large quantities of data. This data can be removed only by an authorized user (the administrator in most cases).

Using the Event Logs

When an application reports an error, or a security incident occurs, Windows generates an appropriate event. These are then recorded in the event log's later analysis. Windows XP, Windows NT, and Windows 2000 have three default event logs collecting information from applications, the operating system, and specialist events pertaining to security. These three logs are as follows:

- Application log

- Security log

- System log

On your SBS 2003 server, there are an additional three logs. These are as follows:

- Directory Service log

- DNS Server log

- File Replication Service log

To view an event log on a Windows XP Professional client computer, you can either connect to the event log over the network from your server or another workstation, or you can log in and access the logs locally.

To view any of the event logs on a Windows XP Professional client computer:

1. Click Start ➤ Settings.

2. Select Control Panel.

3. Double-click Administrative Tools and then double-click Event Viewer.

Viewing the logs on the server is easier. As always, there is an easy link to get to it from Server Management:

1. Click Start ➤ Server Management.

2. Highlight Monitoring and Reporting.

3. On the right-hand window, select View Event Logs.

From either a workstation or server, you can access event logs on another computer by right-clicking Event Viewer (Local) and selecting Connect to Another Computer.

There are many event types that can be recorded in the event logs, each one having its own specific purpose. More detail on event types is covered in Chapter 11, where you are shown a more holistic approach to information security than is appropriate to cover here.

Running the Event Viewer

When you start Event Viewer, you might be surprised to see a vast number of events already recorded in the logs. Don't worry—this is perfectly normal. Windows systems are complicated, and because your systems will have been running for at least a few days, you'll be seeing a whole array of events recorded.

To make things a little clearer and to establish a good baseline to start from, the best thing to do is clear all the events from all the logs and start afresh:

1. In the left window pane, right-click on the Application log and select Properties from the context menu.

2. At the bottom on the properties dialog box, click the Clear Log button. When it asks, "Do you want to save Application before clearing it?" click Yes and save the log to an area on your hard disk.

3. Perform the same operation on all other event logs, in each case choosing to save the legacy logs on a same place on the disk.

4. The log size can be adjusted to hold more information by right-clicking on the appropriate log, selecting Properties, and then increasing the maximum log size to no larger than 65,000 bytes (this upper limit is imposed because backups will fail if this is set too high).

5. Below the log file size, you'll see the choices for what the system will do when a log file fills up. If set to Overwrite Events as Needed, the oldest events will be overwritten as soon as the maximum log file size is reached. If Overwrite Events Older Than x Number of Days is selected, only events older than this number of days can be overwritten. In this case, if the event log fills up before the number of days is reached, new events will not be written to the log. If this happens, you might need to increase the size of the log or alternatively decrease the number of days until an event can be overwritten. If you select to clear the events manually, the log file will fill up and will not record any new events until you manually clear them out yourself.

Performing Backup and Recovery

One of the most important tasks you can undertake on your system is to ensure that you have a good, robust backup regime. Backups should be done properly and regularly, ensuring that the data your business relies on is stored safely and can be recovered in the event of a disaster.

The problem with backing up your system is that no one really does it. Because it's a preventative practice rather than a reaction to a newly presented situation, on many occasions it is the last thing to be thought about. But—and I cannot stress this enough—without a good backup regime, you are in for a pretty harsh reality check when your server's hard disk goes pop. Disk drives don't last forever. They have high-speed spinning disk platters that are vulnerable to shock, containing bearings that wear and moving parts that cease. By not backing up your system, you are effectively turning a blind eye to a chain-smoking child. It's only a matter of time before the inevitable keeling over.

There are many ways to back up your system, from a full backup (which copies the live state of your running server in its entirety to the backup media) right through to backing up only individual data areas where business-related data is stored.

Warning If you intend to use your backup to do a complete restore—and you should at least plan to have one full backup per week—you'll need to make sure you that back up the system state as well as your data files. This ensures that you can recover the Active Directory in a working state from the backup, without which your system will not function properly.

If you have the time and resources, perform a full backup once a week and incremental backups in the interim. This will save you a whole load of hardship and heartache later if your system fails. Full backups every day, although they store all your system data and user data, take time and can be costly because you need a large amount of removable storage media to store the backups when you take them. On a daily basis, an incremental backup takes less time than a full backup, but the downside is that when you recover a system from an incremental backup set, the process takes some time and can be arduous compared to simply recovering the complete system in one go from a full backup.

Backups can be taken by using a tape device, removable hard disks, writable DVDs (on which you back up only small amounts of data), or any other media with enough capacity to store a copy of the files you need to keep safe. In days gone by, it used to be best to use a tape media for your backup because the capacity and robustness of tapes far outweighed the capacity of other kinds of removable media, but nowadays USB-connected hard disks are available with hundreds of gigabytes of disk space, often the entire capacity of your server system.

Warning Although tape storage is more expensive than any other form of backup media, it is definitely the best. Removable media may be a false economy because the mean time between failure (MTBF) ratings for these (due to the high-speed spinning disk platters, bearings, and so on) are much higher than that of tape devices.

The benefit of using a tape backup system comes mainly from the cost of the individual tapes themselves. They are cheap and cheerful and very rarely go wrong, so it doesn't put you out that much to have 10 tapes (incremental backups Monday through Thursday, full backups on Friday, cycling over a further three weeks, and a spare tape in case of tape failure). You can cycle their use and take them off-site for secure storage in a fireproof safe.

The following points should be considered when you design your backup strategy:

- Always store backup tapes off-site.

- Record as much data in your backup as you can.

- If you are doing a full system backup, always record the system state of the server.

- Rotate your backup media over a set number of days, preferably no less than one week.

- If possible, do a full backup once a week, and then incremental backups in the interim.

To set up the SBS 2003 backup facility, do the following:

1. Click Start ➤ Server Management.

2. Under Standard Management, click Backup to reveal the Manage Small Business Server Backup page on the right.

3. Click Configure Backup to start the Backup Configuration Wizard.

4. On the Welcome screen, click Next.

5. On the Backup Location page, select the device you want to use for your backup. Click Next.

6. If you are storing your backup file on a removable disk, select the appropriate removable media drive mapping. Click Next.

7. Now select the files and folders you want to save to the backup and click Next.

8. On the Define Backup Schedule page, select the days you want to perform the backup and then click Next.

9. On the Storage Allocation for Deleted Files and Emails page, accept the defaults and then click Next. (You should set your Exchange item retention to be between 60 and 90 days to ensure that you lose no emails.)

10. On the final page, check your choices. Then click Finish to finalize the configuration of the backup service.

Printing

Configuring shared printing on your SBS 2003 network is really straightforward. The following procedure will allow you to add a printer to the server and share it with any group of users you've defined as a security group:

1. Click Start ➤ Server Management.

2. Under Standard Management, click Printers.

3. Click Add a Printer to start the Add Printer Wizard.

4. On the Welcome screen, click Next.

5. If the printer is a local printer (one that is physically attached to the server), select the top radio button. Otherwise, if you are trying to add a networked printer (one that has its own IP address or is attached to another computer), click the lower of the two radio buttons.

6. Click Next.

7. If the printer is a Plug and Play–compliant device, the drivers will be automatically loaded. Otherwise, you'll have to follow the guidelines to install the device driver from the printer manufacturer, supplied with the device. Click Next.

8. If you are installing a network printer, you must first browse to the network client computer that has the printer physically connected to it, find the shared printer name, and then click Next.

9. You can select to locate a printer in the Active Directory. By default, all SBS 2003 printers will be stored as objects in the Active Directory for ease of finding as a resource on the network. Click Next.

10. To add this printer as the default printer for the server, select the top radio button. Otherwise, select the lower radio button. Then click Next.

11. On the final page of the wizard, review your settings and then click Finish.

To view the printers already created on a system, click the Start menu and select Printers and Faxes. This is the standard printer management interface, where all printing and faxing devices are listed and configured on either your SBS 2003 server or Windows workstations.

To share a printer on the network for other users, right-click on the printer's name and click the Sharing tab. You can give the printer a sensible name to help users find it on the network, and you can add permissions to the share to make sure only authorized users have access to its resources.

■**Note** You can connect printers to users' workstations and share them on the network too. The only problem with doing this is that when the user's computer is not switched on, you cannot print to that printing device. It's better to either connect printers directly to your SBS 2003 server or to buy an IP print server from your local computer store. An IP print server can act as a USB or parallel interface for the printer that can be connected to the server (over TCP/IP), without the printer having to be physically connected to the server itself. This will allow you to house your server in a safe computer room, away from your user (many servers are too noisy to be in the same room as your users anyway), and have the printer in a more accessible office location.

Faxing

Desktop faxing and routing has seen an end to waiting queues at the fax machine. We have reduced our paper usage and been able to track lost faxes in the archives. Our users particularly like the customizable cover sheets and reports once a fax has been sent.

—Michael Jenkin, IT manager, Copyworld

You will have already run through the basic configuration of the fax service during your run-through of the To Do List in Chapter 4. However, there are a few things worth knowing how to configure over and above what you've already done to allow you to completely tailor the faxing service to your needs.

To configure the faxing service further, do the following:

1. Click Start ➤ Server Management.

2. Under Standard Management, click Fax (Local).

Creating Custom Cover Pages

On the right-hand side of the screen, you are presented with the Manage Fax Printers page, where you can opt to rerun the Fax Configuration Wizard, manage fax jobs from the fax console, create customized fax cover pages from the Fax Cover Page Editor, and configure your fax service's hardware support. Because you've already run through the Fax Configuration Wizard, we'll start by looking at creating customized cover pages:

1. Start by clicking the link Manage Cover Pages. This starts the Fax Cover Page Editor and displays a tip on how to get the most out of the editor. Click OK.

2. A great way to get started creating a cover page is to look at the examples. Click File ➤ Open from the menu. You will see various .cov files listed in the explorer box. Pick the generic.cov file and click Open to start with a generic fax template (see Figure 5-19).

3. All you have to do now is edit the fields in the sample cover page, adding in personalized information about your business, and save the new cover page as your own. To save the cover page when you are finished, click File ➤ Save, and then call it something appropriate to its intended use.

4. You can obviously create a cover page from scratch if you so desire, but this will be more time-consuming. When you've saved your cover page and are content you have finished, click File ➤ Exit.

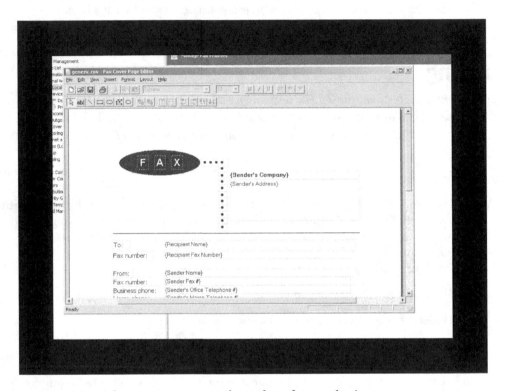

Figure 5-19. *Sample cover pages are good templates for your business.*

Setting Fax Service Properties

With the Fax (Local) node still highlighted in the left-hand window pane, right-click Fax (Local) and select Properties from the context menu. This brings up the Fax (Local) Properties dialog box, from which you will do most of the low-level configuration of the way the service runs (see Figure 5-20). Some of the settings you'll see here were configured when you ran the Fax Configuration Wizard, but there are many options you should further examine to see whether they are relevant to your business environment.

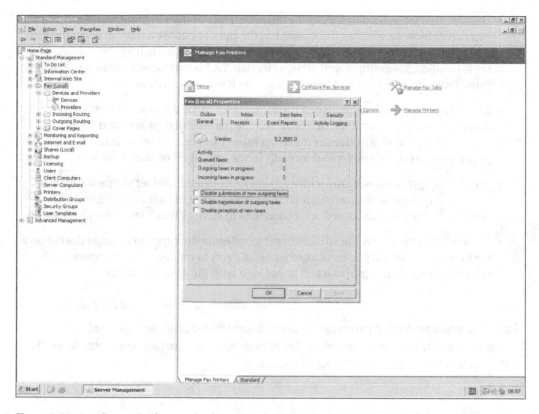

Figure 5-20. *Configure the fax service by using the Fax (Local) Properties dialog.*

There are eight tabs to choose from for configuring what's going on with your faxing service. Here's a brief view of what each can be used for:

- *General*: The General tab shows you how many faxes are currently being processed by your system: the number of incoming, outgoing, and queued faxes are all listed under the Activity heading. From this tab, you can also switch off the ability to send and receive faxes as well as disable the user's ability to submit them into the queue. This can be particularly helpful if your modem or telephone line fails.

- *Receipts*: If you want users to be notified of the progress of a fax being sent, you can select the Enable Message Boxes as Receipts check box. If you'd rather the receipt was sent as an email, you can select the Enable SMTP Email Receipts Delivery check box. Leave the email address as the default—this address is the address the email receipt will appear to have come from when it arrives in the user's inbox.

- *Event Reports*: You can adjust the amount of audit data to be stored in the Windows event logs by using the four parallel slider controls. The further to the right the slider, the more events will be stored for that aspect of the fax service.

- *Activity Logging*: By default, both incoming and outgoing fax activity is logged in a separate log file, specified under the Activity log folder location heading.

- *Outbox*: This tab is used to specify the characteristics of the outgoing fax queue. Here you can determine whether the sender has the right to choose a custom cover page and add a banner to the fax. You can also set thresholds determining how the sending of the fax is handled; for example, you can specify that the fax service will try no more than three times to send a fax, and between each try it will wait 10 minutes.

- *Inbox*: You can specify to archive all incoming faxes to a log and set the parameters for that log to determine its maximum size and the number of days archived faxes are stored. It's a good idea to store as much fax history as possible because this traditionally paper-based service is not stored formally in the way email or files are stored.

- *Sent Items*: You can specify to archive all sent faxes to a log and set the parameters for that log to determine its maximum size and the number of days archived faxes are stored. As I have already stated, it's a good idea to store as much fax history as possible.

- *Security*: This tab allows the administrator to delegate the rights to manage the fax service to specific users. If you want another set of users to manage the fax service, assign a security group for this purpose and populate it with the appropriate users.

Note It is recommended that you set your modem to answer the call after two rings, install a dual fax line, and set a "proper" fax machine to answer after 10 rings. In this way you have a hard-copy backup fax capability in case there is a problem with your IT equipment.

Managing Fax Jobs

From the Manage Fax Printers interface, available through the Server Management console, you can manage the current fax jobs that are incoming, transmitting, or pending in the fax queue. To do this, click the Manage Fax Jobs from the Fax (Local) node in Server Management to run the fax console.

This management console allows you to see which faxes have already been received and stored in your inbox, which faxes are currently incoming, any faxes that have already been sent, and faxes that are waiting for processing (or faxes that have failed to send three consecutive times).

You can right-click on any of the entries listed on the right-hand side of the console and manage each item individually. You can view a fax's properties and if required delete a fax from the queue.

Case Study—Copyworld

Copyworld maintains approximately 70 email accounts across three major states of Australia, running two accounting packages, numerous payroll systems, worksheets, specification documentation, Customer Relationship Management (CRM) files, and many more line-of-business applications.

Making good use of Microsoft Exchange Server email item retention, mailbox retention, Active Directory lost and found, Volume Shadow Copy, and SBS 2003 backup services, the

Copyworld IT support team has never had any issues retrieving lost data from their systems and are extremely happy with the built-in resilience features of SBS 2003.

Using daily SBS 2003 reports and system backup scheduling, Copyworld's backups are automated and checked to a point where the IT support team can simply leave the system alone and let it get on with it.

Copyworld is responsible for looking after its own internal systems as well as its various remote clients across Australia. With the aid of the Microsoft newsgroups and product user groups, the IT support team has tapped into the wealth of talent and experience in the small business community to find answers to any issues that present themselves on the systems. These newsgroups come highly recommended by all the staff in the IT support team. For more information, see a list of troubleshooting resources in Chapter 12.

Case Study—Planthire

Philip Stanley was extremely happy with his new system. Although the change was gradual, he had begun to notice a change in his staff, their daily routine no longer governed by the old ways of working. Now, automation, efficiency, and enhanced communication were pervasive throughout their daily working lives.

One of the things he enjoyed the most about the SBS 2003 solution was its flexibility. The following list exposes a few of the key features that helped Philip improve his business's effectiveness:

- *Accountability*: Philip now knows who is doing what, and more importantly, how long it is taking them. He can use the accurate feedback he gets from the computer system to further hone his business processes and increase efficiency.

- *Automation*: Introduction of the Windows Small Business Server fax service has totally transformed one of Planthire's communication bottlenecks. Each of Philip's workers needs to send faxes to their respective customers and suppliers. To make this possible from their workstations, Philip designed a collection of Microsoft Word documents to act as templates for each of his users needs. When a user needs to send a fax, he simply opens Word, creates a new document by using the template document, and then sends the completed file to the fax printer. This automatically routes the fax to the Windows fax services on the SBS 2003 server, bundles it up with a company cover sheet, and sends it to the recipient.

- *Software distribution*: Using the built-in group policy software distribution methodology, Philip has found sending applications to users' desktops a simple and easily managed service. By copying the source files to the application network share and adding the installation command to the published applications policy, applications are deployed without the need for a visit to the workstation.

Case Study—Servideal

One of the most important aspects of the infrastructure design for Henry and Maria was the implementation of a good backup strategy. Having previously experienced what a poorly managed backup solution can cause, with months' worth of data loss and practically unrecoverable business, Henry didn't want this happening to them.

In response, he decided the best approach for them was a full backup strategy running overnight. In the morning Henry would remove the tape from the backup device and put in the oldest one of his set. He decided to buy enough backup tapes to give him seven full days of full backups, and these backup tapes would all be stored away from the server. His approach was the safest he could think of. He has three places to store tapes in case of emergencies: one in his mother's house (dropped off when they had Sunday dinner), one in a safety deposit box at the bank (he made one trip a week to the bank), and one in his own garage.

In the event of a disaster (fire, flood, and so on), Henry will simply call on his hardware reseller to provide a similarly specified server and then use the most recent good backup to restore his entire business. As long as he has premises with an Internet connection, he can be back in business within a matter of hours.

Case Study—Country Estates

Finally, Alan Smith can rest easy. With the implementation of a hierarchical OU structure that reflects exactly how his business should be running, and a well-structured set of group policies and security groups to control access, rights, and permissions, he is confident that his data is protected, users get access to only what he wants them to access, and virtual teams are working collaboratively on projects right across all four sites.

Management of workstations and servers has never been so easy, and tools such as remote control (terminal services) and remote access have completely reduced the cost of his IT department. His IT guys are now able to work on important development of the SBS 2003 solution to really improve the business rather than continually fixing problems and patching workstations.

Summary

This chapter has covered many of the most important aspects of running your SBS 2003 infrastructure. I can't emphasize enough that the best way to learn how things work is to dig in and use them. There are a lot of low-level details and nuances that simply cannot be covered in detail in this book—we still have to look at the rest of the components included with the package, such as Exchange 2003 and Windows SharePoint Services.

One important point to bear in mind is that the built-in Help and Support facilities within Windows Server 2003 and the additional help content supplied via Server Management in SBS 2003 is really comprehensive. To access the Help and Support facility from Windows Server 2003, click Start ➤ Help and Support. This allows you to search for specific topics, such as network configuration or Internet connectivity, as well as presenting some high-level documentation and walk-throughs of commonly performed tasks.

In addition, Microsoft's website has reams of valuable information on configuration and management, and I'd recommend that you look there for any relevant documentation and white papers on running SBS 2003. You can also obtain all the latest software updates and security patches from the Microsoft website (http://www.microsoft.com/windowsserver2003/sbs).

CHAPTER 6

■ ■ ■

Windows SharePoint Services

SharePoint portal has been our savior. Previously, managers and staff at our various sites have kept in touch via mobile calls and emails. There were many places to locate data and lots of places for it to get lost. We are now able to keep our managers up-to-date no matter where in the world they are. They know they can log on and get access to all the information they need and that it is up-to-date. They can get immediate feedback on users and review discussions. Copyworld has implemented a very large WSS site and it contains multiple sites below it.

—Michael Jenkin, IT manager, Copyworld

Without a doubt, the most important aspect of introducing a good IT infrastructure into your business is to enable effective collaboration services between users. By *collaboration*, I mean any services that allow your users to work more effectively in sharing data, ideas, and strategy.

A prime example of what I mean by collaborative capabilities is the set of services delivered with Exchange Server 2003. Exchange allows users to send information to one another electronically, organize meetings, and view each other's free/busy time so that they always know who's available and where everyone is. Another less-obvious kind of collaboration is that of a simple shared network drive. By using a network share, many users can access data folders to read or contribute to company or team-related information.

Another method of sharing information is to mimic the services provided on the Internet by creating your own internal website. This will allow you to publish corporate information to a shared community, available through the user's standard desktop web browser, such as Microsoft Internet Explorer. Nowadays, intranets are extremely popular and most companies are employing their services for at least some of their total workforce collaboration capability.

So, everyone needs an intranet. That much is clear (I hope). But the question is, *where do you start?* Web development is certainly not as easy as setting up an email server, and nothing like creating a network share. Although there are many good tools available for creating web content, the real trick comes from learning how to create interactive services that allow users not only to read shared information, but to leverage many of the collaborative facilities of the underlying technologies, such as shared file stores, all through one intuitive interface.

Microsoft has yet again come to the rescue. Included with SBS 2003 is a relatively new intranet technology known as *Windows SharePoint Services (WSS)*. WSS is a free download available from the Microsoft website, but it has been integrated into the SBS 2003 product suite to make life easier.

Introducing WSS

The idea behind WSS was for Microsoft to deliver a product that created an out-of-the-box intranet for companies that didn't have the resources to start creating one from scratch. Generating your own intranet site that is capable of offering the collaborative capabilities you'd expect your business to use would easily cost a few months' worth of profits in development time and still might not be good enough to add real benefit.

WSS is a predefined set of collaborative capabilities designed to interface with existing aspects of your infrastructure, such as the file store, Exchange Server 2003, and Internet Information Services.

The features WSS provides to your company are as follows:

- *Document management*: WSS provides a powerful document management system that allows you to share and manage your business documentation, applying version control and a checking in and out system to ensure that documents are maintained in a secure fashion.

- *Idea sharing*: Through the use of discussion forums and lists, WSS allows you to share information, start discussion threads, and communicate with the rest of the business through a single, highly versatile interface.

- *Office integration*: If you use the latest version of Microsoft Office, you'll find that many of the features accessible directly on the WSS website are also integrated into the Microsoft Office menus. This allows you to publish directly to WSS from within Word, for example.

- *Security*: As with all Microsoft products, the WSS system uses a set of tightly controlled groups to assign permissions to users. The hierarchy of site groups allows the data within each site to be associated with varying levels of permission.

SBS 2003 automatically generates an intranet website based on the information provided during the general product installation. Accessing the default WSS site is as easy as opening Internet Explorer and typing the address `http://companyweb` in the address bar at the top of the screen. This takes you to a web page with a list of services available on your SBS 2003 server:

- My Company's Internal Website

- Network Configuration Wizard

- Remote Web Workplace

- Information and Answers

To access the WSS site, click the topmost link, My Company's Internal Website. This will take you to the WSS home page, `http://companyweb/default.aspx` (see Figure 6-1).

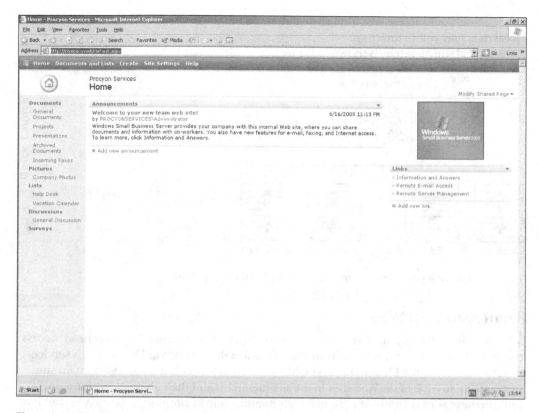

Figure 6-1. *The WSS home page lists links to all collaborative services.*

Microsoft Office Integration

If you are using any of the features of Microsoft Office 2003 (such as Outlook 2003, which comes part and parcel with SBS 2003), you'll immediately gain the advantage of the tightly integrated services connecting client to server. Office applications directly interface to the WSS server system, and your Office menus will list extra capabilities that allow you to perform server-side functions without leaving the Office environment.

If you are using earlier versions of Microsoft Office, you can still use WSS. However, as you move back through the versions, there is less and less integration between the two products. For anything preceding Office 2000, you'll have to rely on accessing the WSS site directly rather than via the Office application menus.

WSS Site Hierarchy

It's possible to generate any number of WSS subsites that sit beneath the default company site, and in each case these subsites can be created for a specific purpose. For example, a company might choose to use the top-level site purely as a way of allowing different departments to access lower sites. In this case, the site administrator would remove all the collaborative capabilities from the top level, create links to the lower levels, and apply the appropriate permissions to these lower levels so that only the appropriate staff in each department could access data.

Management could access data from all departments, but the workers would be constrained to access data only within their own.

A typical site hierarchy is shown in Figure 6-2.

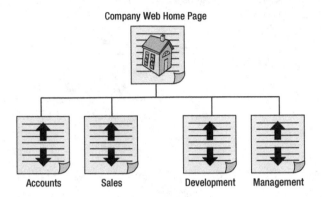

Figure 6-2. *Create a site hierarchy to support your business structure.*

Permissions in WSS

Before delving into the guts of WSS, it's necessary to get a few concepts into your head. Access to your WSS site is controlled by using permissions like those employed by the NTFS service to restrict access to the file system (as you have already seen in Chapter 5). Users attain site membership to each of the WSS sites in the site hierarchy, and their ability to perform operations on these sites is controlled through their membership in *site groups*. Every WSS user is a member of at least one WSS site group, ranging from the least privileged Guest site group to the total control attributed to the Administrator site group.

Table 6-1 shows the site groups that a user can be a member of.

Table 6-1. *Site Groups*

Site Group	Description
Guest	The Guest site group does not permit a user to do anything on the site.
Reader	A user who is a member of the Reader site group can browse the site and read any data held within that site. This user has no right to add information to the site or modify the site itself.
Contributor	A user placed in the Contributor site group can add, edit, and delete items as well as doing anything that a user in the Reader site group can do.
Web Designer	The Web Designer site group adds to the Reader and Contributor permissions by also allowing the user to modify the web pages within the site.
Administrator	Any user placed in the Administrator site group can completely remodel the WSS site, add new subsites, and modify the permissions.

Getting Started

The first time you load the WSS default company home page, you'll see some links down the left side listing the WSS's capabilities. Current company announcements are displayed in the middle of the screen, and various web links to complementary sites and services are shown on the right.

■Note WSS is a highly customizable application. The default libraries and capabilities supplied when the site is first created should be evaluated in light of your specific business requirements. In many cases, the default will be applicable and should remain intact (such as the document library for incoming faxes). In other instances, such as the placement of the Help Desk option under the Lists heading, the default might not be appropriate to your business.

The great thing about WSS is its flexibility. Practically everything you can see on the home page is configurable, right down to the layout of the page itself. By clicking Site Settings in the horizontal menu at the top of the screen, you are taken to the site administration console (see Figure 6-3). Here you can (as long as you have the appropriate permissions) customize the web content, manage your users, and personalize the site for the logged-in user.

Figure 6-3. *SharePoint sites are configurable via the web interface.*

We'll start by exploring the default home page to give you an idea of which services are offered out-of-the-box and how you might exploit these services for your own business environment.

The components you'll find accessible from here are as follows:

- *Libraries*: Libraries are WSS components used to contain collections of files that you wish to control in a more orderly fashion than that of the NTFS files and folders. You can create as many libraries as you need, for files such as Word documents, pictures, spreadsheets, and virtually any other category that's required by your business. The libraries included by default with WSS are Documents and Pictures. You can have subfolders within each library to help you separate data into manageable containers.

- *Lists*: In WSS, lists provide a structured way to publish company data that has an element of order to it. Broadcasts, such as company announcements, for example, would be considered a list because they contain discrete pieces of information placed in order by date. The default lists included in WSS are Announcements (appearing on the home page), Help Desk, Links (also appearing on the home page), and Vacation Calendar.

- *Discussion boards*: Discussion boards are the WSS equivalent of Internet newsgroups. You can post comments, start new threads of conversation, and keep tabs on existing lines of debate. As many discussion boards as necessary for your business can be created, but the default WSS site comes with only one: General Discussion.

- *Surveys*: You can use a survey to solicit opinions from a set of users. Surveys can be created when needed. There are no default surveys because each would have a very different set of questions and responses.

Navigating Your Intranet

A WSS site is no different from any other website you might access on the Internet. You use your web browser (Internet Explorer) to access the data, click links on the pages to move from one place to another, and follow the intuitive advice on each page to navigate around the various services and data stores.

WSS sites have the following items of interest:

- A link bar at the top of the page for accessing the site's main facilities

- Quick Launch bar down the left side also showing links to the site's facilities

- The main form of the page, where information is displayed

The Top Link Bar

At the top of each page on a WSS website, you can at any time access a standard set of links. This section gives you an overview of each of these links (details of each are provided later in this chapter).

Home

You can click Home at any time to bring you right back to the top-level home page. The Home link is available from all web pages on all subsites and can be used at any time during normal site usage or site administration to return you to the top level of the web hierarchy.

Documents and Lists

Clicking Documents and Lists takes you to a new page listing every library and list you've defined on your site (see Figure 6-4). You will also be presented with links to all subsites and workspaces beneath the top-level WSS site.

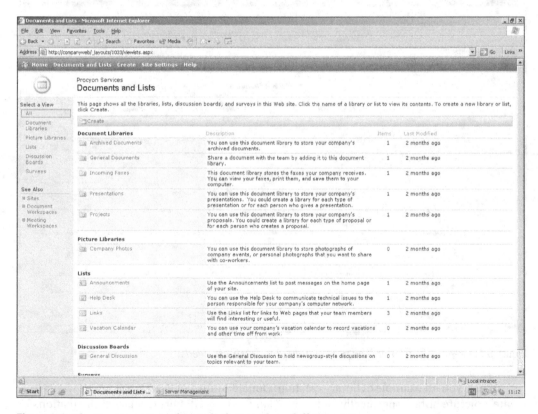

Figure 6-4. *The Documents and Lists link provides a full site map.*

By clicking the Create link at the top of the list, you are taken to the Create Page, from which you have the ability to create new libraries and lists that have a specific focus on your business (see Figure 6-5).

You can also navigate to any of the existing libraries or lists by simply clicking on the relevant name, such as Incoming Faxes.

Note Although you can create and remove any of the default libraries or lists installed on your SBS 2003 WSS system, it's advisable to keep the Incoming Faxes library as installed. You can route all incoming faxes to this library, hence publishing them all automatically to your workforce via the intranet.

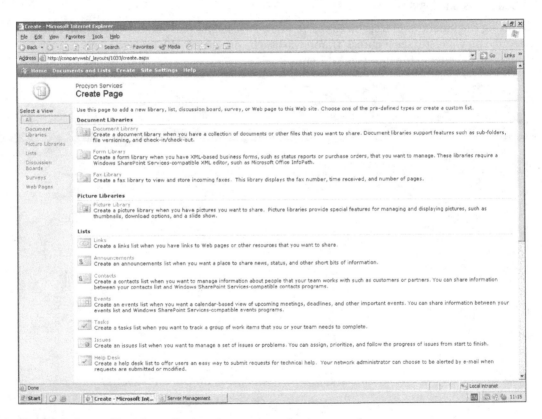

Figure 6-5. *Create libraries or lists pertinent to your business needs.*

To give you an example of library creation, Donald Munro of Practical Gardens wants to create a picture library specifically for his head landscape gardeners to share their creations with each other. He creates a new picture library by clicking the Picture Library link, gives the new library the name Success Stories, and then adds a description of how the library should be used. To make life easy for his users, he selects the option to Display This Picture Library on the Quick Launch bar. To make sure all versions of pictures are stored, he selects a radio button that allows the system to create a version each time a file is edited in this picture library.

To finally create the site, he simply clicks the Create button. WSS pauses for a few seconds while it creates a new library to these specifications, making sure that this library is accessible through the Documents and Lists link as well as via the Quick Launch bar.

New libraries are instantly accessible, and WSS automatically navigates the web browser to the library's main interface, where Donald can subsequently populate the library with whichever information he sees fit (see Figure 6-6).

A picture can be added to the library by any user in the Contribute site group, by clicking Add Picture. Donald can also create any number of subfolders inside the library to split the data into manageable chunks.

Warning Site permissions are not as granular as NTFS is this context. All libraries and lists on a site are controlled by using the permissions of the five top-level site groups. If you need to stop users from accessing data in a particular folder, you can do it in one of two ways. You can create an NTFS share and secure the information by using standard security groups, and in this case you'd create a link on the WSS intranet site to point to the share. The other way to achieve this result is to create a new child site off the main site and limit the users who have access to this site.

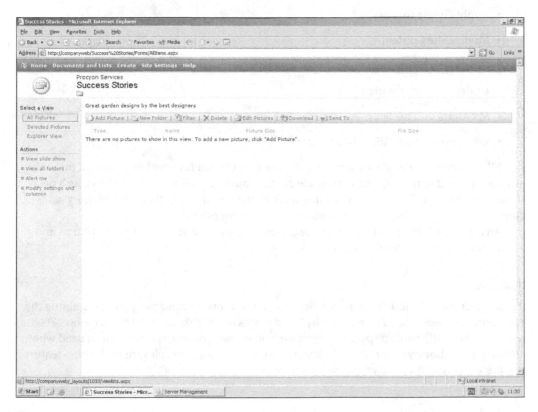

Figure 6-6. *You can populate a new library immediately after creation.*

■**Note** If you are adding new files to a document library, you can use the New Document link only when you have the appropriate Microsoft Office products installed. The most comprehensive integration between WSS and Office comes with Microsoft Office 2003.

Site Settings

If you click the Site Settings link on the top link bar, you are taken to a page where you can administer the rest of the WSS system. From here you are presented with the following options:

- Manage Users

- Manage Sites and Workspaces

- Configure Site and Workspace Creation

- Go to Site Administration

- Change Site Title and Description

- Apply Theme to Site

- Modify Site Content

- Customize Home Page

- Update My Information

- My Alerts on This Site

- View Information About Site Users

I'll go into more detail on each of these options later, but for now keep in mind that this interface is used to manage the overall site configuration as well as the logged-in user's personal configuration. Normal users would use this menu to manage their own identity, and administrators would also use it to customize the site for others.

An additional administration console is available for advanced site administration and will be covered later in more detail (see Figure 6-7).

Help

If you select the Help link from the top link bar, a new browser window opens, containing the WSS help interface. The information displayed in this menu (like many other Windows 2003 help files) is totally context specific. Figure 6-8 shows how context-specific help is used when creating a new library or list. The window displayed will always be relevant to the WSS feature you are viewing at the time when you select Help.

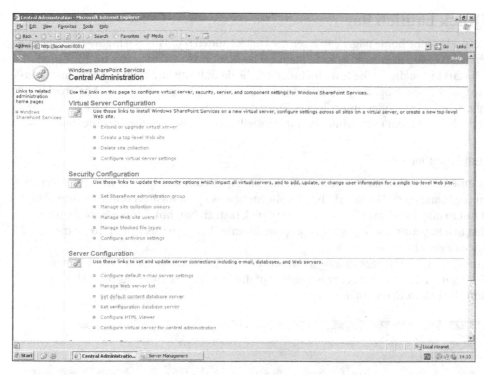

Figure 6-7. *Central Administration is used for advanced management.*

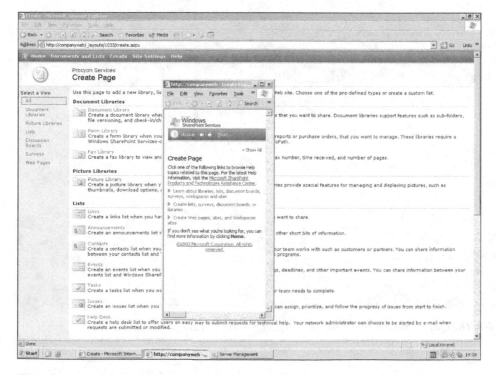

Figure 6-8. *Context-specific help focuses on your current task.*

The Quick Launch Bar

On the left side of the home page, you'll see the Quick Launch bar. This is a highly configurable menu that allows you to publish links to the most commonly used WSS pages on your site.

We'll start by looking at the links included on the default site and then proceed to configuring the Quick Launch bar for your own needs. In all cases, the Quick Launch bar provides two levels of links: categories and subjects. The category (shown in bold) will take you to the full set of subjects of that type, while the subjects will take you only to the specific item.

Document Libraries

The Document Libraries category is used to display the document libraries you want accessible from the home page. The list of libraries shown here is by no means comprehensive. You can opt not to display all your libraries on the Quick Launch bar, but if there is room, it's a good idea to add your most important company libraries because this will improve the users' experience of your intranet.

Figure 6-9 shows the page displayed when you click the Document Libraries category in the Quick Launch bar. This category is a subset of the Documents and Lists page shown when you follow the link from the top link bar.

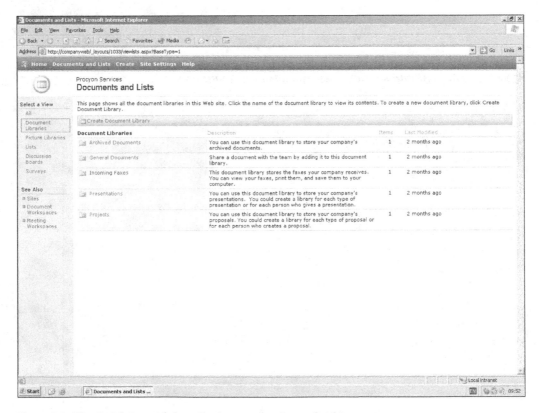

Figure 6-9. *The Quick Launch bar displays categories and subjects.*

Note As with most aspects of the SBS 2003 solution, there are many ways to accomplish the same task. The trick is finding the way that best suits the way you work. Find it and stick to it.

Warning If you don't strive to provide the most optimized interface you can for all your users, you could drive them away from the intranet, and they will seek other ways to collaborate and work. If this happens, the site has failed, and you should reconsider your site design very carefully. The worst thing that can happen to your business is that some of your users end up using the intranet, while others seek a more user-friendly method of collaboration. This split method of working will undermine any aspirations you have in creating an improved collaboration workspace. If in doubt of how your users perceive your intranet, conduct a survey, listen to the results, and update the site accordingly.

Picture Libraries

If you follow the Picture Libraries link on the Quick Launch bar, you will be taken to a list of all the libraries on your site dedicated to digital images. Any digital image libraries you decide to display on the Quick Launch bar during their creation will be displayed beneath this category heading. By default, there is only one of these: Company Photos.

Lists

The Lists link on the Quick Launch bar takes you to a full list of all the WSS lists created for use on your intranet. Any list selected to be displayed on the Quick Launch bar during creation is displayed beneath the category heading. By default, there are two of these: Help Desk and Vacation Calendar.

Discussion Boards

The Discussion Boards link on the Quick Launch bar takes you to a full list of all the discussion forums you've created for your users. Any discussion selected to be displayed on the Quick Launch bar during creation is displayed beneath the category heading. By default, there is only one of these: General Discussion.

Surveys

The bottommost link on the Quick Launch bar is Surveys. There are no default surveys set up on your system, but when you create any, you can opt to have them shown here.

Warning It's a good idea to have only a few surveys active at any one time, and you should be discerning in their use. Although surveys are great tools for soliciting users' opinions on company-related matters, you don't want your company turning into such a democracy that you no longer have any control over what happens. Try to find a happy medium and let users have their say in the things that matter the most to them, not to your business.

The Main Screen

Okay, so we've covered the top link bar and the Quick Launch bar. Now it's time to take a look at the rest of the home page.

Announcements

In the middle of the home page, you'll see the default list, Announcements, shown with a default message to welcome users to the site. If you follow the link ("Welcome to your new team web site!"), the announcement is opened and you can read the complete message.

If you go back to the home page and click Add New Announcement, you are then presented with dialog boxes that allow you to create a brand new company announcement. You'll need to fill in the title of the announcement, the message body, and an expiry date of when the announcement is no longer applicable. You might, for example, be announcing a team meeting that takes place one week from now. When the date passes, the announcement no longer is required, so it will be automatically removed. If you want to attach a file to the announcement, click Attach a File. Then when you are finished, click the Save and Close button.

Note Try not to attach files to announcements. If you need to direct people to a file, try putting the file in a document library and then include the link to the document in the message body. This means that documents will remain in their respective libraries, remaining under change control and appropriate access control.

Links

The following three links are listed on the right-hand side of the home page when you first start WSS:

- *Information and Answers*: Information and Answers is a useful help facility containing myriad information about SBS 2003 and how to use its many services. This covers topics such as remote access, mobile devices, email, and faxes.

- *Remote Email Access*: Clicking this link takes you to your web-based email facility. This is covered in greater detail in Chapter 7.

- *Remote Server Management*: This link is for administrators to allow access to the server that needs managing. If you're trying to access the server from the Internet or via a dial-up link, this is the easiest and quickest way of gaining access to the server's management consoles. Remote Server Management uses a terminal services session on the server to permit access to the standard Windows 2003 desktop, allowing you to run the Server Management console or any other MMC snap-in.

Adding new links to this section allows you to customize the page to include other company-related intranet pages, Internet links to external websites, or even links to file stores somewhere on your server. To add a link, click Add New Link. You will be directed to a new web form where you can enter the URL, a description of the target site, and some notes about the target site.

Note To add a link to a piece of file store somewhere on your server, create a share for that file store and in the URL field type //<servername>/<sharename>. For example, in my case, to map the C: hidden share, I'd type //sbs/c$.

Managing the Intranet

There are two elements of managing WSS that must be covered to make sure you can fully configure the intranet site to your needs:

- To access the site-related administration interface, start at the main WSS home page and click the Site Settings link on the top link bar.

- To configure the entire WSS capability (that is, elements of the WSS system that affect all sites), you need to open Server Management, click Internal Website (under Standard Management), and then select Central Administration.

Site Administration

If you click the Site Settings link on the top link bar, you are presented with various options. Some of them are self explanatory, such as Change Site Title and Description, while some require a more in-depth analysis. This section presents the details of managing your users, and managing your sites and workspaces. It also takes you on a tour of how to perform more-advanced management tasks associated with user permissions.

Manage Users

By clicking the Manage Users link, you are taken to the Manage Users interface (see Figure 6-10).

Figure 6-10. *Manage the capabilities your users have on your intranet.*

You can add a new user to the list of users allowed to access WSS by following these steps:

1. Click the Add Users button. You are offered a page where you can type in an email address, user name, or *cross-site* group. In the case of a cross-site group, you can type the name of a Windows security group, such as Domain Users, to give access to all your SBS 2003 users.

■Warning When you add a Windows group to the Users dialog box, you'll have to use the `<DOMAIN>\` prefix, where `DOMAIN` is the name of your SBS 2003 domain, for example `mybusiness\users`. If you happen to not enter the domain name, WSS will attempt to find the group in your local domain, but if you are trying to add users from a remote domain, they won't be found.

---

2. Select the level of permissions these users will have over your site (selecting from the permissions detailed earlier). After you've finished adding users and attributing permissions to these users, click Next.

3. Provide an email address for the user or users that you can use to notify them that they have permission to your new site. You can also change the name that the group of users would be displayed as within the web interface, making it something more meaningful than the security group name.

4. Create the welcome message for your new users. This is optional, so don't worry if you decide not to bother. When you're done, click Finish.

The web page will revert to the Manage Users page, and you'll see the new users added to the bottom of the list.

To remove users from your WSS site, select the check box next to the user or group and click Remove Selected Users. If you want to change the permissions a user or group has on the WSS site, again select the appropriate check box and click Edit Site Groups of Selected Users.

■Note If your business is very small and you intend for everyone to have the same access to all data (except for the administrator, who will be able to completely modify the whole site), then all you have to do is add the Domain Users built-in security group and give it the Contribute permissions. This means that all users can write to and read from all aspects of your WSS site.

Manage Sites and Workspaces

To create a new child site in the WSS hierarchy, click the Manage Sites and Workspaces link and then click the Create button. This takes you to the New SharePoint Site page, where you can specify the name of the site under the heading of Title, add a description of the site so that users can determine whether they need to visit it, add the URL details of the site so that users can directly access it from their browser, and select the permissions model to be adopted for the site.

The only aspect of creating a new site that you need to consider at this stage is whether the site needs the same permissions model as that of the parent (top-level) site.

When you are ready to create the new WSS site, click Create.

Note If you are creating a child site specifically for access by a certain business unit, and this business unit's data is to be kept private, you should select the Use Unique Permissions radio button before clicking the Create button. If you are simply creating a child site to partition data into more meaningful chunks, and you are sure the permissions defined at the top should be reflected throughout the site, leave the User Permissions radio button as the default (Use Same Permissions as Parent Site) and click Create.

The next phase of site creation is to select the appropriate template to use for that site. Templates are used to adjust the capabilities of each WSS site. There are eight standard templates, each with its own subset of capabilities. For completeness they are listed here:

- *Team Site*: A team site is effectively the same as the default site you have already seen. Selecting this template will create a child site with all the capabilities available from the top-level site. In a business with very separate business units, this template might be more applicable, directing users to their own child site rather than to the top-level site; the child site would contain all information that is relevant to those users. If this were the case, administration of the site would be devolved down to the manager in charge of that business unit.

- *Blank Site*: A blank site is great for advanced users to create whatever kind of look and feel they want. If you are planning to start developing highly customized WSS sites by using Microsoft Office FrontPage 2003, a blank site is the best choice, allowing you to start from scratch.

- *Document Workspace*: A document workspace is a cut-down version of the top-level site, offering document management facilities for document storage as well as a task list for assigning to-do items and a links component for customizing the list of websites made readily available through the site.

- *Basic Meeting Workspace*: A basic meeting workspace offers you a site capable of setting objectives for users, creating attendee lists, publishing meeting agendas, and assigning a new document library to that meeting workspace. This can be used when a business unit needs to focus on one particular task, pulling together the right people and source information into a single collaborative workspace. See Figure 6-11 for an example of a typical basic meeting workspace created for a business unit called Garnes and Bolden.

- *Blank Meeting Workspace*: A blank meeting workspace allows you to completely customize the site in the context of a collaborative meeting workspace. You can add and remove web components that allow you to perform any of the functions inherent to the rest of the site.

- *Decision Meeting Workspace*: Use a decision meeting workspace to create an extremely focused meeting environment for document reviews, process reviews, and marketing initiatives.

- *Social Meeting Workspace*: A social meeting workspace can be used to generate chat among your workers that is related to social events and company policy. This site includes discussion forums, image libraries, and document libraries specifically for event directions.

- *Multipage Meeting Workspace*: A multipage meeting workspace is the most flexible of all the workspaces, containing all the functionality of the other templates but over a multiple-page layout. This means that each page can contain much more information.

Figure 6-11. *Create customized workspaces to facilitate collaboration.*

Note When you go back to the Sites and Workspaces page, you'll see that you now have your new site listed under the appropriate heading. To delete a site, click the X button opposite the site name.

Configure Site and Workspace Creation

By following this link, you can opt to allow users in the Contribute site group, or users in the Web Designer domain security group, to create child sites beneath the parent.

Remember, only site administrators can create sites by default. However, you can delegate this capability to users in the Contribute group or Web Designers group (for FrontPage users) by clicking the Configure Site and Workspace Creation link on the left-hand side of the screen.

On this page you can choose to allow users in either the Contribute site group or in the Web Designer domain security group to create subsites. I prefer to allow only the latter to create sites. If you have a department that needs to do this sort of ad hoc site creation, appoint an administrator and leave the contributors to be responsible for merely contributing to the resources they have been assigned. The problem with offering normal users the ability to create sites is that your governance over your hierarchy disappears and your site structure becomes unwieldy and messy.

Go to Site Administration

This link takes you to another management interface that allows you to perform a more comprehensive set of management tasks on your site:

- Users and Permissions

- Management and Statistics

- Site Collection Galleries

- Site Collection Administration

It wouldn't be a good use of time to list every one of the management facilities available through this interface. Many of the items are intuitive, and the functionality is a straight copy from another part of the site, for example the Manage Users interface. However, some of these lower-level management tasks should be examined in a bit more detail to make sure you understand exactly what's possible with WSS:

- *Manage Site Groups*: Use this interface to create new site groups with very specific low-level permissions. This capability can be likened to the Advanced NTFS permissions that you can apply to security groups and users to offer only very specific capabilities.

- *Manage Anonymous Access*: You can specify whether you allow anonymous users access to your site. This might be useful if you are publishing your website to an Internet-facing interface, such as through ISA Server, and you want anyone on the Internet to access the information.

- *Manage Cross-Site Groups*: Cross-site groups allow you to offer access to other sites where users participate in collaborative work.

- *Save Site as a Template*: You can easily create your own child site templates by creating a generic site that would be suitable for your purposes, and then saving this site as a template to be applied later (much in the way you can create user templates for taking the pain out of creating additional users). New templates appear in the template list when you create a new site.

- *Manage Web Discussions*: This is a good way to expose all the web discussions happening on your server at any one time. Clicking Update will search the entire site hierarchy for these kinds of discussions and list them all under this heading. You can then navigate to any of the displayed discussions and manage them individually.

- *Manage User Alerts*: This link will display an interface for searching the site for all alerts designated for a specific user.

- *Manage Web Part Gallery*: The Web Part Gallery allows you to look at any of the web parts already installed on your system, and if you have some new ones, you can upload them to WSS.

■**Note** A *web part* is a web page object designed with a single purpose in mind. Web parts work together to act as the building blocks that make up a web part page. A web part is made up of two files, with its values stored in a database. I will cover web parts later in this chapter in a bit more detail.

Virtual Server Administration

You've learned how to navigate your way around a WSS site, create new child sites, create site templates, and manage the basic settings for a site. But there is more to managing a WSS system than merely the internal working of the site itself. The underlying server architecture that WSS is built upon is known as *Internet Information Services (IIS)*, a complex subcomponent of the Windows 2003 operating system that WSS exploits for its web-hosting environment.

IIS plays host to items known as *virtual servers*, websites that can be as simple or complex as required. You can run as many virtual servers as you require for your business. Some can be created and populated with content directly (possibly by using Microsoft Office FrontPage 2003) and some, such as WSS, have been already created and are simply running as client-facing services. You can see the Central Administration console shown in Figure 6-12. There are various advanced tasks you can perform on your WSS site from this menu.

Understanding a little about what can be done with the WSS site at the virtual server level is important for one primary reason: you will be constrained in what your WSS site can do by the control imposed on that site by the virtual server. If you learn how the virtual server can be manipulated to your benefit, you can do the following tasks:

- Create, remove, or modify the entire WSS hierarchy

- Change the underlying security settings for the entire site

- Modify how WSS interacts with other aspects of your SBS 2003 system

- Manipulate the site statistics and configure analysis tools, such as quota management

To access the Central Administration interface, do the following:

1. Click the Start menu and then Select Server Management.

2. Under Standard Management, highlight Internal Website.

3. Click the Central Administration link on the right-hand side of the screen.

■**Warning** I strongly advise that any modifications to a WSS virtual server should be performed only when you are completely confident in the consequences of modifying that setting. To learn more about modification of a WSS virtual server, click Help in the top-right corner of the Central Administration web page.

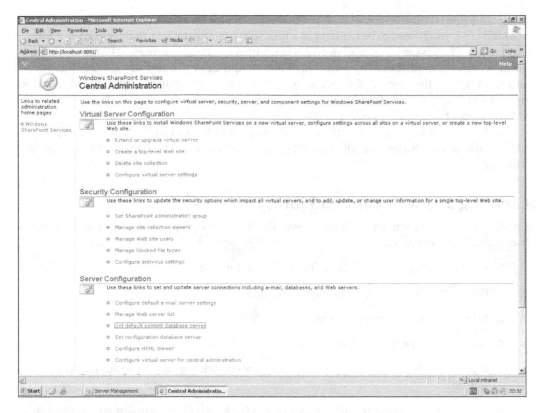

Figure 6-12. *Central Administration manipulates the IIS virtual server.*

Using Document Libraries

Document libraries are one of the most useful features you get with WSS. WSS includes five default document libraries when it's first installed, but these are purely there as examples to show you how these could be used. You can create as many new document libraries as you need for your business and should seriously consider rounding up all extraneous files and file store areas currently used by your users, removing any shares they use to store files, and forcing them to put all their data into WSS. This might sound radical, but a half-hearted approach to using WSS doesn't really work—I'm sorry to say, it's all or nothing.

Probably the most important consideration when deciding whether to start using document libraries is that of backup. Documents are not held in standard file system folders, in the way you store documents in your My Documents folder on a workstation. Instead they are stored within a database file (Microsoft SQL Server database or an MSDE database). This means that unlike files and folders that can be restored selectively in a normal backup, your document libraries, like everything else stored by Windows SharePoint Services, must be restored as one. It is extremely important that you implement a comprehensive backup strategy that can not only store, but easily recover, your Windows SharePoint Services system because its use will soon position it as a business-critical system that you can't afford to lose.

To help get around this problem, Microsoft has developed (and delivered with Windows SharePoint Services on your server) a tool called `stsadmin.exe`. This tool allows you to perform command-line administration of your Windows SharePoint Services installation. To use stsadmin.exe, you'll need to be running as a user with Administrative privileges on your SBS 2003 server. The stsadmin.exe tool provides you with a means of automating Windows Share-Point Services administration by using batch files/scripts or by running discrete commands you execute from the command-line. For more information on using stsadmin.exe for backing up and restoring your Windows SharePoint Services site files, see http://support.microsoft.com/?kbid=889236.

As long as this hasn't put you off using document libraries and you are happy with the backup and restore limitations (all or nothing), it's time to proceed to the next stage: creating a library.

Creating a New Document Library

Creating a new document library is easy. From the WSS home page, for any level of the site hierarchy, do the following:

1. Click the Documents and Lists link on the top link bar.

2. On the Documents and Lists page, click Create.

3. Select Document Library (at the top of the list).

4. Add a name and description for the library.

5. If you want the library to appear on the Quick Launch bar, select the appropriate radio button.

6. At the "Create a version each time you edit a file in this document library?" question, select Yes.

7. The document template selection determines which type of document is stored in this library. Select Microsoft Office Word Document for this exercise.

8. Finally, click Create to make the library.

The web browser is automatically redirected to the new document library's home page, from which you can create a new document, choose to upload a document, create folders inside the library, and filter the list of files displayed within the library.

Warning Reorganizing a document library after it is being used is a lot harder than reorganizing simple folders and files on a hard drive. The checking in and out process that protects the documents inside the database can cause system administrators hours of work that might have taken a few minutes in a standard file store. If you are going to use document folders, make sure to get the design of the folder system right up front.

Using a Document Library

If you have accessed the WSS site from a workstation with Microsoft Office 2003 running on the desktop, you can click the New Document button to launch the appropriate editor for the document template type you selected in the previous section. If you created a library by using the Microsoft Word template, Microsoft Word will open and allow you to create a new document that will be stored in WSS. If you don't have a compatible version of Microsoft Office to use to integrate with WSS, you can still open Word manually, create your document, and then click the Upload Document button to move it into WSS.

To upload a document, follow these steps:

1. Click the Upload Document button.

2. Click Browse to find the file you want to move into WSS.

3. Find the file, highlight it, and click OK.

4. Click the Save and Close button.

You'll see that your file has been uploaded into the library (see Figure 6-13) and can be accessed directly through the web interface.

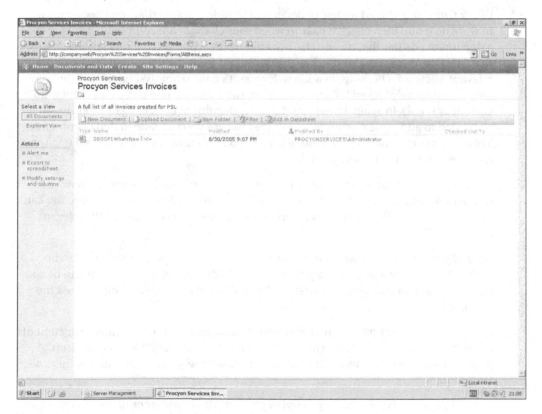

Figure 6-13. *Documents can be better controlled when held in libraries.*

Every document held in a library can be manipulated from the web interface. If you move the mouse over the document title, you'll see a drop-down menu that lists the following options for the document:

- *View Properties*: If you select the View Properties item from this context menu, you are presented with a list of information explaining when the document was created, who it was created by, and when it was last modified.

- *Edit Properties*: You can edit some of the properties of each item by selecting this option. You can modify the name of the document as well as giving it a more meaning-ful title. If you have chosen to maintain version control, a new version is created each time you modify the document's properties.

- *Edit in Microsoft Office Word*: If you choose to edit the document in Word, WSS instructs your system to first run Microsoft Word and then load the document from the library straight into Office. Again, this requires the version of Office to be compatible with this feature.

- *Delete*: You can delete a file by using this option, if you want the file and all previous versions removed from the document library.

- *Check Out*: Some shared folders or document libraries require that you check out a file to work on it and then check it back in when your changes are complete. Checking out a document ensures that no one else can edit the file while you are making any changes to it. You can check out and check in the document from the document library or the relevant Microsoft Office application so long as it's compatible. When a file is checked out, it is effectively locked for access by other users. No one else can check it out until you check it back in again. When you check the document back in again, you are prompted to add some comments about the changes you've made to that document. This allows you to track who has done what to your documents over time and trace any mistakes back to their point of origin.

- *Version History*: If you want to view the version history of a file, this option shows a list of versions ordered from the most recent at the top to the oldest at the bottom. You can opt to open any of the previous versions of the document by clicking on the relevant date.

- *Alert Me*: This option invokes the WSS alerting engine, whereby a user can opt to be alerted by an email when a change to a subscribed document occurs. Alerts can be spe-cific to document changes, new posts in discussion forums, or all changes across the entire site.

- *Discuss*: Clicking this option enables you to insert review comments into the document, as long as it is saved as HTML. This opens a special editor that allows you to insert inline HTML comments into a browser and discuss these comments with another col-laborator.

- *Create Document Workspace*: If you opt to promote the importance of the document to one that demands its very own document workspace, you are effectively creating a WSS child site specifically for this document. Your employees can now collaborate on this document in a way that ensures they have absolute focus.

Customizing Document Libraries

As you're probably beginning to see by now, virtually every aspect of WSS can be customized. Document libraries are certainly no exception. Every library you create can be modified to suit your needs by following the Site Settings link on the top link bar and then selecting Modify Site Content.

You can now select the appropriate library you wish to manipulate from the list shown on the Modify Site Content page (see Figure 6-14).

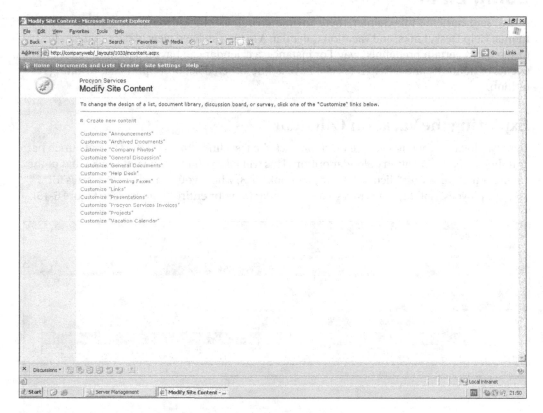

Figure 6-14. *Customize a library's settings to suit your needs.*

When you click on the specific library you need to modify, you can opt to change the settings you selected when the library was first created, such as the name of the library, its description, the file template it is associated with, and its version control standards. You can also opt to change the way the library presents information to the user on the screen.

And If All Else Fails...

You might find that your users simply don't like Windows SharePoint Services for document storage. It is certainly a change of working practice from a standard file store solution. Because of its extra complications of checking files in and out and users' inability to easily browse (Windows Explorer–style) around the entire store, many users revert to having their files stored on a mapped drive on your server.

If document libraries can work for your business, use them. Otherwise, stick with what you know. As with most things, it works for some and not for others. You could always look for a compromise, allowing users to use traditional file stores on a mapped drive, while company-related marketing information and so called "published" material could be posted into a document library and made available through the intranet.

Using Lists

As I've said earlier in this chapter, there are four default lists included in WSS: Announcements, Help Desk, Links, and Vacation Calendar. A list is a stylized view of data that can be ordered in a certain predefined way. For instance, a calendar can have a date-ordered list of events or holidays, and a Help Desk can have a time-ordered list of support calls awaiting resolution.

Exploring the Vacation Calendar

To get an idea of what lists can be used for, click the Lists link shown on the Quick Launch bar and then click the Vacation Calendar option. This will take you to a view not unlike that of the calendar feature within Microsoft Office Outlook 2003, where you can add new entries for your employees' holiday dates to a shared calendar for your entire business (see Figure 6-15).

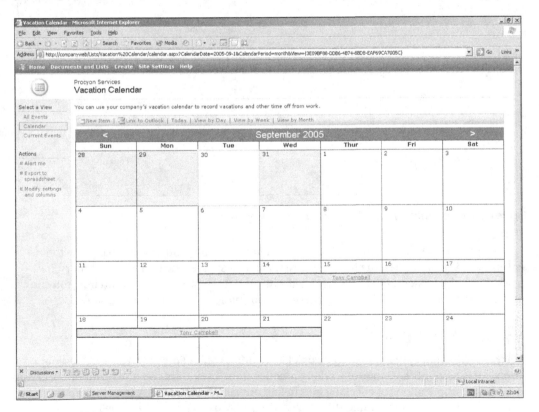

Figure 6-15. *A shared calendar can be used to track employee leave.*

You can opt to share information with your Microsoft Office Outlook 2003 application so that any appointments or vacation information stored in your WSS site can easily be amalgamated into your Microsoft Office Outlook calendar. This means that you still have a single consolidated view of your calendar, although some information might be entered by using Microsoft Outlook, while other information related to the team site might come from WSS.

Creating a New List

As with any new component, to create a new list in WSS, click the Create link on the top link bar and then select the appropriate list type from the selection menu. You can create lists for any of the following topics:

- *Links*: You can add hyperlinks to other websites, whether internal or external to the WSS site.

- *Announcements*: This type of list allows authorized users to create announcements to share company information, news, meeting requests, or social events.

- *Contacts*: A contacts list is a list specifically aimed at allowing you to manage people-related information. You might create separate contacts lists for customers, employees, or suppliers.

- *Events*: The vacation calendar is an example of an events list. These calendar-based views of events can be integrated with Microsoft Office Outlook 2003 and can be used to represent any date-related company information.

Warning Don't expect calendar information from Microsoft Exchange Server to synchronize automatically with Windows SharePoint Services event views. You are expected to manually export and import information into these Windows SharePoint Services lists, and it can become a burden to keep them synchronized. Try to keep your Microsoft Exchange calendar requirement separate from that of Windows SharePoint Services, such as keeping the event view specifically for a WSS site, and you'll avoid this problem. Users need to realize that although Windows SharePoint Services is good, it has not mastered everything just yet.

- *Tasks*: A tasks list can be used to track the work assigned to a group of users or to assign work to individual workers or teams of workers.

- *Issues*: An issues list is used to identify a set of problems that might be facing a project. Think of this as part of your project risk or issues register. If you let workers have access to an issues list, the collective brains of your workforce might help solve these issues quickly and efficiently.

Note Microsoft occasionally releases Windows SharePoint Services templates for enhancing your site's capabilities. Take a look at http://www.microsoft.com/technet/prodtechnol/sppt/wssapps/default.mspx to see the latest list of templates.

- *Help Desk*: The Help Desk list is a very specific kind of tool (see Figure 6-16). It is used to track user problems, assign the problems to a manager, and make sure your users have somewhere to get feedback on any outstanding problems they have with the system.

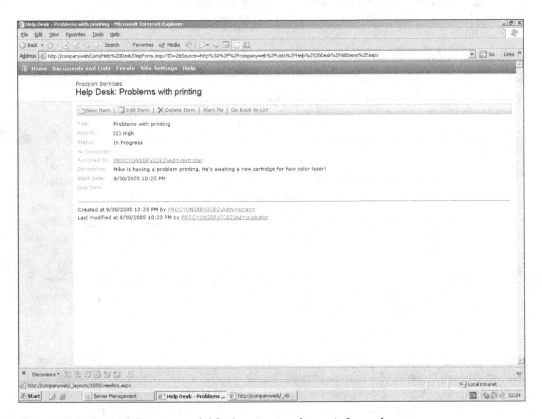

Figure 6-16. *Help Desk lists are useful for keeping employees informed.*

Using Surveys

A survey can be created at any time to take a poll on how users feel about a particular topic. Surveys can be anonymous, or users can respond with their name and contact details if they are to be contacted individually to discuss their opinions.

A good example of when a survey might be of use is about a month after you implement the SBS 2003 server solution for your business. At that time, you might want to take a poll across all your users to see what they really think of your investment. The results might show that they find some aspects of your implementation unwieldy, and this would prove invaluable in feeding in to your system's development plan.

Creating a New Survey

There are two aspects to every survey that you must consider: the survey container, which is the work area that houses the survey, and then the questions that give the survey context.

The process for creating a new survey is very like that of libraries and lists. Follow these steps:

1. Click the Surveys link on the Quick Launch bar.

2. On the Surveys page, click the Create Survey button.

3. On the Create page, click the only option available, Survey, to start the process.

4. On the New Survey page, you need to add a meaningful name and description for the survey, making sure that the purpose of the poll is obvious to your users. I recommend that you choose to display the new poll on the Quick Launch bar to ensure that your users see it as soon as they log in.

Note After you create the survey, I also recommend that you send out an announcement related to the survey, clearly stating the objectives and any timescales you want your staff to adhere to. The announcement will help draw attention to the survey on the home page.

---

5. Under the Survey options, you can select either to show the users' names who respond to the questions or to grant them anonymity by selecting the radio button marked No under the "Show user names in survey results?" question.

6. If you want to stress test a survey and have the same person input multiple answers, you might want to select Yes under the "Allow multiple responses?" question. In most cases, it's best to not allow multiple responses because survey results can be misleading if the same person voices their opinion more than once. After you've filled in all the details on this page, click Next.

Defining Questions

You will now be asked to create the questions that your survey will offer to your users. There are two kinds of questions to consider: those with free-form text answers enabling your users to respond in their own words, and those with a finite set of responses, such as a rating of 1 to 5 or a lookup list of predefined answers for the user to choose from. An example lookup question might be, *What's your favorite time of year?* The four possible answers might be predefined as Spring, Summer, Fall, and Winter.

The Add Question page is shown in Figure 6-17.

Question and Type

In the topmost box in this section, you type the question in plain text. However, this should be the last thing you do, because the context of the question, its type, and responses should all be considered before you word the question.

Warning Creating surveys is an art in itself. You need to make sure that the questions are searching enough, offer enough scope for users to voice their opinions clearly, but also bound the context of the survey in such a way that the answers don't meander and you get a real result at the end of it. A badly constructed survey will lead to ambiguous results, which in turn can lead to inappropriate action.

As you've seen, users can respond in a variety of ways to survey questions, by free-form text, by selecting from a list, by clicking Yes or No, or by entering a numeric value. These answers can be checked in such a way as to ensure that the data is of the right context, but in the case of free-form text, this is impossible. It's worth having as few free-form text answers as possible, because these subjective answers are hard to disseminate into hard results.

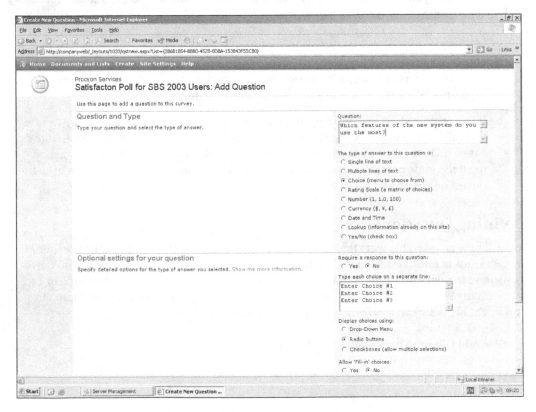

Figure 6-17. *Questions should be unambiguous and have definite answers.*

There are nine types of questions you can ask, and every question must be one of these types. As you select any of the radio buttons next to the question type, you will see the optional settings in the lower part of the screen change in relation to the type of question you want to ask. The question types are as follows:

- *Single Line of Text*: Users are allowed to add only a few words in answer to this question. This limits the ramble factor that some users might be prone to. Questions of this type can be optional. It's possible to limit the character count (the default is 255) and you can add a default text string, such as an example answer.

- *Multiple Lines of Text*: This is the most free-form answer. A user has the flexibility to ramble on and on about what he feels. These answers should be reserved for the end stages of a survey—you know, those Any Further Comments sections. Questions of this type can be optional. It's possible to limit the line count (the default is five), and you can opt for a rich-text answer that allows the user to add some formatting to the answer.

- *Choice (Menu to Choose From)*: When answering a question of this type, a user is presented with a set of choices from a menu. You can add as many choices as you need, entering one on each line in the dialog box. You can configure the method of delivery of the questions, such as drop-down menu, radio button, or check boxes.

- *Rating Scale (a Matrix of Choices)*: This answer type should be used when you want your users to select from a set of choices on a numeric scale. This kind of question is the one you most commonly see on marketing surveys, with the scale from 1 to 5, the answers equating to strongly disagree to strongly agree, with some graded answers in between.

- *Number (1, 1.0, 100)*: This question is purely for a numeric answer. You can set upper and lower thresholds for the answers, set the number of decimal places the answer should be calculated to, display the result as a percentage, and suggest a default value.

- *Currency ($, ¥, £)*: This one is fairly obvious: the response to a question of this kind is a numeric value related to an amount of currency. You can select the appropriate format from the drop-down list, add a default value, and specify whether this question should be optional.

- *Date and Time*: The date and time question should be used to force users to respond with a date and time. You can ask for the date field to be entered without the time or opt to have both. You can also fill in a default date and time to be used as an example.

- *Lookup (Information Already on This Site)*: This question type allows the user to cross-reference other aspects of the WSS site, such as user information, discussions, and libraries.

- *Yes/No (Check Box)*: This question is akin to the typical true/false, yes/no, black/white question type. There are two answers and only one choice.

Each time you complete the details of a question, click the Next Question button at the bottom of the page. After you have entered all the questions you need for your survey, click the Finish button.

After you have finished populating your survey container with the required set of questions, you get a last chance to customize the survey before publishing it to the WSS company home page (see Figure 6-18).

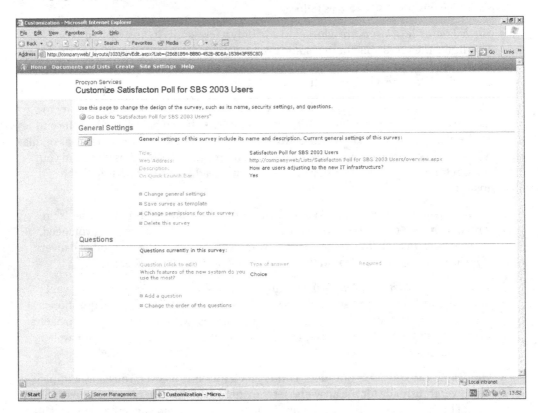

Figure 6-18. *Last-minute customization before the survey goes live*

You can modify the general settings of the survey—the basic survey details such as the name and description—as well as delving into a bit more detail with the survey permissions. You can also go back and add a few more questions at this stage in case you've forgotten anything before finally going live.

To go to the live survey, click the Go Back to <Name of Survey> link at the top of the Customize page. This takes you to the actual survey page.

Obtaining Responses to a Survey

As I've already said, the best way to indicate to users that a new survey has appeared is to create an announcement that will greet them on the WSS home page. Although the survey has been created to appear on the Quick Launch bar, many users, when they become familiar with using WSS, will intuitively click to their area of interest and might miss the new item on the left side. An announcement will always grab attention.

Creating an Announcement

As the site administrator and survey owner, go to the company web home page and click Add New Announcement. Give the announcement a snappy title and make the message body bold. Say something like, "New Survey" and "All Users *must* reply within two weeks of this date." Try using some of the rich-text formatting in the announcement description. Tell your users what the survey is all about, when the results will appear, what effect the results will have on the users, and how much you value their opinion. Make the announcement expire on the date that you want the survey to end.

After you're finished creating your announcement, click Save and Close.

Handing It Over to the Users

When it's time for a user to respond to the survey, he will simply click the relevant link in the Quick Launch bar (Satisfaction Poll for SBS 2003 Users in this case) and then click the Respond to This Survey button. This will start the survey and present the user with the first question (see Figure 6-19).

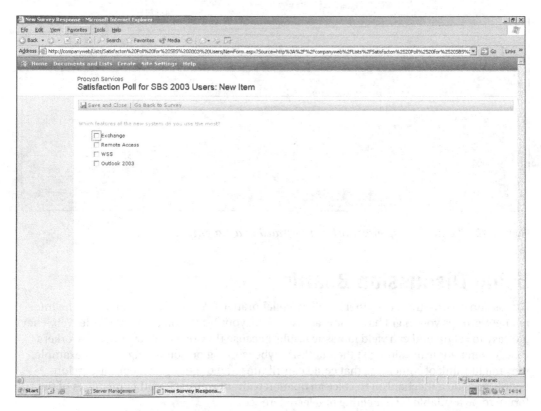

Figure 6-19. *Respond to each question in turn until the survey is done.*

The questions are displayed in a list down the screen. Users are required to respond to all mandatory questions (defined during the Add Question phase), and the answers are validated for use later. After the users have entered all answers to the survey, they click Save and Close.

Viewing Survey Results

Administrators of the survey can look at the results of the survey at any stage. They can either obtain a graphical view of the results (see Figure 6-20) or drill into each user's individual responses to see the answers.

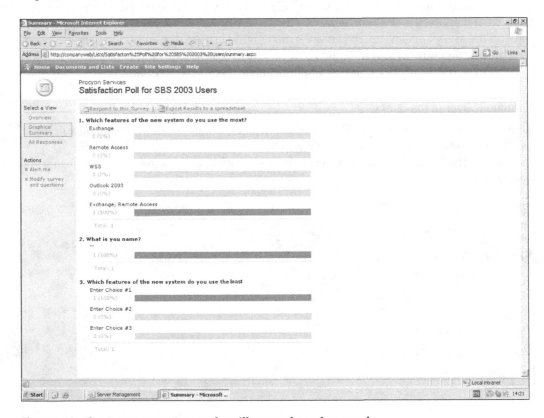

Figure 6-20. *The survey responses are best illustrated as a bar graph.*

Using Discussion Boards

Discussion boards are yet another excellent collaborative feature of WSS, not unlike the Internet newsgroups you might have come across during your travels on the World Wide Web. They are easy to set up and can yield fantastic results because they make effective use of workers' time. When people are sitting at their desks, maybe working on something else, for example, they might think of something that could contribute to an ongoing problem. Discussion boards provide a mechanism to voice an opinion without waiting for other members of the forum to be available for a meeting or teleconference.

Setting up a discussion board is easy. Here are the steps:

1. From the company home page, click Discussions in the Quick Launch bar.

2. On the Discussions page, click the Create Discussion Board button.

3. On the Create page, click Discussion Board. You are asked to supply a name and description for that discussion board and advise whether this discussion should appear on the Quick Launch bar. When ready, click Create.

4. Your browser then focuses on the top-level discussion board page, where you can subsequently begin a thread of discussion on that topic. To create a new thread, click the New Discussion button, give the thread a subject title, and state your point (see Figure 6-21).

5. Click Save and Close to add the thread to the discussion board.

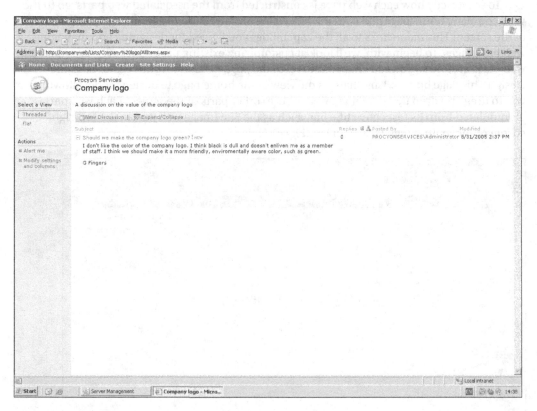

Figure 6-21. *A discussion board can house multiple discussion threads.*

■**Note** You can click the Alert Me link on the left side of the screen to be notified of new postings to any of the threads in this discussion board. Alerts are sent by email to your inbox and will indicate when you should return to a board for an update.

Using Web Parts

WSS is built by using a technology known as *web parts*. These are discrete components of a web page that have a single self-contained function, and can be used on their own or with other web parts to build up an entire multifunctional capability. Web pages created by using web parts are known as *web part pages*, of which there are many under the banner of Windows SharePoint Services.

Web parts are highly reusable and should be thought of in much the same way as real-life objects that have specific parameters and functions, such as an orange: it's round, orange in color, and you can eat it, juice it, or put it in a fruit bowl with other fruit and keep it for later. In the same way, a web part used for inputting data into a database offers a dialog box, a function that context-checks the input, a function that saves the data into the database after it has been verified, and the entire web part can be used as many times as required to perform the same operation in many places on your website.

To see exactly how each web page is constructed from the associated web parts, go to the WSS company home page and click the link called Modify Shared Page at the top-right corner of the screen. This menu links to all the capabilities you'll need for designing and managing web part pages. To begin with, we'll look at customizing existing pages, moving the embedded web parts around so you can change the feel of the page to best suit your users. Click the Design This Page button. This changes the view of the home page to design mode, allowing you to drag and drop the embedded web parts to other parts of the screen. Each web part is manipulated from its respective title bar, such as the Site Image web part in the top-right corner of the main screen (see Figure 6-22).

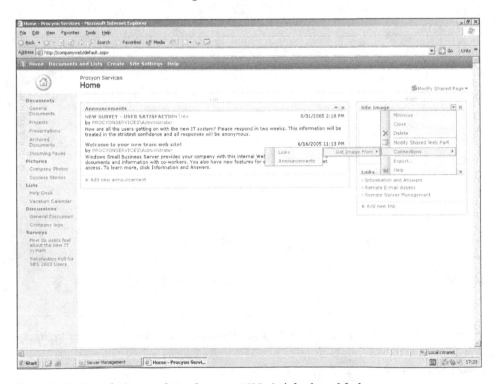

Figure 6-22. *Start design mode to change a WSS site's look and feel.*

Each configurable web part has a thin-lined box drawn around it, emphasizing that it is in fact a configurable object. You can drag and drop any web part to any other part of the screen that the interface will permit, but the underlying page layout limits where exactly you are allowed to drop in web parts. Try dragging the Announcements web part into the Links web part. You'll immediately see a new layout, and an empty web part container at the top of the screen (see Figure 6-23).

If you click the down arrow in the title bar of any of the web parts on the screen, you are presented with another menu, offering some context-specific options.

Note Please remember to use the Help facility provided through the web part context menu. This link will take you to a Help page detailing exactly what the web part does and when it should be used.

Figure 6-23. *Drag and drop web parts to authorized screen areas.*

Clicking the Close button (the button with the X icon) on the web part title bar will delete the web part from that page. If you do delete a web part and want to get it back, or you want to add a new web part to a page where one does not exist, click the Modify Shared Page link, select Add Web Parts, and select Browse. This brings up the web part list, where you can select from a list of categories any of the possible web parts you have available to inset into your site.

To add a new web part, highlight the one you require and click the Add button (see Figure 6-24). After you have finished adding web parts to your page, click the Close button to the right of the Add Web Parts title bar.

Note Another way of reducing the footprint of a web part on the screen without deleting it altogether is to click on the context menu in design mode and select Minimize. This will ensure that only the header for that web part is displayed on the screen and not the entire contents of the web part's body. Users can still follow the header link to the body of the web part, displayed on a separate web page.

There are two further context menu items worth exploring before you finish with web parts:

- Modify Shared Web Part

- Connections

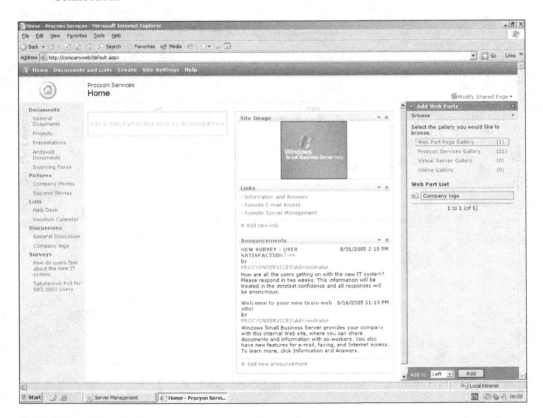

Figure 6-24. *Add predefined web parts to a web page from the gallery.*

Modifying Shared Web Parts

When you add a new web part to a web page, it's not always going to display exactly what you want by default. Each web part is different in functionality, so for each one there is a different set of configurable parameters that define its operation in the environment you put it in.

The example I'll use here is a simple one, but is useful for illustrating the process. To best understand the features of more-complex web parts, refer to the help file for that web part. For this example, we'll use the Site Image web part:

1. Click on the context menu of the Site Image web part and select Modify Shared Web Part.

2. To modify the image file used as the site image (possibly to your own company logo), click the ellipsis (…) icon next to the URL.

3. In the Text Entry dialog box (see Figure 6-25), type the URL of your own site image (this can also be a file system path). Then click OK.

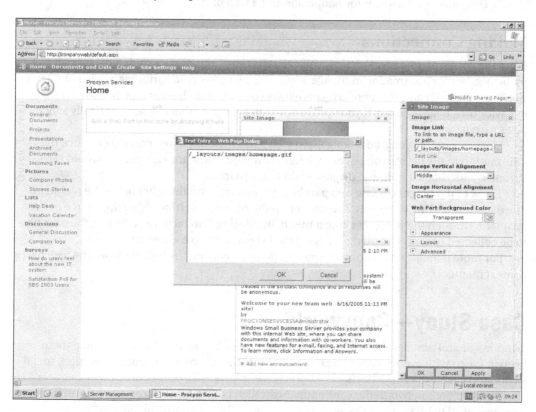

Figure 6-25. *Web parts are highly configurable components of a site.*

4. To change the position of the image as displayed within the bounds of the web part container, click the Image Vertical Alignment drop-down list and select Top, Middle, or Bottom.

5. The background color can be changed if you need a solid color rather than a transparent backing.

6. You can now expand any of the other categories: Appearance, Layout, or Advanced.

7. Under Appearance, you can change features of the image itself, such as its Title, Height, Width, and some aspects of the frame design.

8. Under Layout, you specify whether the web part is visible on the page and its relative position on the page.

9. Under Advanced, you can specify additional features of the web part, such as whether the image can be minimized, closed, or moved, and whether you want to include a Help link and further information about the web part.

Making Connections

From the context menu of a web part, you can select the Connections option to connect web parts together for information exchange, such as drawing specific attributes of a list or discussion from one web part into another. This allows you to glue web parts together so that their behavior on a page is linked; if you update one web part, the other one automatically synchronizes with it.

Most commonly you'd be linking listed web parts with static web parts to enhance the information in the list. As you select each item in the list, the static component would synchronize with that list item and display further information.

Think of the process as one web part being the source and the other being the recipient. The data flow is always one-way. You can set up the connection from either the source or the recipient, through the web part context menu, by clicking Connections, selecting the data type to be collected or sent, and then specifying the list you wish to connect to.

For more details on how connections can be used, consult the help file from the web part context menu.

Case Study—Copyworld

Windows SharePoint Services has been used extensively by Copyworld's staff to help them keep in touch with events, procedures, occupational health and safety documentation, social items, and even work time sheets.

Because their network spans the entire Australian continent, it's been essential that services such as RDP, VPN, and RWW allow users to check the vacation calendar and keep up-to-date. Social functions, company photos, and more items are updated in real-time to staff in hotel rooms, interstate offices, and at home. Users can open saved Word files and publish Microsoft Office Excel records easily and painlessly. Users can see photos of Copyworld staff they have never met before (due to being more than 1,000 miles apart in some cases) and catch up with various function groups of the Copyworld team.

Case Study—Planthire

WSS was something completely new to Philip Stanley. When Philip thought of websites, he thought of informational pages on the Internet or pages selling products or services for companies that have "got with the times." Exploring WSS was slow to begin with as Philip tentatively started clicking links to see what they would do, but it wasn't long before it clicked—WSS is not just any old website; it's a completely new way of working. After running through a few examples with himself, setting up discussion forums and document libraries for solely his own use, he decided to create a user guide for his workforce. It wasn't long before he had a good idea of how WSS would fit within his business and he decided it was time to expose this functionality to everyone else.

To do this, Philip created a survey specifically to try to lure people into looking at the site. He'd already set up some public document libraries and a few high-level discussion forums, as well as a list service for company announcements. Next, he subscribed all his users to the list service and created the survey. After he was finished, he instructed WSS to inform all his users that they had to take part, and a link was subsequently mailed to the entire workforce. It didn't take long for it all to catch on as more and more people started exploring the WSS system. Philip published his user guide to the site and then sent out a message for everyone to read it and comment. The next thing he did was announce the survey results and then call a meeting to discuss the way forward.

Now the entire business runs on WSS. They rarely use a shared file store in the traditional way, and all corporate documentation and information is stored in WSS. Everyone loves the simple interfaces and the integration of things like the shared calendar function for holiday and leave planning, and the routing of faxes to a fax library where automatic notifications are generated has made taking on WSS easy.

The key to the success of the introduction of WSS was in letting his workers see the benefits and allowing natural transitions rather than imposing new ways of working straight away.

Case Study—Servideal

For such a small organization as Servideal, the idea of collaboration didn't seem as key to their success as advertising and increasing revenue. It was then that Henry realized WSS can be published externally to clients who can subsequently participate in discussions and interact with the Servideal staff. This allowed Henry to create a new service, unlike any found elsewhere on the Internet, whereby the customers on the World Wide Web could collaborate and interact with the Servideal business directly, making suggestions, taking part in surveys, even taking part in discussions about product introduction and termination of unwanted product lines. The Servideal customers loved this interactive shopping experience, giving Servideal a really satisfied and loyal customer base.

Case Study—Country Estates

Alan Smith's vision of the future removed the barriers created by the physical separation of his offices, instead creating what he called e-sales teams across all sites and all disciplines. He saw an e-sales group comprising a manager, a team of agents, an administrative clerk, a financial adviser, and a legal adviser. These groups would service different customer requirements, wherever that customer might be, meaning the team of people assigned to a property were not merely the local team in the local office, but rather a team of experts in that line of property from anywhere in his business.

All of his employees were expected to travel when a customer meeting was planned, but for the majority of time, they would work within the bounds of a dedicated WSS site, specifically created for their area of interest. This site would be for not only managing potential and secured contracts, but also for providing a repository for any specialized information in their field. For example, the WSS site for Victorian town houses had discussion forums relating to restoration, national pricing, builders, and location information.

Summary

WSS is extremely powerful. You will probably have realized by now just how powerful it is, but the only way to ensure that you get the most use from it is to educate your users about all its capabilities. It's extremely easy, and very common, for users to stick with what they know, and if you're not careful, you'll end up with only a small portion of your staff using the facilities, while the rest struggle along with shared file stores and long drawn-out meetings where nothing really gets accomplished. I'm not by any means saying that you won't still have unproductive meetings—this is part and parcel of running any business—but if meetings sometimes go down rabbit holes with protracted discussions that might not require an immediate decision, turn these into WSS discussion boards and let your employees interact in their own time.

Note You'll be surprised that some people who are shy in face-to-face meetings will display an amazing talent to contribute to discussion boards. The less formal and far less confrontational view of a discussion board allows all members of staff to voice their opinions openly and honestly without vying for the attention of bosses or peers in a noisy conference room.

So, construct a training program for your users—both old and new—and make it mandatory. If you see a trait to move back to the old way, but you know this will not help business, make the old way of working no longer viable. Upload files from a shared drive into a document library; then remove the users' permissions to access the share. To make it work, you need to adopt a somewhat dictatorial role as company director. If you are a consultant putting this solution into someone else's business, make sure to explain in detail all the benefits WSS will bring to that business. Train the managers as part of your consultancy.

All in all, WSS is whatever you make it: from a simple place to store and version-control your corporate documentation, to a fully integrated and collaborative work environment from which every aspect of your business is run. Some small business managers have found that aside from email and some line-of-business applications, their workforce spends the majority of their day logged in and interoperating with the company.

CHAPTER 7

■ ■ ■

Exchange and Outlook

Nowadays, email forms the heart of many businesses' communications infrastructure and is used for a variety of purposes:

- Arranging meetings

- Delivering products to customers

- Holding ad hoc conversations

- Organizing lunch appointments

- Marketing

- Invoicing

- Advertising and sales

- Conducting surveys

- Broadcasting newsletters

The reason email has become so successful, introduced into virtually everyone's way of life, is that it's a globally accessible form of communication that's independent of time constraints, forcing no immediate reply from the recipients (as telephone calls do) but making sure the message arrives at the destination much quicker than it would if sent by traditional means, such as snail mail.

Note The nickname *snail mail* came about when the traditional method of sending letters and parcels across the planet was compared with the new electronic form of email: the postal service travels the planet at a snail's pace in comparison with the rapid communication now possible with email.

For all these reasons, Microsoft has included their email server product, Exchange Server 2003, in the SBS 2003 product suite, giving you a business-ready email service that not only provides the basics of electronic messaging, but also has a number of additional collaborative features, such as shared calendars and public folders, to help your workforce work better and smarter.

Exchange 2003 is installed as part of the initial configuration of SBS 2003 and comes with both the Standard and Premium editions of the product. It is automatically configured as part of the setup routine, and additional configuration is performed when you run through the To Do List.

On the client side of messaging, Microsoft Office Outlook 2003 is also included with your SBS 2003 product license. Outlook acts as the primary interface into your Exchange 2003 system, providing access to your mailbox, shared calendar (see Figure 7-1), and public folders.

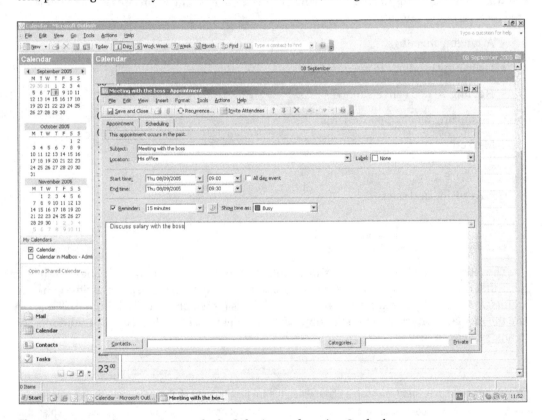

Figure 7-1. *Managing meetings and schedules is easy by using Outlook.*

This aim of this chapter is to introduce you to the Exchange 2003 management interfaces and expose the various collaborative features within the product that can be configured better to suit your business. Throughout the chapter I'll provide practical examples of how the technology can be used, and where appropriate show how configuration affects the client view of the system, through Outlook 2003.

Note You should never install the Outlook 2003 client software on your SBS 2003 server. The functionality Outlook brings to the client can easily be exploited, opening up a direct interface into the server environment for malicious hacker types. If you need to connect an email client to your server (for whatever reason), try using Outlook Express, which would already be installed.

Messaging Basics

Most of the basic configuration of Exchange 2003 is done when you install SBS 2003 and run the To Do List item, Connect to the Internet, as you did in Chapter 4. This runs the Configure Email and Internet Connection Wizard (CEICW), which both enables your server to connect to the Internet and configures your Exchange 2003 server to send and receive emails externally.

Warning If you have not yet run the Configure Email and Internet Connection Wizard, you should do so at this stage. Everything we are going to cover in this chapter relies on SBS 2003 being initially configured by using this wizard. If you have not run it, open Server Management, click To Do List, and select Connect to the Internet.

Before we start delving into the features of Exchange 2003 that you might want to configure in your organization, it's important you understand the basics of what email is, how it works, and where the drawbacks might be.

What Is Email?

Electronic mail, or *email* for short, is a way of sending electronic messages (with or without attachments) to recipients over a network. The principles behind the transit of email are much the same as those of conventional mail. Messages are wrapped in an envelope (the Simple Mail Transfer Protocol, or SMTP), sent to your local post office for sorting (your Exchange 2003 server), forwarded onto remote post offices that deal with mail on a local level for their own clients (someone else's Exchange 2003 server), and finally delivered by a mail carrier to the client (Exchange 2003 transmits the email to the end user's email client). See Figure 7-2 for a representation of how email flows across the Internet.

■**Note** This analogy, comparing email to the postal service, is purely illustrative. There are, of course, many differences (and variations on the theme) when you explore the details of how email traverses networks and is delivered to end clients. However, this analogy will help you grasp the basics.

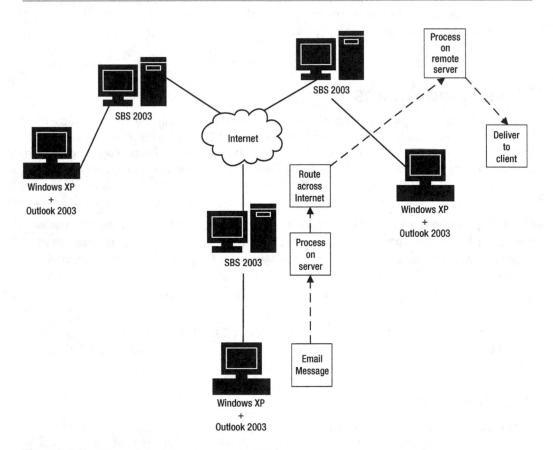

Figure 7-2. *End-to-end mail from across the Internet*

Email has been around in one form or another for almost a quarter of a century now. History recorded the first email ever transmitted over a network to be a message sent by Cambridge, Massachusetts engineer Ray Tomlinson as long ago as in 1971. Ray is also attributed with coming up with the idea to use the @ convention, which symbolizes the location of the message recipient to the email software. Virtually everyone on the planet is familiar with the convention of using the recipient's name concatenated to the @ symbol and suffixed with the destination domain name of the recipient.

Email messages are a lot like parcels, containing a payload of information and attachments, wrapped in some packaging that tells the underlying system where they should be sent. You can send plain old text, or you can send a combination of text and attachments, such as pictures, documents, or applications.

Extensions to the formatting and protocols over the years have extended email's capability to include these bolted-on attachments. However, these are supplementary to the main function, which is still, intrinsically, to transmit text messages from one person to another.

Email Protocols

There are a various *protocols* (the conventions used to package up and send email) available with today's technology that can be employed to send email across a network, but by far the most common and popular is that of Simple Mail Transfer Protocol, or SMTP. SMTP defines the method that a server system would use to send mail across the Internet and was designed specifically for TCP/IP networks.

When you send an email to an email server, the protocol you use is SMTP. At this stage, this is all you should need to know about SMTP.

The Post Office Protocol, or POP, is the second protocol you need to understand. It works in harmony with SMTP for email clients that need to pull mail from the mailbox on the server. POP is currently at version 3, so all references to this protocol are written as POP3. POP3, unlike SMTP, is used specifically to download email from a remote server by using this very specific client/server interface.

Email Clients

If you've ever received an email message, at home or at work, you'll be familiar with using an email client. A *client* is simply a tool used to send or receive email messages, and adheres to the standards needed to package your messages or decode incoming messages to be transmitted. The email clients included with SBS 2003, available for all users, are Microsoft Office Outlook 2003 and Outlook Web Access. In both flavors, Outlook is capable of writing email messages in any number of formats, but the method used on the Internet for sending mail is SMTP. Outlook will wrap up the message and attachments you are transmitting and forward them to the chosen server.

Outlook integrates tightly with Exchange 2003 to provide not only an extensible mail facility but also an array of further collaborative capabilities that can be deployed across your business.

SMTP and POP3

To learn to fully utilize all the facilities of Exchange 2003 would take a lot more than this short chapter. The aim here is to present the management tasks that you need to understand to run a stable email infrastructure, as well as to show you how you might configure some of the extra collaborative features provided by Exchange 2003 above and beyond simple email handling.

Your Exchange 2003 server can be addressed directly from the Internet; you register your domain name as a public email destination, and your ISP registers your IP address as public. In this way, when someone wants to send an email to one of your employees, she would send it to tony@procyon-services.co.uk and the SMTP server representing her company would query the Internet DNS servers for the Mail Exchange (MX) address for the domain procyon-serices.co.uk.

There are two primary methods you can use to collect email from the Internet: If you instructed your ISP to deliver email directly to your Exchange 2003 server, the DNS query would return the address of your mail server (Exchange 2003 in this case) and the email would be delivered directly to Exchange. If, on the other hand, you instructed your ISP that you would pick your email up from their SMTP server (hence you wouldn't be exposing your own IP address to the Internet community), you would use the POP3 connector to download email from the ISP's server.

Note If you instruct your ISP to have email delivered directly to your system, the ISP will create a DNS record known as a Mail Exchange (MX) record on the Internet DNS servers to allow email to be routed directly to your server.

Receiving your email via a POP3 connector has plenty of benefits, especially if you suffer low or intermittent bandwidth connections to the Internet. It is by far the easiest method of transferring email to your small business, and its main benefit is that you can have your ISP manage and hold as many emails on the server as you desire. If your SBS 2003 server becomes unavailable, you could use a web browser to access the ISP's server and continue sending and receiving email. This creates an element of resilience in your email system that is impossible to achieve when running the system entirely on Exchange 2003.

Drawbacks of using the POP3 method include the following:

- If your ISP provides your email address and mailbox space, the ISP will undoubtedly charge you for each mailbox. Having email delivered directly by using SMTP will remove this overhead.

- The POP3 connector requires configuration of all possible misspellings of addressees. To get around this, you can configure a catch-all mailbox that forwards all mail to a specified Exchange mailbox.

Plenty of SBS 2003 users prefer to stage delivery through their ISP and rely on the POP3 connector to download and filter email into the appropriate Exchange mailbox. For these users, POP3 offers benefits that you can't get from SMTP delivery without paying a third-party company to queue emails when the SBS 2003 server is unavailable. SMTP offers total control over your company data, and much faster delivery of email right to your door without it having to be processed by the ISP. The best and most efficient method for email routing is to use solely SMTP, but in some cases the practicalities offered by POP3 win.

If you opt for POP3 delivery in the short term to fix a short-term problem, you should carefully consider your migration strategy for the switch to SMTP. When you move to SMTP delivery, you might want to contract the services of a third party to queue email in the event of your server being unavailable.

Note There are number of advanced configuration aspects of both POP3 and SMTP email delivery that should be considered, such as ETRN/TURN and EHLO/HELO. Both of these settings are found under the SMTP connector's advanced properties page and should be used appropriately if instructed by your ISP. It is advisable to always check your connector configuration with your ISP to make sure email delivery is as efficient and secure as it can be.

Management Interfaces

You can manage your Exchange 2003 system from two locations: Exchange 2003 System Manager and the Users interface. Management functions are focused on the server and on services that directly affect individual users.

Exchange System Manager

To access the Exchange 2003 System Manager, do the following: click Start ➤ All Programs ➤ Microsoft Exchange ➤ System Manager.

From this interface, shown in Figure 7-3, you can do virtually anything in Exchange that you need. This is an extremely powerful administrative tool, and much like other complicated aspects of managing the underlying systems of SBS 2003, you won't need to use this often (if at all) to perform run-of-the-mill configuration tasks, such as modifying users' mailboxes, setting permissions, and changing quotas.

Figure 7-3. *The Exchange System Manager is extremely powerful.*

When you run System Manager, you are presented with an MMC console interface that has several top-level management nodes on the left side of the screen. These are listed as follows:

- *Global Settings*: From the Global Settings menu, you can specify the message formats that you use to send email messages, set thresholds for messages sizes, set recipient and sender filtering (blocking), and also set up mobile device access, such as for a mobile phone.

- *Recipients*: Beneath this node, you can modify the Details templates, Address templates, and address lists; modify recipient policies; and update changes and replication. Details templates are used to define the properties of the dialog boxes that appear when you view the recipient properties in an address list. Address lists are containers of users or groups that define special sets of recipients (see Figure 7-4).

- *Servers*: The Servers node is used to manage any Exchange 2003 server in your infrastructure and check software version numbers and service pack levels. In the case of SBS 2003, there is only a single Exchange server (your SBS 2003 server) and from this node, you can manage many aspects of the server system.

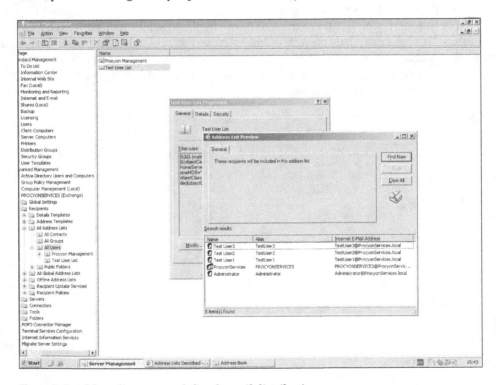

Figure 7-4. *Address lists are predefined email distribution groups.*

- *Connectors*: This node is used to manage the various connectors that Exchange 2003 can have to remote systems. In many cases, SBS 2003 users opt to use the POP3 connector configured to point to their ISP. This will be covered in more detail later in this chapter.

- *Tools*: The Tools node contains access to various advanced tools that can restore corrupt mailboxes, track messages as they flow through the system, and provide monitoring facilities that can be used to troubleshoot Exchange 2003. Many of these tools are quite advanced, and if you are interested in learning more about any of them, try looking in the online Exchange Technical Library, at http://www.microsoft.com/exchange/library.

- *Folders*: Under the Folders node, you can configure your server's public folder list, including the management of the folder permissions and the addition of content to the folders (see Figure 7-5).

Content added to public folders is available to everyone who has permission to view those folders from Outlook. We'll take a more detailed look at setting up and managing public folders a little bit later in this chapter. For now, if there is anything you want more detail on and it's not covered here, don't hesitate to call up the help files or check the Microsoft online library.

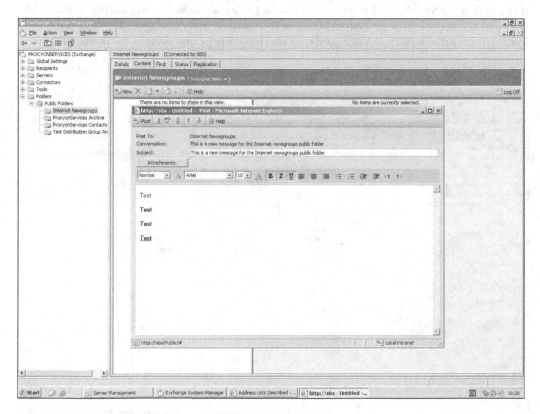

Figure 7-5. *Create public folders on the SBS 2003 server.*

Warning Playing around with Exchange Server 2003 is not for the faint-hearted. There are a lot of things that could go wrong, so make sure you have a good backup and you know what you're doing before you start adjusting any of the underlying configurations that the SBS 2003 setup routine has completed for you. Always consult the online help facility or the Microsoft Exchange Technical Library if you are unsure about anything (http://www.microsoft.com/exchange/library).

Public Folders

Public folders can be used for many purposes. They can be used to store company documents, distribute messages, and make excellent discussion forums, in much the same way as you can create discussions in Windows SharePoint Services. The great thing about public folders is that they are accessible directly through Outlook 2003 or via the web interface with Outlook Web Access. Email can be directed to a public folder as easily as to a normal email recipient, and any number of handling rules can be applied to the message.

If you expand the Folders node in the Exchange System Manager and then expand the Public Folders node, you are shown a list of all public folders currently configured on your system. These public folders are available to users using Outlook 2003, through the Folder List view. If you look at Figure 7-6, you'll see that the Outlook Folder List view displays the four public folders listed inside the Exchange System Manager. You can post new messages to existing public folders from Outlook 2003, as a standard user who has Write permissions to the public folder.

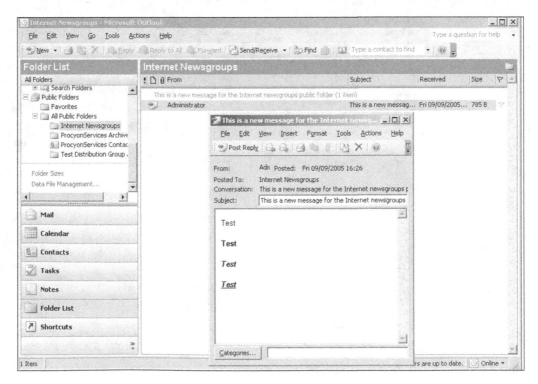

Figure 7-6. *Use Outlook to submit messages to public folders.*

To create a new public folder for a select group of users to access and post to, do the following:

1. From the Exchange System Manager, expand the Folders node.

2. Right-click Public Folders, select New, and then select Public Folder.

3. In the properties dialog box, enter the name of the public folder and a description of the contents or focus of that folder.

4. The Replication tab is not needed because your Exchange infrastructure is based on only one server. Click the Limits tab.

5. If you want to set a maximum size for the folder, you can configure three elements of restriction: the limit at which a capacity warning is issued, the limit at which users may upload no more postings, and a maximum item size. Leave the deletion and age limits as defined because they are optimized for your environment.

6. Click the Details tab. This is purely for administrative purposes, for you to record that you have created this item and to record any extra information you may wish about its usage. When you're finished, click OK. This creates the new public folder and its associated email address. The folder is then added to the list in Exchange System Manager.

7. To modify the settings of your new public folder (including permissions), right-click on the new folder name and select Properties.

8. Under the General tab, you'll see the folder name and description created earlier. If you click the Email Addresses tab, you'll see the SMTP address used to address this public folder. Email sent to this address appears as a new email item in the folder.

9. The most important thing to consider at this stage is the permissions set to be applied to the folder. Click the Permissions tab. There are three types of permissions you can set: Client Permissions, Directory Rights, and Administrative Rights.

10. Clicking the Client Permissions button displays the dialog box shown in Figure 7-7.

11. To add a new user to the access list for this public folder, first click Add. Highlight the user you intend to grant access to and then click Add. This moves the user to the right-hand side of the dialog box. You can select as many users or groups of users as you need. After you've finished, click OK.

12. New users or groups automatically get attributed the Author role. If you want to change the role, select which is most appropriate from Table 7-1.

Note Users get the Author role because this is the default. If you change the default role to None, new users will get none. If you do set the role to None, remember to turn off the Folder Visible attribute. This will ensure that users who are not allowed to access a folder don't get to know of its existence.

---

13. To remove a user or group from the list, highlight the name and click Remove.

14. If you highlight a user or group and click Properties, you'll see some further Active Directory attributes associated with that user.

15. When finished, click OK.

16. If you now click Directory Rights, this allows you to change the Active Directory permissions of this object. I'd advise leaving this as the default unless you really know what you are doing.

17. You can also delegate the right to administer this public folder to any user or security group in your Active Directory. If you want to do this, click Administrative rights and then add the appropriate users or security groups. Click OK when finished.

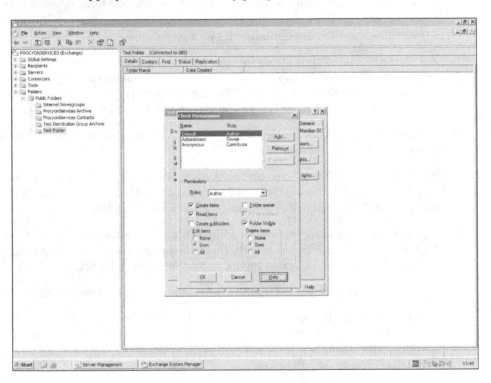

Figure 7-7. *Set appropriate permissions for all new public folders.*

Table 7-1. *Roles That Can Be Assigned to Public Folder Users*

Role Name	Permissions	Description
Owner	Create Items, Read Items, Create Subfolders, Folder Owner, Folder Contact, Folder Visible, Edit All Items, Delete All Items	The Owner of a public folder has effectively Full Control over all folder contents, and any hierarchy beneath this folder. It's possible to assign multiple Owners if required.
Publishing Editor	Create Items, Read Items, Create Subfolders, Folder Visible, Edit All Items, Delete All Items	A Publishing Editor has almost the same level of access as an Owner except for the folder Owner status.
Editor	Create Items, Read Items, Folder Visible, Edit All Items, Delete All Items	An Editor has all the permissions that a Publishing Editor has, minus the Create Subfolders permission.
Publishing Author	Create Items, Read Items, Create Subfolders, Folder Visible, Edit Own Items, Delete Own Items	The emphasis for an Author is shifted from all objects to only the objects created by that author.
Author	Create Items, Read Items, Folder Visible, Edit Own Items, Delete Own Items	An Author has all the permissions that a Publishing Author has, minus the Create Subfolders permission.
Non-editing Author	Create Items, Read Items, Folder Visible, Delete Own Items	A Non-editing Author cannot edit posted items. All he can do is create and delete items.
Reviewer	Read Items, Folder Visible	Reviewers are allowed only to read posts in folders. They have no editing permissions at all.
Contributor	Create Items, Folder Visible	Contributors can create posts but cannot read posts or edit in any way.
None	Folder Visible	A user with the None role can see the folder exists but has no access to the contents.

I think it's wise to explain in a bit more detail the meanings of each of the permissions:

- *Create Items*: The user has the ability to create new posts in the public folder.

- *Read Items*: The user can read the content of posts sent to the public folder.

- *Create Subfolders*: The user can go on to create a hierarchy of subfolders beneath the top-level public folder where the permission was granted.

- *Folder Owner*: This permission makes the user or group the owner of this folder.

- *Folder Contact*: The Folder Contact is attributed only to the folder Owner, and the owner's contact email address is publicized in the public folder when it's browsed using Outlook 2003.

- *Folder Visible*: If a public folder is not visible for a selected user, that user will not even know of its existence when he browses the Public Folder list in Outlook 2003.

- *Edit Items*: The user can modify items already posted to the public folder. You might designate a user as the moderator for a forum, so that the moderator is allowed to take out libel or hurtful comments.

- *Delete Items*: This speaks for itself. The user can delete items from the folder. Again, this might be useful for forum moderators.

Address Lists

Address lists are the lists of users and distribution groups presented to the user through the Exchange Address Book. When a user uses Outlook 2003 to look for a user, he queries the Address Book, possibly the global address list (GAL), to see whether the user exists.

The GAL contains all users' email contact details on your system, but sometimes creating a customized view of the GAL helps users determine which part of your organization users are members of. Instead of having one long list of users and email addresses, you'd split your GAL into departments, with a separate list for management, and potentially another list for suppliers.

The example shown previously in Figure 7-4 showed a new address list created beneath the All Users default list called Test User list. To this list I have added three test user accounts, Test User1, Test User2, and Test User3, as well as the Administrator account and a further distribution group called ProcyonServices. When you use Outlook 2003 to open the Address Book, you are presented with the new address lists, shown in Figure 7-8, and can subsequently send emails to this list.

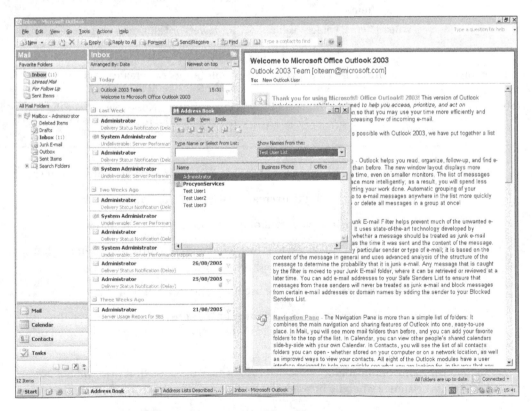

Figure 7-8. *The Address Book displays custom address lists.*

To create your own address lists, do the following:

1. From the Exchange System Manager, expand the Recipients top-level node.

2. Expand All Address Lists.

3. Right-click All Users, select New, and then select Address List.

4. In the Create Exchange Address List dialog box, enter the name of the new address list. Click Filter Rules.

Note The *filter rule* is the rule the system applies to the Active Directory when deciding which users and groups should be included in the address list. Remember that the GAL is better organized by user name than email address, so it's important you get the filter rules right.

---

5. On the Find Exchange Recipients page, make sure all the check boxes under the heading Show These Recipients are selected, and then click Find Now.

6. You are now presented with a complete list of all users, groups, and mail contacts folders on your system (see Figure 7-9).

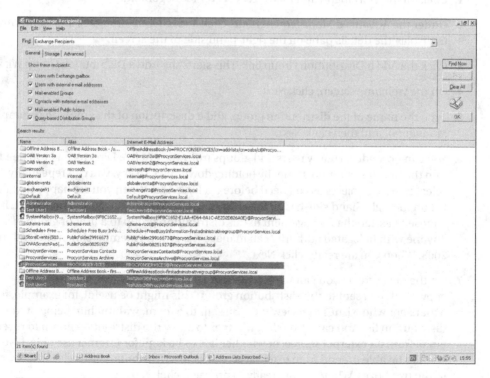

Figure 7-9. *Add multiple objects into each address list.*

7. To add multiple entries at once, hold down the Ctrl key while clicking the mouse on the entities you want included in the address list. When you're finished, click OK.

8. Click Finish.

When you open the Address Book from Outlook, the new address list will be displayed beneath the GAL, as a separate section.

Distribution Groups

Distribution groups are used to enable you to predefine groups of users within your system that have something in common and that you might want to send email to. These can be used to send out team broadcasts, company-wide legislation, or even an itinerary to a social group planning a day out. You can create distribution groups of any users and other distribution groups configured on your system, and doing so is really quite easy. After the distribution group has been created, your users can directly address this as if it were a single recipient and it will appear in the GAL as if it were any other user.

When you first set up Exchange 2003, using the Configure Email and Internet Connection Wizard (CEICW), SBS 2003 creates a single global distribution list for all users on your system, and you can see this if you look in Active Directory Users and Computers.

To create a custom distribution list, do the following:

1. Click on the Start menu and then select Server Management.

2. Under the Advanced Management node, click Active Directory Users and Computers to display the details pane on the right-hand side of the screen.

3. Click the Add a Distribution Group link. This starts the Add a Distribution Group Wizard.

4. On the Welcome screen, click Next.

5. Type the name of the distribution group, add a description of the group (for example, **Managers**), and then click Next.

6. You can now add as many users and groups from your Active Directory as you need to into the new distribution group. By holding down the Ctrl key, you can repeatedly select as many objects as you need before clicking Add. When you are happy that the list on the right-hand side has all the entities you require in the group, click Next. If you choose to assign the management of this distribution group to a user or group of users, anyone with delegated authority can manage the group's membership from Outlook 2003. When you are ready, click Next.

7. On the next screen, you can select whether to create a public folder for storing a copy of all mail sent to this distribution group. This might be useful, for example, for a manager who wishes to review the mail sent to a team, without him being on the distribution list. You can also select whether to allow the distribution group to receive email from an external source, or whether it is to be kept for internal use only. If you want to be able to send from external accounts to a distribution list, select the lower of the two boxes. When you are ready to proceed, click Next.

8. On the last page, click Finish.

The wizard goes on to create the distribution group with all the attributes and members you selected during the last few steps. The new distribution group should be instantly available when Outlook 2003 users query the Address Book.

Note Individual users can create personalized distribution lists themselves by using Outlook 2003. However, the ones created by using the server console are available to everyone, whereas distribution lists created in Outlook 2003 are for personal use only.

The Users Interface

The second place where you can perform most of your Exchange 2003 administration is from the Users interface, available through the standard SBS 2003 Server Management facility.

Open Server Management by clicking Start ➤ Server Management. Then highlight the Users item in Standard Management.

In the details pane on the right, all the users you have configured on your network should be displayed on the screen. By way of example, highlight one of your users by clicking on the user's name: this will show the options available for configuring that user. Click the Change User Properties link to bring up the user's properties dialog box.

There are four significant tabs available in this dialog box that can be used to modify how the user entity operates in Exchange 2003: Email Addresses, Exchange Features, Exchange Advanced, and Exchange General.

Email Addresses

Click the Email Addresses tab to display the list of addresses that has been configured for this user (see Figure 7-10). You'll see two addresses listed in the dialog box: one you are probably familiar with by now—the SMTP address—and the other you are probably not so familiar with. X.400 is not a protocol that you will need to understand for using SBS 2003, and more than likely you will never require it unless you are connecting to a very specialized network environment. Internet email is all based on SMTP, so this is what we'll concentrate on.

You'll see that every user has a single SMTP address associated with his user account. You can easily add a second address if you need to by clicking the New button and then selecting SMTP Address from the list. Click OK and then type in the email address associated with that user.

Note Make sure that any alternate email addresses you assign to your users can be located within your domain. To be sure, give the user an alias address but leave the domain name as your own. There are ways to get around this, but this is a very advanced feature and involves some complicated configuration changes. The other thing to be aware of is that you must not use a name that you might want to assign as the primary name to another user or folder.

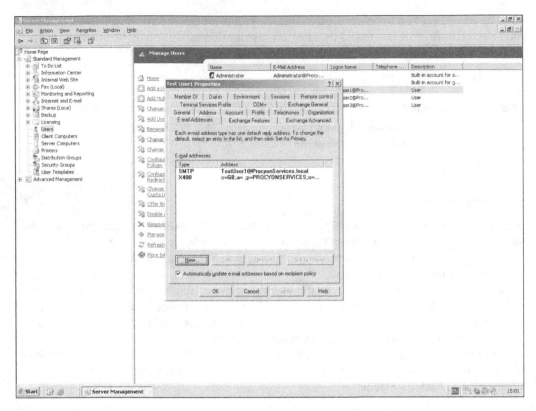

Figure 7-10. *There are two default addresses configured for your users.*

A good example of when you would use a second email address for a user would be if you assigned every user in your organization a role: a role might be salesmanager1 or webmaster. Role-based email names are useful for publishing externally to the Internet community, for example, on your website, so that your employees remain anonymous to the Internet users, while still being named as email recipients internally.

■Note Many SBS 2003 systems are set up to have multiple aliases for each user, handling common misspellings of users' names and nicknames.

Exchange and Mobility

There are extra features on top of the collaborative mail facilities you get with Exchange 2003 that are still governed under the Exchange banner. Click the Exchange Features tab from the user properties page to see which features are enabled for that user (see Figure 7-11).

Exchange Server 2003 can be configured to provide secure access to the user mailbox from a range of mobile devices, such as Pocket PCs and Windows Smartphones. Exchange ActiveSync is an additional service on top of the client-side ActiveSync product that updates every enabled user's Exchange facilities—for example, email, calendar, and contacts are all replicated to the mobile device. To set up a mobility service, speak to your preferred cell phone service provider to see whether they have a gateway and tariff that suits your business.

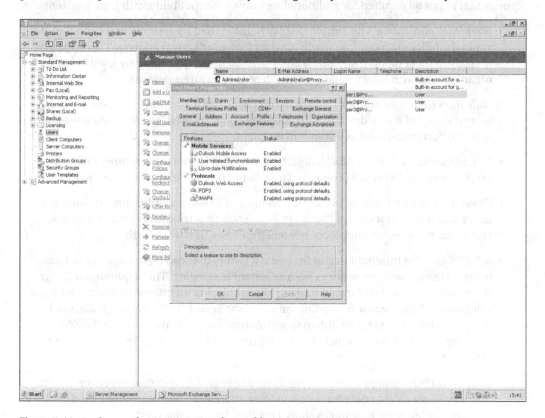

Figure 7-11. *Exchange features are configured by using user properties.*

Note In many countries, such as the US, cell phone companies provide data services by default. Speak to your provider to see whether they offer a data plan on your phone (many of the new cell phones have this capability built in). If this is the case, you won't need a gateway, but only the phone and the mobile device settings, configured according to your provider's instructions.

Advanced User Configuration

Click the Exchange Advanced tab. These settings are used to configure attributes of the user's account that might be required for additional security or compatibility with legacy systems:

- *Simple Display Name*: The Simple Display Name is used by systems that cannot understand the full, long name you might have set for a user's email address. This is extremely unlikely in most modern situations and would be more appropriately used in larger organizations with legacy email systems they need to interoperate with.

- *Hide from Exchange Address List*: Select this check box if you don't want the user to appear in any of the Address Lists. This option could be used for a mail-enabled group that you don't want used as a standard recipient.

- *Downgrade High-Priority Mail Bound for X.400*: This is another interoperability check box for legacy X.400 email protocols. This will not be used in your environment.

- *Custom Attributes*: Clicking this button allows you to add an additional attribute to a user's account for tracking in Exchange 2003. Such an attribute could be the user's social security number, employee reference number, or date of birth.

- *ILS Settings*: The Internet Locator Service is a facility that can be used to better locate users on the network for services such as instant messaging. The requirement for an ILS will present itself if you start looking into employing an internal instant messaging solution, such as Microsoft Live Communications Server (LCS). Although this book does not cover LCS, you can obtain more information on its usage with SBS 2003 from the Microsoft website: http://www.microsoft.com/office/livecomm/prodinfo/default.mspx.

- *Mailbox Rights*: Changing mailbox rights for a user grants or denies user access to that mailbox. There might come an occasion when more than one user might need access to a single mailbox—for example, a shared mailbox for the sales team.

Exchange General Configuration

The Exchange General tab shows you general email information about the user, his name, and where his email is stored on the server. This tab also presents three configuration activities that can change how the user's email function operates:

- *Delivery Restrictions*: You can set limits on the user's email message sizes for both incoming and outgoing traffic as well as setting some message restrictions on what is and isn't permitted. By default, a user is set to be able to receive email from anyone else, including Internet users who are under no governance of you or your system. If you configure a user to receive email from only authenticated users, he'll receive email only from users who are internal to your organization. This is a good way to restrict access to temporary staff whom you don't want exploiting your business's IT resources for personal gain.

- *Deliver Options*: You can designate a Send on Behalf user. This would be someone like a personal assistant who would be required to send an email to a recipient on behalf of a manager. The recipient would see that the message was Sent on Behalf of Manager. You can also automatically forward all email from this mailbox to another mailbox. This could be used to forward all sales team messages to the sales manager, allowing the manager to keep an eye on what her staff is doing.

Warning Because of the differing privacy regulations from country to country, you should set your delivery options based on local legal requirements.

- *Storage Limits*: You can set limits on the user's mailbox size. This interface is fairly intuitive; you set a threshold for a warning, a threshold for when the user can no longer send mail, and finally a threshold for when the mailbox no longer allows sending or receipt of email.

Note Your users' mailboxes will undoubtedly become their desktop filing system unless you do something to make life easier. Recommend that all useful company-related information is stored in SharePoint Services, all personal information (especially large attachments) is stored on the user's local hard drive, leaving only low-capacity (text-only) email in Exchange. In this way, users won't become irate when they cannot send and receive email because of storage limit restrictions.

POP3 Configuration

The following section covers two key aspects of configuring the POP3 service for Exchange 2003: adding mailboxes and defining routing rules. You will be required to configure both of these elements before your POP3 service is fully operable.

Adding POP3 Mailboxes

To use the POP3 connector, the facility that allows you to interface to your mailboxes on the ISP, you need to create POP3 mailboxes on your local Exchange 2003 server. This can be done by using either the CEICW or the POP3 Connection Manager (see Figure 7-12), available from the Server Management console.

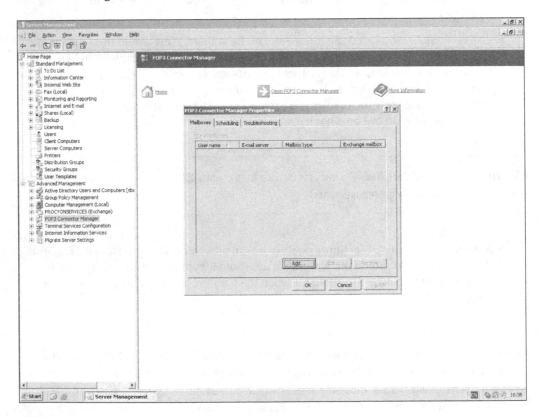

Figure 7-12. *Add POP3 users by using the Connection Manager.*

To add POP3 mailboxes to your SBS 2003 server, do the following:

1. Click Start ➤ Server Management.

2. Under the Advanced Management node, highlight the POP3 Connection Manager item.

3. In the details pane on the right-hand side of the screen, click Open POP3 Connection Manager.

4. Click the Add button.

5. You are now presented with the POP3 Mailbox dialog box (see Figure 7-13). You need to type in the details of the user's ISP email account and the server that the ISP holds the user's mailbox on. You will undoubtedly be required to authenticate at the ISP when you collect mail, so type the user's logon details and then specify which Exchange mailbox this POP3 user account is mapped to. You can select that the user is mapped to an individual or a group account. After you are finished, click OK.

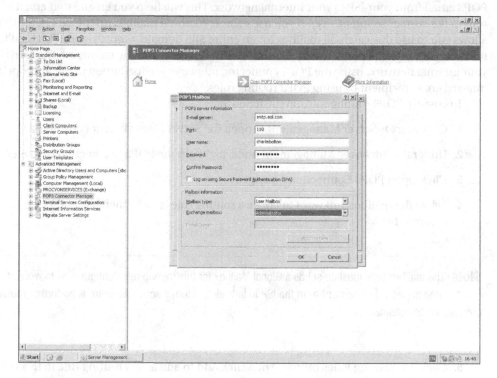

Figure 7-13. *Supply the ISP details for your local users.*

6. Back on the POP3 Connection Manager Properties page, you'll see your new POP3 mailbox listed on the screen. Click the Scheduling tab.

7. You can define how often your system will check on the ISP to see whether any new mail has arrived. When finished, click Apply. Try starting with 15-minute increments or if this is too "fixed" for your environment, opt to connect on demand.

When you create your first POP3 mailbox, SBS 2003 prompts you to start the POP3 Connector service (unless you've used the CEICW and it's done for you). When prompted, click OK. This starts the service and puts the schedule in place that you previously defined.

Note If you want to immediately download your POP3 email from the ISP server, you can use the Retrieve Now button from the Scheduling tab of the POP3 Connection Manager. When you see the information dialog box, click OK to start the download.

Understanding POP3 Email Routing

POP3 routing configuration can be completely automated by using the CEICW. However, it's important to know how to do this manually to fully understand the principles behind routing POP3 email from your ISP to your internal network. This will help you ensure that email is sent to the correct recipient, even if you use a single catch-all mailbox on the server. SBS 2003 allows you to use this catch-all mailbox for an entire SBS domain, with all email destined for users on your internal domain sent to a single ISP mailbox. When the emails are transferred to your internal network, using the POP3 connector, messages are forwarded to the appropriate internal email recipient by using POP3 routing rules.

To create a POP3 routing rule, do the following:

1. Click Start ➤ Server Management to open the Server Management console.

2. Under the Advanced Management node, highlight the POP3 Connection Manager.

3. Click Open POP3 Connection Manager.

4. Select the mailbox you want to create a routing rule for and then click Edit (see Figure 7-14).

Note The mailbox type must be set as a Global Mailbox for this routing rule configuration to work. If you have mapped an individual account from the ISP to individual internal accounts, there is no further routing configuration to consider.

5. Click the Routing Rules button. Then click Add to add a new routing rule to this catch-all account.

6. You now have to type in a piece of text that will be used to filter the email. You can type in the user name, team name, or anything else that might appear in the To or CC fields of incoming email.

7. Add the Exchange 2003 mailbox recipient that the message will be sent to when the filter matches the email to the rule. When you are finished, click OK.

8. Create a new rule for each name you want to filter on.

9. When you are finished, click OK.

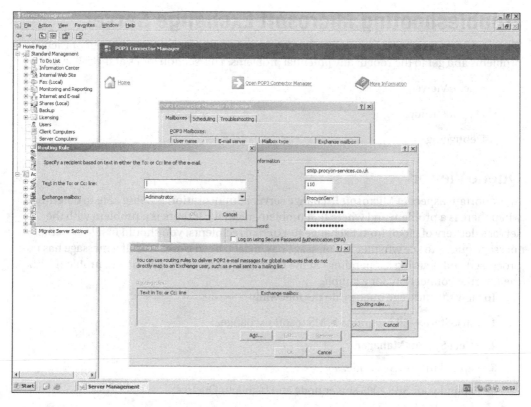

Figure 7-14. *Set up a routing rule for a POP3 catch-all account.*

An example should help put this concept in context: A small IT consultancy company, Nexus Consulting, employing five consultants, has set up a shared SBS 2003 infrastructure to help support their business. The director registered the company and then contacted an ISP to buy some airtime on the Web. The most cost-effective email solution he was offered was a single catch-all email account, whereby all email sent to the domain, destined for any recipient, would be stored in a single mailbox. This mailbox was called catch-all@nexusconsulting.com. Using the POP3 Connection Manager, a single POP3 mailbox was created, called CatchALL, and it was configured as a Global Mailbox. Five routing rules were created, one for each of the users, with the text Mathew, Mark, Luke, John, and Percy, each one with the destination Exchange 2003 mailbox for that user as the destination. Now, if an email is sent to Nexus Consulting, to the address Percy@Nexusconsulting.com, it is stored in the catch-all@nexusconsulting.com mailbox on the server. When it's retrieved by the POP3 connector, the routing rule for Percy sends it to the appropriate internal mailbox.

Troubleshooting Microsoft Exchange Server

There are a few capabilities worth highlighting that can help you better troubleshoot Exchange problems and get to the root of any potential problems. This section looks at the following:

- Queue Viewer
- Diagnostic logging
- Debugging

Queue Viewer

An important aspect of Microsoft Exchange server administration is being able to determine when there is a problem and where that problem might lie. If there is a problem with the server's delivery of email from Exchange to external recipients, you should first look in the message queue to see whether the message has, in fact, been processed. If a message has been processed and is sitting as "pending" in the message queue, you might have a problem with the Internet connection, for example.

To view the message queues, do the following:

1. Click Start ➤ All Programs ➤ Microsoft Exchange.

2. Select System Manager.

3. Expand the Servers node.

4. Expand your SBS 2003 server node and highlight Queues.

You can now view both your internal and outbound SMTP queues through this single consolidated interface as well as perform the following useful functions:

- *Disabling outbound mail*: You can use this feature to instantly disable outbound mail from all SMTP queues. This is particularly useful if you find that your server has become infected with an email virus—you'll be able to quarantine the virus on your own system and deal with it without the concern of infecting customers or partners.

- *Modifying settings*: You can modify the Settings option to change the refresh rate of Queue Viewer if you want a faster update to look at real-time throughput, for example.

- *Finding messages*: You can use Find Messages to search for messages based on the sender, recipient, and message state. This option is similar to enumerating messages in Queue Viewer in Exchange 2000. For detailed instructions, see How to Use the Find Messages Option.

- *Drilling down into the detail*: You can highlight any of the displayed queues to view additional information about that queue.

Diagnostic Logging

Diagnostic logging can help determine the root cause of an email problem because it increases the amount of application error log information generated by Microsoft Exchange.

To modify the diagnostic logging settings on your SBS 2003 server, do the following:

1. Within Exchange System Manager, expand the Servers node.

2. Right-click on the server name and then click Properties.

3. Click the Diagnostics Logging tab.

4. Scroll down through the Services list until you see, for example, POP3Svc for your POP3 service.

5. On the right-hand side of the dialog box under Categories, select the category for which you want to enhance the logging level. For example, a good place to start is to highlight the General category.

6. Under Logging level, click Maximum.

■**Note** The extra information gathered by increasing the diagnostic logging level is collected in the application event log on your SBS 2003 server. It's a good idea to increase the size of the application event log before switching on debugging because an enormous amount of data will be recorded here for diagnostic purposes.

Always remember to set the diagnostic logging level back to the default (None) when you have finished troubleshooting. The higher the level of diagnostic logging selected in the interface, the more work your Exchange server has to do to generate these events. This will degrade the server's capability to operate as responsively as it might have before.

Debugging

If you are still having problems with your email system after modifying the diagnostic logging levels, you can further elevate the logging level by modifying a Registry key on the server that uplifts your event-logging level to the highest value of 7.

■**Note** When you use the diagnostic logging interface and increase the logging level to Maximum, the Registry setting is actually set to 5. The GUI does not allow you to enable debugging.

This is known as the debugging level, which is the highest level of error reporting available on Microsoft Exchange. The default for all diagnostic settings is set to 0.

To enable debugging level 7 for the SMTP protocol, do the following:

1. Click Start ➤ Run.

2. Type **regedit.exe** and press Enter. This starts the Registry Editor.

3. When the Registry Editor appears, locate and then double-click on the following Registry key: `HKEY_LOCAL_MACHINE\System\CurrentControlSet\Services\MSExchangeTransport\Diagnostics\SMTP Protocol`.

4. Set the value to 7 and then click OK.

Warning After you are satisfied that you have found the cause of your problem and no longer need this level of logging, make sure to switch the diagnostic level back to what it was before you increased it. Error logging of this nature can cause an enormous amount of extra work for Exchange and can degrade the responsiveness of a normally operational server.

Note If you want further details on administering and troubleshooting a Microsoft Exchange Server 2003 system, take a look at the online Administration Guide on Microsoft's website: `http://www.microsoft.com/technet/prodtechnol/exchange/guides/E2k3AdminGuide`.

Using Outlook 2003

The Outlook 2003 client will be used by all SBS 2003 users to send and receive email, as well as to update their shared calendar, access public folders, and set tasks. This section covers the basic functions of sending email, setting up meetings, and managing your task lists within Outlook 2003.

Sending and Receiving Email

The most basic and straightforward facility provided by Outlook 2003 is, in essence, its most important and primary task: to send and receive email.

When you first start Outlook 2003 (the first time after installation), you have to tell Outlook that you want to connect to Exchange 2003. Outlook 2003 can be set to connect to web mail systems, such as Hotmail, or POP3 servers, such as one provided directly over a dial-up connection to an ISP. In this case, you will connect Outlook 2003 to the SBS 2003 Exchange server, and it in turn will connect to the ISP.

If you've already run the Connect Computer Wizard for this machine, you can proceed directly to the section on Composing Email.

Connecting Outlook 2003 to Exchange

If you have used the Connect Computer Wizard to connect your Windows XP clients to the SBS 2003 forest, much of the configuration of Microsoft Office Outlook 2003 will already be completed. However, if you have added the computer before completing the Microsoft Office Outlook installation, you'll need to first set up your system to connect to the Exchange server. When Outlook 2003 starts up for the first time, there are no email accounts configured for use. The interface displays only the user's locally stored folders, known as personal folders, without picking up any of the services from the server.

■**Note** *Personal folders* store email and other such data on the user's PC rather than on the server. This can be useful if the administrator imposes limits on users' mailbox space on the Exchange server. Items stored in personal folders are stored locally in files known as .pst files. You can also archive .pst files onto DVD and keep them for future reference. This is a great way of clearing up your mailbox without losing your old messages.

To add a new email account to your Outlook 2003 client, you must close Outlook and configure your mail system from Control Panel on the client computer. To complete this task, do the following:

1. Click Start ➤ Control Panel.

2. From the Control Panel, select Mail.

3. Click Email Accounts.

4. Click the Add a New Email Account radio button. Then click Next.

5. Click the Microsoft Exchange Server radio button (see Figure 7-15). Then click Next.

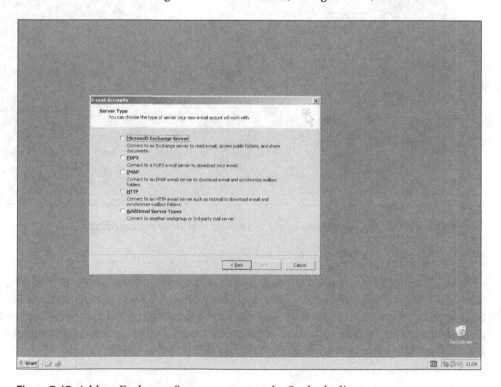

Figure 7-15. *Add an Exchange Server account to the Outlook client.*

6. Type the name of the Exchange 2003 server (your SBS 2003 server name) and then type the name of the user account being accessed. To make sure you have the details correct, click the Check Name button (see Figure 7-16).

7. When you are content that you are ready to proceed, click Next.

8. You now receive an informational message informing you that your email will be sent to your personal folder on your workstation, and not stored on the server. Click Yes to continue.

9. On the last page of the wizard, click Finish.

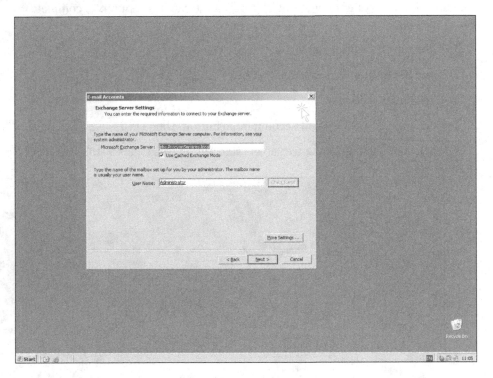

Figure 7-16. *Check the name of the server and user before proceeding.*

■Note Outlook 2003 can connect to Exchange 2003 by using the RPC protocol over HTTP or HTTPS (recommended). By doing this, remote Outlook 2003 users located behind firewalls can connect to the Exchange 2003 server by using the full Outlook 2003 client, meaning no functionality is lost through the web interface (Outlook Web Access). For more information on configuring Outlook 2003 to use RPC over HTTP/S, take a look at the article at http://www.msexchange.org/tutorials/outlookrpchttp.html.

You can now start Outlook 2003 as usual, but you'll see an additional folder beneath the Personal Folders node, titled Mailbox. If you expand this node, you'll see six new folders you have access to: Deleted Items, Drafts, Inbox, Outbox, Sent Items, and Search Folders.

I won't try to present all of Outlook 2003's functionality in this chapter, but I will try to explain the relationship between the Outlook 2003 client and the Microsoft Exchange server. This is important so that users can get to grips with what Exchange 2003 offers end users in terms of functionality and data resilience.

Composing Email

If you send an email, it will be sent from the Microsoft Exchange Mailbox account. To compose a new email to an internal recipient (someone else in your business), highlight the Inbox and click the New button at the top-left of the screen. This opens the Untitled—Message screen where you can compose your email.

Click the To button to select recipients from the Microsoft Exchange Address Book. Select any number of users or distribution groups from the list and then click the Add button.

Note If you hold down the Ctrl key, you can select as many users as you need before pressing the To button. All user recipients will be added to the address bar, separated by a semicolon.

After you have added all the recipients you need to, click OK. A courtesy copy (CC)—also known as a carbon copy—of an email can be sent to a manager or someone who might want to see the email out of interest rather than need. Click the CC button and add users in much the same way as you did for the To recipients.

Note Always add a subject line to an email to ensure that your recipients know the context of the messages they are receiving. This helps users determine which emails are important and which might be simply informational.

Type the body of the message in the large data entry area at the bottom of the email. You have now created your first internal email to your business community.

A number of extra features help you extend the bounds of this simple text-based message to allow you to add attachments, prioritize the message in terms of importance for the recipients, and add a mandatory signature to each message in line with company policy. These features are defined as follows:

- *Add an attachment*: To add an attachment to an email message, click the Insert menu from the email itself and then click File. Select the attachment from the file store.

Warning Never attach files that can contain executable code (code that viruses can exploit). These files have extensions such as .bat, .exe or .vbs. If you need to bring files like this into your system, bring them in explicitly, one by one, by using some other method. You could, for example, use a CD so the file could be explicitly scanned for viruses/malware before introduction to your environment.

- *Add a signature*: Signatures are great for repeating business card details at the bottom of every email without the user having to retype these details. To create a signature, click the Insert menu from an email and then select Signature and More. If you don't already have one, you are prompted to set one up (see Figure 7-17). Follow the simple guidelines to create the signature and append it to each email you send.

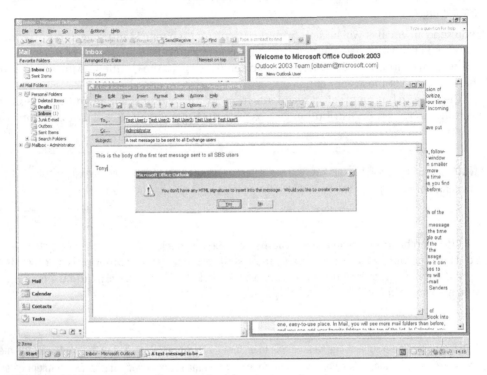

Figure 7-17. *Sign each email you send with a custom signature.*

Warning For security and compatibility reasons, most SBS 2003 users compose email as rich text or plain text. HTML is perceived as a threat by many security system managers and should really be avoided.

- *Set the message importance*: Click the red exclamation mark at the top of the email screen to set the message to high importance. This will display a red exclamation mark in the recipient's inbox to indicate that the message should be treated as more significant than other email.

- *Follow up*: If you click the red flag at the top of the email page, the recipient will be instructed to follow up on the course of action outlined in your email. This should be reserved for use when a follow-up is imperative rather than for normal messages.

- *Set message options*: Additional options are available for customizing an email, and you should explore these to best understand the full capability of Outlook and Exchange. Click the Options button at the top of the email for further information.

New email is delivered automatically to your Microsoft Exchange mailbox, and your Outlook client is notified as soon as the email arrives. If you highlight the Inbox, you'll see a list of all emails sent to your account, any priority settings such as follow-up flags, and a view of the message inside the email shown in the preview pane on the right-hand side of the screen.

To open the email, double-click on the message. You can now reply to the sender, reply to all recipients of the original message, or forward the email to someone not included on the original distribution list.

Creating Appointments

On the bottom-left side of the Outlook main screen, click Calendar. This brings up the personal diary for the logged in-user. The data populating this screen is stored inside the personal folders, but is synchronized by using Exchange. You can add appointments, book leave, schedule meetings with colleagues, and use Internet-based calendars, all from this one interface.

To create a new calendar entry, do the following:

1. From the Outlook 2003 main screen, click Calendar.

2. Click the New button. This brings up a new Appointment form (see Figure 7-18).

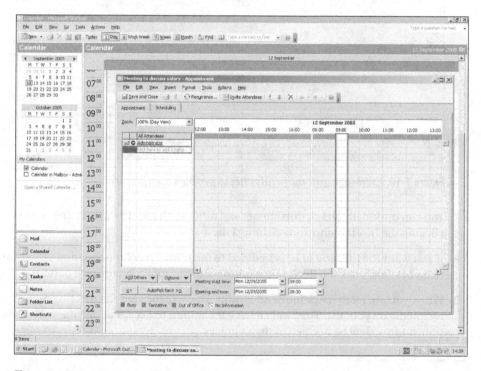

Figure 7-18. *Create entries for yourself or for meetings with others.*

3. Add a Subject and a Location for the appointment and ensure that the date and time of the appointment are set to the correct parameters.

4. Use the Reminder drop-down list to specify how early Outlook will remind you of your appointment. For a meeting on site, you might choose just 15 minutes, whereas for a meeting on a customer's site, you might want a day's notice.

5. Click the Scheduling tab to arrange for other attendees to be contacted by Exchange and invited to the meetings. Exchange will automatically check whether the people you are inviting are available for the meeting and will report clashes if they occur. This gives you the opportunity to reschedule a meeting if there is a clash.

6. Click the Add Others button and then click Add from Address Book (see Figure 7-19). Select the recipients you wish to invite to your meeting and then click OK.

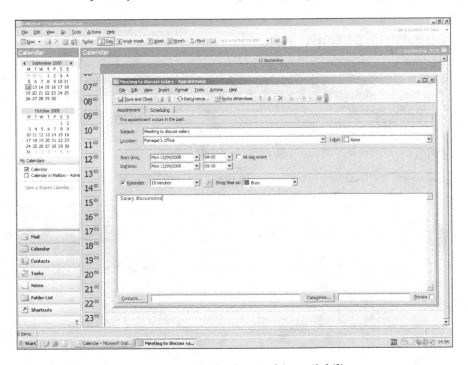

Figure 7-19. *Exchange automatically checks people's availability.*

7. You can optionally attach documents and other such files to the meeting request by clicking the Insert menu and selecting File.

8. If you want the meeting to be scheduled to recur on a regular frequency, say a monthly team briefing, click the Recurrence button and identify a Recurrence pattern.

9. When you are ready, click the Send button. This will forward the meeting request to all recipients on your list. They will all have the option to accept or decline your invitation, and you will be notified of their choices.

▪**Note** It's also possible to create group calendars for user communities and host them in a public folder. If you opt to do this, group calendar appointments can easily be copied back into personal calendars.

Using Tasks

Tasks are Outlook items that allow you to create a To Do list. Tasks take on many forms and priorities, determined by the task creation process, and you will be reminded of approaching deadlines and imminent delivery dates.

To create a new task by using Outlook, do the following:

1. From the Outlook main screen, click the Tasks folder on the left side of the page. This displays the Tasks list, showing which tasks are active and which ones have been completed.

2. To create a new task, click New.

3. Fill in the nature of the task in the Subject field and then fill in the details in the following steps.

4. Assign a due date for when the task has to be completed and a start date for when you will begin work on the task.

5. The status of a task tells a user how the task is proceeding, from Not Started through to Completed. A priority can also be assigned to tasks to differentiate the more-important ones from normal day-to-day activities. You can track how far through a task you are by suggesting how Completed the task is—stated as a percentage—and you can ask Outlook to remind you as often as you like that a task is still outstanding (see Figure 7-20).

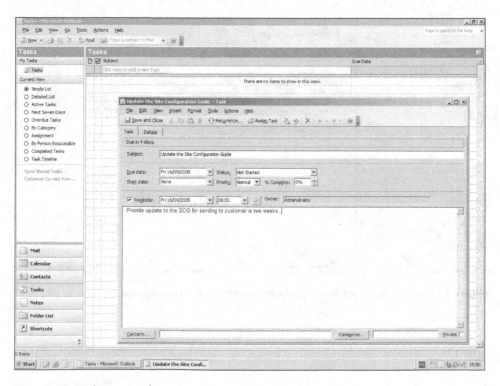

Figure 7-20. *Tasks are used to manage your day-to-day activities.*

In much the same way as Outlook uses Exchange to communicate meeting requests, it will exploit the back-end Exchange server if you decide that a task should be assigned to someone else. In this way, managers can assign tasks to their workforce, and the task is sent as if it were an email. When Outlook pulls the message down, it determines that the message is a task and is inserted in the appropriate folder.

Outlook Web Access

Accessing Outlook from the Internet is easy if you use Outlook Web Access (OWA). OWA is available by default for all remote-access users and is obtained through the top-level company website.

A user who is accessing any computer from the Internet can connect to Outlook Web Access via the business's URL appended with /exchange — in the case of the example shown in Figure 7-21, this would be http://sbs/exchange.

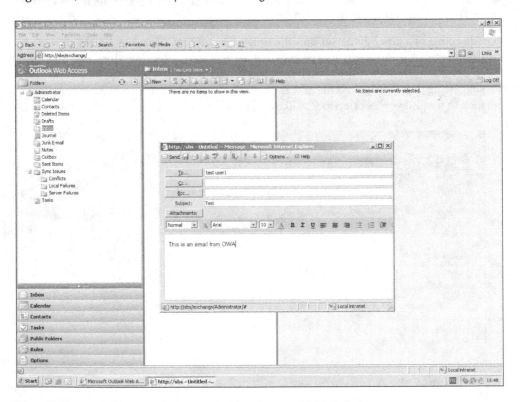

Figure 7-21. *From the server home page, select Remote Web Workplace.*

Note You can also connect directly from the Internet by using traditional web access (using Internet Explorer) as long as you know the DNS name of your SBS 2003 server (the name must be registered to point to your server's IP address), or, if you don't know the name, you can use the IP address of the Internet-facing network interface card on your server.

This displays an interface much like that of the standard Outlook 2003 interface, but it is now running in a web browser environment rather than as a client-based application. By using OWA, you can have your users access most of the facilities of your Exchange server without requiring an Outlook client.

OWA does not require ISA Server 2004 to work; however, if you are using ISA Server 2004 from SBS 2003 Premium Edition, you can easily configure it to publish OWA through the firewall.

Exchange and Security

When you configure Exchange Server 2003, you should be cognizant of the security features that you can enforce through the Exchange interface. There are numerous ways to secure access to your Exchange information store. Some of these measures are designed to stop malicious access, some prevent confidentiality issues, and most simply ensure that the system continues functioning with the level of integrity that it had when first installed. In no particular order, the elements of security we'll look at are as follows:

- Mailbox permissions

- Antivirus

- Shutting down Exchange in the event of an outbreak

Mailbox Permissions

You can modify the permissions on Exchange folders from two places: SBS 2003 Server Management and Outlook 2003. The administrator can modify permissions from the Server Management interface, and users manage permissions through Outlook 2003.

Modifying Permissions from Server Management

To modify permissions from Server Management, an administrator should perform the following steps:

1. Using an administrative account, log into the SBS 2003 server and start Server Management.

2. Highlight the Users node under Standard Management to display the list of users in the details pane.

3. Click on the user you are interested in managing the permissions of and right-click. Select Properties.

4. When you see the properties dialog box for that user, select the Exchange Advanced tab and then click the Mailbox Rights button. This brings up the Permissions dialog box (see Figure 7-22).

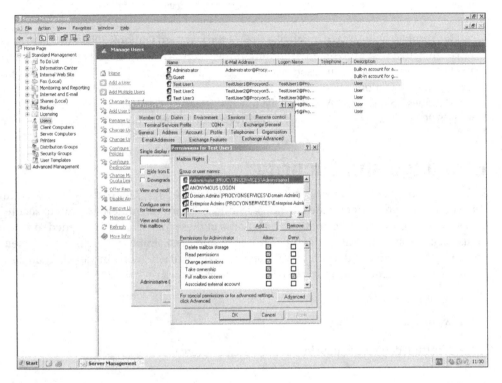

Figure 7-22. *Modify access to a mailbox from Server Management.*

5. To add a new user or group to the access list, click Add.

6. If you know the name of the user or group, or indeed know only part of the name (such as Tony, rather than Tony Campbell), type this in the text box titled Enter the Object Names to Select. Click Check Names.

7. Select the appropriate user or security group from the list and then click OK.

8. Click OK to add this user to the Mailbox Rights list.

9. The user automatically gets the Delete Mailbox Storage permissions, which I'd advise you to remove. You might want to consider the permissions shown in Table 7-2 before you start modifying the list.

Table 7-2. *Permissions That Apply to Exchange Mailboxes*

Permission	Result	Information
Delete Mailbox Storage	This allows the user to delete the mailbox from the mailbox store.	This permission should be granted only to administrators.
Read Permissions	Users with this permission can read items inside this mailbox.	Any user who is required to read mail items in a mailbox should have this permission.
Change Permissions	The user can delete or modify email items in the mailbox.	This permission allows users an element of control over the items in the mailbox.
Take Ownership	The user is attributed the ownership flag for the mailbox.	This should be granted only to the user who is in control of the mailbox.
Full Mailbox Access	This permission gives the user full access to all email items and allows him total control over what happens to those items.	Full control should be reserved for administrators and the user who is designated as the primary user of that mailbox.
Associated External Account	This permission is used if an account is in a remote Windows 2003 forest.	Not applicable to SBS 2003 users.

To further view the advanced permissions that apply to a mailbox, click the Advanced button. In much the same way as you would modify Advanced NTFS permissions to grant a more granular and exact set of access rights to files and folders, you can drill into each individual permission by highlighting it and clicking the Edit button.

Warning Changing permissions as the administrator can be beneficial if users have not been educated to understand what they are doing, but more often it's best to identify what training your users require and explain to them how to modify permissions themselves from the much simpler Outlook 2003 interface. A common time for an administrator to modify the permissions on a mailbox is when a user leaves the company and you need to assign the mailbox to someone else.

Modifying Permissions by Using Outlook 2003

To modify permissions from the Outlook 2003 client, do the following:

1. Open Outlook 2003. Right-click on the folder you want to set permissions for (the Inbox under the Exchange mailbox rather than the Personal Folder inbox) and then select Properties.

2. On the properties page, click the Permissions tab. This displays the current permissions set on your mailbox (see Figure 7-23).

3. Click the Add button to see a full list of all users and groups that can be added to this mailbox. Select the users or groups you want to add to the mailbox permissions list and then click the Add button.

4. When you're finished, click OK.

5. The permissions applied to the user or group are the same as those used for public folders, shown in Table 7-1.

6. When you're finished, click OK.

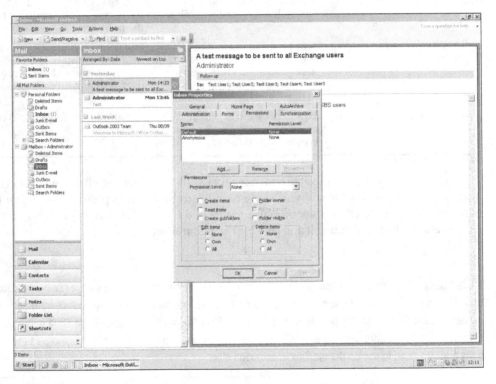

Figure 7-23. *Setting permissions from Outlook 2003 is easy for the user.*

When you grant permissions for a new user or group to access a mailbox, the associated users have the ability to access that mailbox through the Outlook 2003 interface. To access another personal mailbox (as long as you have previously been granted permission), do the following from Outlook 2003:

1. From Outlook 2003, click File ➤ Open.

2. Select Other User's Folder.

3. Type the name of the user whose folder you want to access. Then, using the drop-down list, select that user's folder.

4. Click OK.

Antivirus Products and Exchange

Email is the perfect mechanism for computer virus writers to spread their infection across the entire planet. There is no better and more accessible platform than the underlying infrastructure straddling the connected world of the Internet. The beauty (for the cybercriminals) of using email to proliferate these sorts of malicious code attacks is that even the crudest and ill-conceived viruses stand a chance of creating global chaos if they are unleashed attached to email.

You are probably aware that using antivirus products on workstations is a good way of addressing the problem at the client end, but if a virus is leeching resources from your server or proliferating around the mailboxes inside your Exchange 2003 server, you don't want to wait for it to hit your users before you do something about it.

For this very reason, antivirus products have been created that monitor Exchange 2003 server and can intercept virus signatures in email before they ever arrive in the user's mailbox.

Warning Make sure to configure an exclusion rule in your antivirus system to stop the scanning engine from scanning the Exchange server file store. Antivirus scans of the exchsvr directory have been reported to cause information store corruptions on the Exchange server.

Vendors, such as Trend Micro, McAfee, and Symantec, have created server-based products that do just this: analyze mailbox activity looking for virus signatures, spyware, and spam. If these products detect threats, they can perform a number of countermeasures to ensure that the outbreak is contained and that you suffer no data loss.

To see how McAfee is positioning their small business solution for Internet-based security and email server protection, take a look at http://www.mcafeesecurity.com/uk/products/mcafee/smb/antivirus/mail_protection_smb.htm.

Note If you spot an outbreak of a virus or some sort of spyware, disable your Internet connection, hence protecting your customers. Fight the threat by using the tools you have internally. This is vitally important because your reputation as a company might be blackened if your Exchange 2003 server automatically starts sending viruses to your business contacts. How would *you* feel if a company supplying you with parts or services infected your IT system, rendered your production capability useless, and left your workers without PCs.

Further Investigation

Two further methods of checking the security and integrity of your email system are to use the message tracking logs supplied with Exchange 2003 and to check the event logs on both the user's computer and on the server.

To enable message tracking on your server, do the following:

1. Open Exchange System Manager from the Start menu.

2. Double-click the Servers node. Then right-click on your SBS server and select Properties.

3. Focus on the General tab and then select the Enable Message Tracking check box (see Figure 7-24).

4. Next to the Log File Directory text box, click the Change button.

5. In the Message Tracking Log File Directory, select the location where you'd like the file to be stored. Click OK.

6. Select the Remove Log Files check box and enter the number of days you wish to retain log files for.

7. When you are finished, click OK.

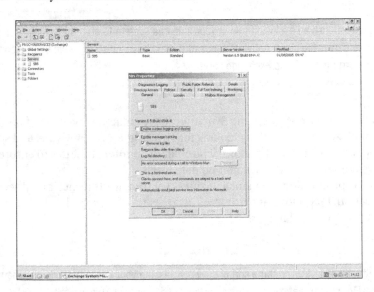

Figure 7-24. *Message tracking helps detect possible security problems.*

To access the information collected by using the message tracking logs, you'll need to use the Exchange System Manager tool called the Message Tracking Center.

■ **Warning** Depending on the level of tracking you configure, message tracking logs can be huge. It is recommended that you use tracking as an investigatory tool rather running it all the time. Keep an eye on the size of your log files and if they get too big, try copying them off to external media.

To run the Message Tracking Center, do the following:

1. Run the Exchange System Manager and then expand the Tools node.

2. Highlight Message Tracking Center to start the application in the details pane on the right.

3. You can search for messages based on the following criteria (see Figure 7-25):

   - *Message ID*: This is a unique number assigned to every email sent by Exchange 2003, and if you know it, you can immediately locate the message and its history within the bounds of your server's infrastructure.

   - *Sender*: This is normally one of your SBS 2003 users and can be located within the Active Directory by clicking Sender and then searching in the usual way for a user resource.

   - *Server*: Because you have only one Exchange 2003 server in your infrastructure, you're best using one of the other search criteria.

   - *Recipients*: You can search the logs for messages sent to particular recipients. This is a good security feature because you can form opinions of how your users might be colluding with one another to achieve some malicious goal.

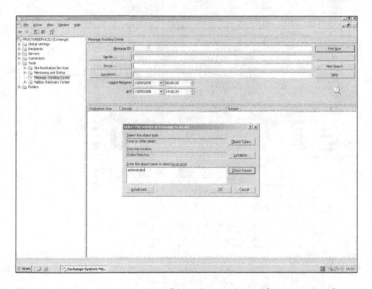

Figure 7-25. *The Message Tracking Center is used to monitor logs.*

4. After you have determined and input your search criteria, click Find Now. Any messages meeting the criteria of your search are displayed in the pane at the bottom of the screen.

Event Logs

On both the user's workstation and the server, there are logs of security events and of application and system events collected to help you diagnose problems and detect security breaches.

Using the event logs is covered in more detail in Chapter 11 but for now we'll take a quick peek at how you access them. The process for opening Event Viewer on the user's workstation is the same as that of the server; the only difference is that an SBS 2003 server has six logs, compared to three on a standard Microsoft Windows XP Professional workstation.

To open the Event Viewer on a server or workstation, do the following:

1. Click Start ➤ Control Panel.

2. Click Administrative Tools and then click Event Viewer. This starts the application for viewing the event logs.

3. Highlight the log you are interested in analyzing to display all currently held events for that log.

4. To see the details of a single event, double-click on the event. This brings up the Event Properties dialog box (see Figure 7-26).

Figure 7-26. *Use the Event Viewer to monitor system security.*

A Windows XP Professional workstation (as well as most of the legacy Microsoft Windows clients based on Windows NT technologies) has three of the preceding event logs collecting information specific to the workstation: the Application log, the Security log, and the System log. These are accessed in the same way as you access the logs on the server.

Case Study—Planthire

Corporate email was a key development for Planthire. Previously, all communication from employees to suppliers and customers (except for Philip Stanley, who emailed from home) was done by using phone calls or traditional mail. With the introduction of the Exchange server, email was available to all employees, both on the shop floor and in the office.

Philip allowed all his users to use email whenever they liked, so they could use it for personal email as well as company email. He was unsure of whether this was a good decision in the beginning as he imagined his employees spending most of their time sending emails to friends, but when he reviewed productivity after running SBS 2003 for just three months, profits were up 40 percent.

This differential told him that business efficiency had dramatically improved and was still increasing month by month. He knew at some point it would settle down as he was in a transition phase, but this enhanced communication with customers and suppliers was improving relationships and securing deals better than he could have expected.

Case Study—Servideal

Henry saw email as one of the prime enablers for his business. No e-commerce site is complete without its email facility: order confirmations, problem resolution, newsletters, brand announcements, and sale information are all customer-related communications that are best serviced by using email.

Email, compared to hard-copy marketing information, is cheap, and as Henry pointed out, much quicker to produce. Customers who receive a leaflet through the mail expect a certain standard to be adhered to, whereas email recipients wouldn't even bat an eyelid at a plain-text, graphics-free mailer. This means press releases can be turned around in a matter of minutes and disseminated to the customer base as fast as the email system will allow, rather than the postal system taking days, if not weeks, to deliver a mass, paper-based mailer to a global marketplace.

The global reach of email significantly reduces the cost of worldwide advertising, and the immediacy of an email compared to traditional correspondence makes it seem a more personal touch.

Case Study—Country Estates

Country Estates has always relied on email to one extent or another. Their goal for employing the centralized and well-managed services that come with SBS 2003 was to bring internal email in-house. This would make the sending and receiving of emails within the company fast, efficient, and safe, and only email destined for external customers would have to traverse the boundary protection of their network.

Because users' mailboxes can be kept on the server, the email database can be backed up as part of normal business so all important email, along with all the other data on the SBS 2003 server, remains safe from corruption. The centralization of email services within the boundary also significantly cut down on the number of viruses getting into the corporate network. Antivirus software scans all incoming and outgoing email at the server, so by the time it reaches a user's desktop, the message should be as clean as it possibly can be.

Summary

As you've probably seen from this chapter, Exchange 2003 is a complex and extremely useful part of the SBS 2003 product set. The POP3 connector is invaluable in the small business environment for speeding up deployment of your email solution (although some would argue that the best way of getting email is SMTP because the POP3 connector is simply a way of disguising a rather cumbersome and unreliable underlying solution really designed for home users). The additional features above and beyond just email, such as public folders and shared calendars, makes this a valuable collaboration capability for your enterprise.

SBS 2003, as usual, does most of the initial configuration required to operate an Exchange 2003 environment internally on your network. With a small amount of configuration, it easily integrates with the rest of the world, offering you global connectivity. But, if you want to go further with Exchange 2003 (and believe me when I say what you've learned here is only the tip of the iceberg), don't hesitate to get more details of Exchange 2003's features and capabilities from the Microsoft technical website: `http://www.microsoft.com/exchange/library`.

■ ■ ■

ISA Server

This chapter concentrates on the features of the industrial-strength firewall capability included with SBS 2003 Premium Edition, known as Microsoft Internet Security and Acceleration (ISA) Server 2004. This upgrade from ISA Server 2000 occurs when you install SBS 2003 Premium Edition Service Pack 1 or is included in newly purchased SBS 2003 Premium Edition systems that include SP1 by default.

Tip In the US, you will need to contact Microsoft to order the CDs for ISA Server 2004. The download for Service Pack 1 from the website does not include this software for Premium edition users. If you obtained your SP1 software as part of another subscription (Microsoft Action Pack or MSDN, for example), you would have received the update with that subscription.

Microsoft ISA Server 2004 is not just a firewall. To put it in context, you must first look at the range of features ISA Server 2004 can bring to your organization before deciding whether it's the right tool for the job. You already should have examined the risks associated with connecting your network to the Internet and assessed the value of your business data held on the systems within your network, and from this, you should have come to the conclusion that a firewall is an essential part of any Internet-connected system.

Understanding ISA Server Capabilities

Firewalls come in many guises, many of which are cheaper and more discrete than ISA Server 2004. Plenty of products on the market provide the same level of firewall protection afforded by ISA Server 2004. So why would you choose ISA Server 2004 over the competition?

First, ISA Server 2004 is most definitely a firewall. It is being utilized in countless classified governmental and high-security environments across the globe (banking, health care, research establishments) and has been accredited with the most rigorous standards to meet the requirements of these customers.

Second, setting ISA Server 2004 apart from the competition, the product delivers several additional, complementary capabilities that can be categorized as follows:

- Packet filtering

- Network address translation

- Web caching

- Web publishing

Packet Filtering

Packet filtering is a capability whereby every TCP/IP packet passing across a protected network interface is scanned for signatures that equate to known network attack patterns. Packet filtering affords a high degree of control over who has access to what on your network and offers the ability to program specific rules pertaining to your access requirements.

An additional feature of ISA Server 2004, not available on the cheaper alternatives, is the capability to perform two types of packet inspection: stateful packet inspection and Application layer inspection. Both of these scan the contents of network traffic, looking inside TCP/IP packets (from two complementary perspectives) for evidence of tampering, hijacking, or brute force attack. Sophisticated hackers have demonstrated their ability to bypass the simpler network defense solutions—although this is uncommon in the small business arena, it is still a growing problem. By using a combination of both packet inspection technologies, by default in ISA Server 2004, you get a deep, intelligent scan of all network communication. The good guys are let in, and the bad guys are kept out.

Network Address Translation

Network address translation (NAT) is a technology used to hide your internal network from the outside world by providing all communications through a middleman—the NAT service. The NAT service sits on the boundary between the internal network and the external network, effectively bridging the gap between the two network interface cards.

The basic premise of how a NAT service works is straightforward:

1. You try to communicate with a computer system that's external to your network (on the Internet).

2. The communication is routed through your default gateway, which just happens to be your SBS 2003 system running ISA Server.

3. The NAT service sees a request coming from an internal network address, trying to speak to an external network address, and it randomly assigns a port number to this connection. This port number uniquely identifies the internal system to the NAT service.

Note Every TPC/IP connection has an associated port number. A port is the application interface in the TCP/IP system that allows multiple communicating services to operate when using the same IP address. For example, you send SMTP mail on port number 25 while you access standard web pages on HTTP port 80.

4. The NAT device adds a new header to the IP packet so the return address is no longer the IP address of the internal system. Instead, the recipient on the Internet will see the address of the sender as the IP address of the external interface of the NAT.

5. All communications coming back from the Internet to the internal system will come first to the NAT device, with the random port number included in the header. This is a feature of how TCP/IP works.

6. The NAT device has kept a record of all randomly assigned port numbers used for external IP connections, and it's a matter of looking up the number in the table and forwarding the packet back to the internal computer.

This process is conceptualized in Figure 8-1.

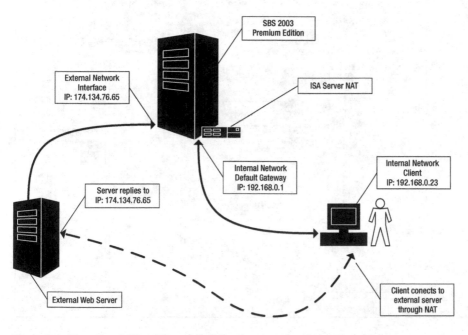

Figure 8-1. *The client's IP address is hidden from external scrutiny.*

Web Caching

The next component of ISA Server to consider is that of *web caching*. ISA Server allows you to specify external systems that are commonly accessed by your users. The target data is stored locally on your ISA Server, allowing it to service client web requests rather than those requests being passed across the Internet.

Web caching can be configured to check that cached components from the target system are up-to-date. Schedules can be set to perform consistency checks on target data elements so that cached components are automatically updated with the latest data.

Configuration of caching is covered later in this chapter, but for now it's sufficient to say that many types of target components can be cached. In describing the cache contents (such as a URL, for example), you can specify the client connection-handling parameters to determine how server requests are handled and how exceptions should be processed. Figure 8-2 shows a cache rule created for CNN's website.

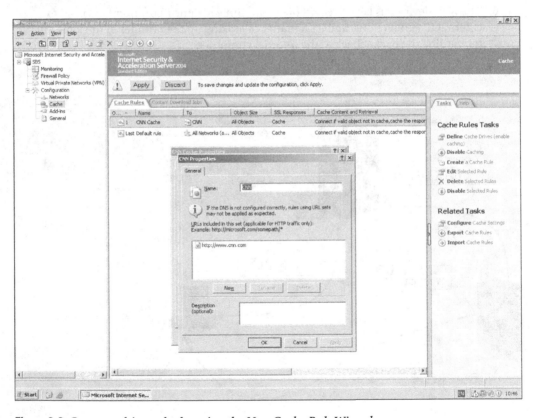

Figure 8-2. *Create caching rules by using the New Cache Rule Wizard.*

The following target components can be cached by using ISA Server:

- Networks
- Computers

- Network address ranges
- Subnets
- Sets of computers
- Domain names and URLs

Web Publishing

Web publishing can be used to make an internal website accessible to authorized users on the Internet. For example, you might publish a small portion of your intranet to the Internet as your home page, keeping the rest of your intranet safely behind your firewall.

Warning Web publishing is not recommended as the best method for getting your website onto the Internet. A better option is to copy the website onto the ISP's server and let the ISP worry about security and resilience. In this way, you don't need to create any potential breaches in your network boundary security.

Web publishing should not be confused with the Remote Web Workplace, which offers access to your actual internal systems over a secure web connection. However, if you want external customers or affiliates to access your website information, web publishing can make those pages available to your external network interface. In this way, your internal web server remains protected behind the firewall while ISA Server is responsible for creating copies of your web pages on the external interface (see Figure 8-3).

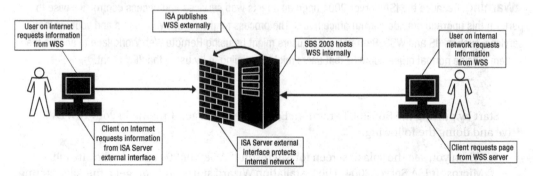

Figure 8-3. *An Internet user browses the website through ISA Server.*

Note For further information on installing, using, and making the most of Microsoft ISA Server 2004, try going to the following websites: http://www.microsoft.com/isaserver/default.mspx and http://www.isaserver.org.

Installing ISA Server 2004

When you first installed SBS 2003, you ran the Configure Email and Internet Connection Wizard (CEICW) from the To Do List (see Chapter 4).

After the installation of ISA Server 2004 has finished, you will have to run the updated version of the CEICW to create the rules and policies necessary to permit your outbound and inbound network traffic to pass across the ISA Server 2004 boundary—features such as email, secure VPNs, Remote Web Workplace, and Outlook Web Access. The CEICW will start automatically when ISA Server 2004 finishes installing.

Note Network settings previously configured with the CEICW will remain unchanged unless explicitly for ISA Server 2004.

ISA Server comes as a separately installable component of SBS 2003 Premium Edition. However, it is much more tightly integrated into SBS 2003 than its predecessor, ISA Server 2000. ISA Server 2004 is enhanced with many additional wizards to aid the SBS 2003 community in the product's configuration.

If you have previously installed ISA Server 2000 as part of your pre-SP1 SBS 2003 Premium Edition solution, you'll have to perform an upgrade to ISA Server 2004 by using your SBS 2003 Premium Edition SP1 installation media. A fresh installation (without performing an upgrade) is extremely straightforward.

Warning Because the ISA Server 2004 upgrade affects web services and access control, it's wise to perform this upgrade outside normal office hours. The process might disrupt your users and your system services, such as IIS and WSS. Remember that users might be using Remote Web Workplace to access the system outside normal office hours or that users might be dialing in by using the VPN client.

Start by putting the SBS 2003 Premium Edition Service Pack 1 media in your CD/DVD drive and doing the following:

1. When you see the splash screen for Microsoft ISA Server 2004 Setup, click Install Microsoft ISA Server 2004. The Installation Wizard starts and you get a message stating that the Windows installer is preparing to install.

2. The next screen you'll see is the Welcome screen. Click Next to continue.

3. Read the End User License Agreement and when you're satisfied, select I Accept the Terms in the License Agreement. Click the Next button.

4. On the Destination Folder page, select the destination disk you want the ISA Server 2004 system to reside on. To change the default, click the Change button and select one of the available hard disks on your system. When you're ready, click Next.

Note Try to install all application software on a separate hard disk from that of the operating system. If you followed the guidelines in Chapter 3 on planning your disk layout, you should use the D: drive.

5. On the next page, Export Microsoft ISA Server 2000 Configuration, you'll need to click the Export button if you are doing an upgrade. This will ensure that all settings from ISA Server 2000 (such as network addressing tables) are copied to ISA Server 2004. This is the simplest and quickest way to ensure that your system continues working when you complete the upgrade. If you are not upgrading, proceed to step 12.

6. You are taken to an embedded wizard known as the Microsoft ISA Server Migration tool. On the Welcome page, click Next to continue.

7. Select the Default Firewall Policy (see Figure 8-4) and then select the radio button labeled Allow Clients on the Internal Network to Access the Microsoft ISA Server 2004 Computer. Click the Next button to continue.

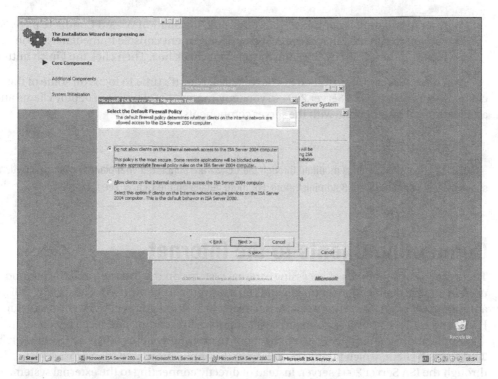

Figure 8-4. *Set the default to allow internal computer access.*

8. On the Create Migration File page, click Create. After the file has been created successfully, click Next.

9. When you see the last page of the migration wizard, click Finish. This returns you to the main Microsoft ISA Server 2004 Installation Wizard.

10. Back on the Export page, click Next.

11. On the next page, click Next.

12. When you see the Ready to Install the Program page, you're nearly there. Click the Install button. ISA Server 2004 is now installed by using either the settings exported from ISA Server 2000 or the default settings that will later be augmented by the running of the CEICW.

Note When working through the CEICW, make sure to select Enable Firewall on the Firewall page. This ensures that the CEICW creates the appropriate ISA Server 2004 rules for the services you need access to via the ISA 2004 firewall.

---

13. After installation is complete, you will see the Installation Wizard Complete page. You can opt to run the Microsoft ISA Server management console immediately upon exiting from the wizard by selecting the relevant check box. Then click the Finish button.

You have successfully installed ISA Server 2004. Now it's time to focus on some of the client aspects of using ISA Server 2004 in your environment and how you deploy clients and applications to interoperate with the server components.

Note Configuration settings modified through the CEICW are annotated with plain-English descriptions specifically aimed at SBS 2003 administrators. For more details on the CEICW, see Chapter 4.

Connecting Clients to the Internet

There are various methods of accessing external systems on the Internet, and the method used in any particular connection depends on the protocols being used. The CEICW will automatically grant users Internet access to reach unsecured and secured websites (using HTTP and HTTPS) as well as configuring the interface for sending and receiving email.

Applications requiring SOCKS connections to external systems must use the ISA Server 2004 firewall client, which intercepts calls from the applications and then proxies them through the ISA Server 2004 server. Instead of directly connecting to the external system, the client connects via the ISA Server 2004 SOCKS proxy.

Note The *SOCKS* protocol is an Internet protocol for connecting client applications to the relevant back-end server application component. SOCKS is an abbreviated form of the word *sockets.*

When you install ISA Server 2004 on SBS 2003, you've built a secure barrier between your internal network and the outside world (the Internet). At this point, only internal systems that require web access and email will have access, and SOCKS applications will be blocked. This, albeit secure, is not acceptable if you need to access line-of-business applications that reside outside your local network.

Warning If you are upgrading from ISA Server 2000 and where you are using the ISA Server 2000 firewall client on your workstations, you should first remove the firewall client before trying to upgrade. After the upgrade you will install the ISA Server 2004 firewall client.

In order for your internal systems to gain access to external network resources beyond the ISA Server 2004 boundary, they will need to be running the Microsoft ISA Server firewall client.

Note The firewall client intercepts TCP/IP calls from SOCKS applications on your workstations and sends them to the ISA Server proxy for relay on to the Internet. By doing this, your applications talk to the external systems via the ISA Server 2004 proxy rather than directly, hence maintaining their anonymity for the duration of the connection.

The firewall client is automatically installed onto your SBS 2003 server in the %systemroot%\ Program Files\Microsoft ISA Server\clients directory. This directory is automatically shared on the network as mspclnt and can be found by using the Client Application Wizard.

To use Group Policy to automatically assign and deploy the firewall client to your workstations, do the following:

1. From the Start menu, click Server Management.

2. Highlight Client Computers on the left side of the screen to display the Manage Client Computers interface in the details pane on the right.

3. Click the Assign Applications to Client Computers option to start the Assign Applications Wizard.

4. On the Welcome page, click Next.

5. Select the client computers that you want firewall client installed on, click Add, and then when you're ready to proceed, click Next.

6. On the Client Application page, click Edit Applications to start the Set Up Client Applications Wizard.

7. On the Welcome page, click Next.

8. On the Available Applications page, click Add.

9. In the Application Name text box, type **Microsoft ISA Server Firewall Client**. Then click the Browse button next to Location of Setup Executable for This Application.

10. You are now asked to browse for the folder location of the application executable. Click on mspclnt to open the firewall client setup folder. Then highlight setup.exe (see Figure 8-5). Click OK to continue.

Note It is recommended that you browse to the folder by using the UNC pathname for the server application share.

---

11. Back on the Application Information page, insert quotation marks around the complete path name so that it reads "\\<servername>\mspclnt\setup.exe" and then click OK.

12. On the Available applications page, click Next.

13. On the last page of the wizard, click Finish.

14. You are now returned to the Client Applications page in the Assign Applications Wizard. Ensure that Microsoft ISA Server firewall client is selected and then click Next.

15. On the Mobile Client and Offline Use page, click Next.

16. Finally, on the last page of the Assign Applications Wizard, click Finish. This will ensure that the firewall client is deployed to all selected workstations on your network.

Note You can use the deployment of the client as an additional security measure, by deploying the client only to users who require connections to external Internet resources. If a client workstation doesn't have firewall client, it can't connect to the Internet unless you opt for using secure NAT. The benefit of Secure NAT is that your clients can be non-Microsoft systems, such as Macintosh or Linux computers (although these are not supported as domain members).

At this stage, you will have completely installed ISA Server 2004. In almost every instance of SBS 2003, you need to do nothing more to ISA Server 2004. Further configuration changes should be made only if you are entirely clear about how those changes will affect your network's security.

The rest of this chapter deals with some of the simpler elements of ISA Server 2004 administration, such as the introduction of schedules into your firewall access rules and creating a web cache.

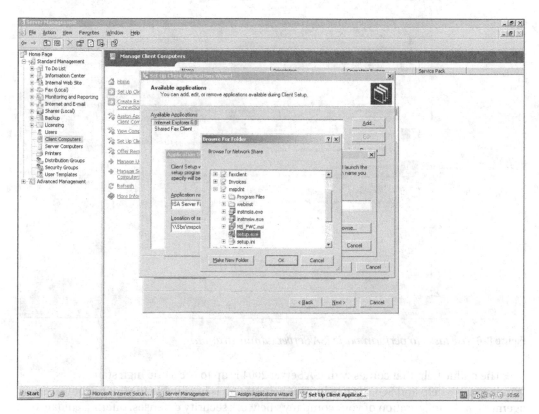

Figure 8-5. *Deploy the firewall client by using Group Policy.*

Exploring ISA Server Administration

Unlike its predecessor, ISA Server 2004 is extremely intuitive. Coupled with a new-look management console and plenty of integrated wizards, running a firewall is no longer a black art. It's just another tool in your toolbox providing a rich set of capabilities.

First, you should start the ISA Server management console. This will allow you to become familiar with the facilities ISA Server 2004 has to offer via this interface (see Figure 8-6).

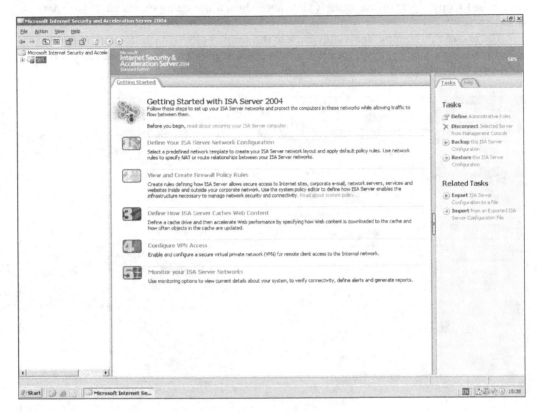

Figure 8-6. *Use tasks to perform basic ISA Server administration.*

The online help that comes with ISA Server 2004 is up to the same high standard as Windows 2003 help and SQL 2000 help. This help system is invaluable to your ongoing management and configuration of your company's network security defenses, offering guidance on all aspects of firewall and caching configuration and a short guide to security best practices that I highly recommend you read.

To start the ISA Server management console, click Start ➤ All Programs ➤ Microsoft ISA Server ➤ ISA Server Management.

You'll immediately see that the ISA Server management console is extremely intuitive, offering guidance on all aspects of running the firewall and caching features.

Configuring Your Network Environment

On the left side of the interface, expand the SBS node and then expand Configuration. Try highlighting the Networks node (see Figure 8-7). You'll see that by default ISA Server 2004 configures your network connection to the Internet as what's called an edge firewall. An *edge firewall* sits between two connected networks and acts as a guard to the internal system.

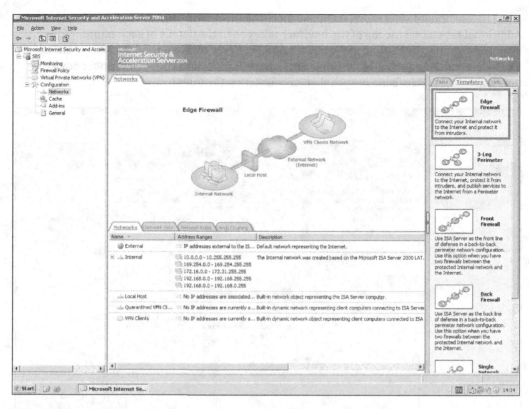

Figure 8-7. *By default, ISA Server configures an edge firewall.*

There are various ways ISA Server 2004 can be used in your environment. For example, if you have an independent firewall on your network, you could opt to use ISA Server to provide only web caching.

Warning Once ISA Server 2004 is working, you should leave it alone. In the SBS 2003 environment, the CEICW has been specially revised to install the most appropriate rules and polices for your small business solution. If you plan to change the mode that ISA Server is running in, you should have enough experience in manipulating ISA Server 2004 to be confident that your reconfiguration is still safe, or you should call in an expert. A badly configured firewall is worse than no firewall at all because you'll be placing trust in inappropriate security-enforcing functions.

Monitoring Your Network

To see how your network and ISA Server solution are performing, click the Monitoring node on the left side of the interface. This starts the ISA Server monitoring interface, shown in Figure 8-8, which defaults to the Dashboard view.

The Dashboard view shows the highlights of all the activity that ISA Server is monitoring. Additional tabs along the top of the interface take you to the details of each monitored section. For example, by clicking the Alerts tab, you get to see the details of any system alerts. Each alert contains a detailed description of what it is reporting and offers further advice on how you might tackle fixing the problem or countering the threat.

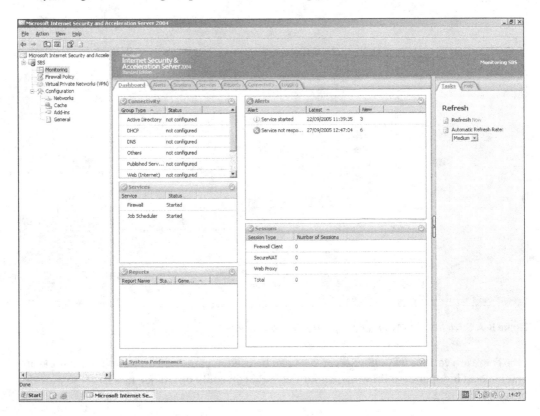

Figure 8-8. *ISA Server monitoring shows security threats and alerts.*

Monitoring Firewall Policy Access Rules

Access rules are the instructions you give to ISA Server that tell it how to handle client requests to access networks under the control of ISA Server. To see a list of your current ISA Server access rules, click the Firewall Policy node on the left side of the main interface. In the details pane, you'll see the default list of access rules created for your system by the CEICW.

These rules will allow all the facilities that you specified in the running of the CEICW to function correctly, such as Remote Web Workplace, Outlook Web Access, and sending and receiving email from your ISP.

Although it's recommended that you don't modify rules dramatically (or at all) or create your own without completely understanding all the consequences, one thing you can do is create a schedule for activating and deactivating rules.

A schedule allows you to control when a rule is applied. Take temporary staff, for example: you might want to configure a rule for temporary staff to have access to the Internet only during lunch breaks while permanent members of staff have access all the time. To do this, create two rules. Have the rule for temporary staff sit above the rule for everyone else and create a schedule to allow access only during the hours of 12 p.m. until 2 p.m.

To define a schedule, do the following from the Schedule tab for the appropriate rule:

1. Click the New button.

2. Give the schedule a meaningful name and description.

3. By default, the rule will always apply. To mark a rule as inactive, highlight the time you want to deny access by clicking on a range of time (dragging a rectangle around the times with the mouse) and then clicking the Inactive radio button. This marks your selection while indicating that the period of time is inactive.

■**Warning** Firewall rules are processed in the order that they appear in the interface, that is, top to bottom. The default rule ensures that any system not explicitly configured to have access in a previously applied rule is automatically banned. It effectively plugs the gaps in your security model. The Access Rules list is processed sequentially until it finds a match for your chosen connection criteria. The first match in the list is always used. When you create rules, be careful that they remain as specific as possible. Catch-all rules used high up in the list mean more-restrictive rules further down are never reached.

Web Caching

The caching of remote websites dramatically decreases the time taken to access Internet web resources. To configure caching on your system, you can create what are known as *cache rules* to define how your system collects external website information and how it treats this information over time in the local store.

To create a new cache rule, do the following:

1. Using the ISA Server management console, highlight the Cache node underneath the Configuration node.

2. From the task pane on the right-hand side of the console, click the Create a Cache Rule link to start the New Cache Rule Wizard.

3. On the Welcome page, type a meaningful name for the cache rule and then click Next.

4. The next page you see is the Cache Rule Destination page. Click the Add button.

5. You'll see the Add Network Entities page appear. Here you can select any combination of IP addresses, DNS domain names, networks, subnets, or computer sets to cache web information from. For this example, click New (top-left corner of the Add Network Entities dialog box) and select URL Set.

6. Give the new URL element a meaningful name. Then click the New button to add the appropriate URLs (see Figure 8-9).

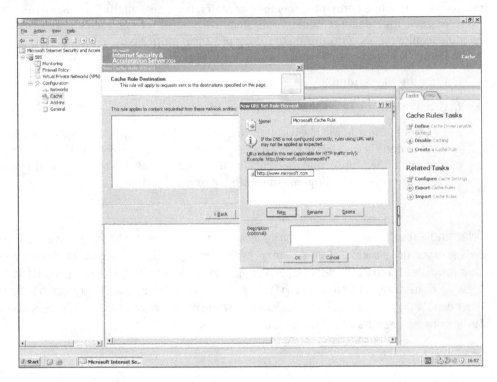

Figure 8-9. *Add a URL to the cache rule to enable active caching.*

7. If you want to add a description of the external site, add this in the bottom part of the dialog box. When you're finished, click OK.

8. Back on the Add Network Entities page, click URL Sets. You'll see your new URL set appear in the list. Highlight this and then click Add.

9. Click the Close button after you've finished adding URLs to the cache rule.

10. On the Cache Rule Destination page, click Next.

11. The next page allows you to specify how cached content is treated by ISA Server. If you select the top option, to use the cache only if a valid version exists, requests for Internet content are serviced internally if the object in the cache is valid (up-to-date); otherwise, the request is routed to the destination Internet server. The middle option delivers the requested information from the ISA Server cache if any version of the object exists locally—this would be useful for static content, such as an online manual or mapping information. If you select the bottom of the three options, the system will return a positive response only if there is something in the cache. If there's nothing in the cache, the request does not go externally and the call will fail. After you've selected the cache mechanism most appropriate to this URL, click Next.

12. On the Cache Content page, make sure you select If Source and Request Headers Indicate to Cache. In addition, select Dynamic Content and Content for Offline Browsing. I don't recommend selecting Content Requiring User Authentication for Retrieval simply because this security measure is better left on the source server on the Internet. Click Next to continue.

13. If you want to limit the size of cached objects (forcing the request to go externally for larger objects), select Do Not Cache Objects Larger Than and then add a value in the text box. Leave Cache SSL Responses selected by default. Then click Next.

14. On the HTTP Caching page, select the Enable HTTP Caching check box. Then set the rest of the policy information for this rule. The TTL (time to live) can be left at 20 percent, meaning the ISA Server expires this content after 20 percent of its age from the point of creation. Add upper and lower boundaries to the TTL (leave the defaults to begin with, and then experiment with the effect of modifying these at a later date). Click Next.

15. On the FTP Caching page, set the time of expiration of FTP (File Transfer Protocol) objects if this is appropriate to this URL. Click Next.

16. On the last page of the wizard, review your selections and then click Finish.

The new cache rule will now appear in the main interface. To modify any of the settings you entered as you ran through the wizard, right-click on the cache rule in question and then select Properties. Try experimenting with aspects of the cache, such as the TTL for the stored objects and the maximum size of these objects. Modifying characteristics such as these will significantly change the experience of web browsing for your users, and after you make changes, try asking around to see what your users think.

Case Study—Copyworld

Copyworld runs multiple divisions across many states of Australia. This means that the company has sales, technical, and accounting teams all needing to share data in a secure manner. Many of their servers are managed by using the Remote Web Workplace, VPN connections, and straightforward terminal server sessions. Their business applications include access to a shopping cart service and the Windows SharePoint Services website. Their intention is to create a business-to-business (B2B) link with all suppliers based on the services provided by SBS 2003.

For all of these reasons, Copyworld has exploited the security features of SBS 2003, implementing the ISA Server 2004 firewall at significantly lower cost than any other military-standard firewall product on the market.

They are using the server-monitoring capabilities of ISA Server 2004 to monitor staff activities, both on the Internet and the local file systems, ensuring that their data is secured and inaccessible to the outside world, yet highly available to all departments of Copyworld.

Using a combination of security technologies, such as NTFS, Active Directory, pass phrases, ISA Server 2004, the client-side Windows Firewall, and file system encryption, they have achieved the level of protection they require.

Security penetration testing by both internal and external parties has proved that their system is secure, and they are delighted with their investment in SBS 2003 Premium Edition.

Case Study—Servideal

Microsoft ISA Server is useful for Henry and Maria for two reasons:

- Boundary protection

- Web publishing

To protect the customer-specific data that any online shop holds, the system must be bulletproof. The boundary device in this case is ISA Server, and Henry has pulled out all the stops in making sure it is as robust as possible. He enabled content checking and stateful packet inspection and created his firewall rules in such a way as to allow only limited connectivity from the inside out, and no connectivity to breach the defenses on the way in.

To make sure no systems could penetrate the network defense, he created publishing rules for all internal services required on the external Internet interface, including email and WSS.

Case Study—Country Estates

In addition to using the firewall features of ISA Server to act as a boundary protection device, Alan also insisted on actively caching external competitors' websites to give his users quicker access to the information on these sites. The active caching rules meant that ISA Server was regularly pulling website material from sources on the Internet, especially during the quiet time of the night. When the users came in the following day to access the Web for studying the competition, they immediately had access to all competitors' sites without ever leaving their internal, high-speed network.

Summary

Microsoft ISA Server 2004 is a vast and comprehensive network security product. It is also extremely complicated (as are most aspects of network defense) and for this reason, Microsoft has taken it upon itself to integrate the product into the SBS 2003 world by replacing the CEICW with an updated version that creates all rules and polices required for an SBS 2003 environment. Microsoft ISA Server 2004 is well ahead of its predecessor, so even novice SBS 2003 users, after a quick run through the CEICW, are up and running (and extremely secure) in no time.

If you want to learn more about ISA Server, there are plenty of resources on the Internet to peruse. Microsoft's own website contains manuals, white papers, troubleshooting guides, and walk-throughs of virtually every aspect of its usage. Many Microsoft Partner companies offer guidance and consultancy on using ISA Server 2004 in any environment, and I'd strongly urge you to consider speaking to an expert if you want to do much more with the product than what the CEICW does for you by default.

Security of your network and your data is paramount to a successful business and as I've stated before, a badly configured firewall is worse than no firewall at all—you think you're protected when you're not. If you don't have a firewall, at least you understand the risks and should have contingency plans for recovery and backup.

CHAPTER 9

∎∎∎

SQL Server

Whether you realize it or not, databases are all around you, helping provide you with access to information that's part of your daily life. A database, in its simplest form, is a place where data is stored. The term *database* comes from the computer industry but has now become more generally used to describe any collection of data that can be mined for information. A telephone directory, for example, is a database, as is your weekly TV guide, or the track listing on a DVD.

The data in a database is structured in such a way as to help you locate the information you need: when you're using the telephone directory, for example, you look up the name of the person you intend to call, and the number appears alongside. The fundamental design issue affecting a database's success is this layout of the data, how the data is structured. Sticking with the telephone directory analogy, all the names are listed in alphabetical order. If, on the other hand, the people in the directory were listed in order of their age, how much easier would looking up a friend's telephone number be? It wouldn't be easy at all; in fact, the job would become so tiresome and drawn out that you'd probably not bother using the directory at all. In this case, the database loses its value as a tool. This leads to the conclusion that the structure of the database is as important as the integrity of the data, and without good structure, the database becomes useless.

Computers can process large quantities of data in complex ways, billions of times faster than a human analyst, and it's for this reason alone that computer database technologies now underpin every IT infrastructure in the world, and your SBS 2003 infrastructure is no different. Standard Windows Server 2003 contains many small-scale databases, such as the Domain Name System (DNS) database and the Active Directory, and these databases are themselves essential for running their supported applications. The data in the DNS server database is ordered in such a way as to allow client systems to look up IP addresses as efficiently as possible. The Active Directory orders information so as to provide a searchable index to the underlying system and the associated users, to allow them to query for computers, users, shares, and other managed directory objects as efficiently as possible.

Understanding Databases

In a Microsoft-centric world, the database system of choice is Microsoft SQL Server, included with the Premium version of the SBS 2003 suite of applications. Microsoft also has a lower-end product known as the Microsoft Desktop Engine (MSDE), which replaces some of the database capability of SQL Server but should not really be considered an enterprise product. Microsoft SQL Server 2000 is but one of a whole range of relational databases on the market; however, the underlying architecture and supported query language is standard (except for a few proprietary extras) across all platforms. To help you better understand the SQL Server, it's important to first understand generically what databases are, how they are organized, and how they perform their functions.

Structure

As I have said, databases have structure. This structure defines the data objects that reside within the database but does not represent any one element of data. Each element of data is known as a *record*, and every record will adhere to the record structure.

For example, in the telephone directory example, the structure might be as follows:

- Name

- Address

- Area code

- Telephone number

- Serial number (a unique reference number identifying each individual record for use in the database)

For every person being listed in the telephone directory, there will be a separate entry containing that person's name, address, area code, telephone number, and unique serial number.

This structure, or *schema* as it's often referred to, acts as the blueprint for each record populated into the database, but without the data, the structure simply expresses how the relationships work within the database.

Relational Databases

The most commonly used database technology in today's IT marketplace is that of the *relational database*. In this model, the data structures are rigidly defined (as with the telephone directory example) and strictly adhere to mathematical principles of set theory that allow database designers to use tried and tested algebraic formulas to manipulate the data.

Entity Relationship Diagrams

When designing a data structure, a database analyst will create what's known as an *entity relationship diagram*, a conceptual design of the data structure represented by interconnected boxes. These diagrams can subsequently be turned into database tables, and relationships can be plumbed into the data to aid with indexing and searching.

There are three kinds of relationships that must be mapped within the modeling of your data:

- *One-to-one relationship*: This relationship has only a single mapping between two data objects, such as the name of a person mapped to the unique serial number for that record entry in the directory.

- *One-to-many relationship*: This relationship allows a single data object to be mapped to many other data objects. A good example in terms of the telephone directory is one telephone number related to many people's names (there might be five people living in one house, using the same telephone number).

- *Many-to-many relationship*: This refers to many instances of one entity being mapped to many instances of another object. In the example of the telephone directory, an office building has five telephone lines with five separate telephone numbers, and each of the five employees can use any phone.

Database Terminology

As with all aspects of IT, there are a few terms and acronyms that need explaining to allow me to write freely about the subject. Here are the ones I think are most important for this chapter:

- *Data type*: The data type of a field is used to identify what kind of information should be stored within that field within each record. In the telephone directory example, the Telephone Number data type would be a number, while the Name would be text.

- *Form*: A form is a client-side device used to display both records and tables to the user. You can create specialized forms for data entry as well as customized views for database designers to link and modify tables.

- *Field*: A data field is a discrete entity in a database table. In the case of the telephone directory, the fields are Name, Address, Area Code, Telephone Number, and Serial Number.

- *Index*: An index is a subset of data that is used for searching for complete records. A good example illustrating the index is a typical index in a textbook. You look up the subject in the index at the back to see the page number that subject is covered on. There is much more detail on the subject on the page itself, but the index helps you locate the data in the first place.

- *Query*: A query in database terms is the crafting of a SQL command to interrogate the database for a specific result. In contrast to a search, a query is normally deep down in the SQL code of an application, whereas a search tends to be a user-fronted facility offering mining capabilities to your database customers.

- *Record*: A record is a complete set of data that makes up a single data entry in the database. The table would define the data fields, and each record thereafter would contain real data.

- *Report*: A report is a structured way of displaying search results. The results are presented in a way that is suited to the user.

- *Search*: A database search uses various criteria for interrogating the database index to find records akin to the subject of the search criteria.

- *SQL (pronounced see-quell)*: Structured Query Language (SQL) is the standard programming language interface used to code simple and complex queries on the database. SQL is extensible and can provide a complete application interface for users as well as performing the data manipulation in the background. SQL is the standard used for querying SQL Server 2000.

- *Stored procedure*: A stored procedure is a compiled executable file containing any number of SQL statements that act as self-contained applets. Stored procedures are usually used for very discrete tasks, such as updating tables or querying an index.

- *Table*: A table is a discrete data structure containing fields, which in turn represent data objects. Tables comprise as many fields as necessary to define that data object. In the telephone directory example, a single table could be used to define the data. More-complex databases can have multiple tables, with relationships crossing between them.

Final Word on Databases in General

We won't look any deeper into database design because it's a fine art destined for the laboratories of the highest-paid help in the IT industry. Database design is a fascinating and extremely rewarding occupation for those people who strive for order and efficiency in their everyday lives. This highly specialized discipline requires hours of complex calculations and modeling before it comes to fruition.

To that end, we'll leave database design to the experts and instead look at how you can use databases in your organization, commission the design of a database (from an expert) that's relevant to your business requirements, and manage your database services to ensure that they operate properly.

Introducing SQL Server

In essence, Microsoft SQL Server is an industrial-strength relational database engine. When I say *engine*, I mean the management and implementation capability that allows you to host databases. This engine manages and facilitates all the functions appropriate to a relational database from this server-side product.

Comparing SQL Server to Other Database Engines

Microsoft SQL Server is one database engine in a family of similar Microsoft products.

The Microsoft Desktop Engine (MSDE) is the second database product in the Microsoft family. It performs the core functions of Microsoft SQL Server but is designed to run on lower-end system platforms such as workstations or servers, where the database requirements are much less than that of Microsoft SQL Server.

Third, there is Microsoft Office Access. This product is also a relational database, capable of servicing queries by using SQL in much the same way as the other products. However, it's much better suited to personal use. It uses a proprietary underlying database architecture never intended to scale beyond a few users. It is the perfect tool for personally developed databases because it provides an easy-to-use development environment that makes the complicated aspects of database design easier for the end user.

Microsoft SQL Server should be thought of as the big brother of these database products, based primarily on the industry standards defining how relational databases should function. It is designed to cope with high-volume, system-intense queries, has multiprocessor support, and easily scales to be a robust enterprise product.

SQL Server offers by far the best resilience capabilities of all in the database family and offers a slicker management interface, making it the best facility for use in a business-wide environment.

We ran an Access database for couriers and company van movements with approximately nine internal van deliveries per day using over 20 couriers. We ran into limitations with Microsoft Office Access as we needed more and more people to connect to the database. Our move to Microsoft SQL Server meant we could allow more people to access the required data and, as an added bonus, we discovered a huge increase in the returned query speed.

—Michael Jenkin, IT manager, Copyworld

Choosing SQL Server

A great example of when you'd be using SQL Server in your organization is if you opted to employ an application such as Microsoft Customer Relationship Management (CRM).

CRM provides a unique interface that brings together all aspects of sales, marketing, and customer service capabilities, providing you with a user-friendly interface for searching and manipulating aspects of your business data. CRM is specifically designed to help small- to medium-sized businesses such as yours to boost sales and service management capabilities (in other words, to help you make good business decisions).

This product can offer enough analytical information to allow you to boost all areas of your business because the data is stored in a complex, well-formed SQL-based relational database, and the underlying reporting capabilities and application layer exposing the data have been designed to deliver added value to your business analysts. This product is specifically designed to exploit the power of Microsoft SQL Server 2000, and benefits immensely from the added resilience and manageability aspects that the database has to offer.

If you've decided to deploy an application requiring the underlying robustness and scalability of Microsoft SQL Server 2000 and you happen to be an SBS 2003 customer, you can get the Premium edition of SBS 2003 for as little as $1,499 (without client access licenses), which also includes Microsoft ISA Server and a Microsoft Office FrontPage 2003 web authoring license. Microsoft SQL Server on its own would cost you a lot more than the entire SBS 2003 Premium suite, so it's certainly worth the expense.

The next section explains how to install SQL Server on your SBS 2003 system because it's not part of the basic installation of the product you encountered in Chapter 4. The SBS 2003 Premium Edition extras (ISA, SQL, and FrontPage) don't integrate in the same way as the core products (because they really are just added extras). However, they work happily in the SBS 2003 environment and are still manageable through their own specialized management interfaces, all of which is covered over the course of this chapter.

Installation of SQL Server

First things first. You need to install SQL Server from your source CD/DVD. To install the product, do the following:

1. Insert you optical media in the drive and wait for the Microsoft Windows Small Business Server 2003 Premium Edition splash screen to offer you a selection of options for installation. In this instance, click Install Microsoft SQL Server 2000.

2. If you receive a warning message saying SQL Server 2000 SP2 and below is not supported by this version of Windows, you can ignore this for now and click Continue. This is a well-known warning and is heavily documented by Microsoft.

3. The next screen is the Welcome page. Click Next to start the installation of SQL Server 2000.

4. On the Computer Name page, you will need to ensure that the Local Computer radio button is selected. Click Next to proceed.

5. When you see the Installation Selection page, choose Create a New Instance of SQL Server, or Install Client Tools (see Figure 9-1). This will install a brand new installation of the SQL Server product on your SBS 2003 server. Click Next to proceed. You could also opt to extend the SharePoint Services instance, or if you prefer, come back and extend the SharePoint one at a later date.

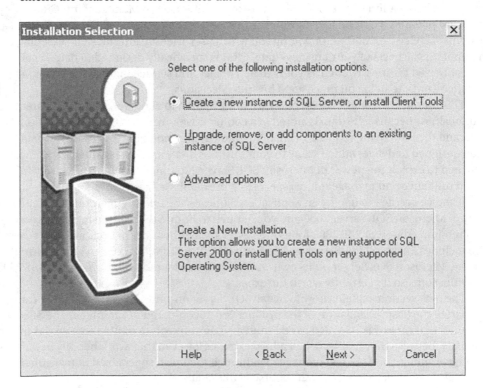

Figure 9-1. *Make sure that you select the option to install a new version of SQL.*

6. On the User Information page, type in your name and the name of your company. Then click Next.

7. Read the license agreement, and when you are ready to proceed to the next stage, click Yes to accept the terms.

8. Type in the CD-key that you got when you purchased the SBS 2003 product suite. This will allow the installation of SQL Server 2000 to proceed. You will have to have bought the Premium edition for your license key to allow you to proceed.

9. On the Installation Definition page, select the Server and Client Tools option and then click Next.

10. Leave the Instance Name as Default and then click Next (unless you have opted to select the SharePoint Services instance as per the instructions on the installation media).

11. Now you have to choose the Setup Type; you can select either Typical, Minimum, or Custom installations. For this installation, you need to select Typical. If you have a data drive (covered in Chapter 4), then locate the Destination Folder Data Files on this drive by clicking Browse. You can install the program files on the system drive. When you're ready to proceed, click Next.

Note If you are extending the SharePoint Services instance, make sure that you select to add the full text search option under the Tools menu.

---

12. On the Services Accounts page shown in Figure 9-2, leave the Use the Same Account for Each Service option selected as the default, and use the domain administrator account as the service account for SQL. You'll see the domain administrator account's user name and domain name automatically filled in the dialog box. You'll need to supply the password for this account. After you've typed the password, click Next to continue.

13. Unless you have specifically been asked as part of an application's functional requirement to start the SQL security model in mixed mode, on the Authentication Mode page, select Windows Authentication Mode. Click Next.

14. On the Start Copying Files page, click Next.

15. The installation progress bar is now displayed, showing you how far through the setup of SQL you are. This takes a while to complete, so be patient and go make some coffee.

Note If you opt for using Mixed Mode security for whatever reasons, your system will be more vulnerable to hacking than it would be if you used Windows authentication. Windows authentication relies on the underlying Windows 2003 security architecture to grant rights and permissions to the database objects. If you opt for Mixed Mode, a separate account managed from within SQL is required and in this case the authentication takes place in an unencrypted fashion on the network.

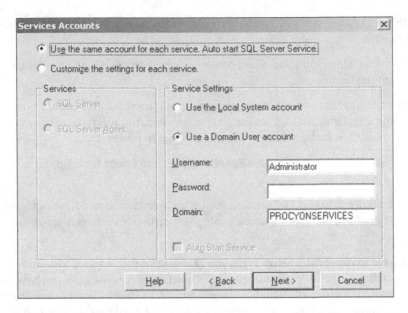

Figure 9-2. *Use the domain administrator account to run SQL services.*

16. Finally, you'll see the Setup Complete page, where you can click Finish to complete the installation.

You've now completed the first part of the SQL Server installation. The next phase installs Service Pack 3a from your installation media:

1. Insert your Premium edition media into your optical drive (if you've for some reason taken it out since the last part).

2. From the splash screen, click the option to Install SQL Server 2000 Service Pack 3a.

3. On the Welcome page, click Next.

4. Assuming you accept the licensing agreement, click Yes.

5. When you see the Instance Name page, make sure Default is checked. Then click Next.

■**Note** MSDE databases running on your SBS 2003 server will already be on Service Pack 3a since the installation of SBS 2003 SP1. Make sure to upgrade all Microsoft SQL database instances to SP3a by running the Microsoft SQL upgrade for each database in turn (with the exception of the monitoring and health databases, which should not be upgraded).

---

6. On the Connect to Server page, ensure that the option labeled The Windows Account Information I use to Log On to My Computer (Windows Authentication) is selected. Then click Next.

7. Next you receive a message stating the system is validating your user account. When the account has been validated, click OK.

Note If you are asked to type in an SA password, you should type a password that you are likely to remember, but make sure this password follows the strong password guidelines described in Chapter 11. (*SA* is an acronym for *system administrator*.) If a hacker could guess your SA password, he would gain access to some very powerful database scripting capabilities from which he could exploit the rest of your system.

8. Accept the default on the Backward Compatibility Checklist page and then click Continue.

9. On the Error Reporting page, click OK.

Note If you want to send error reports directly to Microsoft, you can select the check box to authorize this connection. This means that when SQL experiences a fatal error (one that crashes the database), the error message generated by the underlying operating system and application is wrapped up and automatically forwarded to Microsoft for analysis. This can help Microsoft immensely in prioritizing their bug fixing and analyzing trends that show how users are using SQL Server. If you don't want information about your system being transmitted across the Internet without your explicit authorization, leave the box unchecked.

10. The next phase of the service pack installation gathers some information about your system before the main installation begins. On the Start Copying Files page, click Next. It's now time for another break as the service pack files are copied from the optical media to your system.

11. When the installation process completes, it's a good idea to not only back up your databases (as advised), but do a complete system backup to your preferred backup media (see Chapter 5).

12. When you are asked to back up your master databases, click OK.

13. On the Setup Complete page, you can opt to reboot your server now or later. Select the option to reboot your server immediately. Finally, click the Finish button to reboot the server.

Warning You should plan to reboot SBS 2003 only when you are sure that none of your users are accessing the server or the Internet via the server. If you are doing this update during the day, send a broadcast email to your users informing them to save all work to the server and log off by a certain time; otherwise, they might lose data. Another way of ensuring that no users are using the system is to right-click My Computer (on the desktop) and select Manage. When you see the Manage Computer dialog box, drill down into the Shared Folders node and then click Shares. Next, expand the Sessions node and select Open Files to see whether any client connections are currently made with your server.

Administration of SQL Server

There are a number of administrative tools and facilities you'll need to navigate to fully understand how SQL Server is impacting your SBS 2003 infrastructure. We'll start by looking at the facilities available from the SQL submenu, accessible through the Start menu. Then we'll delve into SQL Server Enterprise Manager, as shown in Figure 9-3.

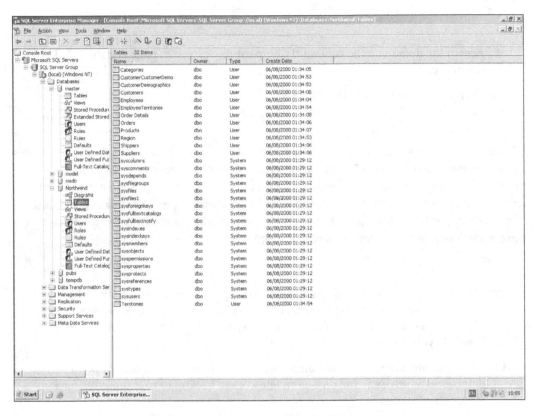

Figure 9-3. *Enterprise Manager is the SQL interface for administration.*

To find out more information about SQL Server 2000, there are countless resources (books, websites, and so forth) available for learning everything you'll ever need to know about database administration, management, and programming. However, the best place to start is right there on your SBS 2003 server, with the built-in SQL Server Books Online.

To access Books Online, click Start ➤ All Programs ➤ Microsoft SQL Server ➤ Books Online.

This fantastic SQL Server resource comes part and parcel with the installation of the product and contains walk-throughs, technical support, SQL white papers, SQL code samples to aid in script and application development, and a web links page referencing many of the best online SQL Server resources, such as TechNet, MSDN (for programming), and the Microsoft SQL newsgroups.

From the SQL Server menu (accessible from the Start menu), you'll also see the following options:

- *Client Network Utility*: This is an advanced option for database administrators (DBAs) to modify how client applications and workstations connect to the SQL database. In the case of an SBS 2003–based SQL Server, there won't be much need to use this facility.

- *Configure SQL XML Support in IIS*: This is used for DBAs to create an IIS virtual directory that can grant HTTP access through to the SQL database. Again, as with the client network utility, this will not be used unless a specific application requires it. If this is the case, the application installation will dictate the settings and may well automate the generation of the virtual directory.

- *Enterprise Manager*: This is covered in greater detail later, but for now suffice it to say it's the primary management tool for all that is SQL Server.

- *Import and Export Data*: This runs a utility known as the Data Transformation Service (DTS), which is primarily used to move data in and out of your SQL Server databases. In the process, this utility prepares the data to be used by other database engines (such as Microsoft Office Access, Microsoft Office Excel, or Oracle) or exports the data as a plain old text file. If you look at Figure 9-4, you'll see that the drop-down list of database destinations is extensive.

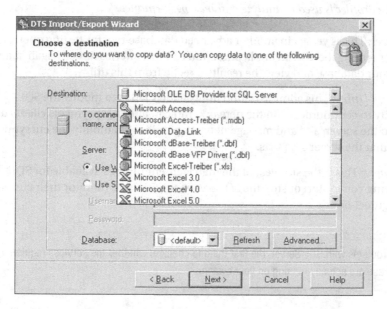

Figure 9-4. *DTS can be used to move data into other database systems.*

- *Profiler*: The Profiler is an advanced DBA tool (see Figure 9-5) used to delve into the inner workings of your databases and to analyze characteristics of database perform-ance and normalization. This tool works in much the same way as Performance Monitor is used to analyze the Windows 2003 operating system.

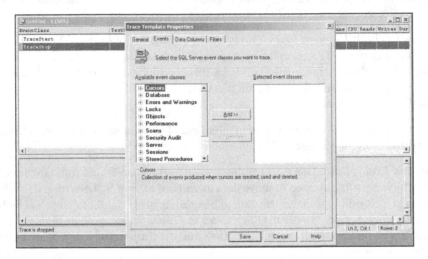

Figure 9-5. *The Profiler is used to analyze database performance.*

- *Query Analyzer*: This is yet again another advanced database tool for testing queries before implementing them in an application. You can run queries directly against any element of your database and view the results directly from this utility.

- *Server Network Utility*: This administration utility allows DBAs to modify the SQL Server's ability to communicate on the network. You can alter the protocols clients use to connect to the server, add and manage network proxies, and modify the encryption capabilities that the server supports.

- *Service Manager*: This is the simplest of the management utilities available for SQL Server, allowing you to start or stop the SQL Server services and monitor their current state (see Figure 9-6).

Note If you have problems with SQL Server, the first thing to check is whether the services required to provide the SQL database are actually running on your system.

To use the SQL Server Service Manager, make sure your SBS 2003 server is selected in the Server text box at the top of the Service Manager console, and then use the Services drop-down box to sequentially select each of the three available SQL services. In order as they appear in the list, the Distributed Transaction Coordinator service should be running, the SQL Server service should be running, and the SQL Server Agent should be stopped. To start a serv-ice that is stopped, click the Start/Continue button. If you decide that you don't want to start the SQL Server or Distributed Transaction Coordinator services when the system boots up, deselect the Autostart Service When OS Starts check box.

Figure 9-6. *Use SQL Server Service Manager to check SQL service status.*

SQL Server Enterprise Manager

Next we'll look at the SQL Server Enterprise Manager console, used for the majority of SQL Server management tasks. To access the console, shown in Figure 9-7, click Start ➤ All Programs ➤ SQL Server ➤ Enterprise Manager.

Viewing the databases installed on your system is straightforward. Expand the Microsoft SQL Servers node beneath the Console Root, expand SQL Server Group, expand (Local)(Windows NT), and then expand Databases. You'll see a list of databases already installed on the system:

- Master

- Model

- Msdb

- Northwind

- Pubs

- Tempdb

Note For the examples in this section, make sure that you are looking at the default database instance rather than any of the other database instances on your system.

To help you get to grips with database administration and operations, Microsoft has included two relatively complicated example databases, called Northwind and Pubs, for you to experiment with. For the rest of this chapter, we'll use the Pubs database to expose the management techniques you need to apply to your SQL databases.

For completeness, I'll first explain the purpose of each of the default databases:

- *Master*: The Master database contains all configuration information for your SQL Server. This database is paramount in the ongoing operational success of your SQL Server and should not be altered in any way by yourself, unless you use the management interfaces. It's essential that you maintain a good backup of your Master database because a corruption may well necessitate a database restore.

- *Model*: When you create a new database, the Model database is used effectively as a template. This Model database contains specific information about your SQL Server system, meaning each new database under its control is based on settings with the appropriate server context. This database should be modified only by experienced DBAs.

- *Msdb*: This database is yet another administrative database used by SQL Server itself to manage the submission of alerts to administrators, the scheduling of administrative batch jobs on the server, and the recording of management operations.

- *Northwind*: This is the first of the example databases included with SQL Server 2000. This corporate database contains a bunch of sales from a company called Northwind Traders that imports and exports specialty foods from around the world.

- *Pubs*: Pubs is the second of the example databases in SQL Server; the data is based on the business of a fictitious book publishing company (see Figure 9-7). This database can be used to experiment with in much the same way as the Northwind database, allowing you to try out SQL queries, scripts, and application front-ends against the data.

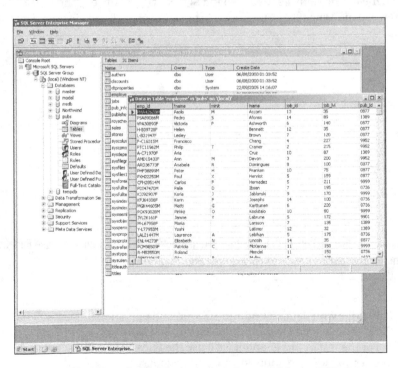

Figure 9-7. *Use the Pubs database to experiment with test SQL scripts.*

- *Tempdb*: Tempdb is created when SQL Server starts up and is used to hold temporary copies of various tables and functions (known as stored procedures).

Accessing the Wizards

Many of the standard tasks you'll need to do when running SQL Server are performed through intuitive wizards. There are 23 wizards available for your use, and the purpose of each is explained in Table 9-1. To access the wizards, do the following:

1. From the SQL Server Enterprise Manager, click the Tools menu and select Wizards from halfway down the menu.

2. You're presented with a Select Wizard page, where you can scroll down through the list to start the one you need (see Figure 9-8).

Note You'll need to be logged in with the right privileges to create and modify SQL Server databases. If you're performing low-level configuration of the database or of SQL Server itself, it's best to use the Administrator account that you used to start the SQL Server service.

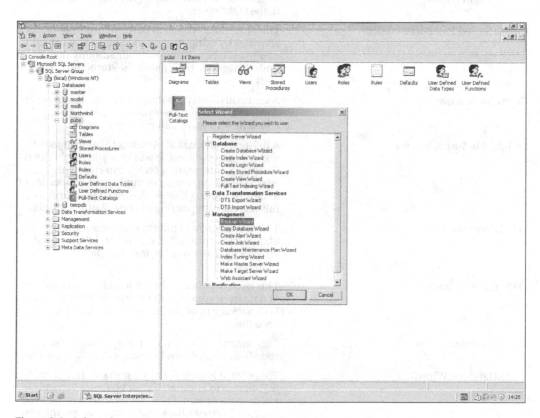

Figure 9-8. *Select the most appropriate wizard for the task.*

Table 9-1. *Wizards Available for Administering SQL Server*

Wizard	Function
Register Server Wizard	In an enterprise environment, you need to register SQL Server before you are allowed to manage it. Because the local server is registered automatically during installation, there is no need to run this any further, unless you want to register the SharePoint Services database or SBS Monitoring and Health instances.
Create Database Wizard	This wizard guides you through the creation of a new database, allowing you to name the database, create files that comprise the data, create the transaction log, and limit database growth.
Create Index Wizard	If you need to create an index of an existing database, you can use this wizard to point the new index at the database, view current indexes, and select the properties of the new index.
Create Login Wizard	This wizard is used to configure User Login Access to the SQL Server.
Create Stored Procedure Wizard	This wizard allows you to perform multiple activities by using stored procedures. You can add new ones, edit existing ones, and modify the underlying code that makes the stored procedure work.
Create View Wizard	A view will display the data within the database in a way that's easy on the eye. Use this wizard to create new views or edit existing views.
Full-Text Indexing Wizard	A full-text index will allow users to query against text strings, much in the way that you might query Google for information on the Internet. This wizard helps you create or modify the properties of a full-text index. (This works only if you turned on full-text indexing during the installation of SP3a).
DTS Export Wizard	This wizard gathers information about the export of data from your SQL database and then uses the DTS package to export it, for example, an Access .mdb file.
DTS Import Wizard	This wizard gathers information about the import of data from your SQL database and then uses the DTS package to import it, for example, an Access .mdb file.
Backup Wizard	This wizard allows you to specify a backup device, specify a schedule, and initiate a database backup.
Copy Database Wizard	This wizard is used to copy databases from one SQL Server to another. If your business expands to encompass a second SQL Server, this may be used to copy databases back and forth between the two.
Create Alert Wizard	By using this wizard, you can define SQL alerts to be generated against certain performance and operational thresholds in your databases.

Wizard	Function
Create Job Wizard	You can use this wizard to generate jobs that are executed on your server based on a defined schedule, including scheduling transaction log cleanup and other such maintenance activities.
Database Maintenance Plan Wizard	Schedule recurring maintenance tasks to automatically perform integrity checks, backups, and transaction log shipping by running this wizard.
Index Tuning Wizard	Streamline the performance of existing database indexes by using this wizard.
Make Master Server Wizard	The concept of Master servers applies to only complex multiserver architectures.
Make Target Server Wizard	Similar to a Master server, a Target server is part of a distributed SQL cluster and is not relevant in the SBS 2003 environment.
Web Assistant Wizard	This wizard allows you to publish the data from a database table to a web page.
Configure Publishing and Distribution Wizard	Replication is necessary only in large-scale environments requiring multiple copies of a database.
Create Publication Wizard	This is where database replication is controlled.
Create Pull Subscription Wizard	This drags information from a replication partner on a schedule.
Create Push Subscription Wizard	This pushes data out to a replication partner on a trigger or schedule.
Disable Pushing and Distribution Wizard	Self-explanatory, but this disables replication from occurring.

The wizards we'll look at in more detail are the DTS Export Wizard and the Backup Wizard, just to give you a flavor of how the wizards are used. In each of the two examples, you'll target the wizard against the Pubs database, but these processes can be carried over to your own corporate databases once you are content that you understand their function.

DTS Export Wizard

Exporting data from a database to use in another application is common, and in the case of SQL Server, the facility for doing this is DTS. The following procedure will export a sample data set from the Pubs database to a text file. To start the DTS Export Wizard, do the following:

1. Start SQL Server Enterprise Manager

2. Click Tools ➤ Wizards.

3. Expand the Data Transformation Wizard node and select DTS Export Wizard.

4. On the Welcome screen, click Next.

5. When you see the Choose a Data Source page, keep the default Data Source, Microsoft OLE DB Provider for SQL Server, and ensure that the Server is set to (Local) and that you've selected the Use Windows Authentication radio button. Ensure that the Pubs database is selected from the drop-down list at the bottom of the screen (see Figure 9-9). Then click Next.

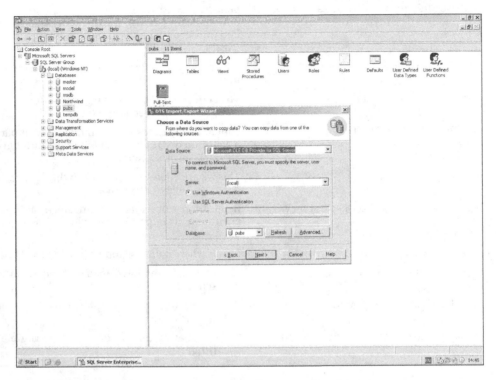

Figure 9-9. *Select the database you want to export your data from.*

6. On the next screen, you need to decide where the data will be exported to. From the drop-down menu at the top, scroll to the bottom and select Text File.

7. Give the export file a name and then click Next.

8. If you want to devise a query to extract a subset of information from the database, such as only the authors and phone number, you can click the Use a Query radio button to specify the data to transfer. In this case, we'll export the entire database, so leave the top radio button selected and click Next.

9. On the Select Destination File Format page, leave the database Source as shown (this should be the correct database as selected earlier); select how the data fields will be separated in the file (delimited by a comma or aligned as a table); and then select the File Type, Row Delimiter, Column Delimiter, and any appropriate Text Qualifiers. Click Next.

10. On the Schedule page, select Run Immediately, and make sure the other two check boxes are not selected. Click Next.

11. On the last page of the wizard, check that you have made all the right selections and then click Finish.

You can now look at the file that's been created by navigating with Explorer to the appropriate directory and opening the file by using Notepad. In the example I've just run through, you'll see the unique author's ID, author's name, phone number, address, and so forth, displayed as comma-separated fields (see Figure 9-10).

Figure 9-10. *The data is exported in your preferred format by using DTS.*

Backup Wizard

Backing up your databases is an important administrative task that should be done as often as you back up the rest of your infrastructure.

To use the Backup Wizard from SQL Server Enterprise Manager, do the following:

1. Start SQL Server Enterprise Manager.

2. Click Tools ➤ Wizards.

3. Expand the Management node and then click Backup Wizard.

4. On the Welcome screen, select Next.

5. Next you are required to select the database you want to back up. Select Pubs from the drop-down list and then click Next.

6. You can change the name of the backup, if you want to, and then provide a meaningful description. Click Next.

7. Select Database Backup—Back Up the Entire Database. Then click Next.

8. On the following page, you need to select the backup device you are using. This can be a tape, a removable drive, or a file somewhere on your server's hard disk (see Figure 9-11). Click Next.

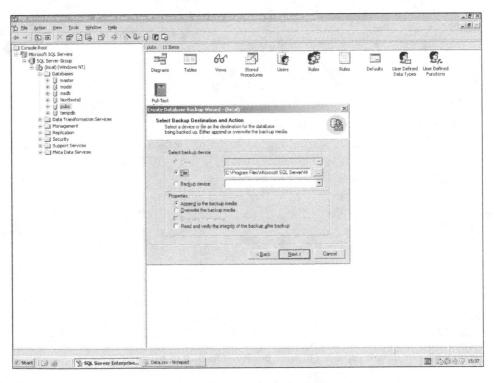

Figure 9-11. *Select the appropriate backup device from the list.*

9. On the Backup Versification and Scheduling page, accept the default settings and then click Next.

10. On the final page, check your selections and then click Finish to start the backup.

After a short time, you'll receive a message stating that the backup has been successful. Click OK to close this dialog box.

CHAPTER 9 ■ SQL SERVER

Into the Future with SQL Server 2005

The SBS 2003 Premium Edition update, Release 2 (R2), includes an upgrade license for SBS 2003 users to upgrade SQL 2000 to SQL Server 2005 Workgroup Edition. There is no doubt that this upgrade will make a huge difference to those SBS 2003 customers who really leverage the underlying power of SQL Server 2000. The upgrade includes a whole heap of new and improved features, such as improved database replication, heightened database resilience (greater database availability leads to less down time), much improved database security with built-in encryption and improved authentication, better reporting, and enhanced data-mining capabilities.

The biggest dilemma facing SBS 2003 users will be whether to buy the upgrade to SBS 2003 R2. The key deciding factor for most will be whether there is a true business requirement to use all the features of SQL Server 2005. If, for example, you are a business using SQL 2000, simply because it's there by default with SBS 2003 Premium Edition, and you are using it for no more than a back-end database for SharePoint, then the real question is, is there any real need to upgrade? I'd say the answer in this case is no. If you positively want (or through the Software Assurance program are getting) SBS 2003 R2 and you are a Premium customer, there is no reason not to upgrade because you are getting the license as part of the R2 license and it's a relatively easy process to follow the upgrade facilities that come with the SQL Server 2005 product.

So, for those of you who are SBS 2003 Premium Edition customers who are getting R2 through Software Assurance or a purchasable license upgrade, here is a little of what you can expect from your investment in SQL Server 2005. For those of you who are in two minds about whether the product is right for your environment, read on and hopefully you'll be swayed far enough either way in order to make an informed decision.

Enhanced Database Availability

These days, business-critical applications are becoming as important to the small business as they are to the large enterprise. If you run a company with a requirement for high server availability, where line-of-business database applications are fundamental to your success, then SQL Server 2005 can be leveraged to increase your current availability to a much better level.

Better Manageability

With every product update Microsoft releases, it always tries to boast improved manageability as one of the primary improvements. In the case of SQL Server 2005, they are absolutely right. With the new management tool (still based loosely on the old SQL Server 2000 tool), you get a much better view of exactly what's going on under the SQL Server hood, and if you want to allow the database to run itself, you can opt to switch on the improved self-tuning facilities for managing database growth and disk allocation.

Improved Security

Security has always been a concern in the SQL Server 2000 arena and in many cases the database has been the primary attack vector for hacking attempts into a Windows system. Microsoft has addressed the previous SQL Server 2000 problems with the introduction of many improvements throughout the entire SQL Server 2005 platform:

- *Secure default*: Microsoft has ensured that the security settings inherent when you install SQL Server 2005 are as secure as they can possibly be. This means that to gain functionality that breaches security guidelines (such as modification to the authentication model), you have to positively relax the security. This means that all risks are understood before security is compromised.

- *Encryption*: All data can be encrypted by native SQL Server 2005 encryption, built right into the software. Information can be encrypted at three levels: in the database itself, in the communication within the database, or on the client computer. The server can be set to deny access to data if the client cannot understand the encryption, allowing administrators to rest assured that no unauthorized eyes are looking into company information. This sort of increased security will be adopted wholeheartedly by e-commerce companies that are responsible for maintaining the privacy of their customers.

- *Policy mapping*: Password policies can now be enforced at the Windows domain level so that group membership will determine access. This means that the product integrates into your corporate policy for access control.

- *Internal access permissions*: The ability to detail permission down to an extremely granular level right inside the database now means that you have the same control over objects inside your database as you do with objects in your NTFS file store.

Quicker Query Response Times

The query-to-response time is a crucial factor in determining performance of your line-of-business application. Changes in the SQL Server 2005 engine have improved the response times of many well-known business applications by more than 70 percent, so in the case of many millions of transactions occurring over the course of a year, the saving would be unprecedented. Whereas a query might have taken half a day with SQL Server 2000, it might take as little as 30 minutes with SQL Server 2005.

Note These are just a few of the myriad features included in the SQL Server 2005 update. To get more information on the complete set of new and improved functionality in this upgrade, refer to http://www.microsoft.com/sql/default.mspx.

Low Price

As you can see, Microsoft has made countless improvements to the SQL Server 2005 product and where appropriate to your business, you will really feel the benefit from this upgrade.

It's worth noting that the product pricing model alone should be enough to convince you of the value of taking the plunge to SQL Server 2005 Workgroup Edition with SBS 2003 R2. Even this low-end version of the product, based on a stand-alone server license (the Workgroup license) retails at $3,900 per processor and is more than double the price of the entire SBS 2003 Premium Edition suite.

Case Study—Copyworld

Copyworld discovered Microsoft SQL Server as the hidden jewel in SBS 2003 Premium Edition. As a separate product, SQL Server is not financially viable for most small businesses; instead most survive on MSDE. Copyworld has found the search capabilities unlocked by SQL Server invaluable, especially in their implementation of Windows SharePoint Services. With most line-of-business applications now able to leverage the facilities of SQL Server, Copyworld has been able to increase its capabilities online and expand in ways not previously conceived.

Case Study—Servideal

The e-commerce package Henry chose to support their business had a number of possible choices he could select for the back-end database. It would have been possible to start running the application on a much smaller-scale solution, such as Microsoft Access or MSDE without much trouble, but Henry knew that as soon as Servideal started trading properly and built an initial customer base, anything less than an enterprise database would begin to show signs of exhaustion. By going straight to SQL Server, the supporting system would scale as easily as Servideal's business grew, with dynamic database growth allowing Henry to worry about running the business and not the IT.

Henry never purported to being a database expert, but by learning the basics of owning and running a SQL Server database solution (not the programming or database design), Henry was able to guarantee that he had good backups, plenty of disk space, and an efficient database to service his customers.

Summary

SQL Server is a massive topic, and this chapter has only scratched the surface of the vast array of capabilities within. There are two discrete disciplines you can excel in where databases are concerned, database management and database design, and both of these are highly skilled and complicated roles. Hopefully this chapter has given you a taste of what SQL Server is all about so that when the time comes for you to use it in your enterprise, you know where to start.

■ ■ ■

CHAPTER 10

Microsoft FrontPage 2003

There used to be a time when creating a website was easy. The first instantiation of the World Wide Web allowed you to disseminate information to end-user systems in a form that made it readily accessible to the reader. The native language of the Web, HyperText Markup Language (HTML), is still the most prevalent coding you'll encounter and remains easy to understand and quick to produce.

HTML is a high-level programming language that your web browser interprets into well-formatted text, presenting the data and images in a way that's pleasing to the eye. The syntax of HTML is easy to understand and to learn, and its inherent portability comes from being interpreted rather than compiled. This means that it's translated into a readable format on the client's web browser rather than at the server end, so the server doesn't have to be concerned about interoperability with every possible operating system that the website is accessed from.

The heterogeneous nature of the systems connected to the Internet has forced web developers to abstract the development of web services away from the underlying operating system, meaning HTML is easily portable from a Windows environment to a Unix environment to a Mac environment. HTML code is quick to develop and easy to test, so even the most novice user can get a site up and running in a short time, albeit rudimentary in function.

HTML can be generated by using any simple text tool, such as Microsoft Notepad or the Unix vi editor. Testing is as easy as opening your completed HTML file with your web browser.

Sounds good, doesn't it? So, where's the catch? The problem is, in the world of the Internet, things don't remain static for long. Soon after the first graphical websites began delivering value-added content to the commercial world, business managers, IT developers, and software vendors such as Microsoft grasped that this limitless resource should be exploited and further enhanced.

The seemingly boundless capabilities offered by today's World Wide Web are far removed from its humble roots, but at its core HTML still provides the underlying structure to every website on the planet. As new programming languages appear on what seems an annual basis, web development has gone from sublime to ridiculous, with dozens of new languages, protocols, and tools available for creating new capabilities such as interactive media broadcasts, news bulletin services, personalized library services, and dynamically linked real-time content.

The thing is, everyone is beginning to see that the value of a website doesn't come from its ability to impress with fancy graphics, snazzy page transitions, or valueless interactivity gimmicks; the real value comes from its ability to get across its message, based on high-value, dynamic, tailored content. I'm not saying that the way data is presented is unimportant, rather that the accuracy and immediacy of the data should be considered first and then backed up with a design that best presents the data to the customer.

Small business customers resent paying web development companies the megabucks they usually charge the corporations for flashy media-rich sites when all they need is a practical answer to getting their message across to their customers. For this reason, DIY web development tools have emerged from many software companies, allowing you to bypass the underlying drudgery of HTML coding and to abstract the design to a user-friendly graphical interface.

Nowadays, business managers, marketing experts, and IT consultants can take a business idea, turn it into a storyboard, and create a functional website, without ever having to delve into the underlying code.

This chapter takes a look at the tools included with SBS 2003 Premium Edition for creating, editing, and publishing your own web solutions. It also delves into the interoperability of FrontPage 2003 with Windows SharePoint Services for enhanced intranet publishing and customization.

Introducing FrontPage 2003

The premier tool from Microsoft for web authoring has been around for some time, but the latest version of the product, Microsoft Office FrontPage 2003, has evolved into a fully fledged development tool that allows you to do two important things:

- *Windows SharePoint Services integration*: FrontPage 2003 fully integrates with Windows SharePoint Services, allowing you to undertake extremely sophisticated customization on the WSS sites to manipulate the content a lot better than what's possible directly from the WSS interface.

- *Traditional web development*: FrontPage 2003 allows you to develop quality websites containing all the latest web technology without having to delve into the coding of each kind of web service. The beauty of FrontPage 2003 in this environment is that you can get as deep into the site development as you feel comfortable. After you become more familiar with development techniques, you can open the code and tinker at the lowest level.

FrontPage 2003 comes as a separately licensed product, but SBS 2003 Premium Edition includes one user license because the product is considered essential for those SBS 2003 customers who are trying to do that little bit more with their corporate marketing and development strategies. These customers have taken the Internet-age initiative: their business strategy deems it necessary to create not only a great intranet site by using Windows SharePoint Services, but also a great Internet presence where the rest of the world will be able to judge the business based on the quality of the website.

It's important to realize that coding a web page is complicated, requiring you to learn the underlying syntax of web page creation (which to get good at is akin to learning Klingon). You'll also find the task extremely repetitive, entailing constantly regurgitating the same old information in different ways to create functionality and content. The key to a good website is not so much the snazzy multimedia gimmicks that many companies have employed; rather the strength comes from the quality of the content used to relate your company messages.

FrontPage 2003's strength comes from doing all the donkey work for you: creating all the underlying HTML code, embedding graphics, and supplying icons and plug-ins for you to use as you please. This makes time for you to consider the quality of the content that you want to publish. The graphical user interface (GUI) for designing web pages is extremely intuitive and allows you to drag and drop web components into whichever area you want on the page. The built-in themes and templates allow you to create complete site hierarchies with a couple of simple clicks. Wizards, such as the Corporate Presence Wizard (see Figure 10-1) generate a site that's ready for you to add the content, and the product even gives you a list of tasks you must complete to finish creating the website. If you have the experience, you can delve down into the code and manipulate the HTML where appropriate. The GUI writes the code on your behalf, allowing you to become more of an editor than a low-level coder, and the beauty of it is, the code is bug free.

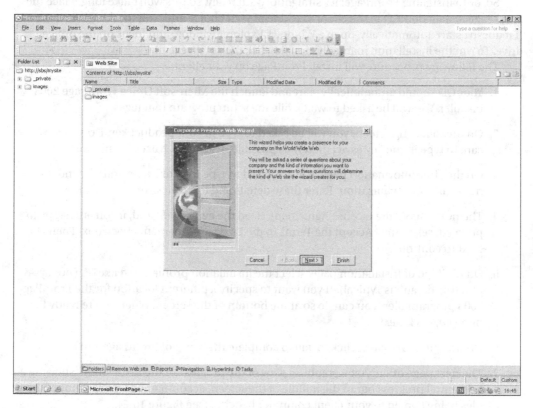

Figure 10-1. *FrontPage 2003 has a diverse range of built-in website templates.*

Installing FrontPage 2003

When you purchase SBS 2003 Premium Edition, you are given one licensed copy of Microsoft Office FrontPage 2003 to install anywhere on your network. Microsoft doesn't expect a small business to have more than one web author in the organization, hence one licensed copy. If you think you do need more licenses, you'll need to purchase these separately.

Warning It's not advisable to install FrontPage on your server, because the server should be reserved for server functions such as processing client requests. You should never do development on a live server of any kind because, by their very nature, things you develop are never right the first time. Through the execution of some unwanted code or script, or simply something that was badly configured or implemented, you could reduce the capability of your server to such an extent as to render it useless. Worst case: you crash the server, leaving your users high and dry.

So, onto installing FrontPage; it's straightforward really, so this won't take long. Place the FrontPage installation CD in the client machine of your choice and wait for the CD to autorun. If it doesn't start automatically, open a Windows Explorer window and focus on the optical drive. To run the installation manually, double-click the setup.exe file.

The following procedure will install FrontPage on your client:

1. Your CD should automatically start and launch the Microsoft Office FrontPage 2003 installer. You will be asked to wait while the setup program initializes.

2. On the following screen, you will be asked to type in your product key. Do so, taking care to type in the key as accurately as possible. Then click Next to continue.

3. On the User Information page, you are asked to type in your name, initials, and the name of your organization. Enter these details and then click Next to continue.

4. The next page is the License Agreement. Read the agreement and, if you are happy to proceed, select the I Accept the Terms in the License Agreement check box. Then click Next to continue.

5. On the Type of Installation page, select the installation profile you'd like on your system (the default is Typical). If you want to specify a different location for the FrontPage 2003 program files, you can do so at the bottom of the screen. When you're ready to proceed, click Next.

6. On the Summary page, click Install to complete the setup of FrontPage 2003.

7. The next page offers you a graphical view of the progress of the installation, showing a horizontal progress bar in the middle of the screen, accompanied by a readout of the files being copied to your client computer beneath (see Figure 10-2).

8. After the installation completes, you get a chance to check the Internet for updates and, if you want to, remove the installation files. I recommend that you check for updates on the Internet because this will ensure that any security patches or vital functionality patches are downloaded and installed before you start doing any real work on web development. You should leave your installation files in place so that you are not asked for the source CD when applying future security patches or hotfixes. When you are ready, click Finish.

FrontPage 2003 is now successfully installed on your client computer. To start using Front-Page 2003, click Start ➤ All Programs ➤ Microsoft Office ➤ Microsoft Office FrontPage 2003.

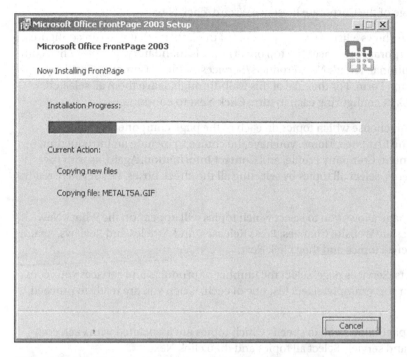

Figure 10-2. *The FrontPage setup routine is intuitive and simple.*

Creating Your First Website

So you've installed the product and you're now itching to start creating quality web content and flashy websites. No problem. The best and most-effective way to get to grips with how FrontPage 2003 works is to dig right in and start creating your own company's website.

This section provides a walk-though of the steps required to create a new website by using the Corporate Presence Wizard. To access the wizard, use the following steps:

1. From FrontPage 2003's main menu, start by clicking File ➤ New.

2. On the right-hand side of the screen, you'll see the New Task pane. Under the New Website heading, select More Website templates.

3. Under the General tab, highlight the Corporate Presence Wizard and then click OK. This starts the process of creating a new, multipage corporate website featuring various predefined pages for typical corporate requirements.

The following procedure will help you work through the steps of the Corporate Presence Wizard and then get you started creating content and working with the task list:

1. On the first page of the Corporate Presence Wizard, click Next.

2. The next screen shows a list of six components of the website that you can configure as part of your corporate presence. The top one, Home, is mandatory. The other five components are optional: What's New, Products/Services, Table of Contents, Feedback Form, and Search Form. For the sake of this walk-through, leave them all selected. We'll take a look at configuring each in turn. Click Next to continue.

3. Now you have to choose which topics on each of the page components will be included. On the first page, Home, you have the choice to include an Introduction, Mission Statement, Company Profile, and Contact Information. Again, as with the page components, select all topics by selecting all the check boxes. When you're ready, click Next.

4. The following page allows you to select which topics will appear on the What's New Page. The topics are Website Changes, Press Releases, and Articles and Reviews. Again, as before, select all topics and then click Next.

5. On the Products/Services page, select the number of products and services your company offers. For this example, select just one of each. When you are ready to proceed, click Next.

6. The following page allows you to specify which topics are associated with each company product and service. Select all topics and then click Next.

7. On the Feedback Form page, you get to select the information fields that the user will be asked to input data into when she provides site feedback. As before, select all items and then click Next.

8. The next page allows you to state whether you display the feedback as a web page or simply record the information that the user enters as a text file. For this example, opt to store the feedback in web-readable form. Click Next.

9. The Table of Contents is a link bar on your home page that offers links to all other aspects of your website. Select all the options available and then click Next.

10. The next page allows you to set the general look and feel of all pages on the site. You can display a company log on each page, a page title, a link bar to the rest of the site, plus some company-specific information at the bottom of the screen, including a contact email address and copyright notice. Select all items and then click Next.

11. A web page that displays the Under Construction symbol tells the reader that the page is not complete. If you want this symbol displayed on all pages that you've not completed, you select Yes. For this example, select Yes and click Next.

12. Next, you need to type some information about your company name and address. When complete, click Next.

13. Type some contact details for your company. When finished, click Next.

14. That's the end of the first phase for creating your company's corporate web presence. Make sure you leave the Show Tasks View After Website is Uploaded check box selected. Then click Finish to generate the website with the details you've entered.

After you've completed running through the wizard and clicked the Finish button, FrontPage 2003 generates the skeleton of your corporate website based on the details you entered during the preceding 14 steps. This may take a few minutes depending on the power of the computer you're doing your web development on.

When the wizard completes, you are left with the Tasks view, showing which aspects of your website still need developing. At this point, the entire site needs editing to personalize it for your own environment (see Figure 10-3).

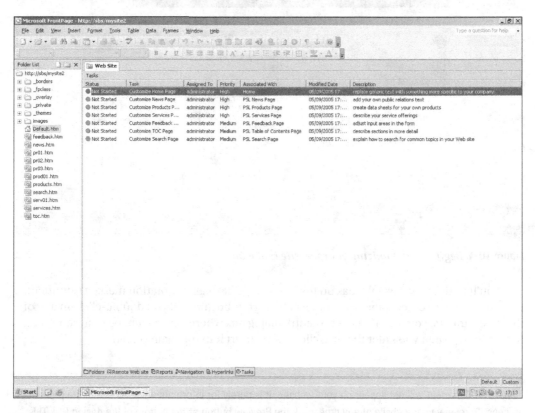

Figure 10-3. *The Tasks view shows which components need editing.*

Customizing Web Pages

FrontPage 2003 makes editing every aspect of your website easy and intuitive. By using the Tasks view, you can click any individual task listed in the dialog box to bring up a properties page where you can modify the description of the task itself. From this dialog box you can also click Start Task to begin the process of customizing that aspect of your website.

To start this example, double-click the Tasks view object Customize Home Page. Then click Start Task. Figure 10-4 shows how your website is presented for customizing.

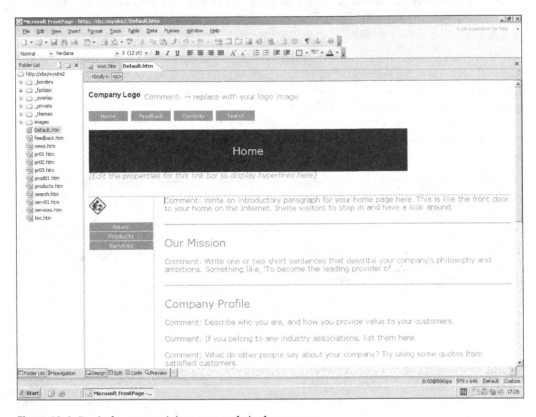

Figure 10-4. *Begin by customizing your website home page.*

You'll notice that several areas on the home page have an annotation marked Comment, prompting you to enter some relevant text about your business. If you double-click on any of these comments, you are offered a text entry dialog box where you can change the comment. In each case, when you enter the text, click OK to insert it in the main screen.

Note A Comment will not appear on your website; it is purely for informational purposes in the production process. To review your website at any time, click the Preview button at the bottom of the design GUI. This displays your web page as it would appear when viewed by using Microsoft Internet Explorer.

You can choose to leave the comments in place. If you'd rather remove them from the Design view, click on them to highlight them and then press the Del key. Either way, you can type your own text in the space provided. This text will appear when you click the Preview button.

Try it. Type a short paragraph about your company beneath the comment at the top of the screen that asks you to type an introductory paragraph about your business. When you're finished, click the Preview button. You'll notice that your text appears and the comment is removed (see Figure 10-5).

After you have finished previewing your website, click the Design button to return to the Design mode. You'll find that as you progress in your understanding of FrontPage 2003, you'll be flicking back and forth between Design view and Preview view more and more. Every time you tweak the site, check the impact in the Preview view. If you're not happy with the change, simply go back to the Design view and click Edit ➤ Undo from the menu at the top of the screen.

Note You can quickly undo any action you've taken in the Design view by clicking Ctrl+Z. Repeatedly pressing Ctrl+Z will step you back through the whole history of changes you've made while editing.

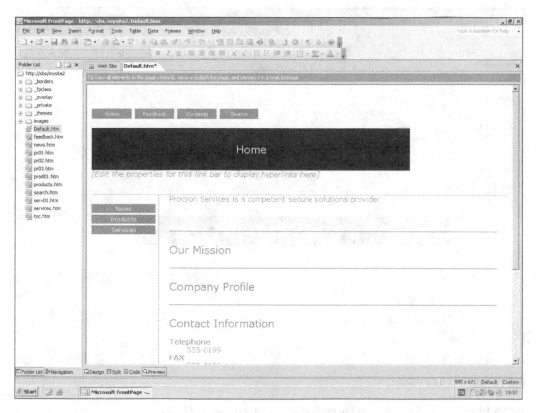

Figure 10-5. *When you preview a site, FrontPage removes all design tags.*

To add your company logo to the page, all you need to do is replace the Company Logo image embedded at the top-left of the Home Page with your own company image.

Note Make sure to shrink the size of the image before you embed it in the Home Page. If you add a large image and resize it in the Design view, the image size remains the same; it's just the way it's shown on the screen that varies. This means that downloading a large image to a client web browser still takes a long time. You can use Microsoft Paint (using the Stretch/Skew option) or any other image editor to resize an image, saving the resultant file as either a `.jpg` or `.gif`.

Two further views worth considering, as you become more familiar with the underlying HTML code, are the Split view and the Code view. The Split view, shown in Figure 10-6, displays both the Design view element and the HTML code that's generated to create the final web page. You can use this view to learn how the code translates to what you see on the screen.

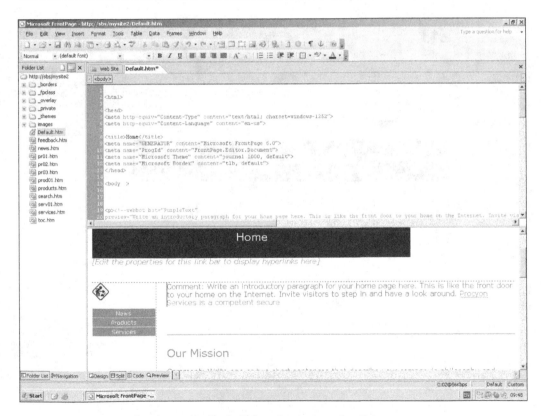

Figure 10-6. *Use the Split view to see both design elements and HTML.*

After you have finished editing the web page and are happy with the content, it's worth saving it locally. This is prior to publishing it to the Web, because you are not yet finished working on the complete site. If you click File ➤ Save, you are asked whether you want to mark this task as completed. If you decide to mark the task as completed, the next time you come back to the Task view menu, you'll see that completed tasks are marked with a green light.

To return to the Tasks view, click View ➤ Tasks from the menu. You can now select another task to start working on. You'll need to work through every element in the Task view to complete work on your website.

The Navigation View

At any time while editing your website, you can click View ➤ Navigation. This will display a hierarchical view of your current website's configuration, showing every page you've added to the site (see Figure 10-7). From here, you can double-click on any page to open that page in the Design view.

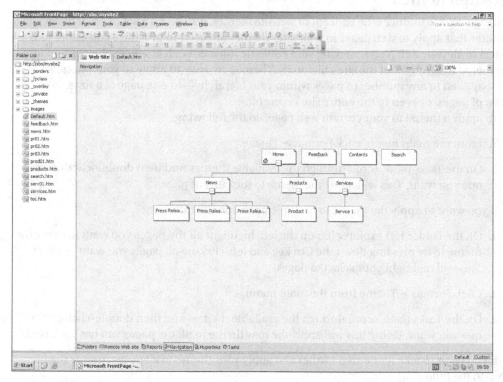

Figure 10-7. *Use the Navigation view to inspect your site's hierarchy.*

The great thing about using the Navigation view is that you immediately see the pages that are linked in your site's hierarchy. To add a new web page to the site's hierarchy is simple: highlight the page that you want to create a new page beneath, one that already has child pages, or one at the bottom of the tree, and then click the New Page icon (the small white folder icon on the top-right control bar in the Navigation view). This creates a page beneath the page you had highlighted.

Note Any new page created from the Navigation view is created with no content. It will, however, inherit the navigation bars associated with the entire site's theme, including the link bar down the left of the screen, a top link bar, and contact details at the bottom.

Website Themes

FrontPage 2003 introduces the concept of website themes. A *theme* is a set of predefined attributes that apply to web pages in your site. Themes are used to provide a consistent look and feel to all your web pages, making sure aesthetic aspects, such as color schemes and fonts, are adhered to throughout the site's hierarchy. Themes are easy to apply to your pages, and can be applied to any number of pages within your hierarchy—to one page at a time, to a collection of pages, or even to the entire site in one hit.

To apply a theme to your current web page, do the following:

1. From the main menu, click Format ➤ Theme.

2. On the Tasks pane, scroll through the available themes and then double-click on the one you want. This will apply the theme to the current page.

If you want to apply the theme to multiple pages, do the following:

1. On the Folder List explorer bar on the left, highlight all the pages you want to apply the theme to by pressing down the Ctrl key and left-clicking all pages you want to affect. This will highlight your selected pages.

2. Click Format ➤ Theme from the main menu.

3. On the Tasks pane, scroll through the available themes and then double-click on the one you want. Doing this will apply the new theme to all the pages you have selected.

If you want to take it one step further and apply your theme to all pages in your site hierarchy, do the following:

1. Click Format ➤ Theme.

2. On the Theme task pane, scroll through the available themes and find the one you want to apply to your site. Hover the mouse pointer over the thumbnail of the theme and then click the down arrow that appears next to the thumbnail. Click Apply as Default Theme from the drop-down menu (see Figure 10-8).

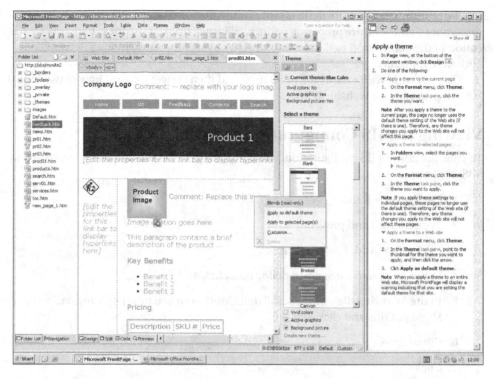

Figure 10-8. *You can easily apply themes to any number of web pages.*

3. You will need to authorize the system to continue because a default theme will change every page on your site, regardless of any formatting you've already applied to your pages. If you are happy to go ahead and apply the selected theme to your entire site, click OK.

Publishing to an Intranet

You can use the services of SBS 2003 to publish your company's website on your local intranet. The enterprise web server product Internet Information Services (IIS) is included as part of the Windows Server 2003 operating system and is a fully operational web server that can provide exactly the same level of web hosting capability that your ISP can provide.

■**Note** There is a limited version of IIS that can run on Windows 2000 and Windows XP clients but it should be avoided as an enterprise web server because of its reduced capability and because it will be running on a workstation. Workstations are designed to be able to be switched off by users, whereas servers should have a higher level of availability and resilience.

Publishing your website to IIS is fairly straightforward once you know how. You have to remember that the entire process is performed locally on your business network, so authentication of the connection to the server is done by using inherent Windows Server 2003 authentication services.

To start with, we'll take a look at IIS itself and then concentrate on how to use FrontPage 2003 to publish your website to IIS.

Viewing the IIS Configuration

To view the current IIS configuration, you'll need to perform the following procedure on your SBS 2003 server:

1. Click Start ➤ Run.

2. Type `mmc.exe` and press Enter.

3. Click File ➤ Add/Remove Snap-in.

4. In the Add/Remove Snap-in dialog box, click Add.

5. In the following dialog box, scroll down until your see Internet Information Services. Highlight this and click Add.

6. Click Close.

7. Click OK.

8. Under Console Root, expand the IIS Manager node and then expand the local computer node.

9. Expand the Websites node to see the complete list of websites you have installed on your server.

Note You'll see that there are at least four default websites already running on your system. Two of these are specifically for SharePoint administration, one is your company's own SharePoint site, and the fourth is the default website always included with any IIS installation.

Creating a Virtual Directory

There are various ways of publishing your website to the IIS server, but the easiest way is certainly to use the default website already created and add a new virtual directory into that site. A *virtual directory* is a repository of web pages that assumes the overarching properties of the site its sits inside. In the case of the default website, which has already been created and is running, adding another directory of pages beneath is as easy as copying the files into the right place. To create a whole new website, from the top-level container, is much more complicated.

To create a new virtual directory beneath the default website container, do the following:

1. Using the IIS Manager, right-click Default Website.

2. From the context menu, select New ➤ Virtual Directory. This starts the Virtual Directory Creation Wizard.

3. On the Welcome page, click Next.

4. On the Virtual Directory Alias page, type the top-level name of the folder structure that you want to copy your website into and then click Next.

5. You are asked to select the folder location where the website files will be stored (this should be a folder on your server). You can browse to an existing folder or create a new one—the choice is entirely your own. When you are finished, click Next.

Note It is good security practice to not leave these files on your C: drive so that "code walkers" cannot trawl the IIS file store and locate back doors into the operating system.

---

6. On the Virtual Directory Access Permissions page, select the permissions most appropriate to your website. In most cases, the only check box you will need selected is the Read permission. All of the other permissions add capability but reduce security. It's best to start with a permissions set that is the most restrictive; then, only if you have to, increase the permissions if your site doesn't function correctly. When ready, click Next.

7. On the last page of the wizard, click Finish.

You have just created a virtual directory container as part of your default website that you can use to publish your own web content into. The easiest way to ensure that you can access the directory is to share it on your network as a standard network file share, albeit a hidden one.

Note Remember, hidden shares are the ones that have a $ on the end of the share name. These are discussed in more detail in Chapter 5.

You should restrict the share permissions to allow access to the directory only when you are logged on as the user authorized to publish content to your website. This restriction will stop any unauthorized users from accessing the site's source files or any accidental corruption of the data by yourself or another user.

After you have shared the directory and applied the appropriate permissions (the directory on the server should have the cupped hand icon underscoring the folder icon), you are ready to publish your website to this directory from FrontPage 2003.

Publishing the Site for Your Workforce

When you are satisfied that your website is ready for public consumption (in this case, I'm referring to your own workforce), do the following from FrontPage 2003:

1. Click File ➤ Publish Site. This brings up the Remote Website Properties dialog box (see Figure 10-9).

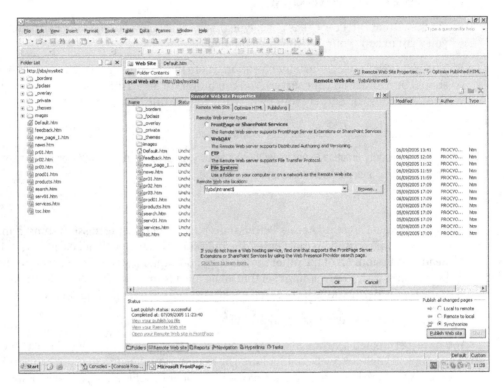

Figure 10-9. *Use FrontPage to publish your intranet to SBS 2003.*

2. Select the File System radio button from the list of remote web server types. You are effectively copying the entire site to the location that you specify in the dialog box.

3. Type the location of your network share in the dialog box (the hidden share you created earlier for your intranet) in the format \\<servername>\<sharename>$. In the example shown in Figure 10-9, the hidden share is \\sbs\intranet$. When you're ready to continue, click OK.

Note If you are having trouble contacting the server, try instead using its IP address: this invariably works when the UNC path name does not.

4. Under the Local Website menu folder, you'll see a compete list of all files in your website. In the Remote Website folder, you'll see that the folder is blank.

5. At this point (before the final act of publication), it's worth opening Microsoft Internet Explorer and typing in the URL of the new virtual directory. You will receive an error when you try to connect because there is currently no content at this location.

6. On the FrontPage 2003 interface, ensure that the Publish All Changed Pages radio button (bottom-left of the screen) is set to Local to Remote. Then click the Publish Website button. This copies all files associated with your website to the server, placing them underneath the selected share, and then reconfigures the URLs embedded in the pages to point to the right place on your server. As the site is copied, progress is shown at the bottom of the screen in a progress bar (see Figure 10-10).

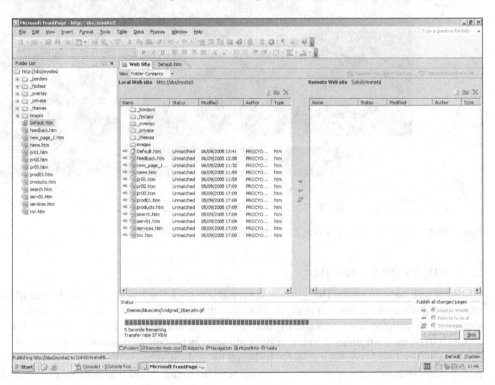

Figure 10-10. *Publishing copies of all website files from PC to server.*

You can now use Internet Explorer to test the website. Run Internet Explorer and type the appropriate URL in the address bar at the top of the screen. The format of the URL is `htpp://<servername>/<intranet alias name>`. In the case of the example I've cited during the last few paragraphs, the URL is `http://sbs/intranet`. Internet Explorer will display the website exactly the same way as it was shown in the Preview view in the FrontPage 2003 editor (see Figure 10-11).

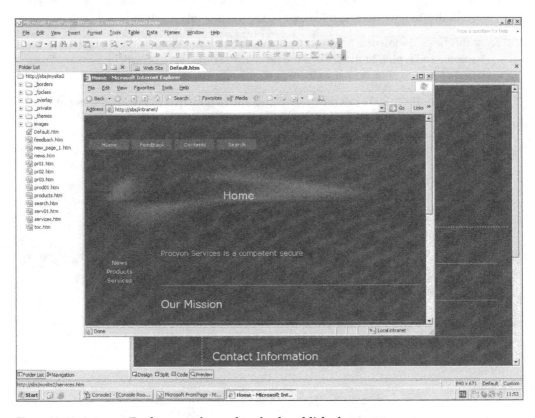

Figure 10-11. *Internet Explorer can be used to check published content.*

Editing Page Content

Editing a web page from the Design view is easy. If you click the Insert menu at the top of the page, you'll see a whole list of objects that can be added to the current page. These range from simple formatting components such as horizontal lines and text breaks, to pictures and text, through to more-complicated web components such as hit counters and spreadsheets. All of these items are highly configurable. Each should be evaluated by using the FrontPage 2003 help facility, which does a great job in explaining exactly how each of these should be configured.

Modifying any of the embedded components already included in your web page is also straightforward, with everything being done via a graphical interface and dialog entry box. For example, if you double-click the Home component (the banner with Home written on it), a small pop-up dialog box appears, allowing you to change the text presented in this component. If you change the text to Home Page and click OK, a new component appears on the screen, with the new title Home Page.

Every object on every web page is configurable to some degree or another, and in every case the way to configure it from the Design view is to double-click on it. To navigate through the website from one page to another, hover the mouse over a link, press the Ctrl key on your keyboard, and click your mouse. This will navigate to that page as the editor remains in Design view.

Publishing to the Internet

Publishing your website internally on your private business network is one thing, but the real test comes when you want to go public, to the rest of the world. The Internet, for all its flaws, does one thing brilliantly: it allows anyone on the planet (with a connection) to communicate with anyone else.

This communication can take the guise of many forms—email, websites, file sharing, conferencing, and more—but the important thing is getting your message heard. To this end, websites are fast becoming the first point of contact that your potential customers will have with your company. Therefore, whatever message you present on the Internet must be clear, concise, unambiguous, and—foremost—literate.

Publishing a website to an ISP is easy (as long as you read all the small print from the ISP on what they support and do not support). This section details exactly how to get your site from the FrontPage 2003 development environment into the environment of the World Wide Web.

Taking Initial Steps

Before sending anything out into the public domain, I strongly urge you consider three important points:

- Be clear about the messages you want to get across about your company. Any messages you present on the Internet should be derived from your business plan's marketing strategy.

- Define your business as the best in its class and, if possible, back your definitions up with real examples of the services you provide or products you supply. Obtain quotes from existing customers and seek their permission to use them as reference sites or satisfied customers.

- Have the entire site proofread for technical, grammar, and punctuation mistakes. There is nothing more off-putting for a customer than a website that reads like it was written by an eight-year-old. If you can't spell or put commas in the right place, how do you expect to provide a quality service or product in the field you purport to be an expert in?

With all that taken care of, and your site looking fabulous in the FrontPage 2003 Design and Preview views, try soak-testing the site on your intranet for a few weeks before going public.

Note You could publish your site on the intranet and then conduct a WSS survey whereby your internal business users can comment on the site's usability, content, and style. Evaluate everyone's opinion and use discretion to include or discount any observations.

Choosing an ISP

First things first: you need an ISP. Choosing the right ISP for your business can be complicated; there are thousands of these companies on the Internet, providing a whole range of services, from global companies such as AOL down to small localized companies with only a small number of clients. You need to ensure that the ISP you choose is reputable, sustainable, and can provide you with the facilities you need to get your business on the World Wide Web. If you are unsure as to which services you need, speak to any of the big companies on the Internet. Often, national telecommunications companies also provide ISP services.

The kinds of services you might be looking for are as follows:

- *Domain name registration*: You will need to register a public domain name with your ISP so that Internet users can find your business's website and send email to you. An ISP should be able to tell you which URLs are available, as well as registering one for your use and informing the Internet community of the new site.

- *Web hosting*: This is the general term for an ISP providing a service enabling you to upload your website to their server. Effectively, their servers play host to your web pages. There are many services that support modern websites, such as databases, server extensions for certain products, streaming media, and support for Microsoft Office FrontPage 2003. If you are using FrontPage 2003 to develop your website, ask about FrontPage server extensions before you sign up, as well as how they provide page counters, hit logs, and other housekeeping functions.

Warning Your website will almost certainly lose functionality if you don't have the server extensions installed.

- *Email*: Most ISPs offer an email service. Make sure that the one you choose meets your needs regarding number of users, number of addresses, routing, and whether they provide remote web mail.

- *Bandwidth*: ISPs also provide the point of presence onto the Internet network, such as a dial-up modem link or a broadband connection. Make sure you quiz the ISP on what it can provide as a package.

- *E-commerce*: If you intend to offer an online shopping experience, many ISPs are now offering predefined services to customers for shopping carts and payment facilities. If you need these, make sure to evaluate whether they'll really do the job you need them to. See if you can get cheap fraud insurance through the ISP to cover any legal action from customers who run into problems. If the ISP provides some sample site links, take a look at them and see how well they work. Look for secure and insecure HTTP pages (the secure ones are indicated by a padlock appearing at the bottom of the browser).

After your ISP contract is signed and sealed, it's time to think about publishing your first website to the public domain.

Note Consider not putting your email details directly on the website. Try using a web form for people to send comments or queries, or try hiding the email address behind an image. This stops spam robots from reading the email address and automatically adding you to a spam distribution list (unfortunately a very common problem these days).

Setting Up an Online Website

Before you proceed with publishing your website, ask your ISP for the following information:

1. The user name and password to be used when you publish your site to their server. You will need to type this in when you contact the server through FrontPage 2003.

2. The method of transfer of the site, that is, are you using FTP, WebDAV, or another method? When you start the Publish Site process from FrontPage 2003, you'll need to instruct FrontPage 2003 on which form of file transfer it should use to connect to the site.

3. You'll need to inform the ISP of the default web page name you are using on your site; in the case of a standard FrontPage 2003 website, the name of the file is default.htm.

Note An ISP using a Unix-based server system will undoubtedly be case sensitive, so make sure you remain consistent with your cases when writing code and creating content.

---

4. If you're using FTP, you'll need to know both the ISP server name and the directory the files should be sent to (see Figure 10-12).

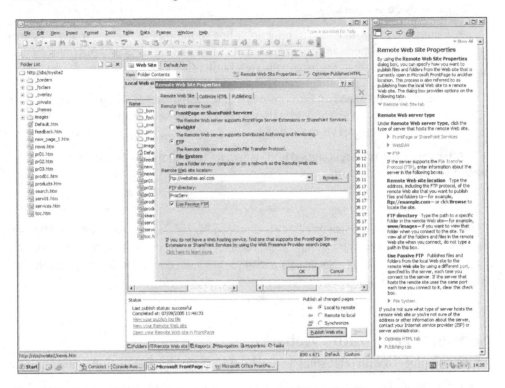

Figure 10-12. *Most ISPs will demand that you use FTP for publishing.*

Note By far the most successful way to publish a website to a web server that supports FrontPage is to use server extensions. Speak to your ISP about enabling FrontPage server extensions on your website.

After you've selected the appropriate publishing method and instructed FrontPage 2003 on which user name and password to use to gain access to the server, you can simply publish the site as if it were local on your network. The only difference will be that the time it takes to upload your site will be determined by how much bandwidth you have on your Internet connection. If your LAN speed is 100 Mbps and your Internet connection is a broadband 1 Mbps connection, uploading your site will take approximately 100 times longer than it would to your SBS 2003 server on your local area network.

After the files are uploaded, use Internet Explorer to check that the content and site structure are as you expected. When you are happy, you can start routing your customers to your site. It's worth registering your site on as many search engines as you can. The following search engines allow you to register your company website on their search engine at no cost, but in some cases you may have to create an online account:

- http://www.google.com

- http://www.altavista.com

- http://www.alltheweb.com

Warning You can also pay search sites to express-list your company site, or place your site in an advantageous position on each user's screen. Ask each search engine in turn which paid services they offer and select the ones that best suit your business: some are paid up front, and others work on a click-through basis. If you select the wrong model, you might end up with extremely high advertising costs that you didn't anticipate. Try choosing less-common words that might mean something to your company and clients but might not be so expensive for accidental hits. This will raise you right up through the search list and keep the costs down.

Using FrontPage with Windows SharePoint Services

The final topic I'd like to cover regarding FrontPage 2003 is how you'd use it to create and modify aspects of your Windows SharePoint Server site that are beyond the scope of what's possible when using the standard browser interfaces provided by WSS.

Using your FrontPage 2003 editor, you can load up your entire WSS site into the editor and have full control over everything it does.

Opening your company's WSS intranet is easy:

1. From the main FrontPage 2003 menu, click File ➤ Open.

2. In the textbox where you might enter a filename, instead type the URL of your company website. In my example, the URL is http://companyweb. Click Open.

3. The first view that you get of the site is a list of files and folders. To move into Design view of the website, double-click the file default.aspx (see Figure 10-13).

You'll see the WSS home page that you are familiar with appear inside the FrontPage 2003 editor, the page appearing first in Design view. You can now do everything you could do before when editing a web page: add objects, change text and links, and modify the layout.

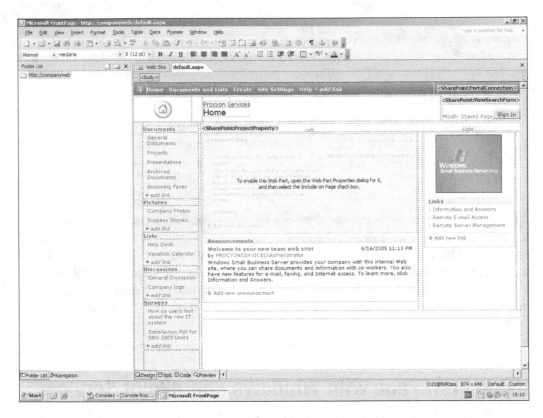

Figure 10-13. *Edit any aspect of your WSS site by using FrontPage 2003.*

If you click on the Split or Code views of the site, you'll see the underlying HTML code that makes the WSS site function. Figure 10-14 shows an example. This code is fairly complicated and it's best you don't fiddle with it without knowing exactly what you are doing. To learn more, check out Microsoft's website on FrontPage 2003: http://www.microsoft.com/frontpage.

After you have finished tinkering with your WSS site, it's as simple as saving it back to the server to make your changes active.

Warning Make sure you back up your server before doing any work on your WSS site. Because the FrontPage 2003 editor is extremely powerful, an inexperienced user could easily delete a valuable web part or function that your business relies on. A reliable backup will allow you to recover any lost functionality relatively easily.

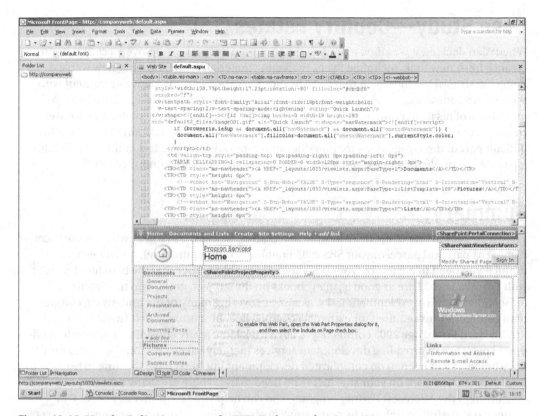

Figure 10-14. *Use the Split view to see the HTML that underpins WSS.*

Case Study—Servideal

Customization of the WSS site was Henry's primary goal when he installed FrontPage. He needed to add corporate logos and rework page content quite significantly to ensure that the site did what he wanted, simply because he couldn't afford for Internet users to have the same level of interactivity with the site as internal users might in another business environment.

FrontPage allowed Henry to create a well-crafted, functionally rich site, personalized to Servideal's business yet still secure enough to allow users access from both the Internet and internally from their home network.

Case Study—Country Estates

When Alan decided it was time to update the corporate image, he employed a contractor to create a fresh new look, including flyers, marketing material, and a stunning new website. Being the shrewd businessman that he is, he didn't take out a maintenance agreement with the website contractor, instead buying total rights to all artwork and design. Next, he promoted one of his junior administrators to the role of web master and installed the licensed copy of FrontPage 2003 on the young lad's computer. Because this assistant already had the difficult part of the design done for him (the contemporary look and feel of the new site), his job was easy, publishing news items, property details, and general announcements.

Summary

FrontPage 2003 is one of the most flexible web editors on today's market (with one user license coming as part and parcel of your SBS 2003 Premium Edition purchase), and it's especially useful if you need to customize your WSS sites. Always remember that the help files included with FrontPage 2003 are as good as many books on the subject, going into the details of the most common web development tasks, as well as covering many of the underlying component configurations required for extremely complicated, functionally rich sites.

To learn FrontPage 2003 completely is not a trivial job. Many consultants and web developers specialize in providing development services that rely solely on FrontPage 2003 for their daily bread. If you need to do complicated development but don't have the time to learn or the local expertise to work on your site, there's no need to fret. There are many professionals available through the Microsoft Partner program who can help you (obviously at a cost). One strategy successfully employed by many small businesses is to contract a web designer to create the initial site and then pass over the content for your own people to manage in the future. In this case, you would add updates to the press releases, the What's New section, and any new services yourself, simply adding to the existing content.

CHAPTER 11

■ ■ ■

A Short Guide to Information Security

The advent of the Internet has completely changed the face of modern businesses, opening up a brand new world of electronic communication to the masses. New methods of business-to-business (B2B) and business-to-consumer (B2C) communications, such as instant messaging, email, data sharing, and web services, are but a few of the plethora of facilities provided to any business that wishes to participate. And all these services complement and enhance business activities, leading to new levels of customer satisfaction and company profitability.

The Need for Security

The remarkable set of services provided on the Internet doesn't come without risk. As with any large community, both real-life environments and virtual ones, the Internet attracts its fair share of criminals, each with the sole intention of preying on innocent users like ourselves for their own criminal gains.

In the real world, law enforcement is localized to the country where the crime is committed and, unless we are talking about large-scale international crime syndicates, crime is normally committed on a local scale and controlled by local police. Conversely, computer-based crime is extremely distributed: criminals operate from every corner of the globe, totally anonymous, completely untraceable, and absolutely untouchable.

The proliferation of e-commerce sites on the Internet has also brought about its own share of associated criminal activities. With e-shopping so commonplace nowadays, shoppers are able to buy high-value items such as cars and vacations almost as readily as they can buy books, CDs, or DVDs—all with the click of a few buttons.

The big players, companies such as Amazon.com, have built their world-class reputations on an underlying trust that their services are secure and reliable. Customers wholeheartedly put their trust in these companies to protect their privacy when they supply personal information, such as credit card details and shipping addresses, into e-commerce websites.

But the question you should be asking yourself is, how safe is it really? The subject of preventing personal information theft, known as *privacy protection*, is very high on the global security agenda, but the buck still stops with the end user. You must ensure that you properly understand the hazards presented in the electronic environment of the Internet, taking care to protect yourself from all the threats that lurk in the recesses of cyberspace.

Note In one case, an employee was given strict instructions that only he and another party could withdraw money from a bank account—and only in person. The employee decided to email the details of the bank account to the other party, not realizing that there were key loggers (rogue software that records all the keys you press on your keyboard) installed on his system. The information about the bank account, including the procedures for withdrawing the cash in person, were sent covertly to a criminal gang. The gang withdrew $9,000 from the account.

Of all the exploits and hacks currently circulating around the online community, one of the most devious is known as *phishing*.

Note An even more targeted version of phishing has emerged recently, known as *spear phishing*, whereby real information about you and the people you deal with is used to lure you into divulging personal and private information back to the criminals.

Hackers can use social engineering practices (see the section later in this chapter) to obtain private information about e-shoppers by impersonating official websites and asking users to reenter user name and password details. Sometimes you are even threatened or led to believe that your account has already been hacked and that unless you act immediately by doing what the message says, you will suffer insurmountable losses. So, hastily you tap in your user name, password, account details, and so on, and are then redirected to the real site and have to do it all again. You think this is just a glitch. But unbeknownst to poor you, your user name, password, and account number are sitting in someone else's database, where they can subsequently be used to do whatever they like with. In this case, they could alter the details of your account, obtain your credit card information, order goods by using your credentials, or even find out where you live. You must always question the intentions of web pop-up windows that proclaim to be from a valid source such as your bank or eBay.

Many attacks are accompanied by serious threats that attempt to play on your trust, coercing you into acting before you realize that the threat might be bogus. If you suspect that you are being targeted by a phishing attack, your best course of action is to pick up the phone and confirm the request with the company in question. If you are still unsure, a quick phone call to your national computer crime unit would do no harm and would certainly put your mind at rest.

More information on phishing can be obtained from the following website: http://www.microsoft.com/athome/security/email/phishing.mspx.

Note How do you ensure that an online store is what it claims to be? There are several governing bodies that offer an official seal of approval for e-commerce sites, such as www.bbonline.org or www.truste.com. If you come across an online store displaying one of these emblems on the front page, follow the link and check the company registration. You could also try a customer satisfaction site such as www.epinions.com or www.bizrate.com to see what previous customers have made of that shop. Finally, if you don't have a good feeling about an online shop, don't use it. You will be certain to find the service or product somewhere else you can trust.

Cybercrime

As a veteran Microsoft consultant, I've spent thousands of hours working on highly secure computer systems over the past 15 years. The one overriding factor I've expressed time and time again while conducting design reviews of these systems is the inability of the system owners to understand what exactly constitutes a secure solution.

Computer-based crime, known by the buzzword *cybercrime*, is on the increase. Government-commissioned computer crime units are springing up in police forces all around the world to try to tackle the proliferation of the more-violent cybercrimes, such as online pornography, pedophilia, and terrorism, as well as to tackle the less-violent but still destructive rackets such as illegal gambling, drug distribution, and fraud. Police forces are also now cooperating through international partnerships with other countries to try to stop some of the more pro-lific of these global criminal enterprises, but the small-time criminals are still operating largely untouched.

Cases have arisen over the last few years of people being coerced into parting with their money for bogus products and fraudulent lottery tickets. More recently, impersonation of certain online services such as eBay or banks has become rife.

Two US government law enforcement agencies, the Federal Bureau of Investigation and the National White Collar Crime Center, formed a coalition partnership in May 2000 now called the Internet Crime Complaint Center (IC3), whose goal is to offer businesses and private Internet users some method of contacting an official investigatory body if they suspect they've been targeted by Internet fraudsters. In the first year alone they received over 30,000 calls.

The toughest challenge faced by law enforcement today is to figure out how to prosecute cybercriminals who are operating outside the jurisdictional control of national anticybercrime units. Without the ability to prosecute these perpetrators, the mere existence of law enforce-ment organizations would not hold enough weight to be a deterrent to criminal activities. Although hacking is illegal in countries such as the US and the UK, it is not illegal in every country the Internet connects to. Hackers exploit this loophole, cleverly routing their attacks through countries where their practices are not deemed illegal and therefore gaining this stag-ing advantage over local law enforcement agencies.

The best way for you to actively help in this long struggle against cybercriminals is to work with the authorities who manage and enforce your national Internet infrastructure. The following organizations are useful contacts if you want more information on cybercrime and what you can do to help:

- *ISP*: Try contacting the ISP you use for Internet connectivity. These guys will have their own connection policies and spam and email rules, and most ISPs will clamp down hard on anyone misusing their facilities. ISPs are governed under license from higher authorities on the Internet. It is the direct responsibility of the ISP to ensure that their portion of the Internet is safe. Because their ongoing success as a business depends on it, they will usually be more than happy to help.

- *IC3*: The Internet Crime Complaint Center can be contacted through their website at http://www.ic3.gov.

- *Cybersnitch*: For terrorist-related cybercrime, you can contact a unique online resource called Cybersnitch, where you can report potential terrorist threats or offer leads that might need investigating. Look at http://www.cybersnitch.net.

- *NHTCU*: In the UK, the National Hi-Tech Crime Unit is a multiagency initiative set up to tackle all aspects of serious and organized crime in the UK. They also work with counterpart initiatives in countries all over the world to combat threats such as bribery, corruption, hacking, and illegal drug trafficking. The NHTCU is now part of the Serious Organised Crime Agency (SOCA) and can be contacted at http://www.soca.gov.uk.

- *WiredSafety*: Organizations such as WiredSafety, as shown in Figure 11-1, act as the man-in-the-middle between you and the police forces who might investigate reports of online crime. They offer consultations and help for victims of cybercrime as well as a comprehensive education program on all aspects of online security. WiredSafety can be contacted through their website at http://www.wiredsafety.org.

Although this message might lead you to think that the Internet is some sort of gangster-run empire of crime and racketeering, it's not as bad as all that. The important thing to remember is that criminals do operate on the Internet, as in all walks of life, but as long as you take the appropriate measures and maintain a sensible defense (as you would in every aspect of life), you'll maintain a healthy, hack-free system, and your money and data will stay protected.

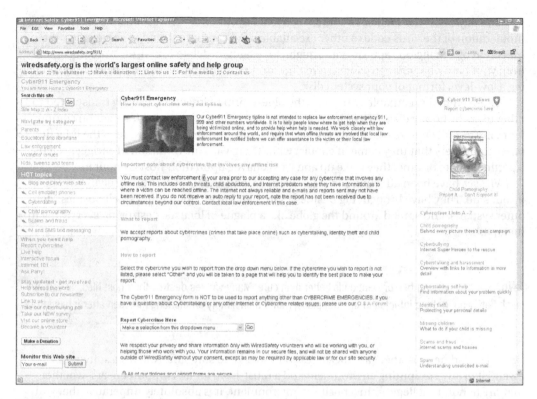

Figure 11-1. *Use an online intermediary to help beat the criminals.*

Viruses, Trojans, and Malware

It's virtually impossible to switch on the news without hearing a report about the latest computer virus to hit the Information Superhighway. The very name, *computer virus*, conjures up images of rogue fragments of DNA flying about, infecting every computer they come in contact with, and in many ways, those images are accurate.

A computer virus is a small piece of computer code piggybacking on an existing application and using aspects of that application's execution environment to perpetuate itself.

■**Note** By *execution environment*, I mean the allocation of protected memory, disk space, and system privileges offered to a legitimate application by the computer. A virus exploits these aspects of the legitimate application to run its hostile code.

The payload—the malicious content delivered by the virus—is responsible for two things: proliferation of the virus code to other executables and computers, and in some cases, the execution of a malicious act. The virus might, for example, delete Microsoft Word documents from your hard disk, change your system time, or do something even as destructive as initiating a low-level format of your system disk.

These kind of executable viruses are the oldest form of infection, usually transported to other users by floppy disk, CD, or Internet downloads. Some viruses lie dormant on computers for many months before executing any malicious code, running only to spread the infection to other computers that they come in contact with. Then, with the initiation of a trigger, such as a pertinent date or time, they wake up and wreak havoc upon their host computers.

Viruses have been affecting computer users as long as computers themselves have been by our side. They have brought big businesses to their knees, obliterated small business computer systems, and spread around the globe like a plague of locusts, destroying everything in their path.

Note Always remember, prevention is better than cure. Many viruses destroy their host files, so you are much better not getting infected in the first place, rather than simply eradicating infection after it has struck.

The good news is: there are measures you can take to stay safe. Antivirus software is essential in any computing environment and a must-have for all computer users, whether they are at home, college, or in a business environment. It is absolutely imperative that you invest in a reliable antivirus system such as Symantec's Norton AntiVirus or Trend Micro PC-cillin, which are both comprehensive and extremely reliable products with the backing of large, multinational companies.

These products are especially good because of their online live update features, whereby the virus signature file (the data that the antivirus product uses when it searches your system for viruses) is updated every time a new signature is released. This process is also used to update the software engine (the software that drives the scanning system) when a new strain of virus comes out that needs an updated approach to scanning rather than just a new signature.

Antivirus software scans for traditional viruses, Trojan horses, worms, and other less-known annoyances known as malware, spyware, and adware.

Note Take a look at http://www.symantec.com and http://www.trendmicro.com for more information on Symantec's and Trend Micro's small business antivirus solutions.

One of the most dangerous pieces of malicious software being perpetuated on the Internet is the Trojan horse. As its namesake suggests (from the gift delivered from the Greeks to the Trojans and containing a regiment of Greek soldiers), a *Trojan horse* in computerese is a piece of what might seem, at first, innocuous code that is capable of doing something more after the payload is activated.

These Trojan horses can come from websites or software downloads and can be used for various malicious reasons by cybercriminals. Trojans (also called *Bots*) can be used to harvest email addresses for advertising, or might be used to log your keystrokes and send these logs to a third party on the Internet. More-dangerous Trojan horse infections have been known to be capable of receiving commands from a central source, to be updated automatically and to carry out whatever functions the owner wishes. Networks of Trojans have been found, all communicating with each other, and money is now being made on the black market by criminals who hire out Botnets (networks of Bots) for specific targeting campaigns.

■**Note** Botnets are big business in the cybercrime underworld. The best advice I can give is to ensure that you have active, real-time scanning on your server at all times, which is possible with most server-quality antivirus/antispyware products.

Finally, it's worth mentioning rootkits. *Rootkits* are toolboxes (a collection of scripts and utilities) used by hackers to crack into a computer system. They are available for virtually every operating system on the market (Windows, Linux, Solaris, and Macintosh) and are used to help the hacker gain access to systems at the system administrator level, whereby the hacker can then exploit any element of the system he desires. Good antivirus/antispyware software will perform a thorough scan of your system for rootkit tool signatures and remove the offending software.

Spam

If you've ever used electronic mail, you have definitely been exposed to spam at some point. The lack of control that regulatory bodies have over the distribution of electronic mail and the associated mail server infrastructures has allowed the perpetrators of spam to send billions of unsolicited advertising and marketing messages to beleaguered users such as you and I. The lack of a consolidated approach to fixing this problem has led to spam proliferating to an almost biblical scale, with projection from industry giants reckoning that without a proper initiative for controlling spam, the Internet as we known it will cease to be of any use.

This might sound like scaremongering, but the reality is that spammers waste a huge amount of Internet resources, as well as wasting the time of the users who have to sift them from their inboxes. However, the good news is, with careful configuration, you can all but eradicate spam from your system.

■**Note** The term *spam* came from a Monty Python sketch (episode number 25 to be precise) in which a menu is presented to a diner with every meal accompanied by some sort of side order of Spam processed meat. Spam, spam, spam, email from work, spam, email from son, spam, spam, and more spam. The analogy fits the bill perfectly because the point is this: you end up with 80 percent of your mailbox containing rubbish, but you have to read through it all just in case some of it might be from your bank manager.

In the early days, it was a lot easier to separate the wheat from the chaff. Strap lines such as *You've won a million dollars* or *Click here to continue* were as intelligent as it got. But as the spammers have become more devious, they've adopted more penetrating tactics, personalizing their efforts with much more innocuous opening lines such as, *Hi friend, hope you are well*, or *I tried calling you but it went to voicemail.*

It's an ongoing battle, but as with anything else, as you bolster your system's defenses to catch today's spam, there's always someone out there dreaming up the next generation of countermeasures to make sure that the junk still gets through.

If you could employ someone to open all your mail, instructing them to delete any unwanted junk before forwarding it to you, you'd be 100 percent sure that you wouldn't have to deal with the chaff. The reason that assertion works is simple: this kind of filtering is subjective.

As a human being, it's easy to evaluate information in a subjective way, determining its relevance as you scan all the content and meaning as a whole. This evaluation is founded in your own personal experience, education, things you might have heard on the evening news, or even something your mother-in-law told you. This is *subjective filtering*, and the problem faced is that it's difficult to build subjective capabilities into a machine that works purely on logic. Writing computer software is probably the most logical thing a person can do. To turn logic into a subjective, warm feeling, capable of deciding which email you want to trash is the Holy Grail of computer science research. If researchers could crack this puzzle, the next stage would be to develop a fully functional, reasoning replacement for the human brain (scary thought), or possibly a computer that we could download our own intelligence into.

For all these reasons, spam filtering is a difficult egg to crack, especially to make it 100 percent effective. The tighter you create logical rules, the more false positives you're likely to receive. A *false positive* occurs when an innocent email, one that you don't want deleted, gets mistaken as a piece of spam and put in your junk mail.

When you are considering a way of dealing with spam within your own organization, there are a few rules you should obey to make sure as little as possible breaks through:

1. Never respond to requests from emails that ask you to reply. The spammers are attempting to get their hands on two things: your money and your email address. The money one is obvious (it's how they make their living), but the reason for the email address is slightly less obvious. Spammers communicate with other spammers and sell email lists to each other. After you're on a spammer's for-sale list, you can expect the amount of unsolicited email you receive to increase exponentially.

2. At some stage, all spammers must rely on an ISP to proliferate their junk across the Internet. Spammers are clever, hiding much of the information related to their communication, but it's possible to determine some information, such as IP addresses, by looking at the message header. ISPs normally promulgate an antispam policy, most doing their best to deal with complaints from their paying customers. Contact your ISP to see what their spam policy is, and in some cases, you can forward spam messages to your ISP for them to decipher and deal with on your behalf.

3. The final tool in the fight against spam is for all inhabitants of the Internet—both users and ISPs—to get a software solution. The long-term goal is to make spamming impossible, and only when the cost of perpetrating the techniques far outweighs the gains, finally will we see its demise. The junk mail filter provided by Microsoft is good, and it's free once you have Outlook. Other vendors out there also sell dedicated countermeasures, such as Trend Micro's Network Anti-Spam (http://www.trendmicro.com) and NwTech's MailMarshal (http://www.nwtechusa.com).

■**Tip** You can do some investigation yourself by using Microsoft Office Outlook to view the spam message headers. Right-click on the message in question and select Options. You are presented with a screen showing the entire message header. The IP addresses shown allow you to track the source of the message. Look at the Received From field and you'll see several IP addresses. As email passes through the Internet, each server stamps the message with its own address. The address at the top of the message header is your own ISP's mail server address. The rest of the addresses are mail servers in between yours and the one responsible for initially sending it. Most importantly, the one at the bottom of the list could be an ISP used by the spammer. To discover the last legitimate IP address in the list, you can use an email look-up server on the Internet. When you find an address that does not correspond to a real, registered address, you can take a guess that this one is the spammer's. You can now write a letter of complaint, explaining your findings, to the appropriate ISP.

■**Note** There is a built-in spam-filtering capability supplied with Microsoft Exchange Server 2003 Service Pack 1. This filter becomes your first line of defense, augmenting the capabilities of your antispam products in eliminating spam once and for all.

Security software provider McAfee has taken the lead in producing software tools dedicated to eradicating spam from the Internet. McAfee's flagship antispam product, SpamKiller, introduces intelligent filtering capabilities, such as filtering on the originating country. The value of this product comes from its built-in, regularly updated set of predefined filters based on the analysis of the existing spam currently hitting your inbox. McAfee delivers live updates to clients to ensure that they are as up-to-date as possible. Another nice feature of SpamKiller is the automated complaint-generation facility, which you can configure to discover the relevant email address that a complaint should be sent to and to send a predefined message on your behalf.

A Matter of Privacy

I think I'd be safe to assume that most of you, at one time or another, have used a PC in a public place to access the Internet or send email. These facilities, typically available in designated Internet cafés or local libraries, are invaluable if you are travelling away from your usual place of business, especially where there might not be an alternative method of connecting to online services.

The problem with publicly accessible services such as these is that they are notoriously unsafe. Public computers are not always what they seem. In some cases, unbeknownst to the system owner, a computer could have become infected by a virus or Trojan horse. The Trojan might be configured to send keystrokes to a central system where all PC activity is logged. In this case, if you logged on to your online banking service, your user name, password, and PIN might have been recorded for unsolicited use.

It's also worth noting that, although the service is cheap and handy, you can attribute no trust to the infrastructure or the management of the PC systems on this infrastructure. There could be countless back doors and loggers installed on the PCs by the system owners, also capturing keystrokes, email addresses, and so on.

Imagine this scenario: you go into an Internet café while on vacation to reach back to your SBS 2003 server to manage a bank account, access some company-specific information, or check on some invoices. A system scanner on the computer that you are using captures your SBS 2003 domain credentials, your email address, your SBS 2003 server's IP address, and any other information you might offer up to the malicious software-listening device. It doesn't take long to see that the person with access to this collected data now has complete access to your business network, your bank accounts, your customer information, and anything else they want to pry into.

Warning Don't use public PCs for anything that you might want to keep private. Don't send passwords from a public PC and certainly don't access any bank accounts. If you need to communicate by using email, set up a separate email account with an online web service such as Hotmail and use it only for insecure communications. If this account is compromised, it should present little concern. When you return from your trip, change your online passwords, just to be on the safe side. If you must access your systems from a public PC, change all passwords as soon as possible and monitor all security event logs and firewall logs when you return.

Protecting Privacy with Internet Explorer

From a purely Microsoft perspective, privacy can be controlled by using appropriate Internet Explorer settings (especially in the latest iteration of the product that shipped with Windows XP Service Pack 2). These settings allow you to select a threshold for the Internet Zone while you cruise around the Internet.

This threshold permits only the information you specify to be made available publicly as you connect to websites. This information is controlled, in web-browser-speak, by the way Internet Explorer processes objects known as cookies.

Cookies are used by many websites to replay information that you would otherwise have to retype. They are also used to create a personalized environment for you, setting up screen information or taking you to the place where you spent the most time during your last visit. The concept behind the cookie is to facilitate a much more fluid surfing experience so that using sites over time becomes a personalized experience. You likely have already experienced this on sites such as that of Amazon.com. When you return to this site to do more shopping, the site greets you with your own name.

The problem with cookies, however, as with many technologies that attempt to make life easier, is that there are ways they can be exploited.

To set the threshold within Internet Explorer, click Tools ➤ Options and then select the Privacy tab. Move the slider to set the threshold that you are most comfortable with (see Figure 11-2). Be aware, the higher security you use, the more retyping you'll have to do on authentic websites.

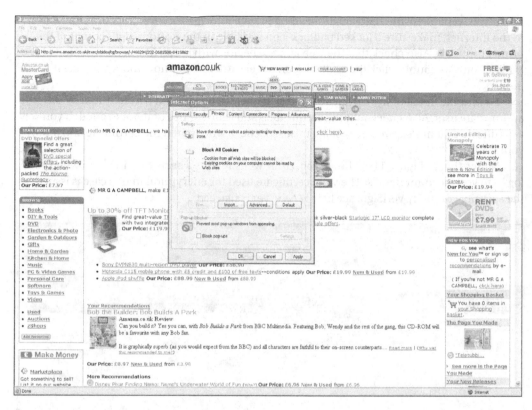

Figure 11-2. *Use privacy thresholds to control the use of cookies.*

Securing the Connection

When you are content that a website can be trusted, you should also think about the wire-level connection to that site. Think of it in the context of a telephone conversation. You telephone your bank and are happy that you are talking to someone you trust. That's great. But what if the line were tapped? Your password, account number, and PIN would be offered over the wire, and anyone listening could simply replay them to gain access to your account.

Warning Wireless networking is even more susceptible to being "sniffed." Make sure that you secure all wireless network connections with the strongest possible encryption available to you. If you are unsure of the strength of a connection, don't use it to transmit sensitive information.

To counteract this threat on a computer system, a method of enforcing confidentiality is needed. This is known as *encryption*, whereby the two end systems wishing to chat over the public network make an initial secure connection, share a key (for example, a single-use shared password), and all communications forthwith are secured by using this key. The keys are big, complex numbers that are difficult to crack. Most speculative criminals are not capable of cracking these codes. From a small business perspective, the computing power required to crack the codes is far greater than the capabilities of the hackers that might threaten you.

If you want to ensure that you are sending private information over a secure connection to the Internet, make sure a locked padlock icon is visible in the bottom-right corner of the browser window. Also check that the web address begins with https (the secure version of HTTP). You can double-click the padlock icon to get extra information about the trust it implies.

Look at the detail of the certificate to see whether it's being used correctly and by the appropriate user. Also check that the certificate is still valid for use and not expired. If you see a certificate that has expired or is being misused, check who issued the certificate and report your findings.

Notice that in Figure 11-3, the Amazon.co.uk website uses a secure connection when you log in to your account details. The valid certificate used for encryption in this case is issued by the security company VeriSign; see http://www.verisign.com.

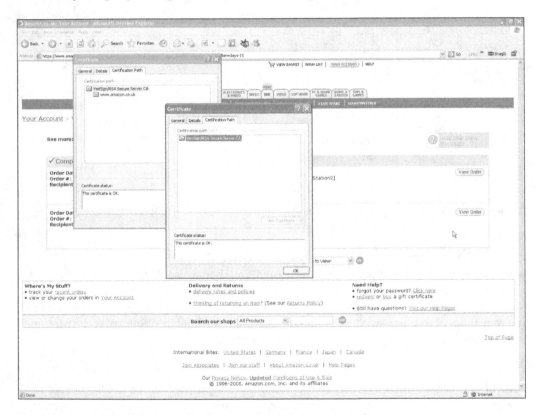

Figure 11-3. *Double-click the padlock to reveal website security info.*

Social Engineering

Social engineering is the term used to describe the method that a hacker might use to retrieve information about you or your system by relying on your weaknesses as a person.

A social engineer is effectively a technology-savvy con artist. These people rely on their innate ability to exploit the confidence of their target, applying pressure on their "marks" to elicit guilt, sympathy, remorse, or pity. These psychological triggers are extremely powerful for the confidence trickster in gaining access to passwords, PINs, addresses, bank details, or even money paid for a product or service that never materializes.

Passwords are the underlying identification and authentication method for gaining access to the vast majority of computer system services around the world. You log on to your PC by using a username and password, you access your telephone banking system by using a password, and you use a password in the form of a PIN in conjunction with your bank card to extract money from an ATM. For this reason, the majority of social engineering attacks are geared toward extracting certain passwords from you by leveraging your emotions and compelling you to divulge passwords at their request.

It's in our nature to trust each other and we don't expect that when we get a call from the bank manager that the person on the end of the phone might not be who they say they are. How many times has the bank called you and asked for your password before they will proceed? This is exactly what I'm talking about. In most cases, the immediacy of the request puts you on the spot and forces a decision, and in these cases, again part of our nature is to avoid confrontation. To answer, "No, I'm not going to tell you that. I'll phone the bank back on the number I always use to confirm that this call is legitimate," isn't the first thought that springs to mind.

Another example of a more-elaborate scam might be a hacker who telephones you claiming to be from a company selling children's books. The hacker asks whether you have children, inquires about their ages, dates of birth, and the kinds of books they like, and inadvertently during the conversation you've already given away their names, your partner's name, your pet's name, and your own date of birth. All this information could offer the hacker an advantage for getting into your bank account. He might phone the bank and say he's you but has forgotten his password. They run through the usual verification checks, date of birth, address, wife's name, and pet's name, and bingo, he's got access to your funds.

Also consider this: a person's date of birth is often used as a memorable date for account transfer authorizations. A pet's name is often used as a password in your home, and might also be used in the office.

Combining Social Engineering and Technology

The best example of social engineering being combined directly with the use of technology was the ILOVEYOU email worm. Although you might not have been expecting to receive an email with the phrase *I love you* in the subject line, the phase itself is evocative enough to compel you to open it. Unless you knew that this particular exploit was doing the rounds, you might easily have fallen for it, wondering who indeed loves you. As a result of this clever emotional con, infection spread like wildfire right around the world in record time.

Other cons are orchestrated through the use of web links that drag your browser to a website that offers something for free or some secret information that will make you rich. As soon as you follow that link, your system is marked with a cookie. It might ask you to register for a free download, where you must give an email address, a user name, and a password. How many times have you used the same password for systems scattered over the web? Is your online banking password used anywhere else?

Often the social engineer cons you into installing a piece of software that can be exploited by either the con artist himself or someone they sell your information/identity to. For example, the information from a key logger might be sold for hundreds of dollars to a third party who in turn uses the information to hack into your bank account.

All these technology mitigations work only when it's a technology-delivered con. If a con artist telephones you and puts you on the spot, try to remain calm and verify all credentials. If you cannot verify the credentials, call back on a number you know, not a number they give you.

Fighting Back

The way to counteract the con artist is to be aware of the threat. The fact you are reading this book has opened your mind to the possibility that you might be approached by an electronic con artist. This is the first step in preventing future cons.

The following steps will help you fight back against the social engineers:

1. Keep your guard up at all times.

2. Spread awareness throughout your business by email, security notices, and so on.

3. Consider a high-quality anti-malware solution, including antivirus software, and adware- and spyware-scanning engines.

4. Give nothing out over the phone unless you initiate the call.

5. Don't respond to spam email.

6. Never fill in online forms with personal details unless you are sure the form is legitimate.

7. Do not use bank account details anywhere else.

8. Commission a security penetration test from an ethical hacking organization to attack your IT and expose any weaknesses.

9. Consider hiring a security consultant to look specifically at the physical security countermeasures on your premises.

Hacking

Although hacking is not considered as high a risk to the small business community as that of viruses and spyware, it is still a threat, and small business systems still get hacked every day of the week.

It's important that you are completely aware of the risk of your system being hacked and understand how to best to counteract the threat. To gain a better understanding of what hacking is all about, this section describes it from the perspective of the perpetrator.

Many reasons drive a person to hack a computer system: some of them are authorized and some are illegal. The term *hacking* is used to describe the act of breaking into a computer system and gaining access to resources by bypassing the inherent security of the target system. Sometimes hackers work under commission from the system owner as a way of penetration-testing a system's security defenses, while other hackers operate illegally to gain unauthorized access to remote systems.

Hackers who work illegally are usually known as *black hat* hackers, whereas hackers working under legitimate authorization are known as *white hat* hackers.

■**Note** White hat hacking is also defined as hacking to locate vulnerabilities in systems to gain a better understanding of that system by the hacker.

Many hackers simply enjoy the thrill of cracking a complicated puzzle. These guys are normally the caffeine-driven techno-wizards who sit in darkened basements in their parents' house and live for their online communities. Their nicknames or CB Radio–style "handles" attribute almost superhero status to their activities, and their exploits are used to acquire fame and kudos with their peers in the hacking underworld. Their activities rarely cause malicious or criminal damage, and their presence is often only felt through their leaving a trademark on a defaced website to identify them to the rest of the hacking community. Many of the best hackers grow up to become legitimate employees of IT security companies, where they can continue their trade while earning a good living.

■**Warning** Hacking, even when there is no malicious intent, is still illegal, so don't try this at home (or in the office).

The final kind of hacker worth mentioning is the most sinister. These are the cybercriminals whose intention is to perpetrate industrial espionage, instigate threats or briberies, or steal money or data from the unsuspecting public.

Hacker Tools

Whatever the kind of hacker, they all have one thing in common: the tools they use to pursue their exploits. The following is just a short list of some of the facilities available to hackers today, giving you an idea of what these guys are capable of doing to your system from anywhere in the world.

War Dialers

War dialing is a term that was coined to describe the act of scanning sets of telephone numbers for computer systems. A *war dialer* is a telephony device that connects to your computer and allows you to select a batch of telephone numbers and then sequentially dial each number until a computer responds at the other end. The results are then logged by the war dialer software and kept by the hacker for future use.

If your computer is connected to your phone line on an analog modem, and if the system is configured to accept incoming connections, a war dialer could easily obtain your number, and even get to the point where the hacker might obtain a login prompt. This is where you need a strict regime for user names, passwords, and access control.

Note A company once had a network-attached fax machine. This machine was definitely not a PC, just a plain old fax machine. A war dialer calling the fax machine's number tricked the machine into identifying itself. Then (using some techno-wizardry), it tripped the fax machine into diagnostics mode (this is not that complicated). From here, the war dialer determined the fax machine's IP address. Finally, using some further information available from the fax diagnostics, the hacker found it was a short hop over to the company's server.

Password Grabbers / Key Loggers

Some hackers have developed software applications that, once installed on your computer (typically through some seemingly legitimate download), can record every keystroke you make. The results are sent via your email system to the recipient somewhere out in cyberspace. Many password grabbers and keystroke loggers can be eliminated by scanning your system with an antivirus or antispyware tool.

Password Revealers

When you see a password in a login dialog box, it normally appears as **********. This is the operating system's attempt at concealing the password from someone looking over your shoulder when you type. A password revealer can scan your screen for windows containing password dialog boxes, and then by using a simple algorithm, it can display the password to the hacker.

If you left your computer logged in and a hacker came by, he might install one of these revealers and look in your Internet Explorer history file to see if you've visited any secure sites. Say, for example, you recently logged in to your Amazon.com account and ordered a CD. All the hacker needs to do is navigate to the login page and click Log In. If you've saved your login credentials, the dialog is presented with the ********* next to the password field. He can run the "revealer" to obtain your password. And like a lot of people, the password you use for Amazon might be the same as the password you use for your bank, your ISP dial-in, or your remote-access connection to your business.

Brute Force Password Crackers

The password for your Windows system is stored in a secure part of the file system called the Security Account Manager (SAM) database, where it is encrypted by using a complicated algorithm that should theoretically keep your password safe. The problem is, because the source code for the algorithm was made publicly available, hack developers were able to develop a tool that uses the algorithm to sequentially look for passwords. The tool either starts at A, B, C, D, and so on, or uses a dictionary to run the algorithm again and match the encrypted word against those stored on your system. In this way, it is only a matter of time before the password is revealed for each account on the system.

Unwanted Network Connection Dialers

The last item worth mentioning is probably one of the most common types of exploit out there and it's one of the most annoying. It's possible for a piece of malicious code to install a network connection on your system that automatically dials a premium rate telephone number somewhere out in cyberspace. This cunning piece of software relies on your embarrassment of being connected to such a site and the fact that it's easier to simply pay the phone bill than explain yourself. Be careful, checking your network connections often, that you don't have any of these intruder dialers installed on your systems.

Hacking Resources

If you are interested in looking at some of the tools available on the Internet that can be used by hackers, take a look at the following list of websites:

- *Darknet.org*: This is one of the UK's leading hacker resources. See `http://www.darknet.org.uk/` for more information.

- *2600*: To read up on the exploits of contemporary hackers (although not strictly related to SBS 2003), have a look at the quarterly hacking magazine *2600* at `http://www.2600.com/`.

- *Disinfo*: A good site for all things conspiracy related, this contains hacking links, tools, and contacts at `http://www.disinfo.com/site/`.

- *SecureRoot*: For a more-official look at all things related to computer security, take a look at `http://www.secureroot.com/`.

Warning Countless websites in cyberspace tout hacking exploits and security-related information. It's advisable to steer clear of these sites and to go only to the more-reputable vendors such as Microsoft because many are riddled with debilitating malware, viruses, and adware.

Microsoft and Security

As with any complex computer system, Microsoft's portfolio of operating systems and applications is not without its own set of problems. Some of these problems manifest as operational bugs as an aspect of the software doesn't function quite as it should. In these cases, the bugs are usually spotted before the product is released.

Less-obvious bugs or *development oversights* in software functionality are much harder to spot during Microsoft's product-testing phase. In these cases, the software might be doing its job properly, yet still be inadvertently opening up an exploitable security vulnerability. These particular bugs are the most dangerous ones because they usually escape from Microsoft unchecked until a clever hacker lurking on the Internet manages to find the loophole, develop an exploit, and subsequently hack into some unsuspecting user's system.

Bugs have varying degrees of impact on your systems, ranging from the totally innocuous right through to downright dangerous. If a bug is innocuous and has slipped through the Microsoft testing net, it's a simple matter of when you find it, you see if a fix exists and implement that fix. However, if the bug manifests as a serious security threat, it's essential that you patch the system as soon as possible, because you can bet your bottom dollar that for every system that is patched, there are 1,000 other systems still open to hackers that now know and understand how to exploit this security hole.

Being the largest supplier of business and home computer technology, Microsoft is probably the top target for all hackers and criminals trying to prove their worth on the black hat circuit. Over the years, Microsoft has been party to many attempts to hack into their inner citadel, and in some cases, the bad guys have succeeded, causing great loss of data and kudos to Microsoft and undermining the trust you have in their products.

All these attacks have one thing in common: they rely on the ability to exploit an inherent vulnerability in the underlying software products being used. To counteract this ever-increasing threat, a new initiative known as *trustworthy computing* was set up to look at the Microsoft business as a whole in an attempt to change the way the company developed, fixed, tested, and managed their software.

Trustworthy computing now pushes its principles into the core of everything Microsoft does as a company. It has been responsible for large-scale initiatives throughout Microsoft, such as the development of Windows XP Service Pack 2 (an entire remodeling of the Windows XP client operating system), and Microsoft's latest weapon in its antispyware arsenal, Microsoft Windows AntiSpyware. Get AntiSpyware from the downloads section of Microsoft's website or by following the link at `http://www.microsoft.com/athome/security/spyware/software/default.mspx`.

Note Microsoft has a whole stash of useful information related to IT security on their website. Although most of this stuff is geared toward Microsoft products, there are some interesting white papers on general IT security concerns as well as some free utilities that can scan your systems for potential vulnerabilities. Visit the Microsoft TechNet Security Center at `http://www.microsoft.com/technet/security/default.mspx`.

Security Patches and Hotfixes

Keeping Windows systems up-to-date with all the latest security patches is essential if you want to maintain a solid security baseline. As new vulnerabilities are discovered within the billions of lines of code that make up your Microsoft systems, security patches are released almost immediately from the respective development teams.

A timely approach to implementing these fixes should stop these threats in their tracks, meaning that vulnerabilities such as the Sasser worm that completely rely on inherent problems with your software are eradicated before they spiral out of control.

To make life easier, Microsoft has introduced the Windows Update service. This utility interfaces with an online database and scans your system against the baseline of what should be installed from an update point of view. You can then choose which, if any, of the patches you want to download onto your systems.

Note For your server systems, it's better to download the Windows Server Update Services from `http://www.microsoft.com/windowsserversystem/updateservices/default.mspx`.

This service can interface to virtually every supported Microsoft product, including server operating systems such as your SBS 2003 server, and workstation operating systems such as Windows XP and Windows 2000. The service will also scan productivity software such as the Microsoft Office 2003 suite for known vulnerabilities.

Check the Windows Update site regularly, to make sure your system is up-to-date (see Figure 11-4).

To access Windows Update:

1. Click Start ➤ All Programs ➤ Windows Update.

2. Install Windows Update by following the link on the right-hand side of the web page (see Figure 11-4). This is the latest and best version of the update software.

After you've installed the Windows Update software, it will scan your system and offer a list of updates that you might want to install. The installation of patches can be set to automatic by selecting Express Install, or you can selectively choose which patches to apply by choosing Custom Install.

You will then be able to set the Windows Update service to act automatically on your behalf. If you have an always-on Internet connection, the service can be configured to automatically download and install patches during quiet periods, such as overnight.

Warning It's possible to set your server to automatically install and reboot patches, but this is not recommended because server maintenance should be done on a known and understood schedule. Try to keep server security patching and hotfix application as a manual activity.

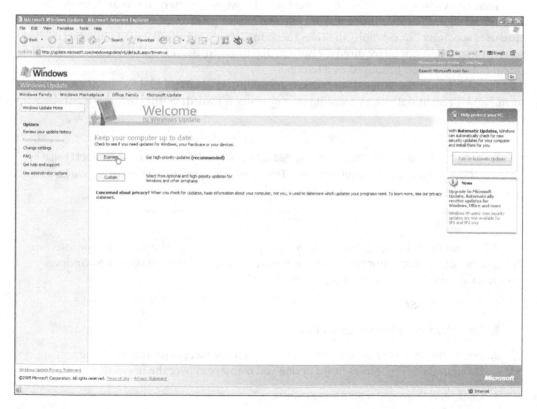

Figure 11-4. *Use Windows Update to keep Windows systems up-to-date.*

The Microsoft Baseline Security Analyzer

Aside from keeping your systems up-to-date, the other big factor in determining whether your system is secure is how its configured. The Windows Update service has the patching angle covered, but what about system configuration?

To tackle this problem, Microsoft developed a tool called the *Microsoft Baseline Security Analyzer (MBSA)*, which can be used to scan every computer system on your network (workstations and servers). It combines a comprehensive sweep of your operating system for missing security patches with a detailed look at your configuration and assistance on how best to configure aspects of your system to eliminate better understood vulnerabilities. The result of running a system scan with the MBSA is a detailed breakdown of all vulnerabilities, with comprehensive descriptions of how to mitigate the threat attached to each.

The MBSA is completely network capable, meaning that after you've installed it on a system on your network (a workstation or server), you can target any other networked machine that you have access to.

Note Download the MBSA from Microsoft's website at `http://www.microsoft.com/technet/security/tools/mbsahome.mspx`.

The MBSA scans each of the computers you choose for a variety of security threats. It looks at configuration items such as your use of complex passwords and disables certain insecure user accounts (for example, the Guest account). It also offers advice on removing certain services that might not be required for normal day-to-day use—services that might pose a threat if they were compromised by a hacker.

Microsoft touts the MBSA as the "free vulnerability assessment tool for the Microsoft platform," and for an initial stab at securing your systems, it's worth getting to know it.

Note If you had access to the network and wanted to hack into a Windows system, you would begin by using the MBSA to scan for obvious vulnerabilities. This would give you a quick heads-up on how hard the system will be to attack.

When you first run the MBSA setup, you are presented with a simple web-style interface that guides you through your first system assessment. To run a system scan of a Windows computer system by using the MBSA, do the following:

1. Start the MBSA.

2. Click the Scan a Computer option.

3. Select the computer to scan. This can be either the local computer (the one you are running the MBSA utility from) or one you connect to over the network.

4. Click Start Scan and wait for the results.

After the scan has finished, you are offered a security report containing all the vulnerabilities discovered on your computer. The report is in the form of an ordered list of hyperlinks explaining exactly what was scanned. The details of the findings can be retrieved by following the hyperlink to the relevant advice (see Figure 11-5).

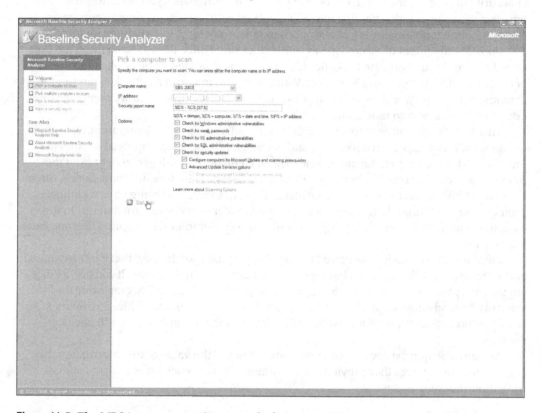

Figure 11-5. *The MBSA can scan entire networks for vulnerabilities.*

Designing a Secure System

The methodology for designing a secure computer system follows the same process whether you're designing for a small business or a massive enterprise. The only thing that changes is the number of times you need to follow the set process that defines security boundaries, threats, and mitigations within your systems.

The most important thing to bear in mind when designing a secure system is that the purpose of security is to protect you. Security must be seen as a business enabler rather than some sort of evil curse placed on your business systems. It certainly should not become so imposing that it cripples the systems you've lovingly invested time and money in to bring to fruition. If you let IT security rule your design, this threat mitigation might start acting like a self-made denial-of-service attack.

Scoping

There are many industry methodologies that define the *best way* of putting together a secure infrastructure solution, and all will lead to a secure system. However, the key to implementing IT security in your business is to not overdo the security; otherwise, you take away from the business capability. Understanding the risk associated with *not* locking down a service or removing some functionality is just as important as knowing how to switch the security on.

Consider the threat of macro viruses within Microsoft Office files. *Macro viruses* are executable pieces of code attached to Office files that run as an added value application on top of the file itself. In the case of a Microsoft Word document, macros can check databases for dynamic fields, run system code to pull out special workstation information, populate tables, offer user interfaces, and much, much more.

Microsoft Office comes with a Visual Basic for Applications (VBA) programming environment that allows application developers and power users to develop improved document interfaces. This means that documents can deliver elements of intelligence right from the moment of inception from the template. With all this added functionality comes a new threat: the macro virus. A macro virus is a rogue piece of VBA developed by using virus techniques, proliferating itself through the opening and execution of infected Word documents. In this case, the virus quickly spreads throughout your Office environment, corrupting files and causing mayhem.

But is the answer really to switch off the capability? If you take the view that it is not required and switch it off, you'll end up not having that added capability in the future. If you take a different tact, to try to reduce the risk by closing down the proliferation methods, employing the services of a good antivirus product, and heightening the security of your Office environment, you have successfully reduced the risk enough to still maintain a capability yet still mitigate the threat.

A security scoping study of your IT systems will reveal the value of the information they contain and the services they provide. It's important to look at each aspect of your system from three different angles:

- Confidentiality

- Integrity

- Availability

Confidentiality deals with the value of the data itself. What is the data worth if it falls into the wrong hands? Could the leakage of this information compromise any aspects of your customers or your staff, or give away valuable company secrets or your secret recipe for fudge? The point is, where confidentiality is a consideration, you must look at security methods for protecting the information's secrecy. When you decide that a piece of information requires this level of protection, you are looking at employing encryption techniques of some sort to protect the data. You might encrypt emails to clients to stop them from being sniffed over the Internet. You might protect files on your server by using the Encrypting File System (EFS). You might consider full disk encryption on mobile devices (such as laptops) if the information on the hard disks contains confidential company information.

Integrity is the security term describing the inherent level of trust you must place in a piece of data. In the example of sending an email to a colleague, you want the information transmitted in that email to be exactly as you typed it when your colleague receives it. It's possible for a third party to intercept and modify your email in a way that compromises some aspect of your communication. They might add themselves to a distribution list or change a billing address, for example. In this case, it's not the confidentiality of the message that's important, it's that the message needs to remain as it was intended. In this case, a technique known as digitally signing the information comes into play: the message is scanned by the sending system, and then a checksum of the message contents is created and signed by using a digital signature. When the recipient receives the email, his system verifies the digital signature and recalculates the checksum. If the one transmitted with the sender's credentials and the one received are the same, message integrity is assumed.

Availability is the term describing the level of service that you expect from your systems. A denial-of-service attack against your server directly affects your system's availability. Many attacks of this nature come as a result of virus infection or poor boundary protection. To mitigate this threat, the most important things are a good antivirus regime and firewall protection at the boundary.

Cost vs. Security vs. Functionality

Think of your business as an equilateral triangle. The three apexes of the triangle are labeled cost, functionality, and security (see Figure 11-6).

Take any two of the apexes, work on them together, and the third suffers. If you want a secure system that maintains all your functionality, the cost of the solution exponentially increases. If you want low cost and high security, your functionality will be adversely affected. Similarly, if you want maximum functionality at a lower cost, you can achieve this only through a relaxed security policy.

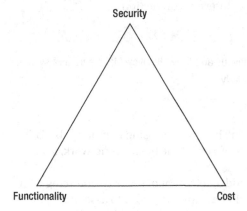

Figure 11-6. *Your business can be represented as an equilateral triangle.*

Work from the Outside In

I've always favored the approach of starting at the outside and working your way in when securing a computer system because the boundary of your network is where most attacks originate. When I say *boundary*, I mean any connection from your internal systems to the outside world. This could be your Internet connection with a firewall device to protect you from the rest of the world. But it also includes protection against viruses coming in through CD-ROMs and floppy disks. Rogue files might also come through the email system and must be sought out and destroyed before they cause any harm.

The Boundary

A good system for modeling your network boundary is called *domain-based security (DBS)*. It looks at the big picture, at a high-enough level, to determine exactly where the dividing line lies between the systems under your direct control and those you have no responsibility for.

Note DBS should not be confused with the Microsoft definition of a domain; instead it refers to a logical grouping of people, resources, and infrastructure from the point of view of how the business operates.

DBS provides a method of defining the security-relevant zones that an infrastructure relies on, allowing you to easily see where you'll need to strengthen connections and apply tighter rules, and where threats originate from.

First things first: get a blank sheet of paper and draw a large circle in the middle of the page. Write the name of your business in the circle. This represents the security domain applicable to your business.

Next, consider each of the systems you connect to externally. This will include connections to the Internet, to other businesses, and to home users needing dial-in access as well as any other dial-up systems such as modems installed in workstations and fax machines.

Give each of these external systems a domain of its own and then connect them logically in the way they interface with each other. In the example shown in Figure 11-7, the small business domain has a direct connection to the Internet as well as a connection to a home user's system. This particular home user also has a separate Internet connection.

Note All home-based systems should adhere to your antivirus and firewall policy. Make sure that systems are up-to-date and firewall configurations are checked regularly.

The Internet VPN home user connects to the small business by using Remote Web Workplace, tunneling over the Internet. So although she connects to the business network, it's via her Internet connection.

At each of the interconnections, you'll need to add an element of security-enforcing technology. The way to determine what technology should be implemented is to assess the threats posed by the connection with regard to *confidentiality*, *integrity*, and *availability*. Study each service required through your external interfaces and determine the impact of loss of that service.

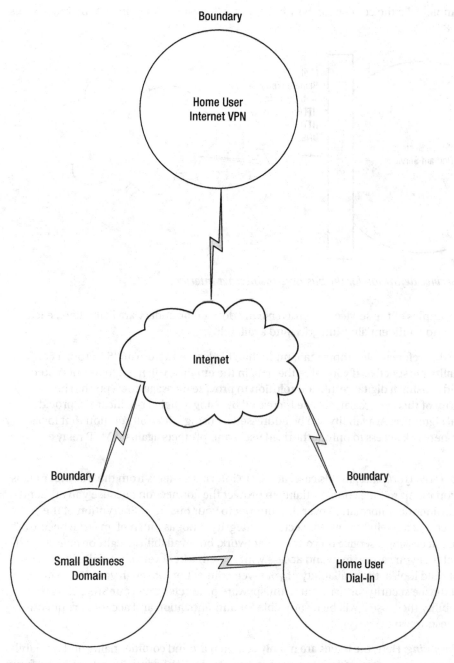

Figure 11-7. *Domain security model for a typical small business*

For example, take the connection between the small business domain and the Internet, as in Figure 11-8.

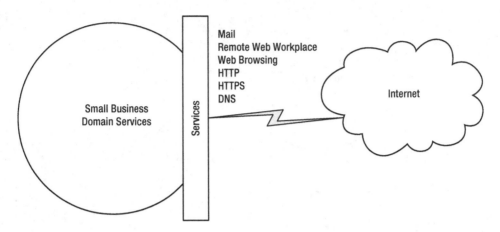

Figure 11-8. *Service definition for the business-to-Internet interface*

Three examples of the services that traverse the domain boundary are listed here, each with reference to confidentiality, integrity, and availability:

- *Mail*: Mail refers to electronic mail, more than likely to and from an ISP. From a confidentiality perspective, if you value the data in the email, it will need to be encrypted. Consider using a digital certificate solution to provide message encryption. The integrity of this service can also be increased by using a digital certificate to provide a digital signature. Availability can be addressed by using a firewall solution that locks down network access to only authorized users and protects against SMTP relay and spam.

- *Remote Web Workplace*: In this case, access to internal systems from the Internet means that you might require confidentiality to protect the connection because you are sending confidential information over the Internet to your business. Encryption of the connection can help bolster this security. Integrity is not as much of an issue because you are accessing a service on your own network, but availability might be an issue if it's critical that you can log in to and access your system whenever you require. In this case, you should look at the availability of your web connection (through your ISP), your client device security (antivirus and antispyware products), and your SBS 2003 server availability (because it will be responsible for authentication and access to your company resources).

- *Web browsing*: Here, the issues are mainly centered around confidentiality and availability. Integrity is not required when you visit a web page. Confidentiality comes in the form of the details you might transmit to a web page, and the way a web service might interrogate your computer for information, such as accessing your cookies for personal logon information. Ensure that all web connections requiring any element of confidentiality use the SSL protocol—denoted by the padlock appearing in the browser window at the bottom of the screen. Internet availability is enhanced by ensuring that you have a well-configured boundary device such as a firewall stopping your systems from being hacked.

As you can see from these examples, you will start to build up a profile of all the security measures you need to employ, and you'll also get a picture of the ones that, although helpful, might be unnecessary or unwieldy. The underlying message is that security costs money. Security can also cost you functionality.

Tabulate each risk in terms of confidentiality, integrity, and availability (known as an *infrastructure risk analysis*) and attribute a high, medium, or low weighting to each. This table is the beginning of your security policy—the policy that defines all the steps you've taken in mitigating the threats you've defined in your domain model.

Within Each Domain

The systems inside your boundary should now be considered by using the same methodology used at the boundary. You should carry out a risk analysis of the following aspects of your system, each time referring to confidentiality, integrity, and availability:

- *Local files*: These are files held in users' personal file stores on both servers and workstations (and laptops in offline mode). Systems such as EFS can be used to encrypt the users' personal files. Ensure that any files users deem important are stored on the server so they are backed up. Antivirus products will scan all files on demand and clean them of corruption.

- *Shared files*: These are files held in shared collaborative systems such as network drives and Windows SharePoint sites. Make sure all server directories are backed up, and where appropriate, ensure that files are encrypted using EFS. Antivirus products will scan all files on demand and clean them of corruption.

- *Local email*: This is email stored on the Exchange system. Make sure you have an email antivirus product that scans attachments on arrival in the Exchange system. The client-side antivirus product will also scan messages created on the client before they are sent to the Exchange system. This will stop email virus proliferation within your business or out to your customers.

- *Remote email*: This is email stored on end-user systems, either in offline storage files or exported to disk. If email is required to be stored long-term, it should be exported from the system and stored on either tape or optical systems.

- *System security/patch levels*: Use automatic updates and the MBSA to ensure that all security configurations are applied and patches are installed.

Warning SBS 2003 administrators advise you to always update your workstations automatically, but servers should be updated manually. This allows administrators to maintain full control of the server's patch levels and decide themselves on maintenance reboots and other issues.

- *System security/logging on*: Securing identification and authentication to your systems is done by ensuring that you use strong passwords and remove unnecessary accounts such as the Guest account. Don't give users higher permissions than they need to do their jobs. Use Windows authentication in your SQL databases rather than Mixed Mode authentication.

- *User's ability to introduce threats*: Control access to floppy disks, USB pen drives, and optical devices for importing data. All import and export of data should be explicitly checked for viruses, and if you are interested in the data being exported from a confidentiality perspective, use a utility that audits all data transfer for your later scrutiny.

- *Social engineering*: Create awareness for mitigating spam and phishing attacks. A plan should be put in place to train all your computer system users in understanding what they are dealing with when they use the Internet. All procedures defined for a business must be adhered to and should form a clause in the employment contract of every employee.

- *Network security/firewalls*: Ensure proper configuration. Ongoing management should include monitoring the firewall logs on a regular basis.

- *Network security/wireless security*: Make sure to follow all guidelines for changing WPA/WEP passphrases and ensuring that no rogue systems have been authorized by your access point. When possible, use WPA encryption or one of the more-robust wireless protection mechanisms.

At the end of your risk analysis, you will end up with a long list of risks and subsequent countermeasures that will help mitigate the threats imposed.

SBS 2003 Security

It wouldn't be right to have a chapter on information security without looking directly at the features provided by the SBS 2003 product suite. The security features included in SBS 2003 are comprehensive and wide-ranging and if used correctly can secure your system to the point where only an extremely determined hacker might gain unauthorized access.

It's true to say that no security system is totally unbreakable, and for this reason security solutions providers are constantly updating, improving, and revising software and hardware to cope with ever more devious and elaborate exploits.

SBS 2003 allows you to enforce security policy through your domain policies from the central server, meaning you can create strong password policies, configure the user's desktop environment, map shared drives to relevant permissions, and manage system backups all through simple-to-use GUI interfaces.

Implementing a Security Program

The following is a 10-step program that should help your SBS 2003 domain and network remain as safe as possible. Follow each step, referring to each of the relevant sections in this book that covers the functionality in question. After you've worked your way through the list, you'll have a well-rounded and robust security policy that can be used as your network's configuration baseline. After that, it's a simple case of maintaining the baseline by regularly auditing your systems for change.

Step 1: Implement a Strong Password Policy

Users are authenticated to the operating system by entering a unique user name and password. Most of the time, users are responsible for selecting their own secret passwords to be used for logging in. The key to making this security mechanism strong is to prevent users from selecting easily guessable passwords while still making them select ones that can be remembered. A password written in a notebook is only as secure as the physical access to the notebook.

Try implementing strong password policies by using the following method:

1. Log on to the SBS 2003 server as an Administrator.

2. Click Start ➤ Server Management.

3. In the details pane, click Users.

4. In the console, click Configure Password Policies.

5. Select the check boxes labeled Minimum Length, Complexity, and Maximum Age. Then change Configure Password Policies to Immediately.

6. Click OK to close the console.

The Minimum Length option indicates the least number of characters a password can contain. This helps protect against users selecting very short passwords that would easily be cracked by a brute force attack. It's recommended that you opt for passwords more than 12 characters in length.

Note Any password stored on the network can theoretically be cracked by using brute force attacks. However, the longer the password, the more time it will take this method to work. For each extra character you add to the password length, you exponentially increase the number of possibilities the attacker has to cycle through before finding the right combination. In other words, the longer, the better!

The Complexity option forces passwords to contain a variety of character types. You can use this to ensure that passwords cannot contain the user's account name, and passwords must contain characters from three of four categories: uppercase letters, lowercase letters, numerals, and nonalphanumeric characters such as !, $, #, or %.

Note It's a good idea to tell your users to change their password before the very last reminder on the last day of the cycle. This will stop them from being locked out of the system. Also, make sure that your users know to shut down their workstations at night because the password reminder appears only after a reboot.

The Maximum Age option sets the lifetime of the password in days. Passwords older that the maximum age must be changed when the user next logs on.

Step 2: Use NTFS (on Workstations and Servers)

A *file system* is the method used by the operating system to control access to the data on the hard disk. Windows systems can use a variety of file systems to control access to data; the simplest one, and the default after installation, is FAT32. FAT32 offers little protection to the data on the system, so any protection you inherit is from the secure logon mechanism covered in step 1.

To enhance the security of the file system, it should be converted to NTFS. This is a more configurable model, granting access control permissions to individual files and folders. This means you gain access to files and folders on the server only if specific rights have been granted.

To see what file system you are using:

1. Double-click My Computer to open the Explorer window.

2. In the details pane, right-click the hard drive that you wish to check and select Properties.

3. Look at the General tab to see which file system is being used.

If you are not currently using NTFS and wish to convert to it, click Start ➤ Run, type **convert C: /FS:NTFS** and then press Enter.

Step 3: Set File and Folder Permissions

Access control to all shared files and folders should be set to allow only the most appropriate access to these resources.

Now that you are running an NTFS file system, you can set granular access permission of data items:

1. Using Windows Explorer, locate any directory to which you want to add permissions.

2. Right-click on the directory or filename and select Properties.

3. Select the Security tab.

4. By clicking Add or Remove, you can modify the list of users who have access to the resources.

5. Highlight a specific user or group to modify the individual rights that user has to the files.

Permissions such as Full Control offer the greatest privilege over file system objects, whereas permissions such as Read offer limited privilege, granting only the ability to read the contents of the file or folder.

Step 4: Use a Firewall

If you are using the Premium edition of SBS 2003, you should be using the enhanced security features of ISA Server to secure your network boundary. For a detailed look at configuring ISA Server, see Chapter 8.

If you are not using ISA Server to secure your boundary connection, you can use the software firewall provided by default on SBS 2003 Standard Edition, much like that supplied on

Windows XP SP2. Your server would need two network adapters, one for the internal network and one for the Internet connection.

The recommended way to set up the SBS 2003 software firewall is to run the Configure Email and Internet Connection Wizard. This will set up the firewall on your broadband connection automatically. Follow these steps:

1. Click Start ➤ Server Management.

2. In the console, click Internet and Email.

3. In the details pane, click Connect to the Internet.

4. On the Connection Type page, select Broadband.

5. For the Broadband Connection Type entry, choose A Direct Broadband Connection and carefully follow the rest of the on-screen instructions.

Step 5: Install an Antivirus Tool

Make sure to buy an enterprise antivirus tool capable of integrating with both your NTFS file system and your Exchange 2003 email system. This will allow you to ensure that viruses cannot get into your system through either of the two most likely methods of infection.

For more information on enterprise antivirus solutions, check out http://www.mcafee.com/ and http://www.trendmicro.com.

Step 6: Install an Antispyware Tool on Workstations

Antispyware software will mop up the rest of the rogue files that antivirus products don't. Not all malicious software is considered a virus threat, and although antivirus products are getting better at stopping spyware infestations, they aren't quite there yet. Microsoft now offers its own utility called AntiSpyware, available for free download from http://www.microsoft.com/ athome/security/spyware/software/default.mspx.

Warning Because you should never be surfing the Internet from the server, it's recommended that you don't install anything but your antivirus product on SBS 2003. Antispyware might flag something that you inadvertently delete without realizing it's critical to your server's operation.

Step 7: Use a Comprehensive Patch Management Policy

Update your system to the latest version of the Windows Update services and Windows Server Update Services and download the Microsoft Baseline Security Analyzer onto the SBS 2003 server. Use both automatic updates and regular MBSA scans to ensure that your system is up-to-date and you are maintaining a good security patch baseline.

See the following three websites for more details:

- http://windowsupdate.com

- http://www.microsoft.com/technet/security/tools/mbsahome.mspx

- http://www.microsoft.com/windowsserversystem/updateservices/default.mspx

Step 8: Restrict User Permissions

SBS 2003 comes with a set of templates that give users the level of access they require to do their jobs. The *user template*, for example, does not let the user who has logged in with one of these account types have remote access to the network. Users who come under the control of the Mobile User template do have this privilege. When you first set up a user by using the Add User Wizard (discussed in Chapter 5), you automatically assign them to the appropriate template.

However, to reassign templates to users or reclassify a user, do the following:

1. Click Start ➤ Server Management.

2. In the console, click Users.

3. In the details pane, look at the description for each user.

4. Click on the user you wish to change the privileges for.

5. Click Change User Permissions to launch the wizard.

6. On the Template Selection page, select the template you are interested in assigning.

7. Exit the wizard by clicking Finish.

Step 9: Secure Wireless Networks

If you are using a Wi-Fi network in your business, make sure to set it up by using the security features that your equipment provides.

If your access point supports WPA, make sure to use this because it is certainly the most secure method of controlling wireless networks. However, if you are stuck with WEP, make sure that you manually configure the secret key (the shared secret between clients and the access point) rather than letting the system assign one automatically. Make sure that the key you assign is the longest possible length.

If there are additional security capabilities on your wireless devices, make sure to configure all of them, and where possible, check for firmware updates.

Step 10: Use the Event Logs

Setting up your SBS 2003 system to audit everything that goes on will allow you to look back over the history of your system's usage and determine where malicious or unauthorized access has occurred.

To switch monitoring on:

1. Click Start ➤ Server Manager.

2. In the details pane, click Monitoring and Reporting.

3. On the console page, click Set Up Monitoring Reports and Alerts.

4. Follow the instructions in the Monitoring Configuration Wizard.

There are five event types that can be recorded in the Windows event logs, each having its own specific purpose; the last two event types are security events and are exclusive to the security event log:

- An *error event* is denoted by a red circle emblazoned with a white cross and indicates a serious system problem.

- A *warning event* is not necessarily significant but might indicate something to be investigated. A warning event is denoted by a yellow triangle emblazoned with a black exclamation mark.

- An *information event* denotes successful operations and is useful in tracing problems where you can eliminate things that are working properly. Information events are displayed as small, white speech bubbles emblazoned with a lowercase *i*.

- A *success audit event*, denoted by a gold key, indicates that a security-related function proceeded successfully (for example, when you log on).

- A *failure audit event*, denoted by a gold padlock, indicates that SBS 2003 has blocked an action from occurring. This might indicate an attempt to gain unauthorized access to your system.

Glossary of Security-Related Terms

Like every other aspect of information technology, IT security has its own set of acronyms and buzzwords that you'll need to understand before you can get to grips with the subject.

The following list of definitions should help you understand at least some of these security concerns pertinent to the small business environment. Many of these are terms you might have heard before, but it's important that you properly understand what each means in its proper context so that you can build your defenses in such a way as to mitigate each of the threats.

- *Adware* is the electronic equivalent of junk mail. It takes the form of applications that run on your system and receive advertisements from Internet marketing companies. These advertisements are forced onto your screen either through Internet Explorer browser pop-ups or in some cases Windows Messenger service dialog boxes.

- *Denial-of-service, or DOS attacks*, are attacks on your system that intend to cause disruption. A typical DOS attack will make your system run extremely slowly or block access to a server. Anything that reduces your ability to use the system in the way that you normally would use it could be considered a denial of service. More-contrived attacks are distributed denial-of-service (DDOS) attacks, whereby the perpetrator places exploits on many systems, all working with the same sole purpose of slowing down and stopping your services.

- A *digital signature* is a means of ensuring that the integrity of a piece of data is maintained and that the sender whom a message is coming from is actually who he claims to be.

- *Malware* is a generic term describing any malicious software that has been installed on your system. This includes Trojan horse applications, innocuous adware, and the more invasive spyware. Viruses can also be described as malware.

- *Phishing* is the act of enticing information such as logon credentials or credit card information from you by using social engineering principles that prey on your sensitivity or obligation to obey certain rules. You may be asked to verify your account by reentering your username and password. In addition to phishing, there are other data collection techniques, such as spear phishing, key loggers, rootkits, ransom ware, and dialers.

- *Pop-ups* are unsolicited advertisements appearing on your desktop, usually triggered by some external source that is out of your control. These are commonly encountered when using Internet Explorer to view websites, and are often initiated by websites that are partaking in click-through marketing campaigns.

- *Social engineering* is a term used to describe how a hacker would interact with you outside the IT environment to obtain information that would help him achieve his goals, such as guessing your password. This might be as simple as someone calling you up and pretending to be from your bank, or could form some part of an elaborate plot to completely discredit your services in front of your customers.

- *Spyware* is software installed on your computer without your knowledge, used to capture information about your system, about you, about your surfing habits, or any other snippets of useful information it can lay its hands on. All this is then transmitted back across the Internet to the originator of the spyware and used for direct-marketing campaigns and phishing attacks.

- *Threats* are the exploits that can be leveraged by criminals to undermine your system for some form of unauthorized use. The goal of a security architecture is to eliminate as many threats as possible from your internal systems and to create a barrier that keeps out the remainder of threats.

- A *Trojan horse* is a piece of malicious code that masks its intentions under the guise of something less dangerous. Trojan horse code is typically used to spy on your system operation, possible running a keystroke logger or a password logger and sending its findings to someone over the Internet.

- *Viruses* are the rogue pieces of code traversing the Internet whose sole aim seems to be creating chaos. They tend to be written by hackers and code buffs who thrive on the upset they cause, and in many cases they are purely written for the author to receive notoriety within his own black hat circle.

- *Worms* are yet another member of the virus family, identified by their innate ability to replicate themselves from one machine to another over the network without any form of user interaction. Many worms have been known to detect and use computer networks to proliferate themselves. If your computers are not protected or patched to prevent these sorts of attacks, the worm can spread at dramatic speed. A good example of the devastation caused by this form of virus was the attack of the Code Red worm launched on July 19, 2001. Within just nine hours of this worm hitting the wires, more than 250,000 machines were infected. Another example was the Slammer worm, which exploited a security hole in Microsoft's SQL Server product and managed to effectively bring the Internet to its knees by using a piece of computer code just 376 bytes in length. Worms, like most other viruses, can be eradicated from our systems by using a comprehensive antivirus product such as Norton AntiVirus. So long as you keep your systems patched and up-to-date and have a decent antivirus regime, you should remain safe and sound.

Case Study—Country Estates

One of the most important things required by Country Estates' new IT solution was to distribute the workforce yet allow better teamwork and collaboration. In any distributed environment, the boundaries that require securing become more difficult to control—some staff are working from home, some are working from hotels, and some are working from the train. Country Estates decided that the best way to make sure that the core system back in the head office remained secure was to create an inner enclave that mobile workers would have to enter using VPNs before they could use business data. In this way, any compromise on the end system, such as a laptop being stolen, would not affect the business. A replacement mobile would follow the same password-protected VPN route into the core network, and the employee would resume working without any problem.

Summary

Enforcing a good Information Security policy in your business is vital to your maintaining a stable system and productive workforce. It's a tough fact of life that criminals have woken up to the virtues of the Internet, but as long as you are careful about how you build your walls, your staff should be able to continue working while the criminals are left on the outside looking in. If you are unsure about securing your system, seek help through Microsoft on the security home page: http://www.microsoft.com/security.

CHAPTER 12

■■■

Troubleshooting SBS 2003 Standard and Premium Editions

With the vast array of products and capabilities built into both SBS 2003 Standard and Premium editions, there is no way I can cover every eventuality of what might go wrong and how to fix it when it does. It's a fact of modern IT systems that they do go wrong from time to time, possibly through some inadvertent misconfiguration, or perhaps through the introduction of some new software on the server. Whatever the reason, you need to learn the tricks of the trade to be able to fix these problems.

What I've done in this chapter is try to expose the most common tools used in diagnosing each element of the solution stack that makes up your business infrastructure. (Recall the ground-up approach to defining your IT solution described in Chapter 1.) In each case, I offer guidance on how to best use that tool.

Be warned, however, that not all problems are resolved easily. There will undoubtedly come a time when you need to call in the big guns, Microsoft consultants who are experts in the components that make up the SBS 2003 family of products (probably a Microsoft Small Business Specialist available through Microsoft's website: `http://www.microsoft.com/ smallbusiness/partner/vendorsearch.mspx`). These specialists are well versed in the most complicated of problem-resolution techniques, so your best course of action is to gather as much information as you can about how your system is running, including bringing out your planning guide, before contacting them.

Note If you are calling in an expert, your first point of contact is Microsoft. You can find the correct contact details for your location on the Microsoft website. Another great resource to try is the Microsoft Most Valuable Professionals community:

- `http://mvp.support.microsoft.com`
- `https://mvp.support.microsoft.com/communities/ mvplist.aspx?Product=Windows+Server+System+-+Small+Business+Server`

I'll start by presenting the techniques used for gathering and interrogating diagnostic information on your system before going on to example problems that might affect each of your SBS 2003 applications. I'll show you the most common problem/resolution scenarios facing users today and then finish off by listing the best command-line tools available to Windows 2003 users.

The Event Viewer

Virtually every service, application, and function of SBS 2003 can be audited or logged, either in the native Windows event logs or in customized logs particular to that application. You have looked at the event logs already in Chapter 11 from a security angle, but the information in these logs goes a whole lot further than for detecting security breaches.

Accessing the Event Viewer on your server is easy. Do the following:

1. Click Start ➤ Control Panel ➤ Administrative Tools ➤ Event Viewer.

2. Highlight the event log that you wish to view.

3. Double-click on any individual event to see the event details (see Figure 12-1).

You can also access the Event Viewer directly from the SBS 2003 Server Management interface. If you run Server Management (by clicking Start ➤ Server Management) and highlight Monitoring and Reporting, you'll see the Server Performance Report in the details pane. To the left of the report, you'll see a list of links to various systems management and monitoring facilities, one of which is the Event Viewer.

Note A shortcut to the Event Viewer is to click Start ➤ Run, type `eventvwr` in the dialog box, and press Enter.

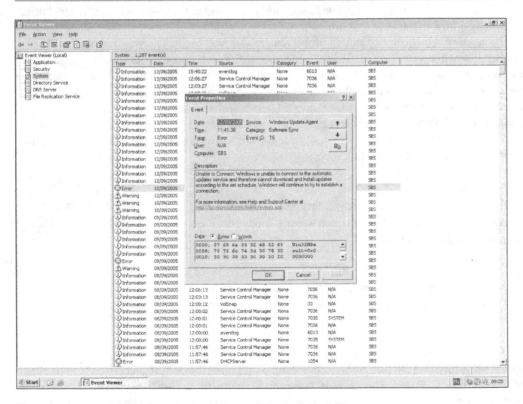

Figure 12-1. *Event Viewer has six server logs, each one full of clues.*

On my example system, I've found an error event in the System log, and it's definitely worth checking into and trying to fix. The Event Properties dialog box shown in Figure 12-1 shows that the error reported on my SBS 2003 server occurred recently and that it's a critical error. The Source field shows that the Windows 2003 service generating the event was the Windows Update Agent. The Description section provides a plain-English description of the problem: "Unable to Connect: Windows is unable to connect to the automatic updates service and therefore cannot download and install updates according to the schedule. Windows will continue to try to establish a connection. For more information, see Help and Support Center at http://go.microsoft.com/fwlink/events.asp."

Aside from this description, the two most important pieces of information that you can use to diagnose the reasons why this problem might be occurring are the event ID (in this case, 16) and the category of error (Software Sync).

■**Note** Try looking at http://www.eventid.net for the most comprehensive and useful list of Windows events on the Internet.

To start with, follow the link to the Help and Support Center. A dialog box will pop up and show you the details of the event being transmitted to the Microsoft website (see Figure 12-2). You should click the Yes button to accept that this information will be sent to the Microsoft website, because this will bring back a series of help and troubleshooting files specifically tailored for this event.

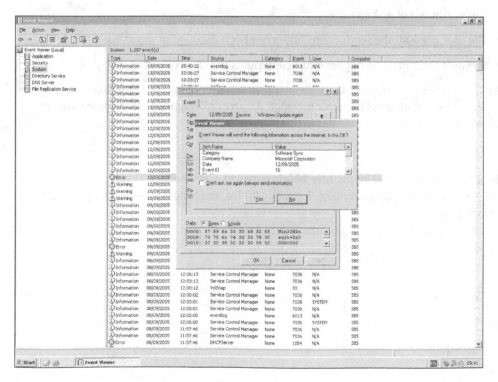

Figure 12-2. *Search Microsoft's website for event-specific information.*

If you don't get a good enough response from the automatic search on Microsoft's website, try using Google, searching on the event ID and the source. In this case, your search would be as follows:

"Event ID: 16" and "Windows Update Agent"

There are plenty of online resources around that will help you diagnose system problems, and many websites contain a complete list of pretty much every event ID and description you can think of.

In this case, the event ID 16 from the Windows Update Agent means that my SBS 2003 system was unable to contact the online Windows Server Update Services server. The reasons behind this error could be many and varied, and this is more of a symptom than a cause. To get to the bottom of the problem, you'll need to dig deeper.

The problem could be generated because of any of the following reasons:

- There is no Internet connection.

- There is a problem with DNS.

- TCP/IP is not working properly.

- The Microsoft website is not working properly.

- The service has been switched off on the server.

- Your firewall is blocking the connection.

- You have a virus or malicious code intrusion causing a service failure.

- You've run out of disk space.

- The user account the service runs under has been disabled or removed.

- The user account does not have sufficient rights to act on behalf of the system.

As you can see from this list, there are plenty of avenues of investigation that you can pursue to get to the root cause of the error message. An array of diagnostic techniques used by the experts will be explained in detail later in this chapter.

Note If the event log files get too big, save them to some sort of removable media (such as DVD) with a filename that tells you what the log contains. Try naming the file something like `sys02102005.log` or `sec01012006.log`.

Monitoring and Reporting

By successfully setting up monitoring and reporting facilities on your SBS 2003 server, you will be able to capture and analyze vital statistics about the health and well-being of your system, and more importantly, act on this information before a disaster strikes.

Performance Report

From the SBS 2003 Server Management console, you can view your server's performance report, which gives a great view of exactly how your system is running (see Figure 12-3). This shows that there are in fact two services that have not started on the SBS 2003 server and two critical alerts that have been raised against the system. If you follow the Details hyperlink beside any of the Summary items, you are taken to the appropriate location in the report.

Critical alerts are listed with a detailed explanation of each one, and in most cases you are prompted to further investigate the alert through the Event Viewer, as shown previously.

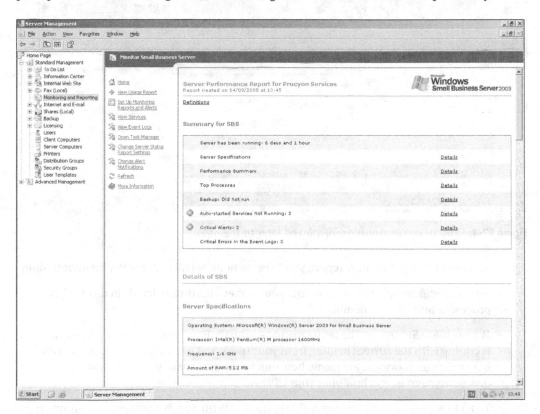

Figure 12-3. *Review the report summary for critical server errors.*

The example Critical Alerts page shown in Figure 12-4 shows two alerts for my server, Microsoft Exchange Management and DHCP Server. In both cases the alerts are reporting that these services are not working properly.

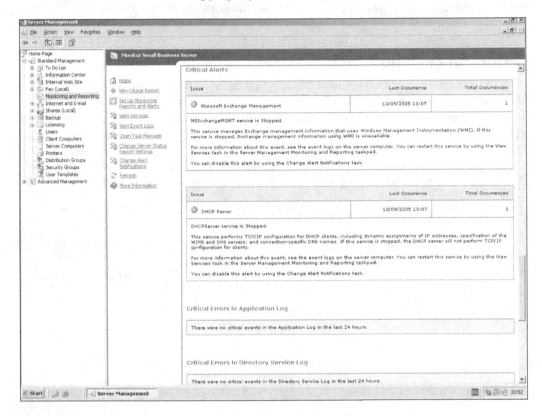

Figure 12-4. *Critical server events are displayed later in the report.*

If you scroll through the entire report, you'll see sections detailing the following information:

- *Server Specifications*: This section lists your server's hardware details in terms of your processor and system memory.

- *Performance Summary*: The performance summary is an overview of how your system is coping with the current loading from your users and network services. It tells you how much memory you are using, how much free disk space you have, how busy your disk subsystem is, and how busy your CPU is.

- *Top 5 Processes by Memory Usage*: This section lists the top five processes running on your server that have been grabbing system memory. If a process is misbehaving, it often appears at the top of this list.

- *Top 5 Processes by CPU Usage*: This section lists the top five processes running on your server that have been grabbing system CPU time. If a process is misbehaving, it often appears at the top of this list.

- *Backup*: This section reports on the success or failure of your latest backup.

- *Autostarted Services Not Running*: You'll find any services that have not started auto-matically listed here. Note: the services listed are only those that are set to start automatically, not all services that are not started.

- *Critical Alerts*: All alerts deemed critical (typically ones that appear as errors in the event logs) will be displayed here in detail. You can modify alerts through the Change Alert Notifications interface, described later in this chapter.

- *Critical Errors in Application Log*: All errors reported in the application log are exposed here for convenience.

- *Critical Errors in Directory Service Log*: All errors reported in the Directory Service log are exposed here for convenience.

- *Critical Errors in DNS Server Log*: All errors reported in the DNS Server log are exposed here for convenience.

- *Critical Errors in File Replication Service Log*: All errors reported in the File Replication Service log are exposed here for convenience.

- *Critical Errors in Security Log*: All errors reported in the Security log are exposed here for convenience.

- *Critical Errors in System Log*: All errors reported in the System log are exposed here for convenience.

View Services

If you click the View Services link from the Monitoring and Reporting interface, this starts the Services management console. This is used to manage system and application services (the code that runs in the background of your system and makes your server work). The list of serv-ices installed on your system is shown in the details pane, with a description of what each service does and a statement of whether that service is running.

To examine the details of a service that may be reporting errors, right-click on the service name and select Properties.

The example in Figure 12-5 shows the service properties for the SBS 2003 DHCP service as running on my example machine. As you can see from the dialog box, this service is set to start automatically when the system starts. The error being reported is that the server cannot start. If you click the Log On tab, you can see that this service is set to start with the Local System account. This account should always work and is by far the best account for services such as DHCP (hence this is the default). Many services run under special user accounts that have special privileges and rights attributed to the account. If you are checking a service that uses a specific user account that's either a domain or a user account, make sure that the account is still operational through Active Directory Users and Computers and make sure that the user account has a current, correct password.

If you click the Dependencies tab, you'll see whether there are any other services that this service is dependent on. If, for example, the service that you are investigating is relies on another service that has a problem, this might be the reason this service is failing.

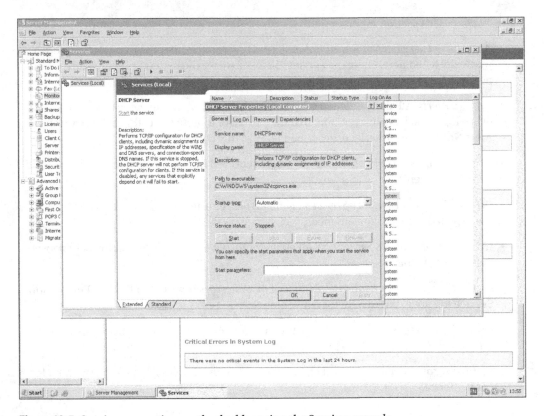

Figure 12-5. *Service properties are checked by using the Services console.*

You can configure special recovery options for any service by clicking the Recovery tab. There are five trigger-points for which you can specify the actions SBS 2003 will take in the event of a service failure:

- *First Failure*: The first time a service fails after the system boots up, you can instruct SBS 2003 to do one of the following: take no action, try to restart the service, run an independent program, or reboot the server.

- *Second Failure*: You can subsequently modify the action if the service fails a second time to the same set of instructions: take no action, try to restart the service, run an independent program, or reboot the server.

- *Subsequent Failures*: On subsequent failures, the service can be configured to again perform any of these actions.

- *Reset Fail Count After*: This parameter is the number of days for which a service must successfully function before the fail count is set to zero. This fail count determines the first, second, and subsequent actions as described previously.

- *Restart Service After*: You can delay the restarting of a service based on this parameter. The value is expressed in minutes.

Task Manager

The Windows Task Manager is often overlooked for its usefulness. However, it makes a great diagnostic tool and can help with all sorts of problems, from networking bottlenecks, to memory usage problems, to rogue processes that might be spyware or viruses.

You can start the Task Manager in various ways, through the Monitoring and Reporting interface, or clicking Alt+Ctrl+Del and then clicking Task Manager, or right-clicking on the taskbar at the bottom of the screen and selecting Task Manager from the context menu (see Figure 12-6).

■**Note** Advanced users will find the free downloadable tool from http://www.sysinternals.com useful for extending Task Manager's capabilities beyond what's delivered out of the box. Connect to the website and look for Process Explorer.

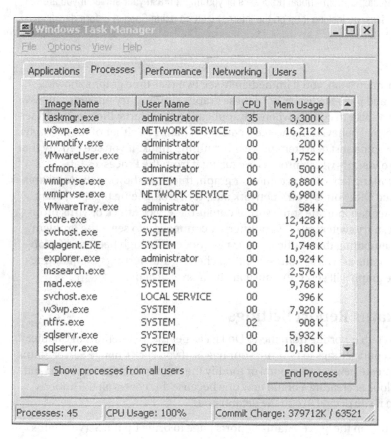

Figure 12-6. *Task Manager is great for diagnosing system problems.*

You can view information from five tabs: Applications, Processes, Performance, Networking, and Users.

The Applications tab displays all running foreground applications, such as Microsoft Outlook Express or Microsoft Internet Explorer. If you highlight an application in the list, you can opt to end the task, hence killing the application. This is most useful if an application has crashed for some reason and cannot be stopped using the normal method.

If you click the Processes tab, you'll see a list of all system processes running on your server. Any application listed in the Applications tab will also be shown here, but instead of seeing the application's name, you're presented with the actual name of the running executable. When you first start Internet Explorer, the application is listed as the name of the website, while the process is called `iexplore.exe`. If you order the process list by CPU usage (by clicking the CPU heading at the top of the column), you'll see which processes are consuming the most CPU power. This can be useful if your system is running slow and a rogue process is hijacking CPU time. To kill off a process that you think is causing harm, you can highlight the process and click End Process.

Warning Be careful not to stop system-critical processes or you might crash your server. If you are unsure as to what a process does, try looking it up on the Internet (search using Google) before deciding what to do.

If you click the Performance tab, you'll immediately see two real-time graphs showing your system's CPU usage and page file usage. With these graphs running, try opening a new application. You'll notice a spike in activity when the application first starts; then it should settle down again. This is normal behavior. If you see a constant spiking in either of these graphs, it's a good indication that some sort of system process is running amok. If you see activity that causes you concern, try to identify which process is causing it from the Processes tab.

If you click the Networking tab, you'll see another graph, this time showing the local area network activity associated with your server's network adapter cards. Seeing high, constant usage on a network adapter can indicate some sort of denial-of-service attack or virus problem. If you see this, you can try switching off your Internet connection to see if the problem goes away. It's worth remembering that traffic on your network can be high because of problems with your network clients as well as your server. If a client is transferring vast quantities of data to your server, the graph will show an unusually high level of activity.

Change Server Status Report Settings

Assuming that you have set up reporting from the To Do List as per the instructions in Chapter 4, you can now change the report settings to best suit your needs. If you click Change Server Status Report Settings, you can create new server reports or modify the standard one set up by default for SBS 2003. We'll take a look at creating a brand new one because this covers all the options available for modification if you decide to edit the default one:

1. Click the Add button on the Server Status Reports page to bring up the Server Status Report Properties.

2. On the General tab, type the report name (something meaningful that tells you what the report is for) and add a description of the items you report on. This description is best left to the end because you might want to summarize everything the report generates.

3. Click the Content tab.

4. To concentrate this report on usage statistics, click the Usage Statistics radio button; otherwise, leave the Performance radio button selected for system-related information.

Note If you opt for a performance report, the report will generate details about your system services, performance counters, and system-related alerts, in much the same way as you've see before. If you opt for a usage statistics report, the information reported is related to your users' email usage, Internet connectivity, fax usage, document sharing, and remote access.

---

5. You should highlight the logs that are to be used in this report. You can add extra logs for applications, for example, simply by clicking Add and then typing in the filename and location of the log file. This will allow you to append any log you like to a report.

6. Click the Email Options tab. Type in an email address for the report to be sent to as well as a reply address for the email in case the person who receives it wishes to comment on the report.

7. Click the Task tab. This is the automatic scheduled task for generating the report. There is no need to change this.

8. Click the Schedule tab (see Figure 12-7).

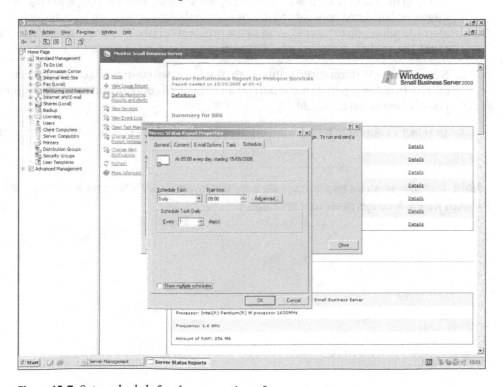

Figure 12-7. *Set a schedule for the generation of your report.*

9. Now you can state whether the report is generated daily, weekly, monthly, once, at system start-up, at logon, or when the system is idle. Add a start time (for example, midnight) and then add an interval to the next running of the report. If you click the Advanced button, you can create a more-granular schedule for the running of your report.

10. When you're finished, click OK to return to the report list.

11. The final thing to note is that the Send Now button will send the latest version of a highlighted report to the recipient in the email address box in the report properties. When you're finished, click the Close button.

Change Alert Notifications

Alerts can be generated and sent automatically to an email recipient when some form of important activity occurs on your system. Alerts take many forms, based on the operation of system services, thresholds set around performance counters, and events appearing in the event logs.

To configure the alerting mechanism of SBS 2003, do the following:

1. From the Monitoring and Reporting interface, click Change Alert Notifications.

2. The default tab displayed is Services. From here you can select which system services running on your SBS 2003 server will notify an email recipient when they stop. Services can stop for a variety of reasons, but if they are stopping outside your knowing, it might explain some unusual activity, or even malicious activity, on your system. An alert will allow you to react as soon as the problem occurs. To report on a service, the check box to the left of it must be selected.

3. Now click the Performance Counters tab. You have two courses of action: you can choose to either report or not report on an individual counter, and for each counter you can adjust the threshold.

4. To select a counter to be reported on, simply select the check box next to that counter.

Note To change whom the email address alerts are sent to, you'll need to rerun the Monitoring and Configuration Wizard. To do this, please refer to Chapter 4.

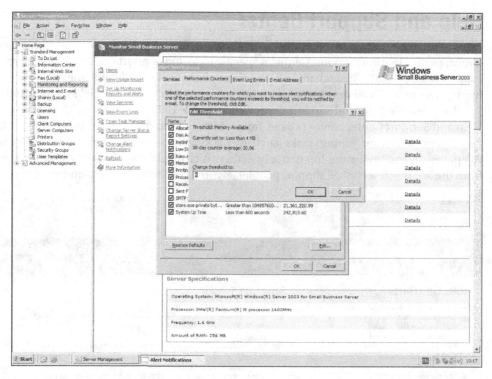

Figure 12-8. *Change the reported thresholds of performance counters.*

5. To change its threshold, click the Edit button and then adjust the value in the Change Threshold To textbox (see Figure 12-8). Each counter is different and works on different units depending on what that counter is measuring. Make sure you read the description of the counter before you change the threshold. When you're finished, click OK.

6. Click the Event Log Errors tab. You'll see only two events that are alerted on. This list cannot be changed. You can, however, opt to switch off these alerts by deselecting the check box.

7. When you're finished, click OK.

Help and Support Center

All of Microsoft's most recent operation systems for desktops and servers come with a facility known as the Help and Support Center. A specific Help and Support Center has been created especially for SBS 2003 customers and contains a plethora of useful guidelines and troubleshooters to walk you through some of the most commonly encountered system problems.

To access the Help and Support Center, click Start ➤ Help and Support. This brings up the Help and Support Center contents page, from which you can drill down into specific problems areas, perform routine support tasks (such as checking the Windows Update website for security patches), and review the Top Issues bulletin (which displays recent support news direct from the Microsoft technical support people). Figure 12-9 shows the Help and Support Center.

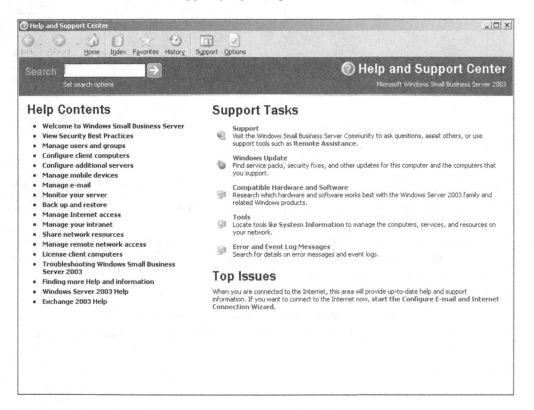

Figure 12-9. *The Help and Support Center has to be tailored for SBS 2003.*

■Note To get the most out of the Help and Support Center, you will need an active Internet connection. You can still run the troubleshooters and view the locally stored SBS 2003 information resources, but to use any of the other facilities available through the Help Contents section, such as the Error and Event Log Messages facility or the Windows Update service, you'll need to be connected.

Click on any of the items under Help Contents to access specific help information on that topic. For example, if you click View Security Best Practices, you are presented with informational bulletins and walk-throughs that will help you protect your network, server, and users from security threats (see Figure 12-10).

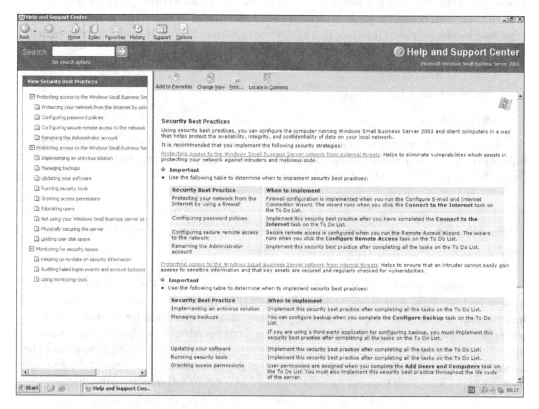

Figure 12-10. *Drill into any Help topic for more detail on SBS specifics.*

The best way to get to know the Help and Support Center is to play with it. There is lots of great information about getting the most out of SBS 2003, and there's no point in reiterating any of it in this chapter. What I will draw your attention to, however, is the Troubleshooting Windows Small Business Server 2003 item listed near the bottom of the Help Contents section. If you click on this, you are taken to a new page with several subjects listed in the details pane, and each subject is broken down into discrete questions about the operation of that aspect of your server. For example, if your users are having trouble sending or receiving email for whatever reason, try running through the troubleshooter labeled Email Cannot Be Received or Sent (beneath the Troubleshooting Users and Groups heading). In this example, SBS 2003 offers one possible reason why your user might be having this problem. Obviously, the list of resolutions is not exhaustive, but what it does give you is a place to start your investigations.

TechNet

Another great resource for troubleshooting your system is TechNet. TechNet is effectively a Microsoft professional's resource for troubleshooting and maintaining Microsoft systems. The Knowledge Base, a database of technical questions and answers and problem resolutions, is probably the most complete guide to all things Microsoft available. You can search the Knowledge Base by using a clever interface that allows you to ask a question. The results are weighted for their relevance based on an intelligent search and index engine.

There are two ways to get hold of TechNet:

- TechNet online

- Subscription

If you go to Microsoft's TechNet website, you can perform a search on any desired help topic by using the Search For box in the top-left corner of the web page. The website for TechNet is http://technet.microsoft.com/default.aspx.

■**Note** Knowledge Base articles from TechNet also appear at http://support.microsoft.com.

If you want a more-comprehensive support package, you can subscribe to TechNet Standard or TechNet Plus. Both subscriptions give you a DVD version of the entire Knowledge Base that you can run on any of your systems, as well as evaluation products for all of Microsoft's server and client software, beta software of products not yet released to the general community, updates and security patches supplied with the subscription, and monthly updates to all aspects of the package. TechNet Plus gives you all of the above but also augments the package with extended Microsoft support through managed newsgroups and prepaid incidents.

■**Note** Microsoft Developer Network (MSDN) and Partner Action Packs are also available and can be found listed on the Microsoft website. Search for MSDN subscriptions or Action Pack subscriptions.

Other Online Resources for SBS 2003

There are plenty of online resources for the SBS 2003 community, but here are a few of the resources I rate the highest:

- http://www.smallbizserver.net/Default.aspx

- http://www.microsoft.com/smallbusiness/hub.mspx

- http://www.microsoft.com/smallbusiness/hub.mspx

- http://www.microsoft.com/technet/prodtechnol/sbs/2003/deploy/ SBSSetupBestPractices.mspx

- http://www.microsoft.com/sbs

- http://download.microsoft.com/download/5/6/1/561c9fd7-0e27-4525-94ec-
  4d2d38f61aa3/TSHT_SBS.htm

- http://www.mickyj.com

System Performance

You can further monitor your server over a period of time in relation to discrete activities it carries out during operation. The facility used to collect and analyze this system data is known as the Performance Monitor.

To start the Performance Monitor, click Start ➤ Administrative Tools ➤ Performance.

Monitoring Processes

Internal processes on a Windows 2003 server computer can be analyzed over time by using system-level objects known as *counters*. The System Monitor, shown in Figure 12-11, can be configured to display the output of this data-collection process as a diagnostic chart based on the feedback from each of the counters you specify for collection.

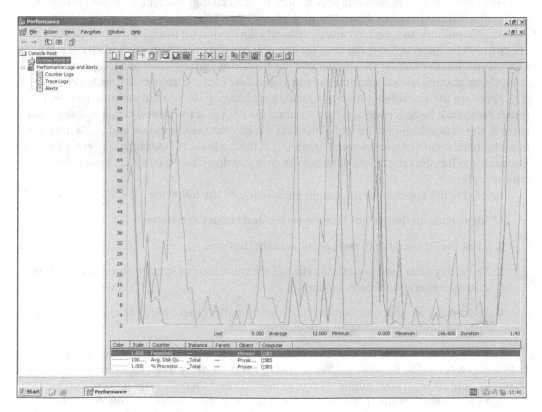

Figure 12-11. *The System Monitor displays real-time counter results.*

If you look closely at Figure 12-11, at the bottom of the System Monitor graph, you'll see a list of the counters you've currently selected for scrutiny. The key beneath the graph shows the counters and the color they are represented by on the rolling graph. The scale for each counter is also shown to give you an idea of what the graph represents. The rest of the description of the counter contains details of the class the counter is in, and the name of the computer you're monitoring—it's possible to connect to a remote computer and monitor it over the network.

If you want to add a new counter to the set you are monitoring, do the following:

1. Right-click anywhere on the System Monitor screen and select Add Counters.

2. If you are selecting counters from your SBS 2003 computer, select the Use Local Computer Counters radio button.

3. The Performance Object is the category of information you wish to monitor, with objects such as Processor, Memory, and Network available for selection. When you select a new object, the list of available counters for that object is displayed below. You can then scroll through the list of counters and use the Add button to add each new counter to the graph. If you are unsure about what any of these counters will report on, highlight the counter and click Explain.

If you have a large number of counters shown in the System Monitor, you can adjust the display to achieve a more readable appearance. You can change the type of graphical display to that of a histogram rather than a line graph (see Figure 12-12).

It's also possible to switch off any peripheral information on the screen by deselecting the check boxes for Legend, Value Bar, and Toolbar. You can also modify the periodicity of the counter output, depending on whether you need real-time information or a long-term trend analysis, by altering the sample time between each data capture from each selected counter.

There are two considerations when looking at changing the sample periodicity: how much data you'll be collecting and how accurate the data is. If the periodicity is low, say every second, the data volume will be high. This data will be extremely accurate and you'll have a blow-by-blow record of your system's operation. If the periodicity is set high, say every five minutes, you'll collect much less data, but the data you do collect might miss important counter spikes.

To modify the appearance or counter periodicity, do the following:

1. Right-click on the System Monitor screen and choose Properties.

2. Click the General tab to see a list of available options.

3. To modify collection periodicity, change the value next to Sample Automatically Every, and the value should be in seconds.

4. To modify the color and font attributes used on the System Monitor, click the Appearance tab and select the appropriate items.

The other aspect of the Performance Monitor that you can exploit is the Performance Logs and Alerts facility. By using Performance Logs and Alerts, you can collect the output from selected counters from any computer on your network and then play this information back through the system monitor to view what's been going on during the data collection phase. You can also opt to export data into another application, such as a spreadsheet or database, for further analysis.

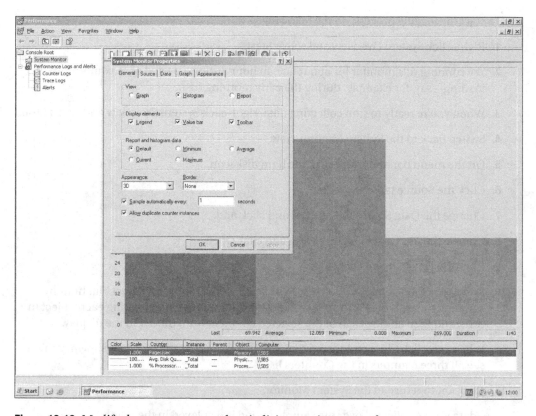

Figure 12-12. *Modify the appearance and periodicity to suit your needs.*

To look at this in more detail, expand the Performance Logs and Alerts node to reveal the three subcomponents: Counter Logs, Trace Logs, and Alerts.

If you highlight the Counter Logs menu item, in the details pane you'll see a sample set called System Overview. Double-click on this to see which counters are included in this collection. These counters offer a good overall picture of how your system is running:

- *\Memory\Pages\sec* is the rate at which pages are read from or written to disk. This is used to give an overall view as to what might be causing systemwide delays.

- *\PhysicalDisk[_Total]\Avg* is the disk queue length, used to show the average number of Read and Write requests queued for the selected hard disk during the sample interval (in this case 15 seconds). This offers a view of how your hard disk system is coping with its workload.

- *\Processor[_Total]\%Processor Time* is the percentage of elapsed time that your processor spends executing an application thread. This summarizes the percentage of time your system spends doing work during the 15-second sample period.

To set up your system to log against these counters, leave the default settings as listed and click Cancel.

To start the logging process, do the following:

1. Right-click System Overview and select Start.

2. Try running this monitor for about half an hour during a period of maximum server loading—say, for example, during the early morning rush.

3. When you're ready to stop collecting data, right-click System Overview and select Stop.

4. Switch back to the System Monitor view.

5. On the menu bar at the top, click the hard disk icon.

6. Click the Source tab.

7. Change the Data Source to Log Files and click Add.

8. Choose the file `System_Overview.blg` and click Open.

9. Click the Data tab and click Add.

10. Add each of the counters you've been collecting data for over the past half hour by scrolling through the Performance Object drop-down list, highlighting each object in turn, and then adding each of the selected counters from the list to the display.

11. When you click Close and the System Monitor Properties dialog box is shown, you'll see all three counters in the Counters list.

12. Click OK to return to the System Monitor.

The data you've collected over the sample period is displayed in the graph.

Alerting

The final thing we'll cover in Performance Monitor is the creation of alerts. You can send alerts to your SBS 2003 system's Application event log.

To configure alerts, do the following:

1. Under Performance Logs and Alerts, highlight Alerts. In the right-hand details pane, right-click and select New Alert Settings.

2. Give the alert a meaningful name and click OK.

3. Add the counters you wish to alert on—for example, Processor Time.

4. Add a limit—for example, 50 percent.

5. Click the Action tab.

6. Click Log an Entry in the Application event log. If you want to, you can also send the alert to a specified email address. In the example shown in Figure 12-13, I've sent the alert to the administrator's email address.

7. When you're finished, click OK.

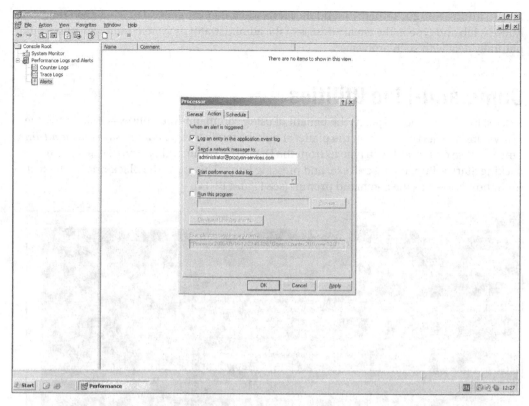

Figure 12-13. *Create custom alerts for the Application event log.*

Health Monitor in SBS 2003

An additional and extremely useful facility provided with SBS 2003 is a utility called Health Monitor. By using Health Monitor, you can actively monitor your server via a set of predefined thresholds and counters. When these thresholds are breached, such as your available disk space running below a predefined limit, you can generate an alert to be sent directly to an administrator warning of this imminent concern.

To configure Health Monitor alerting, do the following:

1. Click Start ➤ Server Management.

2. Click on the performance report within the console.

3. Click the Change Alert Notifications link to access the list of available Alert Notifications.

There are four tabs at the top of the Alert Notifications screen: Services, Performance Counters, Event Log Errors, and Email Address. You can create alerts based on the services listed under the Services tab, allowing you to alert on system and application services defined in this list, such as your DHCP server and the DNS server. By clicking the Performance Counters tab, you can set thresholds for certain information, such as low disk space or memory. Clicking the Event Log Errors tab allows you to send alerts based on events stored in your system's event logs.

To inform SBS 2003 where to send the alerts when they are generated, click the Email Address tab and type in the email address of the administrator or system manager who would naturally deal with such problems.

Command-Line Utilities

Finally, this last section explains the benefit of using command-line utilities—a skill I believe every Windows server owner on the planet should be familiar with. When I say *command-line*, I mean those commands you type in from the DOS-style command prompt, accessible by clicking Start ➤ Run, typing cmd.exe, and pressing Enter. This starts the black-and-white text input box, known as the command prompt (see Figure 12-14).

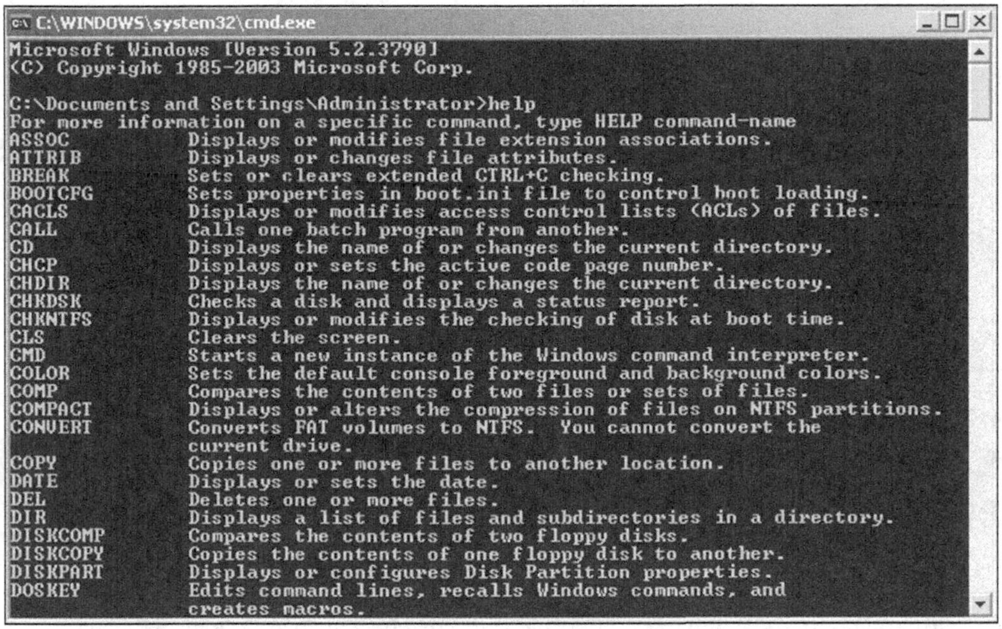

```
C:\WINDOWS\system32\cmd.exe
Microsoft Windows [Version 5.2.3790]
(C) Copyright 1985-2003 Microsoft Corp.

C:\Documents and Settings\Administrator>help
For more information on a specific command, type HELP command-name
ASSOC          Displays or modifies file extension associations.
ATTRIB         Displays or changes file attributes.
BREAK          Sets or clears extended CTRL+C checking.
BOOTCFG        Sets properties in boot.ini file to control boot loading.
CACLS          Displays or modifies access control lists (ACLs) of files.
CALL           Calls one batch program from another.
CD             Displays the name of or changes the current directory.
CHCP           Displays or sets the active code page number.
CHDIR          Displays the name of or changes the current directory.
CHKDSK         Checks a disk and displays a status report.
CHKNTFS        Displays or modifies the checking of disk at boot time.
CLS            Clears the screen.
CMD            Starts a new instance of the Windows command interpreter.
COLOR          Sets the default console foreground and background colors.
COMP           Compares the contents of two files or sets of files.
COMPACT        Displays or alters the compression of files on NTFS partitions.
CONVERT        Converts FAT volumes to NTFS.  You cannot convert the
               current drive.
COPY           Copies one or more files to another location.
DATE           Displays or sets the date.
DEL            Deletes one or more files.
DIR            Displays a list of files and subdirectories in a directory.
DISKCOMP       Compares the contents of two floppy disks.
DISKCOPY       Copies the contents of one floppy disk to another.
DISKPART       Displays or configures Disk Partition properties.
DOSKEY         Edits command lines, recalls Windows commands, and
               creates macros.
```

Figure 12-14. *The command prompt is extremely understated.*

Most of the utilities available through this interface are text-based commands that, at first glance, might seem archaic and behind the times—no fancy graphical user interface, and the syntax is esoteric to say the least. However, the value of these tools comes from their ability to dig deep into the operating system and expose much more of the inner workings of Windows 2003 than the majority of GUI-based management tools.

To see a list of some of the available commands that you can exploit from the command prompt, type **help** and press Enter.

Conventions

There are a few conventions you'll need to get to grips with before you can start experimenting with these commands. The syntax can be complicated and the switches and data can be somewhat obscure, so the following guidelines will help you decipher what you get from a command:

- Where you see the word *volume*, you should replace this with the intended target drive letter.

- Switches cause the command to perform different operations depending on what switches are selected. Switches are normally prefixed by a / and in most cases are optional. An example switch is [/a].

Note To view syntax for any command not mentioned, open the command prompt and type the command name followed by a space and then a slash and question mark (**/?**). For example, type **dir /?** to obtain help on the dir command.

A Few Commands to Get You Started

Here are two useful commands to give you an idea of how these work and how they are affected by the various switches and variables that you can append to the command.

Defrag

You can use this utility to initiate a hard disk defragmentation. Defragmenting the files on your hard disk will free up disk space and make your file system operate more efficiently. You should do this at least once every few months. The defrag command would be used from the command-line interface in the following way:

```
defrag volume [/a] [/v]
defrag volume [/f]
```

The following switches are used to modify the command's operation:

- [/a]: Analyze only, perform no action.

- [/v]: Provide verbose output, more information on what happens than the standard output.

- [/f]: Force defragmentation if the available space is low. This should be used only in an emergency.

> **Warning** Before defragmenting a hard disk on your server, make sure the target disk is not your Microsoft Exchange Server volume (commonly the D: drive). This can cause data on your email server to become corrupt.

Ipconfig

The `ipconfig` command is used to obtain details about your current TCP/IP settings for all network interfaces on your system, and is useful in diagnosing problems that are network related. The following are just a few of the switches used most commonly with this command:

```
ipconfig [/all] | [/release] | [/renew]
```

The following switches can be used to affect the operation of the `ipconfig` command:

- `[/all]`: This causes the `ipconfig` command to show all networking information for your IP adapters rather than just IP address, subnet mask, and default gateway. You'll see DNS servers, WINS servers, and much, much more.

- `[/release]`: This switch is used to release a DHCP-assigned address from a client adapter. This can be used if your system does not have a current address or there is a problem with the IP address detail, such as incorrect DNS server address or gateway information.

- `[/renew/]`: Using this renew switch forces the network adapter to ask the DCHP server for a new IP address.

For more information, use the `/?` switch to view the help information.

More on Windows Commands

A complete reference for all command-line utilities available on the Windows 2003 operating system is available at the following Microsoft website: `http://www.microsoft.com/technet/prodtechnol/windowsserver2003/library/ServerHelp/552ed70a-208d-48c4-8da8-2e27b530eac7.mspx`.

Try looking up the following commands to help you get an idea of what you can do and what might be useful for you:

- `arp`
- `attrib`
- `chkntfs`
- `cls`
- `cmdkey`
- `copy`
- `del`

- dsadd computer

- eventcreate

- format

- net computer

- net group

- net use

- net user

- ping

- runas

- shutdown

- tracert

- whoami

Case Study—Servideal

Maria had been using her laptop over a wireless connection to access the server from another room. For no apparent reason, she stopped having network access to the Internet even through she could still contact the SBS 2003 server and access her files. This led her to believe there was a problem with the wireless network system, but the question was, where should she start investigating the problem?

By using the ping command, she tried contacting Microsoft's homepage (ping www.microsoft.com). She found that there was no response. Next, she tried contacting her external router interface. Again, no response. Next, she tried the internal interface. This time there was a connection. So the problem lay in the interface to the Internet. After a simple power cycle of the Internet router, her connection resumed and she was able to start working again.

With pragmatic use of the ping command, you can determine where the fault lies in the network and start your main investigations there.

Summary

There are countless groups on the Internet that you can subscribe to and that have experts in practically every field ready to help you with your problems. If you look at http://groups.google.com, you'll find the Microsoft public SBS 2003 groups available free of charge and without registration requirements. You can also register for access to Yahoo! SBS 2003 users groups, where you can post questions and have them answered, usually by Microsoft Most Valuable Professionals (MVPs).

Index

You Need the Companion eBook

Your purchase of this book entitles you to buy the companion PDF-version eBook for only $10. Take the weightless companion with you anywhere.

We believe this Apress title will prove so indispensable that you'll want to carry it with you everywhere, which is why we are offering the companion eBook (in PDF format) for $10 to customers who purchase this book now. Convenient and fully searchable, the PDF version of any content-rich, page-heavy Apress book makes a valuable addition to your programming library. You can easily find and copy code—or perform examples by quickly toggling between instructions and the application. Even simultaneously tackling a donut, diet soda, and complex code becomes simplified with hands-free eBooks!

Once you purchase your book, getting the $10 companion eBook is simple:

❶ Visit **www.apress.com/promo/tendollars/**.

❷ Complete a basic registration form to receive a randomly generated question about this title.

❸ Answer the question correctly in 60 seconds, and you will receive a promotional code to redeem for the $10.00 eBook.

2560 Ninth Street • Suite 219 • Berkeley, CA 94710

eBookshop

THE EXPERT'S VOICE™

Offer valid through 1/24/07.